REPRESENTING CLIENTS IN MEDIATION

A guide to optimal results based on insights from counsel, mediators, and program administrators

BY SPENCER PUNNETT

Foreword by John Lande
Isidor Loeb Professor of Law
Former Director, LL.M. program in Dispute Resolution
University of Missouri

AMERICAN BAR ASSOCIATION Section of Litigation

Cover by Jill Tedhams/ABA Publishing.

Printed in the United States of America

17 16 15 14 13 5 4 3 2 1

Library of Congress Cataloging-in-Publication Data

Punnett, Spencer.
Representing clients in mediation : a guide to optimal results based on insights from counsel, mediators and program administrators / By Spencer Punnett.—First edition.
pages cm
Includes bibliographical references and index.
ISBN 978-1-61438-757-2 (print : alk. paper) 1. Mediation—United States. 2. Dispute resolution (Law)—United States. 3. Attorney and client—United States. 4. Practice of law—United States. I. Title.
KF9084.P86 2012
347.73'9—dc23

2012044921

Summary Table of Contents

For Expanded Table of Contents, see page 507.

INVITATION TO READERS

Would you like to share a memorable, instructive personal experience on the topic of representing clients in mediation? Do you have any thoughts or comments for improvement of this book? You might be able to join the voices of other mediation advocates and mediators in an expanded second edition. Contact the author at spencerpunnett@earthlink.net.

Publisher's Note

The ABA Section of Litigation is the premier association for U.S. lawyers involved in litigation and trial practice. More than 50,000 lawyers representing countless areas of practice turn to the ABA Section of Litigation for member-only access to the latest news, information, and thinking on legal strategy, bringing all sides to one place to form a comprehensive view of the profession.

The Litigation Book Publishing Board has been helping authors develop litigation-related books since the Section of Litigation was founded in 1973. All board members are current or former litigators. Our mission is to help serve the profession by publishing books with strong practical value to lawyers whose practice includes litigation.

To my wife, Mercy

Acknowledgments

Lawyers are busy people, and every hour they spend helping with a project like mine is one less hour available to practice law or enjoy their family. Those whom I interviewed in my research for this book took time not only for the interview itself, but later to review the quotes I gleaned, and often to make edits for the purpose of clarifying or expanding on thoughts they had tried to express orally. My deepest thanks for their contribution. Their ideas form the backbone and flesh of this book, which would have been impossible without them.

As my writing progressed, I also found myself quoting widely from other published authors on the topic of mediation, bringing their advice into the "conversation" along with the interview participants. Those from whom I borrowed most include Hildy Bowbeer, Prof. Charles B. Craver, Prof. Dwight Golann, Louise A. LaMothe, Laura H. Kennedy, J. Anderson Little, Bennett G. Picker, Gary P. Poon, and Lawrence M. Watson Jr. I appreciate the generosity that they and many other authors showed in reviewing and blessing my use of excerpts from their works. Also, C. Timothy Corcoran, III kindly allowed me to draw from very useful unpublished materials he had prepared for a presentation. Richard M. Shusterman, after my interview with him, wrote a sidebar article on complex multiparty mediations especially for this book.

This project proved vastly more arduous and time consuming than I initially imagined, and I am grateful to my wife, Mercy Jiménez, for supporting and encouraging (and sometimes pushing) me to go the distance and finally finish the manuscript. Janet S. Kole, whose judgment I respect and trust, lent her experienced eye as my editor.

Given the variety of opinions expressed in this book, it is inevitable that none of the interview participants or authors quoted will agree with every statement or recommendation it contains. I credit them with the book's best ideas; any faults or shortcomings are mine.

Foreword

By John Lande
Isidor Loeb Professor of Law
Former Director, LLM Program in Dispute Resolution
University of Missouri

Representing Clients in Mediation is an important book that should be read by practicing attorneys, law students, scholars, and policy makers interested in modern mediation practice in the United States. Practicing attorneys undoubtedly will benefit from the suggestions from experts experienced in mediation. Although mediation theory is deceptively simple, contemporary mediation procedures and norms are not obvious. Since the vast majority of mediated cases in some contexts are finally resolved in mediation, lawyers have a strong interest in understanding the mediation process and how they can most effectively advocate their clients' interests in mediation. While this is certainly of value to law students and less-experienced lawyers, even veteran lawyers who have represented clients in many mediations will learn practical lessons from this clearly written book. Scholars and policy makers will also gain a deeper understanding of the realities of modern mediation practice in the United States, which can lead to sophisticated insights and wise mediation policies.

Most people wouldn't think of this book as an empirical study of techniques of legal representation of clients in mediation. But that's exactly what it is. Many people think of empirical or scientific research as being limited to standardized surveys of randomly selected samples. Of course, that is a scientific research design that can produce helpful data. But systematically studying a subject using qualitative interviews, as Spencer Punnett did for this book, is also an important form of scientific research, which can provide deeper understandings than are possible with research methods such as surveys. As a lawyer and social scientist who used the same methods in my book *Lawyering with Planned Early Negotiation*, I appreciate that he has done an excellent and thorough job. Social-science research cannot provide "the truth" about dispute resolution. The best that research can do is to provide clearer glimpses. In my opinion, *Representing Clients in Mediation* presents the best approximation of reality of good civil mediation practice in the United States these days.

To present a clear portrait of mediation, the author interviewed some of the most experienced mediation experts (including lawyers who represent clients in mediation) to get their recommendations about representing clients most effectively. He summarizes their prescriptions, noting differences between them. While the book is full of advice, it does not represent the author's own personal philosophy as much as a distillation of the wisdom of the experts he interviewed.

The book is extremely thorough, starting with advice about initiating a mediation process. Given the importance of mediation in modern litigation practice, *Representing Clients in Mediation* appropriately devotes a lot of attention to preparatory steps before all the participants convene for the ultimate resolution of a case. Of course, it also addresses numerous questions about how to be most effective once a mediation conference begins. No detail seems too small to escape the analysis of experts here. Although lawyers normally will not follow all the steps in every case, the book provides a useful checklist for individual cases and a prudent general approach.

Ideally, lawyers would be able to resolve all their litigated cases without the help of mediators. In practice, this is not possible in a substantial proportion of cases. Even in cases that would otherwise settle without mediation, mediation can contribute to fairer, more efficient, and more satisfying process and results. In addition to providing benefits to individual litigants, it can help court systems manage their caseloads given their limited resources in a time of significant financial cutbacks. For better and worse, mediation is the closest that many litigants will have to a "day in court" with a competent, neutral dispute resolution professional. This is not to suggest that people inevitably use mediation properly or that it always realizes its full potential in every case. In fact, this doesn't always happen. In some cases, parties feel abused in a mediation process. It is precisely because the quality of mediation is not assured—and, indeed, is quite variable—that lawyers need to be on their "best game" when representing their clients in mediation.

In my view, the best way to become proficient as an advocate in mediation is to participate in many mediations and seriously reflect on one's experiences. *Representing Clients in Mediation* is one of the next best substitutes, enabling lawyers to take advantage of the experience of many thoughtful mediation experts. The subtitle of my book is "How You Can Get Good Results for Clients and Make Money," which is fitting for this book as well. Lawyers who do a good job for their clients in mediation are likely to earn favorable reputations, repeat business, referrals of new clients, and considerable incomes. Good mediation advocates also help improve the justice system by making mediation a desirable dispute resolution option that satisfies parties' legitimate expectations.

INTRODUCTION

The Big Picture

As mediation has become commonplace, litigators think they know all about it. As a result, they have been trying to make the mediation process an adjunct of litigation without realizing that it is a different process. They fail to use mediation to its full potential and can instead impede settlement.

—Louise LaMothe, mediator (2010, p.66)

Representing Clients in Mediation is designed for lawyers who need to help their clients mediate legal disputes that typically involve a claim for damages. This book probably differs in at least two ways from others you have seen on the subject.

First, this book offers multiple perspectives on all aspects of the mediation process. My research included almost 40 interviews with a variety of experienced mediation players—litigators in private practice, inside counsel, mediators, mediation program administrators, and law professors specializing in the field.[1] You will hear their voices throughout these pages, talking about what works and what doesn't. They are joined by the voices of dozens of other mediation players who have written or publicly spoken on the topic, whose advice is also incorporated here.

These multiple perspectives create a conversation that gives you the benefit of differing opinions on the best way to handle certain aspects of mediation advocacy. As with litigation, mediation is an art, not a science. The practitioners I've interviewed provide insight into how mediation of legal disputes may vary in a range of settings and contexts—for example, mediation of a securities claim under a contractual ADR

1. In addition to elite, distinguished veterans, I also sought lawyers whose backgrounds reflect the workaday world of mediation practice "in the trenches."

clause versus court-ordered mediation of a personal injury claim versus voluntary mediation of a complex, high-stakes business case.

Second, *Representing Clients in Mediation* provides step-by-step advice covering the entire mediation process in detail from beginning to end. Despite variations in how mediation of legal disputes is carried out in different jurisdictions, forums, and practice areas, there are wide areas of agreement among experienced mediation players—including those whose perspectives are reflected in these pages—as to how to get the best results. If you follow the 12 steps outlined here, you can feel confident that you have cost-effectively done all you can to ensure the best possible outcome for your client.

Another unusual and useful feature of this book is that, in addition to the main text, every chapter includes a variety of sidebars—stand-alone pieces that are often just a page or so in length. Many of these sidebars are excerpted from interviews, containing the words and viewpoint of a single mediation player. They range from instructive anecdotes to direct "me-to-you" advice on specific mediation topics.

For example, three sidebars are included in this introduction. In Sidebar I-1 ("Andrew Berry's Rules for Success in Mediation"), a former law-firm chairman offers mediation advice at the culmination of his 40-year career. In Sidebar I-2 ("How to Doom a Mediation"), three mediators provide tongue-in-cheek guidance on how lawyers can most efficiently *poison* the mediation process. Just do the opposite and you'll be fine! Sidebar I-3 ("What One Partner Tells Associates About Successful Mediation Advocacy") distills what new lawyers at one firm are taught about mediation and negotiation.

As you will see, seven of the 12 steps described in this book must be taken before the mediation session begins. In that sense, the session itself is the tip of the iceberg. That does *not* mean you have to spend many hours preparing to mediate a nickel-and-dime dispute. The actual amount of time will be in reasonable proportion to the size and complexity of the case—but it is essential to touch all the bases along the way.

Here is a preview of the 12 steps, along with a sample of what you will find in the chapters that discuss them.

Step One: Check Out the Governing Rules and Plan Accordingly

Although mediation is less standardized and more flexible than litigation, there are still rules—and the specifics can vary significantly. Step One includes four substeps, from locating the applicable rules to learning about the local realities of mediation practice in your forum. Along the way, you will find a discussion of court-ordered ("court-annexed"), contractual, and purely voluntary mediation in terms of key rules that may potentially apply (and what you should check for at the outset.)

Among this chapter's seven sidebars: In Sidebar 1-4, mediators, counsel, and mediation program administrators discuss the problem of parties who participate in court-ordered mediation solely for the purpose of "punching their ticket." In Sidebar 1-7, a prominent construction lawyer talks about mediation in complex cases where many parties are involved.

Step Two: Agree on a Mediator (If You Have a Choice)

Where you have the right to choose, selecting the right mediator for your case may be the single most important decision to increase the likelihood of a good outcome. An effective selection process involves substeps that culminate in execution of a mediation agreement and filing a notice (where applicable), all set forth in Step Two. The substeps include a discussion of deciding with opposing counsel on one of the six possible ways to arrive at a mutually acceptable candidate, followed by agreement and buy-in on the best person for the job. Of course, the chapter also deals with familiar distinctions between facilitative and evaluative mediator styles (as well as some other approaches), offering advice in deciding what approach along that spectrum might be most beneficial in your case.

Sidebars include Sidebar 2-2, in which experienced players discuss the pros and cons of selecting a former judge as your mediator. Sidebar 2-5 describes the potential benefits of a "judo maneuver": deliberately opting for your opponent's preferred choice for the mediator.

Step Three: Agree on Tailored Ground Rules (As Needed)

The fact that most mediation systems have relatively few procedural rules makes them very flexible—but it also puts the burden on the participants to agree on more detailed and specific ground rules to suit their particular case. As an ABA task force has noted, "sophisticated repeat users [want] to have substantive input into the mediation process itself." The chapter covering Step Three offers detailed advice on what specific aspects you may want to tailor with your opponent and the mediator, and why. It also discusses effective use of a pre-mediation conference or its equivalent.

A sampling of sidebars: In Sidebar 3-3, national mediator John Bickerman talks about under what circumstances planning to hold a joint opening session may not be a good idea. Sidebar 3-4 describes an alternative model for mediation where the parties spend the entire mediation session at the same table, with no private caucuses. Sidebar 3-7 addresses the topic of ex parte communications with the mediator.

Step Four: Exchange Information With Your Opponent, Including an Exchanged Memo for the Mediator (As Warranted)

For best results in mediation, experienced players agree that besides obtaining key information about your opponent's case, it is in your client's best interest to ensure that your adversaries also have key information *they* will need in advance of a mediation session. In addition to activities such as direct exchange of documents, exchanged mediation memos—which are required in some forums—can be a means to exchange information as well as to bring the mediator up to speed. The chapter covering Step Four looks in detail at exchanged mediation memos, including their functions, ideal content, style, and timing.

Also, Sidebar 4-2 offers first-person advice on how an associate can best help a senior lawyer with the exchange of documents and memos. In Sidebar 4-3, a mediator tips you off on phrases to avoid in your mediation memo.

Step Five: Confidentially Brief the Mediator (As Allowed or Required)

In addition to or instead of a memo exchanged between the parties, you may be required (or allowed) to submit a confidential memo for the mediator's eyes only. The chapter on Step Five includes a discussion of why it is important to help shape the mediator's view of your case as early as possible (even though she will not be acting as a judge) and how to make an "eyes-only" memo work best for you. You will also find advice on when it may be worth drafting both an exchanged memorandum and a confidential brief.

The chapter's eight sidebars include "A Clerk's-Eye View of Confidential Mediation Briefs" and a longtime mediator's explanation of the characteristics that prompt him to read the briefs of one particular lawyer before the rest.

Step Six: Prepare Yourself for the Mediation Session

In preparing for an upcoming mediation session, there are some tasks that you will likely perform on your own, while others will be completed in the course of preparing your client. Step Six involves the first set of tasks. The chapter on this step describes seven substeps, from moving toward calculating a financial value for your case to preparing a skeleton settlement memorandum.

Among topics of the chapter's eight sidebars: using Litigation Risk Analysis as a mediation tool, preparing "zingers" for use in the mediation session, and determining how to proceed if your mediation team for a corporate client includes an executive who was the alleged wrongdoer in the case.

Step Seven: Prepare With Your Client for the Mediation Session

At least one experienced mediator lists inadequate advance client preparation as the number-one mistake that inexperienced lawyers make in mediation. Adding to the advice in Step Six, the chapter covering Step Seven describes seven substeps to help you avoid this mistake. One important substep is to agree on a negotiating plan for the session. Coverage of this substep includes a discussion of negotiation theory—not just the now-familiar concept of interest-based negotiation, but a critique that this concept has limited practical application in mediating many legal disputes.

Along the way, you will find specific advice on how to arrive at a starting number for negotiations, as well as one mediator's model of how to plan in advance a series of offers to make in an upcoming mediation session that is not dependent on your opponent's responses. Sidebars in this chapter include an inside counsel's advice on preparing business executives, a mediator's views on worthwhile objectives besides settlement to discuss with clients before the session, and an example from a litigator of how good communication with her client made a difference while preparing for a mediation session.

Step Eight: Start the Mediation Session Strategically

The initial joint part of a mediation session—where the parties typically convene together with the mediator and each side makes an opening statement—is an example of a topic where multiple perspectives make a big difference. Are opening statements really worth doing? In the chapter on Step Eight, seasoned mediation players make reasoned arguments on each side of that issue, while others describe why they believe the answer depends on certain variables. If you make an opening statement, what should you try to achieve, and how? Should your client participate? What about visual aids? These are just a few of the questions this chapter deals with in the course of describing seven substeps to make the most of the start of your mediation session.

On the topic of information or evidence that your opponent doesn't know about yet, Sidebar 8-5 deals with the question, "Should I hold something back for trial?" In Sidebar 8-6, a mediator recalls a plaintiff's video exhibit so effective that the other side was stunned. Sidebar 8-7 tells the story of "The Initial Joint Session That Swallowed a Mediation."

Step Nine: Position Your Negotiations at the Initial Private Caucuses

In the series of private caucuses between each party and the mediator that typically follows the opening session, the first one or two are often qualitatively different from the rest. The chapter on Step Nine tells you what the mediator's goals and techniques are likely to be for her initial private caucuses with your side, and offers guidance—in eight substeps—on what *you* should be trying to achieve (and how).

The sidebars to this chapter include a dramatic example of the power of client venting, a mediator's explanation of what he hopes to get from a party during first caucus, and a discussion of the roles of outside lawyers in relation to inside counsel during the caucus stage of mediation.

Step Ten: Pursue Your Plan for Movement Through Caucus Rounds to Settlement or Impasse

From the point that a party puts an offer on the table, the negotiating can potentially begin in earnest. You will find a range of guidance in the chapter covering Step Ten on how to move toward your goal proactively rather than reactively and ultimately bridge the inevitable gap to settlement. You will also find concrete advice on how to lower the danger of impasse, as well as perspectives on when the best course of action is to cease efforts to settle at the session and focus instead on ways to advance the ball afterward.

Among the many sidebars, you will find an illustration of how opposing parties sometimes miscommunicate through numbers; an example of how the "fatigue factor" can wreak havoc in a session; the story of a mediation where both parties unexpectedly came out ahead; and "What Maralee Eriksen Learned From Watching 40 Mediated Settlement Conferences."

Step Eleven: Seal the Deal, Plan for Future Resolution, or Disengage at the Closing Joint Session

Regardless of how the negotiating rounds of caucuses end, the closing joint session requires careful handling for best results. Step Eleven outlines helpful substeps to follow for each of three possible scenarios: (a) the parties have reached an agreement on all issues; (b) the parties have made progress, but there are still outstanding issues to be resolved; or (c) the parties have reached an insurmountable impasse, and any further mediation efforts at this stage look unproductive.

This chapter has three sidebars. Two discuss items you need to consider for inclusion in any settlement agreement. The third discusses a hybrid of mediation and arbitration that has sometimes been used to sidestep the parties' impasse.

Step Twelve: Follow Up as Needed in the Postsession Period

Under scenarios (a) and (b) in Step Eleven, you very likely have more work after the mediation session ends. Step Twelve offers advice on how to proceed if you signed a term sheet (but not a full-fledged settlement agreement) at the closing joint session, or if you and the other side agreed on further steps to help reach a settlement down the line.

Now that you have seen the big picture, you are ready to start reading Step One—or simply dive into whatever part of the book seems likely to help you the most at this moment.

SIDEBAR I-1

Andrew T. Berry's Rules for Success in Mediation

In more than 40 years of law practice, the late Andrew Berry's experience as an advocate in mediation ranged from the ordinary to mass-tort insurance coverage behemoths involving 50 or so different entities. In an interview years ago, I asked him: "If you were asked to give a speech on the 10 secrets to successful mediation, what would be secret number one?" He jokingly replied, "Get a piece of paper with numbers 1 to 10 so you [can] keep track." Berry then proceeded to surprise himself (and me) by actually coming up with seven "rules" off the top of his head. Here they are, along with some of his explanations.

Rule #1: Understand that nobody, including the mediator, is going to be completely candid.

This rule has nothing to do with ethics; it arises from the simple fact that negotiations in mediation are what Berry called a sub-optimal candor environment. "The parties trust the mediator as a general proposition, but understand that the mediator may take minor liberties with the truth. So you won't—and the other side won't—be completely candid with the mediator until you really get down to short strokes."

An example of the mediator's minor liberties: "A good mediator will not give you his candid opinion of how good your case is. A good mediator will tell you your case is worse than you think it is—and probably worse than *he* thinks it is. He will do the same thing to the other side."

Similarly, "when the mediator says, 'I think I can get the other side to X [dollars],' it may mean that the other side is already at X, or that the other side has said there's no way on earth they're ever going to get to X. But if the mediator is candid in revealing either one of those positions, it will make it harder to settle the case."

Meanwhile, you may take minor liberties when talking to the mediator. (This does *not* include playing fast and loose with the facts of the case; see Rule #3.) For example, if there are four items up for negotiation, you might "spend a lot of time explaining why piece number four is critically important" to you, so that "when it comes time to trading and you trade piece four, you increase the chances you'll get something for it. You'll either get credit for it that's usable in 'buying up' *their* pieces, or they will think that they have won something and psychologically be more agreeable."

And of course, you know that the other side will be doing the same thing with *you*.

Rule #2: While you want to negotiate to "yes," it's okay to say no.

This rule is based on the premise that "sometimes even the best mediator can't get the other party to a place which roughly approximates the litigation risk alternative dispute resolution analysis." There is a danger that you (and your client) may nevertheless become so caught up in the process that you give away too much in order to get a resolution.

To be able to know when to say "no," it is essential to do a good litigation risk analysis before walking into the mediation session. If you do, and you and your client have communicated well with each other in advance, "you know what your stopping point is."

Of course, sometimes facts can emerge during the mediation that may raise a defendant's estimation of the settlement value. And for either party, other considerations may justify a higher settlement than the strict value of the case. For instance, your client may be willing to pay somewhat more (or accept less) just to be done with it or to save the time of company executives. But this should be the result of a calculated decision—not getting swept away in the moment.

However, that doesn't change the basic rule: "It's okay to say no, even if you disappoint the [mediator], and even if it makes the other side crazy."

Rule #3: Appear to be entirely candid—and actually be quite candid.

Although this rule may seem to contradict Rule #1, Berry called it a corollary, because he was talking about a different kind of candor. It is one thing to obscure your views and intentions in the negotiation process; it is quite another to misrepresent facts or break promises.

"In mediation, getting caught up in a small exaggeration is an almost trivial event. Getting caught in a big, fat lie is bad for your client in that mediation, bad for you in that mediation, and bad for you in other mediations—at least if any of these mediators talks to another."

An example of breaking Rule #3 during a private caucus with the mediator would be to somewhat misstate the content of certain e-mails in order to exaggerate how much they help your position in a contract dispute. A competent mediator will then bring up those e-mails in his caucus with the other side—and your credibility takes a nosedive. "Believability is very important in mediation, as in life."

Rule #4: Keep careful track of the "bid" and "ask"—and the reasons asserted.

As figures start to be exchanged back and forth during the mediation session, don't just rely on your memory. You will want a complete record of how the offers and counteroffers evolve. This will help you develop a clear picture of "what's negotiating to the middle, how you signal what the middle is," and "what's a false middle." It will also enable you to say things to the mediator like, "You know, that's a movement of less than two percent. If that's what they really mean, we're not going anywhere."

By "the reasons asserted," Berry meant the rationale that an opponent (or you) may give for putting a certain number on the table. At a minimum, this will help you stay clear. In an ideal case, you might even be able to put your hands on facts or legal precedent that undermines your opponent's rationale—and thus weakens his number.

Rule #5: Come in with a really good, readable mediation statement.

This rule refers to the memoranda or letters that parties often provide to the mediator in advance of a session. "Any time you tell your story in a lucid and persuasive way, you're advantaged.

I mean at the margin, mediators are human! They prefer to be dealing with people who are relatively candid and relatively intelligent and relatively open about their needs and their willingness to make compromise."

Even though the mediator has no power to force settlement decisions, his assessment of the strength of your case may help shape his idea of where the negotiated numbers should end up. Beyond this, "virtually all mediations at some point turn into evaluative mediations" to some degree, "even if they weren't set up as such."

Rule #6: Either have good stamina or refuse to work late at night.

"It's amazing how many deals you get done when people are exhausted," Berry said. "Sometimes that's right and sometimes it's not right."

From Berry's perspective, it's right to the extent that fatigue helps foster a momentum in favor of getting the case settled and done. At the same time, "fatigue does affect one's judgment." If your opponent's judgment is affected (to your advantage), then great—but if fatigue causes you or your client to lose sight of your proper stopping point (see Rule #2), it's bad.[2]

One of Berry's favorite classic movies was *The Hustler*, starring Jackie Gleason as a legendary pool player and Paul Newman the young rival who ultimately wears him down. You want to be Fast Eddie—not Minnesota Fats.

Rule #7: Start out by being more respectful to the [mediator] than he [or] she might expect.

If you don't know the mediator personally, you don't know how much deference he wants to receive. For example, does the mediator who is a retired judge (which is common) prefer to be called Judge Jones or Charlie?

Better to start with Judge Jones. If the former judge then says, "Please, call me Charlie," you can become less formal and

---

2. For an anecdote illustrating this, see Sidebar 10-5: "The Fatigue Factor."

everything will continue to go smoothly. But if you call him Charlie and he corrects you—"That's 'Judge Jones'"—you've started on the wrong foot.

"You can always get more casual and friendly as the mediation proceeds. It's very hard to go in the opposite direction."

Even if the mediator is someone you know well—perhaps someone you've mediated previous cases with—you should still start with an air of formality. This is especially true where your opponents do not have the same previous background with the mediator.

"If you go in and say, 'Hi, Charlie,' in the presence of the other side, that could be read as suggesting a level of familiarity with the mediator—and either an accurate or a false suggestion that your friendship with the mediator will be to your advantage and to their disadvantage. And because the mediator understands that it could be read that way, the mediator will be angry at you."

SIDEBAR I-2

How to Doom a Mediation

By John J. Upchurch, Kimberly Sands, and Michael S. Orfinger

A panel of mediators from across the United States compiled a boldface list of mistakes that often cause failure. Mediators John Upchurch, Kimberly Sands, and Michael Orfinger (whose firm has offices in Florida and Alabama) added commentary to write an article (2011), from which this sidebar is adapted. It is worth noting that at least four of the featured paths to doom involve inadequate preparation for the mediation session.

1. Fail to prepare the client and/or decision maker for mediation.

Participants should be prepared for the process itself; i.e., be fully briefed as to the dynamics of the mediation process, the nature and extent of mediation confidentiality and privilege and the underlying policy rationale for its existence, and an idea of the basic procedural aspects of the mediation experience. Evaluations and strategies should be sufficiently flexible to be responsive to opportunities and new information learned during the mediation. This capability is predicated on a thorough discussion and analysis of the parties' strengths and weaknesses leading into the mediation. There is no effective alternative to a meeting in advance of the mediation session itself.

2. Fail to prepare your *adversary* for mediation.

It is important to precondition your adversary as much as possible in order to set the stage for a successful outcome. This requires timely, effective communications in advance of the mediation date. Often, despite the requirement that representatives with "full authority" attend, in actuality the representatives in attendance must "call the home office" to get additional authority to settle. The safest strategy is to assume that you must educate some distant authority figure in advance. Hence, a judgment should be made as to what critical evidence will be shared in advance, most often in the form of the mediation summary. Timing is critical. Assume it will take several days, at a minimum, for the "claims committee" to meet, compare notes, and set an appropriate reserve on the file.

3. Fail to involve the mediator in pre-mediation preparation.

Many mediators will, as a matter of course, interview all counsel in advance. However, if this doesn't appear to be your mediator's practice, engage the mediator to meet in advance, whether in person or by telephone. This affords counsel an advance opportunity to prepare the mediator for the peculiar dynamics at play in a given case that are likely to affect the outcome. Also, this is an opportunity for counsel and the mediator to identify and be well prepared for special complexities such as coverage disputes, estimates, or expert reports.

4. Fail to consider your audience.

It is critical that the advocate determine in advance who will attend on behalf of his or her adversary. The identity and background of the decision maker is particularly important, and worth some independent inquiry if there is information available from colleagues, or even a Google search. This applies both to counsel as well as the client representatives. Your research into the character and background of your audience will influence your approach in the opening, with the goal of securing maximum persuasive impact.

5. Make ineffective use of posturing.

Mediation is the business of managing ambiguity, vague signals, and even shifting goals on the part of the participants. Frequently a party will become frustrated with the process, or become anxious to wind things up, and declare in absolute terms something like, "This is my bottom line—and if you don't agree to pay it, this mediation is over." Should you be the advocate who resorts to this tactic, you will almost certainly experience (a) a failed mediation plus (b) an untenable position from which to restart negotiations later should your client's interests so dictate. A more enlightened strategy is to advise the mediator that you have reached the end of the line for this session—and ask for an adjournment. Let emotions cool.

6. Allow absence of the decision maker.

We are all aware of the practice of insurance carriers to send representatives who do not have the independent discretion to increase their authority absent "phoning home." But lack-of-authority problems are not limited to insurance companies. Encourage the personal attendance of as highly ranked a representative as possible. At a minimum, it is important to have the ultimate authority figure available by telephone to consult during the mediation. Encourage that person to let the mediator participate in the discussion, even with the understanding that he or she will be excused at some point for private consultations.

7. Resort to offensive or unethical practices.

Perhaps it is asking a lot to require counsel for the litigants, engaged in the "war" of litigation, to suddenly become friendly delegates to a peace conference. Yet for mediation to work, this transformation is a necessity. Mediation is often an appropriate forum for a party to vent and "blow off steam"; this process often provides the cathartic effect the client needs to reach a settlement. Sometimes, however, mediation becomes a forum for the *attorneys* to vent—casting the opposing counsel or client in a negative light and generally sabotaging any realistic chances of settlement. No legitimate interest of the client is served by blowing up a mediation by engaging in overtly offensive or unethical behavior. Counsel should also bear in mind that unethical conduct or conduct falling below the standard of care may not necessarily enjoy the blanket of confidentiality and privilege generally afforded to mediation communications.

8. Negotiate reactively.

Merely reacting to the tactics of your adversary, as opposed to taking concrete steps in light of your own strategy, is unlikely to lead to a successful outcome. Ask the mediator to present settlement options as his or her idea if you are concerned about "reactive devaluation" or a reduction in authority because of perceived weakness in your bargaining position.

9. Impose unilateral conditions on mediation.

It is difficult to lure an adversary to the mediation bargaining table while seeking to impose seemingly inflexible conditions. One example is insisting on a particular mediator. This raises a suspicion of "inside baseball" and should be avoided. Another example: attempting to require an opening offer above a certain level, or a demand below some arbitrary figure. This never works. It is a naked attempt to seize control of the negotiations, and ordinarily sinks the mediation initiative before it gets off the ground.

10. Fail to plan and prepare adequately for the mediation process.

Mediation should involve the same level of planning and preparation that goes into any other method of dispute resolution, including trial. Mediation preparation is particularly important because mediation is the only method of dispute resolution in which the parties can control the outcome, rather than simply being bound by it. A negotiating plan is critical to a successful mediation. Fine-tuning as the session progresses is normal, and is often a consequence of new information received during the process. Don't overlook the importance of taking into account the observations and suggestions of the mediator, who provides the benefit of his or her exposure to many similar cases, as well as appropriate observations and disclosures from your adversary.

SIDEBAR I-3

What One Partner Tells Associates About Successful Mediation Advocacy

Christopher R. Carroll (interview)

Christopher Carroll is a founding member of a law firm with offices in New York and New Jersey, with a practice focusing on resolution of insurance coverage issues. Here he describes three key points he likes to make when teaching associates about negotiation and mediation.

I give a negotiation seminar to the newer lawyers when they come in to start work at our firm. When I talk about what I would like from my associates, I try to impart a few key points.

Point #1 is, "*Be prepared*." You can't wing it. Going into a mediation session, there is no substitute for knowing as much as you can and showing your adversary you are ready, and that, if there is going to be a mediated resolution, it is going to be on the merits—there will be no corners cut. There is a huge value in demonstrating that you are prepared to address things on any level, on any issue—properly and well versed. In the end, you can negotiate, and there are games that can be played, and there are personality issues. But there is really no substitute for knowing your stuff.

Point #2 is, "*Bring creativity*." In my experience, among mediators, clients, and advocates, all too often there's a relatively rote approach to how you proceed in a mediation. You know—numbers back and forth. The good mediators and good advocates are those who recognize when the routine is just not going to work, for whatever reason. Rather than continue down that road—knowing full well that you are going to get to a dead end at some point, and probably create more damage than good in that process—they have the ability to jettison the process that was adopted and implement a new one. Go a different route. Try to come up with something different, something more creative as a resolution plan.

A different route could be something as simple as identifying the issues that actually separate you—forget numbers and try to drill down on an issue-by-issue basis. Maybe, in the end, you are going to narrow the case and come up with some highs and lows depending on different outcomes on different issues, you get to a resolution point, just not a straight number. Creativity and flexibility—being able to bend and weave based upon what you are seeing and hearing and the roadblocks in front of you—that's probably the most critical part of good advocacy in mediation.

Point #3 is, "*Take care in listening*"—listening to and kind of reading the other side. Hear what they are saying, hear *how* they are saying it, and respond accordingly. Too often, people send the wrong signals, or don't read the right signals, or aren't reading the signals at all, or are just not listening. It might not be an overt signal—it could just be something that is somewhat subtle. If you are focused in on the persons you are talking to—their personalities, their messages—and if you deliver your own messages properly, you can get further along than otherwise in a mediation process.

See what the important points are from the perspective of your adversary. One of those points might not be something that you believe is really outcome determinative, but it is important to them. Perhaps you can deliver some peace on issues that may not be of import to you. If it has value to your adversary, for whatever reason, be prepared to address and recognize that.

Not every mediation is successful. Certainly, not every mediation I am part of is successful. But I am not going to leave a mediation unless I've overturned every stone—unless I've kind of gone down every avenue that I think needs to be explored.

STEP ONE

Check Out the Governing Rules and Plan Accordingly

> Q: *I'm thinking Step One will probably be "take a look and familiarize yourself with the governing rules." Do you think that's a good idea?*
>
> A: *Yes.*
>
> Q: *Why?*
>
> A: *Well, to begin with, because most people don't! You can very likely have an advantage, because you may know something that other people don't.*
>
> —From an interview with Susan Yates,
> mediation program consultant

Wait. Rules? Isn't mediation supposed to be an informal process?

Compared to the procedural intricacies of civil litigation, sure. But there are still rules. For best results—and to keep yourself out of trouble—you need to know what the applicable rules are and make them work for you.

As you probably know, there are three basic kinds of mediation: (1) mediations required by a court for the parties to lawsuits filed in that jurisdiction (aka "court annexed"), (2) mediations required by a contract between parties, and (3) "voluntary" mediations agreed upon between or among disputing parties. Of the three, court-annexed mediation is where you are likely to encounter the most detailed rules.

But formal rules are only part of the story. You need to recognize that local practice—the customs in a particular legal community—may actually conflict somewhat with the written rules. You don't want to be surprised by those differences.

Also, court-annexed mediation often gives participants a choice to opt out of their rules in whole or in part, which offers the possibility of flexibilities like those associated with "voluntary" mediation.

Step One involves four basic substeps:

1. Locate the applicable mediation rules.
2. Check key provisions in the mediation rules.
3. In court-annexed mediation, decide whether to "opt out" for private mediation or customize rules by stipulation (if allowed), and proceed accordingly.
4. Learn about the local realities of mediation practice.

As with all the other steps in this book, how much time you devote will naturally depend on factors including the size of your case. Ideally, if you are interested in maximizing your competence in mediation advocacy, you should spend some time on your own to increase your understanding of the mediation rules that apply where you usually practice. In any event, whatever time you do spend could pay dividends down the line.

1.1 Locate the applicable mediation rules.

Rules applicable to court-annexed mediation are often promulgated by courts for use in their jurisdiction, but they may also be found in statutes and other materials. For contractual mediation, the primary document is the contract in question, whose ADR clause will often incorporate by reference the rules of a particular "private" ADR organization. In theory, purely voluntary mediation does not have any rules except those that the parties agree on to help solve that particular dispute, but in practice, this usually means turning to a "private" ADR organization and its rules.

A. Rules applying to court-annexed mediation

Rules of court-annexed mediation are comparable to rules of civil procedure in litigation, and may be included as such (*see, e.g.*, Fla. R. Civ. P. 1.700–1.750). They may be more detailed and potentially more rigid than the mediation rules promulgated by alternative dispute resolution organizations for "private" mediation. Their provisions may reflect varying and sometimes opposing interests within the bodies that formulated and approved them. Once codified, they are not necessarily easy to change even with experience and even as ideas about effective mediation practice evolve over time.

The latter point was made by the director of one state court system's ADR commission, who was appointed just when mediation rules for the jurisdiction were about to be adopted. "I looked at the planned rules, and they were not remotely the rules that I would have written," the director recalls. But at that point, it was too late in the process to push for change. "I am where I am and I work with what I've got."

However, as alluded to earlier, the mediation rules in some court systems allow the parties to opt out of court rules in whole or part if certain requirements are met. See Substeps 1.2 and 1.3 for more discussion of this.

For mediation annexed to a state court system, applicable rules may be found in state statutes, unified court rules, or local rules. To use Florida as an example, statutory provisions can be found in Chapter 44 of the *Florida Statutes,* which governs "mediation alternatives to judicial action." Among other things, the statutes contain important provisions regarding confidentiality and privilege in the mediation process (§§ 44.401–44.403).

Florida's statutes, like those of some other states, also provide for court-ordered mediation to be conducted according to rules adopted by the state's highest court (*see* Fla. R. Civ. P. 1.700–1.750). But other rules can also have a direct bearing, such as rules on mediator conduct. For example, Rule 10.330(b) requires a mediator to withdraw "if the mediator is no longer impartial." (Most mediators also belong to voluntary associations that impose rules of conduct on their members.) Rule 10.420(c) puts the burden on the mediator to "cause the terms of any agreement reached to be memorialized appropriately."

Another source of authority on mediations may be ethics opinions, which in some instances may have a direct bearing on procedure. To take another example from Florida, Opinion

2008-006 of the Florida Mediation Ethics Advisory Committee (2008, p.1) states: "It is not permissible for a mediator to dictate, over the parties' objections, who participates in a mediation caucus." (For a discussion of mediation caucuses, see Steps Nine and Ten.)

In some jurisdictions, the rules governing court-annexed mediation are essentially uniform statewide. In others, the applicable rules may be much more decentralized.

For example, the judicial system in the state of New York is divided into departments and further into districts. "Usually the mediation rules are local to those districts," according to Daniel Weitz, although there are uniform commercial division rules. Weitz is Deputy Director, Division of Professional and Court Services and Coordinator, Office of ADR and Court Improvement Programs for the New York State Unified Court System. There are no uniform court rules on confidentiality—that topic is typically addressed in local rules—but there is a state statute regarding confidentiality in settlement discussions (*see* CPLR § 4547).

Federal district courts. In federal court, pursuant to a federal authorization statute, each district promulgates its own rules governing court-annexed mediation (and other forms of alternative dispute resolution). But in diversity cases, some elements of state law may apply to federal mediation in ways that might not be immediately obvious. For more on that topic, see Sidebar 1-5: "Confidentiality: State Law in Federal Mediations."

B. Rules applying to contractual and voluntary mediation

Of course, if the contract underlying your dispute contains a mediation clause, you will know exactly what it says. For example, the American Arbitration Association (AAA) recommends this model clause (among others) for general commercial use (2007, p.11):

> If a dispute arises out of or relates to this contract, or the breach thereof, and if the dispute cannot be settled through negotiation, the parties agree first to try in good faith to settle the dispute by mediation admin-

> istered by the American Arbitration Association under its Commercial Mediation Procedures before resorting to arbitration, litigation, or some other dispute resolution procedure.

By its terms, this clause incorporates the AAA's Commercial Mediation Procedures.

More commonly, your ADR clause may require arbitration (in lieu of litigation) according the rules of the AAA or another major private ADR organization. In that case, the organization's mediation rules will come into play if the parties opt for (or are required to engage in) mediation as a pre-arbitration measure.

Even in a purely voluntary mediation, an ADR organization may be involved, so that its mediation rules will apply. An example of this might be voluntary mediation in conjunction with contractual mandatory arbitration in a dispute between a stock investor and her brokerage.

"Usually what happens is that the customer or former customer will file an arbitration claim with FINRA [Financial Industry Regulatory Authority], and the matter will proceed on that track," says Tracey Salmon-Smith (New Jersey and New York), who used to work as inside counsel for a major brokerage firm. "At the same time, FINRA has a mediation track that you can go on as well, and the two are not mutually exclusive—you can do both." The dispute is resolved through the arbitration process if the mediation fails.

In all mediations, another source of rules may be your engagement agreement with the mediator, but you will not be dealing with that until a mediator is selected (*see* Step Two). Beyond this, don't forget that in some places (as was noted for Florida), rules governing mediators certified for court-annexed mediation may apply even when that mediator is conducting a mediation outside the court-annexed system. The same goes for confidentiality statutes.

1.2 Check key provisions in the mediation rules.

Now, at the very outset, is the time for you to get a good grip on the mediation process ahead, including the decisions and advance planning you will need to make. The following list of questions is tailored to court-annexed mediation:

(a) Are the parties allowed to opt out of court-annexed mediation in whole or part?

A threshold question is whether you are actually required to mediate, or to mediate within the confines of the court-annexed rules. If the choice is there, you might prefer to opt for private mediation instead, or to modify a particular mediation rule in your case by agreement of the parties. Or you might decide it is best to proceed totally in accordance with the default court-annexed mediation procedure. (For more on this decision, see Substep 1.3, as well as Sidebar 1-2: "Why 20% in the Northern District of California Opt for 'Private' Mediation.")

- In some jurisdictions, like Maryland, court-annexed mediation is built into the system but not mandatory. After receiving a judicial order for mediation, the parties have the option to decline—but that is not common, according to Rachel Wohl, who heads the Maryland Judiciary's Mediation and Conflict Resolution Office. "Most people go," she says, "because it has become an expected part of the litigation process, and in some instances, lawyers know that a particular judge really wants them to go—and lawyers don't like to buck judges."
- In the court-annexed mediation programs of some jurisdictions, ADR is mandatory but parties are allowed to opt out of mediation in favor of another form (such as arbitration) if they desire. For example, Rule 8(a) of the New York County (Commercial Division) ADR rules provides: "Parties referred to the Program are free to choose the form of ADR they wish to undergo. Unless otherwise agreed by the parties, cases shall be mediated."
- Parties in some other jurisdictions are allowed to opt out of mandatory court-annexed mediation procedures in favor of a private mediation process. For example, Rule 9019-2(k) of the local rules for the bankruptcy court of Florida's Middle District pro-

vides: "Nothing in this rule is intended to limit the authority of the presiding judge to order, or the parties to agree, to mediation . . . by procedure different from those set forth in this rule." Likewise, stipulation for private mediation (or another form of private ADR) is an option in the Northern District of California (*see* ADR Local Rules 3-4(b) and 8-2).

- A total opt-out is not the only possibility you may encounter. The rules for court-annexed mediation in some jurisdictions allow selective opt-out of certain procedures. For example Prof. Sharon Press (St. Paul, MN), former Director of the Florida Dispute Resolution Center, notes that "a lot of procedural rules in Florida have the phrase, 'unless otherwise agreed to by the parties.'" In her view, the rationale for this is probably to "be consistent with the spirit of mediation as a flexible process."

(b) Specifically, may the parties "opt out" of a court-appointed mediator and choose their own instead?

Among partial opt-out flexibilities, the parties' option to stipulate a mediator of their choice may be one of the most common. For example, this is done in the "vast, vast majority" of cases within Florida's court-annexed system, according to Prof. Press.

In some jurisdictions, a stipulated mediator must be qualified by certification (unless an exemption is obtained). But this is not true everywhere. For example, "in Maryland, if both sides agree, they can choose anyone to be their mediator," notes Rachel Wohl. "The mediator doesn't have to meet court qualifications—if both parties decide they want Uncle Joe to be the mediator, they can do it."

(c) What key time frames and deadlines do the mediation rules contain?

"Time frames—that would be one of the most important things to know," says Susan Yates (Chicago), who helped establish court-annexed mediation programs in Illinois. Sometimes the effect of missing a deadline can be to miss an opportunity.

For example, in New York County's Commercial Division (Rule 4), the program administrator appoints a mediator from the designated panel after receiving a referral order. The parties then have an opportunity to select a mediator of their own choosing instead—but only if they notify the program administrator of their alternative selection and the scheduled mediation date within a specified period of days after receiving the name of the court-appointed neutral.

(d) What are the procedures and criteria by which a mediator is appointed?

Susan Yates poses the following questions: "Selecting the mediator, how much authority do you have? Does it need to be somebody from a roster or can you pick anyone? How do you do that in terms of the other party?"

(e) Who pays for the mediator? If a court-appointed mediator provides some time at no charge to the parties, how much time?

Obviously, these points are of particular concern where the financial stakes are small or the clients' resources slim. Some court-annexed programs provide a certain number of "free" mediation hours. In the District Court in the Northern District of California, for example, the arrangement works like this (2011, p.11; *see* ADR Local Rule 6-3(C)):

> The mediator volunteers preparation time and the first four hours of the mediation. After four hours of mediation, the mediator may either (1) continue to volunteer his or her time or (2) give the parties the option of concluding the procedure or paying the mediator for additional time at an hourly rate of $300, to be split among the parties as they determine. The mediation continues only if all parties and the mediator agree. After eight hours in one or more mediation sessions, if all parties agree, the mediator may charge his or her hourly rate or such other rate that the parties agree to pay.

By contrast, in the Middle District of Florida (Local Rule 9.02(f)), the parties are normally expected to pay from the beginning:

> Absent agreement of the parties and the mediator, mediators shall be compensated at a reasonable hourly rate provided by order of the Court after consideration of the amount in controversy, the nature of the dispute, the resources of the parties, the prevailing market rate for mediators in the applicable market, the skill and experience of the mediator, and other pertinent factors. Unless altered by order of the Court, the cost of the mediator's services shall be borne equally by the parties to the mediation conference.

(f) Are there limitations on the techniques a mediator may employ?

As will be discussed more in Step Two, some mediators take a purely "facilitative" approach, while others may give more evaluative input to encourage movement in the parties' positions during a session. If you think a strong evaluative style might be best for your case, be aware that the rules in at least one jurisdiction apparently require court-appointed mediators to avoid this. Rule 17-102(d) of the Maryland Rules of Procedure provides in part (italics added):

> A mediator may identify issues and options, assist the parties or their attorneys in exploring the needs underlying their respective positions, and, upon request, record points of agreement reached by the parties. While acting as a mediator, the mediator *does not engage in* arbitration, *neutral case evaluation*, neutral fact-finding, or other alternative dispute resolution processes and does not recommend the terms of an agreement.

In practice, a provision such as this may be honored more in the breach than the observance, but in some circumstances it might prompt you to seek a private mediation instead.

(g) Do any rules restrict the parties' ability to communicate freely with the mediator in advance of the mediation session?

Pre-mediation conferences are covered in Step Three, and confidential presession communications with the mediator are covered in Step Five. As discussed there (and other places), such conferences and other communication before the mediation session can be very useful. Yet not all court-annexed programs may allow them. A study from the ABA Section of Dispute Resolution's Task Force on Mediation Quality (2008a, p.6) reported that while many mediators schedule pre-mediation discussion as a regular practice, "some mediators participate in court programs that require the mediator not to communicate with any participant prior to an actual mediation session."

You may also want to be aware of any rule that might affect your ability to communicate privately with a mediator before the mediation session, without the opposing party present (i.e., ex parte). A small survey by the Task Force on Mediation Quality (2008a, p.7) found that a majority of survey participants found ex parte calls acceptable (although not necessarily preferable) for both procedural and substantive matters. Florida's court-annexed system specifically allows mediators to "meet and consult privately with any party or parties or their counsel" (Rule 1.720(i)), but this may not be universal. For more on the issue of ex parte communication between one party and the mediator before the mediation session, read Sidebar 3-7: "Ex Parte Communications With the Mediator."

(h) Is a pre-mediation conference mandatory?

An example of a rule requiring pre-mediation conferences: "The mediator shall schedule a brief joint telephone conference before the mediation session with counsel who will attend the mediation session to discuss matters such as the scheduling of the mediation, the procedures to be followed, the nature of the case, the content of the written mediation statements, and which client representatives will attend" (District Court, N.D. CA, ADR Local Rule 6-6). If your jurisdiction has such a requirement, you know that the discussion of such conferences in Step Three will absolutely apply to you.

rules patterned on" Federal Rule of Evidence 408," which is the principal federal provision protecting confidentiality of settlement talks (2009a, p.218). Although there is no general mediation privilege in the federal courts, many states have gone further with statutes providing for confidentiality of the entire mediation process (p.219).

(m) Will the underlying litigation be stayed during the mediation process?

Discovery and other elements of the litigation process may likely continue on a parallel track during the mediation process. If you believe it would be beneficial to halt the litigation side for a period of time, you may need to obtain an order from the judge.

1.3 In court-annexed mediation, decide whether to "opt out" for private mediation or customize rules by stipulation (if allowed), and proceed accordingly.

As discussed in Substep 1.2, the applicable court-annexed rules may permit you to "opt out" completely in favor of a private mediation process (though this is probably unusual) or—much more commonly—to customize your court-annexed mediation experience by stipulation. The latter approach allows you to modify individual provisions of the rules if both parties agree.

Where the parties in a court-annexed mediation are permitted to stipulate to a mediator of their choice, you should consider this option very seriously, for several reasons:

- In many court-annexed systems, the court-appointed mediator may simply be the next one in line on the roster, with no matching of background or abilities to the needs of your particular case.
- Many court-appointed mediators may have relatively little experience in that role. Certification may require completion of a training program and a certain amount of hands-on work as a mediator, but

minimum qualifications required are limited. "I think most of the roster managers would also tell you that on their rosters they have some outstanding mediators—and they have some pretty green mediators," says Rachel Wohl.

- The parties and lawyers involved in a dispute may be more committed to the mediation process when the mediator is someone they have affirmatively chosen for themselves. "[T]he first way to really get everybody bought into the process is to get everybody to buy into the mediator," says V. Heather Sibbison (Washington, DC). "And you need everybody to feel that the mediator is somebody that they have participated in hiring; otherwise, they're less likely to really want to participate. . . . [T]hat works much better than when a court appoints a mediator on their own, because everybody is hostile to the mediator in that situation" (Sibbison speaking in Bickerman et al., 2003, p.2).

It probably goes without saying that you should consult with your client on this issue. Going through the process described in Step 2 (selecting a mediator) will certainly involve some additional time (and thus expense) on your part. In addition, in jurisdictions where some free mediation hours are provided by a court-appointed mediator, a private alternative could also involve more mediator fees.

Obviously, you and your client cannot decide on your own whether to seek an alternative to the court-appointed mediator (or customize any other rule in the court-annexed program); your opponent must also agree. Your opponent's degree of interest in pursuing this option may also provide an early signal of the degree to which he is committed to the mediation process.

Stipulations may require lead time and be subject to deadlines—particularly with regard to mediator choice. So figure out right from the start what stipulations you may want to obtain and take action as needed.

1.4 Learn about the local realities of mediation practice.

"Oh, well, that's what the rules say, but that's not what we do here." Susan Yates has heard this sentence more than once in her work helping to set up court-annexed mediation programs in Illinois. "While it's important to know the rules, it's also important to ask around and find out how people really practice," she says.

As an example of how custom may differ from the rules, she points to mediation memoranda: "The rules may specifically say that parties will provide the mediator with pre-mediation statements. It may be that the way practice has evolved, they don't do that. Or it could be the other way around. It could be that there's nothing in the rules about providing written statements to the mediator, and it's turned out that the parties do that."

Because so many of Florida's court-annexed mediation rules can be "otherwise agreed" (*see* the discussion in Substep 1.2), Prof. Sharon Press thinks it is hard to know when local practice in that state actually conflicts with the rules. But she does note that in practice, some rules appear to be blurred more frequently than others. For example, if the parties opt for their own choice of mediator, the rules require them to stipulate "with the court" within 10 days after the order of referral. But the actual practice may be more relaxed, within limits:

> Typically the way it works in large civil cases is the court orders the parties to mediation and then doesn't really expect to hear from them until they come back either with a report of the mediation agreement or a report of no agreement. I don't think anybody closely monitors the ten-day period for stipulation on a mediator, and I don't think there's really a strong expectation that the parties are going to come back to the court and say, "Here's our mediator. Can we have this stipulation with the court that this is our mediator?"

> The unwritten rule is that assuming you're doing everything that you're supposed to do, no one's going to come back and bother you about it. On the other hand, if for example nobody schedules the required mediation, somebody from the mediation program is going to come back and say, "What's going on? You've not complied with the rules/order."

There may also be notable variation in practices within states that do not have a unified court system, such as Maryland. In that state, there is a set of statewide ADR rules, but there are no local court rules. The differences in practice from one jurisdiction to the next can be significant. "One county, for example, may send motor torts to mediation and another county may not," notes Rachel Wohl. "One county might send everything to mediation and another county might only send employment cases or contract cases." While acknowledging that "uniformity might be easier and preferable for some reasons," Wohl also points out that some differences may be better adapted to "jurisdiction-to-jurisdiction differences in the bench, the bar, and the demographics of the public they serve."

Bottom line: After reviewing the written rules applicable to your mediation, you should talk with other lawyers who have significant experience with mediation in the arena where your case will be mediated. Then factor what you learn into your planning.

SIDEBAR 1-1

Definitions of "Mediation"

Here are some definitions of "mediation" found in various court rules, a statute, and the Uniform Mediation Act. Although they share a common thread, there are differences in emphasis and nuance.

Uniform Mediation Act

"'Mediation' means a process in which a mediator facilitates communication and negotiation between parties to assist them in reaching a voluntary agreement regarding their dispute." (§ 2(1))

United States District Court, Northern District of California

"Mediation is a flexible, non-binding, confidential process in which a neutral person (the mediator) facilitates settlement negotiations. The mediator improves communication across party lines, helps parties articulate their interests and understand those of their opponent, probes the strengths and weaknesses of each party's legal positions, identifies areas of agreement and helps generate options for a mutually agreeable resolution to the dispute. The mediator generally does not give an overall evaluation of the case. A hallmark of mediation is its capacity to expand traditional settlement discussion and broaden resolution options, often by exploring litigant needs and interests that may be formally independent of the legal issues in controversy." (ADR Local Rule 6-1)

Florida

"'Mediation' means a process whereby a neutral third person called a mediator acts to encourage and facilitate the resolution of a dispute between two or more parties. It is an informal and nonadversarial process with the objective of helping the disputing parties reach a mutually acceptable and voluntary agreement. In mediation, decisionmaking authority rests with the parties. The role of the mediator includes, but is not limited to, assisting the parties in identifying issues, fostering joint problem solving, and exploring settlement alternatives." (Fla. Stat. § 44.1011(2))

Maryland

"'Mediation' means a process in which the parties work with one or more impartial mediators who, without providing legal advice, assist the parties in reaching their own voluntary agreement for the resolution of the dispute or issues in the dispute. A mediator may identify issues and options, assist the parties or their attorneys in exploring the needs underlying their respective positions, and, upon request, record points of agreement reached by the parties. While acting as a mediator, the mediator does not engage in arbitration, neutral case evaluation, neutral fact-finding, or other alternative dispute resolution processes and does not recommend the terms of an agreement."
(Md. R. Civ. P. 17-102(d))

SIDEBAR 1-2

Why 20% in the Northern District of California Opt for "Private" Mediation

The ADR Program for the U.S. District Court, Northern District of California, has a reputation as a model in the federal system. Its mediation element features a very detailed set of procedural rules—along with considerable freedom for participants to opt out (with consent of both sides) in favor of "private" mediation that can largely sidestep those formal rules.

According to the program's current director, Howard A. Herman, a great majority sticks with the court mediation system, which entitles participants to (among other things) four free hours of the court-appointed mediator's time. Nevertheless, Herman says, in roughly 20% of cases the parties select a "private" provider instead.

Why? "You have more control of everything related to your ADR process," he notes. A major flexibility concerns the choice of mediators. In "private" mediation, "you can choose whomever you want, on whatever basis you want," in a locality that is endowed with "a very vibrant and competent private ADR sector."

Another flexibility is that "you are not governed by the requirements of the ADR local rules for exactly how sessions will be held." In this context, Herman points to court requirements for what types of individuals must appear in person at the mediation session: "So, for example, if there are parties or lawyers who want to appear by telephone or to simply be on phone standby, we have some very specific rules about that and procedures that have to be followed in order to obtain permission. The parties can't simply agree among themselves that someone is going to be on the telephone. And the mediators and neutral evaluators don't have the authority to just allow that." By contrast, "if you opt for a private ADR proceeding, you are not governed by that rule."

Herman says that in some ways, the court mediation system is actually more flexible than it may look on paper. Notably, in practice, program administrators "are willing to work with people to try to ensure that they get a neutral who is to their satisfaction," although this may not be fully apparent from the rules. Nevertheless, "ultimately it's up to the ADR Program's discretion."

SIDEBAR 1-3

Early Neutral Evaluation Versus "True" Mediation

There is some continuing confusion over the difference between "true" mediation and a form sometimes known as early neutral evaluation—which is also sometimes loosely called mediation. What the two always have in common is that the "neutral" or mediator has no power to decide the case. If there is a resolution, it must come through a settlement deal by the parties.

However, the basic concept of early neutral evaluation is for the neutral to evaluate the case—to give an opinion on the likely outcomes, with the intent of aiding the parties to settle. By contrast, some court-annexed mediation programs may expressly prohibit the mediator from offering any evaluation and limit her solely to facilitative techniques. In other forums, mediators may provide varying degrees of evaluation, but this is not a central part of the process.

New York County is an example of a jurisdiction where early neutral evaluation is extensively employed in certain types of disputes—particularly for personal injury. According to Daniel Weitz, who helps oversee ADR in New York state, most neutral evaluation work there is done by court-employed staff, who conduct sessions in probably several thousand cases each year.

"What's going to really move and settle that type of case," he says, "is a credible neutral who understands the value of certain injuries in certain contexts and can give a realistic assessment of the merits of the claims—both plaintiff's and defense claims."

The focus of this book is on so-called true mediation. However, given that even "true" mediation may involve some evaluation by the mediator, and early neutral evaluation may involve a facilitative approach by the neutral, there is definite overlap.

SIDEBAR 1-4

"Punching Your Ticket" and Good Faith Requirements

Does your client—or your opponent—resent having to spend the time and money to participate in mediation, wanting to do nothing more than the absolute minimum? Or do you yourself believe that your case is not yet ripe for settlement, through mediation or otherwise? Under those circumstances, what is the best way to proceed?

Jay Cohen calls unwilling participation by a party in the mediation process just to meet a legal requirement "punching your ticket." Cohen is a mediator based in Winter Park, Florida (near Orlando), who has conducted more than 4,000 mediations since 1990. When he senses that type of situation in a mediation session, he sometimes tells the participants: "Look, if I'm just here to punch your ticket, let me know." Not surprisingly, he reports that disputes where a ticket-punching attitude is involved are "very difficult to resolve" in mediation.

Based on focus groups composed of people who have had experience with mediation (mostly as lawyers or mediators), the ABA Section of Dispute Resolution's Task Force on Improving Mediation Quality (2008a, p.33) reported:

> Several participants expressed frustration about mediations where one side was not ready to mediate, whether due to lack of preparation and/or unwillingness to negotiate seriously and take reasonable positions. Some complained about use of mediation as "cheap discovery." . . . One participant talks informally with opposing counsel in advance to determine whether they are serious about mediating and will not mediate if they do not seem to be serious.

Several interviewees for this book pointed to mandatory court-annexed mediation programs—especially relatively recent ones—as being particularly prone to this problem. Paul Sandars (New Jersey) is a litigator with a strong construction law practice who has served extensively as both a mediator and an advocate. Painting with a broad brush, he contrasts his experience in court-annexed mediation with mediation of construction disputes—where alternative dispute resolution has a long history:

> The construction mediations that I do either as an advocate or a neutral, I find that the parties are more familiar with the process and the expectations are different. In the state court program, people don't want to be there. They don't know what it is, they have never done it before, and they don't how to prepare

> their clients. . . . I've had very few of the state court-ordered mediations that I would consider to be a true mediation. Whereas in the private side, people retain me who are serious; they understand the process, they prepare their clients, and their clients have the right expectations. They come ready to spend as much time as it takes to settle the case. . . . The state system, it's like herding cattle.

An observer who explored litigators' attitudes in a Rocky Mountain city a few years ago encountered "resentment among the lawyers and not a lot of respect" toward a mandatory court-annexed mediation program that they felt had been forced upon them. The observer found that lawyers in the area saw mediation as an unwanted obstacle in litigation, paraphrasing their view like this: "We have to go through this hurdle in lots of cases that [are] inappropriate, and we know we are not going to settle, where we know the insurance company has offered a price and they are not budging—but we still have to go."

There is reason to think acceptance of court-annexed mediation may tend to grow with experience over time. In Florida, where mandatory mediation is long established, Edward M. Mullins finds the greatest resistance from out-of-state lawyers. They are the ones who say (in Mullins's paraphrase), "Why do we got to go to mediation? This is ridiculous!" But even among Florida lawyers, he still sees many who view mediation as just a hoop to be jumped through, which he considers "really unfortunate."

To the extent that lawyers see mediation as just a ticket to be punched—with minimal willingness to perform—the question of good faith naturally arises. Some mediation rules expressly impose a good-faith requirement. An example from the bankruptcy court of Florida's Middle District: "The mediator shall report to the Court willful failure to attend the mediation conference or to participate in the mediation process in good faith, which may result in the imposition of sanctions by the Court" (Local Rule 9019-2(d)(2)).

Good-faith requirements tend to be associated with jurisdictions that developed court-annexed programs early, according to Daniel Weitz. From his perspective helping to run New York's court-annexed ADR programs, the problem with this approach is "the elusive nature of good faith," which is "subjective and difficult to judge."

Because of this, Weitz says, the trend has been to focus more on mediation-program design and education initiatives. The latter can include "training mediators to facilitate document exchange and information exchange in a way that's just as meaningful as it could be in discovery" without going through formal discovery procedures.

Now let's circle back to you and your case. At the start of the mediation process, you may want to get a read on the opposing party's attitude. Informal conversation with opposing counsel may quickly give you a sense as to the seriousness (or not) with which she views mediation. If her attitude indicates that her side is just punching their ticket, you may have to adjust your own effort accordingly, so as not to put too much costly effort into a process whose prospects look dim.

If your own client has a negative attitude toward mediation, you can consider whether this view is ingrained or might improve with input from you. If your client is adamant, or your own assessment of the prospects for settlement at this stage through mediation is negative, likewise you will want to calibrate carefully the amount of time and effort you expend.

Despite any of these assessments, it may still be worth your while to put enough into each of the steps in this book so that something good *could* come out of the mediation. You might be pleasantly surprised.

SIDEBAR 1-5

Confidentiality: State Law in Federal Mediations

While most rules governing mediation annexed to a federal district court can be found in that district's local rules, some elements of state law may also apply. The most notable such element concerns confidentiality.

"You may be surprised to learn that Florida's Mediation Confidentiality and Privilege Act applies to many federal district and bankruptcy court mediations" conducted in that state, wrote C. Timothy Corcoran, III—a former bankruptcy judge—in seminar materials prepared for bankruptcy practitioners (2007, § 2e.i.8). Although his comments were directed to a Florida statute, the same issue could be relevant to confidentiality provisions in other jurisdictions.

By its terms, the Mediation Confidentiality and Privilege Act applies (inter alia) to "[m]ediations conducted pursuant to 'statute, court rule, agency rule or order, oral or written case-specific court order, or court administrative order,'" he noted. "It is unclear whether that means only state courts to the exclusion of federal courts." The act also covers "[m]ediations facilitated by Florida Supreme Court certified mediators, unless the mediation parties expressly agree otherwise."

On the opposite side of the country, the application of state confidentiality law to federal mediation also strikes a chord with Howard A. Herman, Director of the ADR Program for the U.S. District Court, Northern District of California.

"We believe that state confidentiality law sometimes applies in federal court proceedings," Herman says. "We instruct all of the neutrals on our panel in the training for mediators that they need to be conversant with both federal mediation law and our local rules and with the state confidentiality rules."

Asked for an example of how this could make a difference, Herman notes that in California, "there is a specific statute that declares that a mediator is incompetent to testify in a later civil proceeding in court. And that is at least arguably a much broader prohibition on mediator testimony than one would find if one just examined the federal law to that point."

From a practical standpoint, mediator testimony could be important in legal enforcement of an agreement allegedly made at the end of a court-annexed mediation session. Herman says:

> If an agreement is reached in a mediation in our program in federal court, and then there is an argument later about whether to enforce that agreement, that enforcement action is essentially a contract action

which is going to be governed by California contract principles. The federal court will look to the California mediation confidentiality statutes—not to our own local rules—in determining whether to admit certain evidence. In contrast, at least in a federal question case, if the matter does not settle and a party tries to introduce evidence from the mediation in a federal court trial, the court would ordinarily look to the ADR local rules on confidentiality—not state law—to determine whether to admit the evidence. One could write an extended law review article on these topics.

SIDEBAR 1-6

Mediation in Securities Disputes

Albert S. Watkins (interview)

Although court-annexed mediations are common, they are by no means the only important arena. Mediation also plays a major role in construction and securities disputes, sometimes on a voluntary basis in connection with a contractual arbitration clause. This discussion by Albert Watkins (St. Louis, MO), whose practice includes representing claimants and industry members in securities disputes, will give you a glimpse of the mediation process in that arena.

By and large, across the board in the securities industry, when investors sign a new account opening form, they are agreeing to compulsory or mandatory arbitration of their dispute, subject to the rules of the Financial Industry Regulatory Authority (FINRA).

If you have that arbitration, you have to follow FINRA's protocol for the selection of arbitrators. When you get your selection of arbitrators, you go through a relatively limited discovery process. The parties start to get a grasp of the underlying fact situation and understand where the opposition is coming from. Generally you can tell what the range of damages is in fairly short order on the accounts in question.

Once discovery is done, I will write a letter on behalf of an investor to opposing counsel, suggesting that at this point it might be worthwhile for the parties to consider mediation as an alternative—or a condition precedent—to arbitration. Generally speaking that type of overture is received favorably, if you have a claim that has any degree of color to it at all.

You bring the claimant-investor up the learning curve about not only the claim that they have in particular, but the uncertainties that correspond to arbitration. In truth and fact, a disproportionate percentage of these claims give rise to an award of nothing for the investor. Once you get them up that learning curve, if you couple that with a mediator who has taken the time to actually learn about the investor and learn about the investor's claim—and then during the mediation gives the claimant time to air and vent their side of the story—the odds of a claim being reconciled in relatively short order thereafter are astronomical.

SIDEBAR 1-7

Multiparty Mediation in Construction Disputes

Paul Alain Sandars III (interview)

For simplicity, this book often uses language that implies there are only two parties to a mediation, one on each side. But two parties is just the minimum: There may be several parties, even several dozen. Construction law is one of the practice areas where multiparty mediation is most common and developed earliest, mostly on a voluntary basis. Here, Paul Sandars (Roseland, New Jersey), whose practice includes work as both a mediation advocate and a mediator, talks about such multiparty disputes.

My view of construction law is kind of like spokes in a wheel: everybody's got a claim against everybody else. The plaintiff just happens to be the first one who got to the courthouse. Everybody has a counter-claim and cross-claim and indemnity up and down the line. Just with insurance, there are principals' types of groups,

CGL [comprehensive general liability] carriers, and excess carriers. It's not unusual in these cases to have 50 or 60 parties.

These complex cases require a lot of pre-mediation planning. I am not talking about submissions; I am talking about groups. Meeting with attorneys and clients, like for dinner. Talking about expectations before the mediation, so that when we are all in the room, we are all on the same page.

As a mediator, normally I'll go out to dinner with the plaintiffs first, to try and get a sense of what it is they are looking to achieve and what I can bring to the table. A lot of my cases involve condominium associations, which are very difficult because you've got a board of directors. You have a bunch of angry people who have spent millions of dollars on these units, and they are leaking. So, you try and get a feel: Are they really going to fix this? Do they really need all that money? Is there a cheaper way? Should we design a fix in the mediation?

There are a lot of creative ways to settle these cases. If you get the engineering defendants in a room, and they come up with a fix, and they sign off on it, and you get the contractors to agree to do it—settle the case!

STEP TWO

Agree on a Mediator (If You Have a Choice)

> *Q: If you were going to give a speech on 10 secrets to successful mediation, what would your number one be?*
>
> *A: I guess the number one would be: Pick a good mediator.*
>
> —From an interview with Nate Cade, litigator

Where you have the right to choose,[1] selecting the right mediator for your case may be the single most important decision to increase the likelihood of a positive outcome. "As a mediator, one of the biggest mistakes I see is that attorneys don't give enough thought to the type of mediation and the type of mediator they want, and the one that will best suit their client's needs," John Bickerman told a CLE audience in a panel presentation (Bickerman et al., 2003, p.1). His national mediation practice, based in Washington, DC, is focused on big-ticket cases.

Among professionals in the same chorus is Horace "Hob" Jordan, cofounder and general counsel of a closely held company in Lake Forest, Illinois. "Choose your mediator very carefully, because that person will really have a big impact on whether the dispute settles or not," he advises.

Despite this importance, how much time and energy you should reasonably devote to selecting a mediator will be related to the size and budget of your case (as with all other steps in the mediation process). Also, if the mediation rules impose a tight deadline for choosing an alternative to the mediator assigned through a court-annexed program (*see* Substeps 1.2 and 1.3 in the preceding chapter), there may be built-in time constraints.

1. *See* the discussion in Substeps 1.2 and 1.3 in the preceding chapter.

An effective process to secure the best mediator for your dispute may involve five substeps:

1. Find out how much involvement your client wants in the mediator selection process and get input as appropriate.
2. Agree with opposing counsel on one of six basic ways to arrive at a mutually acceptable mediator candidate.
3. Achieve agreement and buy-in on a mutually acceptable mediator.
4. Execute a mediation agreement.
5. File a notice of mediator selection (if required).

2.1 Find out how much involvement your client wants in the mediator selection process and get input as appropriate.

Clients vary greatly in how much involvement they expect (or want) in the mediator selection process. This can depend on factors including the legal sophistication of the client, the client's general temperament and attitude, and the field of law involved.

For example if you are representing a company in a specialized area of mediation (such as securities disputes), in-house counsel may have good knowledge of mediators in the field and strong ideas as to who should be on the short list. At the other extreme, a client may put the decisions entirely in your hands.

In *The Corporate Counsel's Guide to Mediation* (Poon, 2010, pp.41–58), mediator Gary Poon (Washington, DC) offers a systematic approach to guide inside counsel in selecting a mediator, including various factors that should be taken into account (or not) and the mediation style of the potential candidates. At the same time, he recognizes the importance of outside counsel's local knowledge (p.42):

> Your outside counsel may have a list of mediators that he likes to use because he may have had good experiences with those mediators in the past. If that is the case, you should defer to your outside counsel's judgment.

Of course, in any case the inside counsel will have final sign-off authority on choice of mediator.

Robert Craig (Houston) is an example of an inside lawyer who insists on a dominant role. Outside counsel is "not going to name some guy that I don't like or don't know," he says. "It's ultimately my decision, if we have the opportunity to select." (Of course you wouldn't want a mediator your client doesn't like, anyway.)

From your previous interactions in this representation, you may already have developed a sense of how hands-on your client will want to be in mediator selection. The obvious way to find out for sure is to ask. This will probably include discussing which of the ways of arriving at a mutually acceptable mediator candidate (*see* Substep 2.2) your client would prefer—and certainly if you think options 3 or 4 should be considered.

2.2 Agree with opposing counsel on one of six basic ways to arrive at a mutually acceptable mediator candidate.

When it comes to choosing a mutually acceptable mediator candidate, there are basically six possible options:

1. You and your opponent exchange lists of mediator candidates (*see* Picker, 2003, p.73).
2. You have a conversation in which you and opposing counsel raise mediator possibilities one by one until you both agree on one (*see* Sidebar 2-6: "How Sara Soto Selects").
3. You agree to accept any mediator that your opponent wants (*see* Watson, 2002, p.5).
4. Your opponent submits a list of mediator candidates and you pick one from that list (*see* Watson, 2002, p.5).
5. Your opponent agrees to accept any mediator that you want.
6. You submit a list of mediator candidates and your opponent picks one from that list.

In an exchange of lists under option 1, there is a chance that at least one mediator will happen to appear on both lists. This is probably more likely to occur when the lists are relatively long and the number of reputable mediators in the relevant locality or practice area is relatively small. It is also possible that you will see a mediator on your opponent's list that you like but had not thought of (or your opponent will have a similar reaction to a name on your list). Otherwise, you may still end up resorting to one of the other options.

Option 2 may be suited to situations where the relationship with opposing counsel is collegial and both sides already have a thorough knowledge of the mediators whose names may be likely to come up. It envisions a scenario where you may say, "Well, what about Jane Smith? She's got a pretty good rep," and your opponent might reply, "Sure, why not?" (or the other way around). Option 2 seems much less likely to work with truculent opposing counsel who—to quote Sara Soto (Miami)—"have this thing that if I said, 'I want Mr. X,' they must say no to Mr. X" (*see* Sidebar 2-6: "How Sara Soto Selects").

Both options 1 and 2 are predicated on the principle that your primary goal is to obtain a mediator who, in your opinion, offers the mediation style, experience, talent, and skills that are best suited to your particular case. But a very different consideration can also be critically important: your opponent's confidence and trust in the mediator. If you put this consideration at the top of the list, you might decide simply to agree on any mediator your opponent would prefer, using option 3. This possible course of action is discussed in Sidebar 2-5: "A Judo Maneuver: Opting for Your Opponent's Choice of Mediator."

Option 4 is also discussed in Sidebar 2-5. It is a hybrid that can put primary emphasis on your opponent's preferences while still preserving some choice on your part. It goes without saying that options 3 and 4 should only be considered if your client *fully understands and agrees in advance* with this type of strategic move.

At least hypothetically, the concept of options 3 and 4 can also be turned around in your direction, listed here as options 5 and 6. Under these options—however unlikely—your opponent may agree to give *your* side the primary say in choosing the mediator. Your opponent theoretically might decide this is strategic for *his* side, if he sees your client's trust and confidence in the mediator as a key element for success.

2.3 Achieve agreement and buy-in on a mutually acceptable mediator.

In terms of the process required, option 3 (*see* Substep 2.2) is sort of a no-brainer: Your opponent names a mediator and you say okay. The other options all require some exercise of choice on your part. Where you are actively involved in the choice, here are the bases to touch for a very thorough search and evaluation: (1) Decide whether the mediator needs to have special familiarity with the substantive law or practice area involved; (2) decide where your mediator should fit on the spectrum of mediation styles and models; (3) identify the pool of eligible mediators; (4) surface promising candidates through other lawyers; (5) utilize online resources to surface or research candidates; (6) review paper credentials; (7) interview promising candidates; (8) follow up with references; and (9) make the ultimate decision with client buy-in. The exact order of some of these substeps may vary with the case.

A. Decide whether the mediator needs to have special familiarity with the substantive law or practice area involved

In focus groups of experienced mediation users, the ABA Section of Dispute Resolution's Task Force on Mediation Quality found that "[t]o a very substantial degree, users endorsed the importance of subject matter knowledge" (2008a, p.9). This preference (or even prerequisite) appears to be especially strong in relatively specialized types of practice.

For example, in an article on mediating mass tort class actions, Robert Gary writes, "Because of the uniqueness of the issues to class actions, the mediator must be someone who is intimately familiar with, and has had hands-on experience in, class action litigation" (2004, p.4). Similarly, in an article on representing highly paid executives (HPEs), Richard Fincher notes that increasingly, "mediators in HPE litigation are expected to possess subject-matter expertise in executive compensation, benefit design, and taxation, in addition to case and statutory law concerning duties of executive enforcement" (2010, p.4). Sara Soto (Miami) takes it for granted that the mediator in her securities-dispute cases will come from that "relatively small world" where "everybody knows who everybody is" (*see* Sidebar 2-6: "How Sara Soto Selects").

But the priority of a special background is not equally important in all arenas or to all experienced mediation advocates, and such a background cannot substitute for skill in the mediation process. Hob Jordan emphasizes this point:

> Some people say you really need to be subject-matter oriented for whatever the dispute is. I don't feel that way to the same degree. I think the skills of the mediator are oftentimes the most important factor.

William Jentes, a Chicago-based mediator, offers similar advice. Although "special expertise may sometimes be required," he writes, "be sure you put mediation skills at the top of your list of mediator qualifications" (2010, p.3).

As inside counsel in charge of intellectual property litigation for a large corporation, Hildy Bowbeer (St. Paul, MN) questions the assumption that it is always important for a mediator to have expertise in the technology area involved. She writes (2011, p.177):

> [T]he mediator's primary role will be to make sure the parties have come to grips with the strengths and weaknesses of their own cases, and to help them search for creative, mutually beneficial options for resolution. To be effective in that role, the mediator ordinarily will not need to have a Ph.D. in polymer chemistry or be an expert in the optical properties of multilayer films, for example. In fact, in many cases, you may want a mediator who is *not* a technical expert and can give you some insight into how well or how poorly a jury is likely to understand your case.

Even so, Bowbeer acknowledges that "in cases where the parties differ greatly in their assessment of the likelihood of success on a complex technical issue, a mediator who comes with some familiarity with the technology may be able to provide a needed 'reality check' for the parties" (p.177).

Specialized knowledge or experience may be most important in cases where the mediator will need it in order to understand the legal issues thoroughly, assess the potential damages knowledgeably, or communicate with the parties in a way that commands attention and respect. The utility of specialized knowledge or experience on the mediator's part may be greatest where a strong evaluative approach is desired by the parties (*see* Substep 2.3B). Having a mediator with specialized knowledge may also save time in a mediation by eliminating the extra step of educating the mediator on applicable law or practice. Since mediators typically charge by the hour, this may also save money.

B. Decide where your mediator should fit on the spectrum of mediation styles and models

If you have read anything at all about mediators, you probably know something about the distinction between facilitative and evaluative techniques. The bedrock mediation techniques in which all mediators need to be adept are *facilitative*—that is, "assist[ing] the parties in identifying and exploring interests, concerns, motivations, goals, common ground and possible resolutions" (Picker, 2003, p.40). The mediator seeks to encourage movement mainly "through probing and open-ended inquiries."

Particularly in mediation of business disputes, *evaluative* (or analytical) techniques historically have played a major role, although they remain controversial in the larger mediation world. In varying degrees and by various methods, the mediator "evaluates the strengths and weaknesses of each party's case and provides his view on the likely outcome in litigation or arbitration" (Poon, 2010, p.51).

In the early days of mediation, there was a much more distinct divide between facilitative and evaluative approaches. Today, some experts favor a mixed approach that skillfully blends facilitative techniques with subtler evaluative techniques than were used in the past. Still, by personality and background, some mediators who are highly effective in facilitative techniques may be less effective with evaluative techniques, and vice versa.

Beyond the distinction between facilitative and evaluative, there are at least two other mediation approaches you should be aware of. The "*Understanding-based model* of mediation" gained recognition with the publication of a seminal book on the topic: *Challenging Conflict: Mediation Through Understanding* (Friedman & Himmelstein, 2008). From a procedural standpoint, a major feature of this model is that Understanding-based mediation sessions never include private caucuses between each one side and the mediator; both sides are always present at the same table. Regarding mediation philosophy, the authors write: "Where we are likely to differ from many mediators is that we work hard with the parties to help them find and articulate what is important to them, rather than the mediator concluding it for them, and we stress the importance of including the emotional significance to the parties more than many mediators might" (Friedman & Himmelstein, 2008, p.131). For more on Understanding-based mediation, read Sidebar 3-4: ("A Non-Caucus Approach to Mediation") and Sidebar 9-3: ("The Problems with Caucusing").

A *transformative* approach "emphasizes empowerment of the parties and their mutual recognition of each other instead of focusing on the solution of the immediate problem" (Goldberg & Sander, 2007, p.42). This approach is not generally a focus in mediation of commercial disputes, although some argue it should be more utilized (*see, e.g.,* Goldberg & Sander, 2007, p.40). Mediator David Hoffman offers an example of a session that turned out to have a transformative element in Sidebar 2-4: "The Power of Good Listening." Although such experiences are memorable, "truly transformational mediations are very much the exception," writes mediator Eleanor Barr (Los Angeles). "For every single mediation that facilitates deep encounter and transformation, there are twenty that focus on factual and legal positions and money; and as the mediator, it's not my role to force a different agenda" (2012, p.178).[2]

---

2. Other conceptual terms used to describe mediation approaches include a distinction among distributive, integrative, and negotiation principles (*see* Holbrook, 2006, p.1).

Because the vast majority of mediators in the legal field today are trained in a caucus-based model using facilitative and evaluative techniques, the remainder of this substep will focus on those approaches. We will begin by looking more in depth at the facilitative approach, then look more at the evaluative style, and finally discuss how these two relate to your considerations in selecting a mediator for your particular case.

(1) Facilitative approach

With its focus on the parties' "interests" rather than positions, the basic philosophy of facilitative mediation should be familiar to anyone who has read the highly influential book on negotiation *Getting to Yes* (1981), by Roger Fisher and William Ury.[3] Here is another description of the facilitative approach, from the late Chicago mediator and adjunct law professor John Cooley (2002, p.18):

> In a facilitative mediation, the mediator neither offers an opinion on the value of the case nor recommends how it should be settled. Rather, the facilitative mediator assists the parties and their counsel, through information interchange and creativity, to reach their own joint decision on a reasonable settlement or solution.

Take a look at Sidebar 2-1 in this chapter, where P. Jean Baker of the American Arbitration Association emphasizes facilitative techniques in a list of behaviors that she sees as characterizing an effective mediator. The list includes restating the parties' differing points of view "as suggestions rather than contentions," facilitating open exchanges of information, maintaining "active listening skills," and displaying "sensitivity to psychological movements" during the mediation session.

Hob Jordan recalls an example where one of these facilitative techniques—active listening—was used with particular skill. It happened in mediation of a big construction case on the West Coast, which he attended as inside counsel:

3. For a discussion of *Getting to Yes*, read Step 7.4A.

> In the opening caucus, the mediator took extremely good notes. He had a great memory, and he actually repeated just about everything both sides said, and added, "Do I have it right? Did I listen to you correctly?"
>
> I thought that was a great way to start a mediation, because both sides got the impression that, "I am not sure where the mediator is going to go, whether he agrees or disagrees with me, but at least he heard me." The party representative wants to feel, "Oh, you heard me, you heard my pain, now let's bridge the gap."

Since by definition a mediator does not have the power to force a settlement, techniques designed to facilitate the parties' efforts in that direction are essential for success. But Dwight Golann (Boston), a law professor and mediator, gives several reasons to support a view that an evaluative element is also needed for optimum mediation of business cases (2007, p.19):

- "People in a serious dispute with legal implications, especially after talking to lawyers, tend to assume that the 'right' way to approach the matter is by applying legal standards." The client's perception of the likely outcome of his case at trial often serves as his starting-point in assessing any settlement proposals. It is thus natural for a client to seek an evaluation from the mediator, who may be seen as a neutral, experienced authority.
- "A second, more substantive, reason to evaluate is an antidote to litigants' distorted viewpoints about their adjudication alternative." Clients may be more receptive to a reality check from the mediator than from their own lawyer, who is supposed to be on their side.
- "A neutral evaluation also helps parties to avoid responsibility for compromising. At the simplest level it can be comforting for a mediator to explain why compromise is the right thing to do."
- "Finally and not least important, lawyers use mediator evaluations to deliver bad news to clients—that a case is not as good as the party thinks it is, or

perhaps as the lawyer had suggested at the outset." Lawyers are always in a problematic situation when discussing the strength of a case with their client. If their initial assessment is not positive enough, they may never get the representation in the first place. If lawyers emphasize their case's weaknesses too much for purposes of evaluating a settlement proposal, the client may even consider replacing them as trial counsel if the mediation fails. By contrast, the mediator does not face any of these constraints."

(2) Evaluative approach

Compared to a facilitative approach, what an evaluative mediation means in practice is somewhat harder to pin down. "The term itself is understood to mean many different things to many different people," observes a report from the ABA Section of Dispute Resolution's Task Force on Improving Mediation Quality (2008a, p.15).

In part, this is because the nature of the evaluative approach has changed over time (Golann, 2007, p.16). In the early days of alternative dispute resolution (ADR), the centerpiece of mediation of disputes in the litigation context tended to be the issuance of a nonbinding opinion on the merits or a valuation by a neutral. This orientation was formalized in court-annexed programs such as early neutral evaluation, which still operate alongside other ADR modes in some jurisdictions (*see* Sidebar 1-3: "Early Neutral Evaluation Versus 'True' Mediation").

However, too much emphasis on this type of evaluation carries its own drawbacks in a mediation session. Two of those drawbacks are described in an article by law professors (and mediators) Stephen Goldberg and Frank Sander (2007, p.42):

- "[O]ne risk of evaluative mediation is that the mediator's evaluation will fail to persuade the party viewed by the mediator as the weaker and the parties will be back where they were before the mediation began, each seeking to persuade the other that it has the stronger claim." For example, a party who receives a negative evaluation from the mediator may believe that a favorable forum or his lawyer's superior skills will lead to a better result at trial.

- "Another drawback is that, as a result of its focus on the legal strengths and weaknesses of each party, evaluative mediation may fail to uncover a totally different and mutually satisfactory resolution of the dispute, one not wholly dependent on which party is "right" and which is "wrong." For a discussion of such "creative" settlements, see Step Ten.

Prof. Golann adds a third drawback of starkly evaluative mediation (2007, p.18):

> When a neutral states that a case is worth X dollars, it can become a take-it-or-leave-it offer to both sides. Parties are reluctant to accept an outcome higher or lower than the evaluator's number because doing so stimulates painful feelings of loss and exposes the settler to criticism from outsiders.

In the early days of business mediation, former judges were sought after as mediators precisely because of their evaluative authority. Experience of problems over time actually led to a backlash against using former judges in that role (Golann, 2007, p.19). (For more on former judges as mediators see Sidebar 2-2: "Should the Mediator Be a Former Judge?")

Experience also prompted the rise of subtler, less divisive evaluation techniques in mediation. Prof. Golann writes (2007, p.19, italics in original):

> The term [evaluation] is now understood to include more than simply estimating the trial outcome in a case. Most neutral evaluation that I have observed focuses on the *bargaining situation*, not the merits. A mediator might, for example, tell a defendant, "To get the plaintiff to drop to six figures, my sense is that you need to get to $______."
>
> * * *
>
> Indeed, evaluations now often do not take the form of explicit opinions at all. Instead mediators have learned

to use a spectrum of interventions that include pointed questions, tone of voice, and other indirect signals to nudge stalled negotiations back on track.

In view of the confusion about just what "evaluative" mediation means (or should mean), the ABA Section of Dispute Resolution's Task Force on Improving Mediator Quality suggests replacing the term with the phrases "analytical inputs" and "analytical techniques." Here are the Task Force's examples of what those terms may include (2008a, pp.15–16):

- Mediator discussion and analysis of legal and factual issues (including strengths, weaknesses, or both) without necessarily articulating conclusions and opinions;
- Mediator questioning about specific legal or factual issues, sometimes referred to as "reality testing": E.g., how do you think a jury will evaluate your testimony about an oral agreement, when the other side has a writing that seems to say something very different? Will the court permit any testimony about the oral agreement? Isn't that case you rely upon substantially distinguishable from these facts based upon . . . ?;
- Mediator "opinions" or observations of this sort: Who knows what a jury might do with this case, but based on what I have learned about this case . . . it looks like a horse race to me that either side could win. Or, who knows . . . but I like the other side of this case better than yours. Or, who knows . . . but I would agree with you that you should win this case, but I am having a very hard time with your damages claims—I wonder if a judge or jury might have the same difficulties that I have?;
- Mediator suggestions or proposals about settlement, sometimes based upon the mediator's views of the "value" of the case, sometimes based upon the mediator's views of "what the parties might accept," and sometimes based upon both; and
- Specific mediator opinions, delivered to all sides, or delivered selectively only to one side or the other,

> about potential outcomes, dispositive factual or legal issues or settlement values.

Recalling his decades of experience participating in mediations on behalf of a *Fortune* 500 company, former inside counsel Robert Craig expresses his expectation like this:

> I'm often pushing the mediator not to just be a numbers carrier. . . . I want mediators yelling at me if they think our side is way off base as much as I want them yelling at the other side. I mean, they should be expressing their opinion when stupid things are said. And they should know enough about the case through their preliminary work to be in a position to do that.

(3) Controversy over approaches

Despite the entrenched use of evaluative or analytical mediation in commercial cases, the Task Force on Mediation Quality (2008b) declined to take a position on its appropriateness. The reason: "[M]any mediators consider some analytical assistance to be inappropriate and do not offer it, and a minority of lawyers and perhaps a higher percentage of parties either do not want analytical assistance or only want particular kinds of it under specific circumstances" (p.4).

Some insight on this controversy comes from Task Force member John Lande, the Isidor Loeb Professor and former Director of the LLM Program in Dispute Resolution at the University of Missouri School of Law (Columbia, MO). In 2006–2008, the Task Force conducted 10 focus groups—with participants including outside counsel, inside lawyers, and nonlawyer client representatives—in nine cities across the United States and Canada (2008a, pp.2–3). From his experience with those focus groups, Prof. Lande says:

> People generally recognize that in a lot of civil mediation, there is a very strong expectation that mediators will be giving analytical input in a variety of ways. We saw that in the response by lawyers: The people who are primarily advocates in mediation clearly want it a lot. That did not surprise me, including wanting the mediators to pressure parties.

> What did surprise me was that how reticent many of the *mediators* were in feeling that this was appropriate. I guess in some ways, that's comporting with classic mediation theory—that mediators shouldn't be doing evaluations or putting pressure on parties. But given the market environment where that's what is expected by many people, it's interesting that many experienced, sophisticated mediators are still reluctant to do it. For me, that was a surprise.

The attitude of mediators toward evaluative techniques may vary depending upon the region or practice area. For example, Sara Soto (Miami) says, "I find that any [mediator] you ever ask that question will tell you that they are evaluative." (*See* Sidebar 2-6: "How Sara Soto Selects.")

(4) Application to considerations in choosing a mediator

So how do these considerations about evaluative and facilitative techniques apply to your decision about selection criteria?

"I think the best mediators are those who are able to move between different styles as the needs of the parties change," says mediator John Bickerman (in Bickerman et al., 2003, p.1). In the best of all possible worlds, your mediator would have equal and absolute mastery of all mediation techniques, so that in your mediation she[4] could deploy the perfect blend to suit the temperaments of the parties, the nature of the case, and the shifting psychological dynamics of the mediation session.

Unfortunately, you are unlikely to encounter such perfection. So in arriving at mediator candidates to discuss with your opponent, you will have to make some trade-offs based on what is most important in your particular case.

The most obvious choices are at the extremes. For example, if you believe that bitter feelings between the parties to a dispute are a big potential stumbling block to settlement, you

---

4. For the sake of consistency, I use the female gender in this chapter whenever referring to a hypothetical mediator. Of course, I still use *he* when referring to an actual male mediator.

might want a mediator whose facilitative skills are tip-top. A strongly facilitative mediator might also be the best choice where it could be very important to co-operate in coming up with creative settlement ideas rather than to butt heads over the size of a settlement check.

At the other extreme, if you are convinced that your client's case is very strong on its merits, and your main challenge is to make your opponent perceive this too, you might want a mediator with unusually strong evaluative credentials (*see* Bickerman et al., 2003, p.1). In a similar vein, take a look at the part of Sidebar 2-2 ("Should the Mediator Be a Former Judge?") where Walter Stuart and Andrew Berry describe the types of cases for which they might want a former judge in the mediator role.

Of course, most disputes will fall somewhere in the middle. In that case, following Substeps 2.3C through 2.3H, you can simply seek the mediator candidates who seem reasonably competent with a reasonably broad array of techniques.

C. Identify the pool of eligible mediators

If you followed Substep 1.2 in the previous chapter, you already know the basic pool of mediators from which the rules governing your mediation will allow you to choose. For example, if you are opting not to use a mediator randomly assigned in a court-annexed mediation program, you may nonetheless be required to choose someone who has obtained court certification as a mediator. Or in private mediation held under the rules of an alternative dispute resolution organization, you may be restricted to mediators on that organization's list.

The important point to understand is that out of the large pool of people who have obtained the technical qualifications to serve as a mediator in a particular forum, only a handful are likely to have conducted a large number of mediations. As full-time Florida mediator Peter Grilli (Tampa) casually remarked about mediation practice in his state: "Many years ago I heard there were five thousand Circuit-Civil Court mediators in Florida, and there couldn't be more than fifty or a hundred of us who were really making a living out of it." Those are just off-the-cuff numbers, nothing more, but the essence of Grilli's remark would probably strike a chord with experienced mediators and mediation advocates in many jurisdictions. The best mediator for your case may or may not do that work full-time, but in making a selection, you will need to distinguish the truly proficient from among a much larger pool of wannabes.

D. Surface promising candidates through other lawyers

Other lawyers you know or work with can be a major source of information about mediator candidates. This applies to your efforts both to surface promising names in the first place and to assess candidates that have already been surfaced.

If you work at a law firm, the process of surfacing good candidates may be as simple as walking down the hall or bringing up the subject at a lunch meeting. Otherwise (or in addition), you may want to call on whatever network of lawyer friends you have developed, or turn to members of lawyer groups you belong to.

"The usual way to vet a potential mediator is to contact partners and colleagues, usually via email," writes Beatrice O'Donnell (Philadelphia; 2010, para. 4). But she adds this caution: "While this is a quick and easy method to gain valuable information about a potential mediator, make sure that the intelligence that you obtain is recent, reliable, and in the context of a mediation. Many wonderful attorneys may not make excellent mediators."

E. Utilize online resources to surface or research candidates

If you have trouble surfacing the mediator contacts you need, the websites of mediators' professional associations can provide another search resource. For example, the active membership of the American College of Civil Trial Mediators is segmented into Emeritus Fellows, Distinguished Fellows, and Fellows (as well as Honorary Fellows and Retired Fellows). The organization's website makes it easy to view the credentials (*see* Substep 2.3F) of all members and to search by geographic area and types of cases mediated.

Another example is the National Academy of Distinguished Neutrals, whose website states that membership is "by invitation only" and that members "are amongst the most in-demand neutrals in their respective states, as selected by both local peers and litigation firms." The search feature allows you to filter by criteria including type of case experience, gender, status as a former judge, number of years in practice, and even language skills (e.g., fluency in Spanish or Mandarin Chinese).

Similar search features are offered on the websites of other alternative resolution organizations or societies, such as JAMS (which describes itself as the "largest private alternative dispute resolution (ADR) provider in the world") and the CPR Institute for Dispute Resolution (which describes its neutrals as "the most highly qualified mediators . . . from throughout the world").

Of course, much of the value of such a website in surfacing mediator candidates depends on how much (and what kind of) selectivity the organization behind it actually applies. An assessment of that is beyond the scope of this book.

For candidates you have already surfaced (e.g., from communications with other lawyers), online resources are also useful in learning more about them, often including their paper credentials.

F. Review paper credentials

Paper credentials here means the type of information about a mediator's qualifications and attributes that can be gleaned from a web bio, résumé, or curriculum vitae (CV)—such as a certification, published articles, or academic degree—as contrasted with (for example) assessments of a mediator's qualities and abilities from people who have worked with the mediator. This type of information can be very useful, although it is also inherently limited in some ways. The information provided on a résumé or CV falls into a variety of categories, all of which help form a picture of the mediator and her practice:

(1) Credential elements to review

(a) Employment history as a mediator

If a mediator's employer is an ADR firm, the implication, at least, is that she devotes her full time to dispute resolution. This potentially has a bearing on the quantity of her experience as a mediator. For example, the CV of a nationally prominent mediator in Washington, DC, shows that he has practiced for more than a decade at an ADR firm that bears his name. Although his previous workplace was a law firm, the CV specifically notes that his mediation practice there was full-time for about eight years.

If a mediator currently works at a law firm, it is fair to assume that mediation comprises only a portion of her practice (unless otherwise stated). However, this does not prevent some part-timers from establishing strong reputations as mediators.

(b) Certifications to serve as mediator

Since many court-annexed mediation programs include requirements for certification, mediators frequently list such certifications in their credentials. Example: The online bio of a well-known Orlando-based mediator shows mediator certification by the Florida Supreme Court, two of Florida's three federal district courts, and the federal Fifth Circuit Court of Appeals.

(c) Mediator training received

An example of a training credential may be found on the online résumé of a Calabasas, California, mediator (accessed at random on the website of one of the professional organizations mentioned in Substep 2.2D), which states that she received training in advanced mediation skills from the Straus Institute for Dispute Resolution at Pepperdine University School of Law. But a listing of mediator training is by no means universal. Some of the longest established mediators do not list mediation training in their paper credentials; in some cases, such mediators have been practicing in the field longer than most legal mediation programs have existed.

(d) Service as mediation educator or trainer

It almost goes without saying that teaching alternative dispute resolution as an adjunct professor at a law school or in some other reputable context is a likely indicator that a mediator has established some prominence in the field. For example, one longtime mediator's online bio states that she has taught at Georgetown, Harvard, and five other law schools, as well as serving as a trainer at the CPR International Institute for Conflict Prevention and Resolution.

(e) Membership in ADR professional organizations; ADR honors and awards

Membership in an ADR professional organization may not mean much in itself, except to the extent that significant qualifications are required for membership. Honors and elected positions in ADR professional organizations may tend to show that a mediator has achieved a degree of recognition among her peers. Of course, not all ADR organizations enjoy equal status in the field.

(f) Specifics of experience as mediator (i.e., number of years, number of cases, or specific examples of cases)

Paper credentials often indicate (directly or indirectly) how many years someone has served as a mediator, but they do not always provide an indication of the number of mediations that person has under her belt. This can make the volume of mediation experience difficult to gauge—especially with regard to those who continue to practice law as well as mediation. On the other hand, some paper credentials address this question with various degrees of specificity, stating that the mediator has helped resolve more than X number of cases or achieved settlements totaling more than X dollars.

Listings of representative mediations can be particularly helpful in gauging whether your matter would be a good fit, especially where you have determined that the mediator in your case should be experienced and credible in a specific practice area (*see* Substep 2.3A). At the extreme of granularity, the CV of one nationally prominent mediator includes

psychologists in the 1970s. This approach tends to focus on questions related to a candidate's past behavior as a predictor of future performance. The following examples of possible questions for mediator candidates—either in person or by phone—were developed with help from someone whose career in business and government included an assignment as director of recruitment:

- What was the most difficult moment you have experienced in a mediation session, and how did you deal with it?
- What particular dispute do you look back on as your greatest mediation success so far? What aspects of your approach as a mediator made that outcome possible?
- From your experience, what is the most common way that mediation sessions get derailed? What have you found to be the best ways to get things back on track?
- Can you give me an example of a time when evaluative input from you was critical to advancing the ball in a mediation session? Was there a time when you specifically decided to *avoid* giving an evaluation?
- What do you understand now about the mediation process that you wish you had known when you first started?
- If you had to give a presentation on the three most important keys to a positive result in mediation, what would you say?

The purpose of listing these questions here is not to imply that you should ask all—or any—of them when talking to a mediator candidate. Rather, it is to help stimulate your own ideas as to how to tailor your own questions designed to elicit insights into a mediator candidate's values, style, and personal qualities.[6]

In the context of mediator-candidate interviews, Picker (2003) expresses some concern that, "especially if there are

6. For an exploration of how the personal qualities of a mediator can impact a mediation, see Bowling & Hoffman (2000).

any lengthy conversations of substance," an initial private conversation "may create the appearance of bias" (p.73). He suggests that it "may be advisable" for the mediator candidate to be interviewed jointly by counsel for both sides. In the same vein, John Phillips (Kansas City, MO) has said in a panel presentation that for one side to have a discussion with a mediator candidate before retention "may be somewhat controversial," although he did not recommend against it (Bickerman et al., 2003, p.10).

There are several possible responses. One is that it should be possible to gain a great deal of insight about a mediator in an initial interview without talking at all about the case at hand. Another is that it may hardly seem practical to invite opposing counsel to participate if (for example) you are engaging in a phone interview to help decide whether to include a mediator on your proposed list under options 1 or 6 in Substep 2.2.

A third and most important response is that since the mediator is not a decision maker, communications without both sides present do not raise the same types of objections as with a judge. This is highlighted by the fact that confidential briefs by each side to the mediator are common (or required) in many jurisdictions (*see* Step Five). Strikingly, a survey by the ABA Section of Dispute Resolution's Task Force on Improving Mediation Quality (2008a, p.7) found that 85% of respondents approved of private phone calls between one party and the mediator "at least for procedural matters"—and 76% approved even for "substantive matters." (For further discussion, see Sidebar 3-7: "Ex Parte Communications With the Mediator.") Interviewing a mediator candidate, you don't have to discuss either procedural or substantive matters; you don't really have to talk about the case at all!

(1) Client participation

Larry Watson (2002, p.5) suggests that in some cases you may want to include your client in mediator interviews: "Including the client in those sessions will not only go a long way to help determine the best person for the job, but get the client to buy into the process as well."

(2) Information via e-mail

Some other types of necessary information about a mediator candidate, which you may not have been able to learn from review of paper credentials or other materials on websites, may perhaps be obtained via e-mail rather than an interview. This includes information on the mediator's rates, availability on the date of possible sessions, and participants in recent sessions (for follow-up in the next substep).

H. Follow up with references

An inherent problem with references is that the mediator, being human, would prefer to supply only the names of people she believes are inclined to have a favorable view. Rather than start by asking for references as such, you might ask her to name some recent cases she has mediated, then ask who the lawyers were.

In her decades of litigation practice, Edna Epstein has taken that approach: "I ask for people that mediated [with] the mediator candidate and call to see if they would choose him again." During the call, she asks about what the strengths and weaknesses were in the mediator's performance.

"People are generally pretty good about giving you a few minutes of their time and sharing with you" what they know about a mediator, says Nate Cade (Milwaukee). When he wants to assess a candidate he is not familiar with, he will sometimes call other lawyers who have had mediations with that person and ask, "What's this person's posture as a mediator? What type of person are they?"

Richard Spencer (Los Angeles) is a solo practitioner whose practice has included plaintiffs' personal injury cases. For input on specific mediators, he frequently turns to the electronic mailing list of a local organization of trial lawyers, "circulating that name among the organization to see what kind of feedback I get." Warning signs in such comments may include comments like "short-tempered," "doesn't work hard," or "tends to favor" a particular type of party.

Such input from other lawyers when it results in a consensus is "probably one of the most reliable ways of getting some insight into the mediator," Spencer says, "because the paper credentials only take you part way there."

I. Make a final decision on the mediator with client buy-in

You will recall that Substep 2.1 called for you to find out how much involvement your client wants in the mediator selection process and to proceed accordingly. If the client wants a high participation level, by this point in the process she may have reviewed paper credentials along the way and even possibly participated in interviews (in person or by phone) with promising candidates.

Even if you learned in Substep 2.1 that your client prefers a relatively hands-off role in the mediator selection process, you will want to make sure that she feels fully invested in the ultimate decision. Sidebar 2-5 underscores that for best results, you want a mediator whom your opponent trusts and respects—but the same principle also applies to your own client. The simple act of deciding in favor of a particular mediator may increase the client's sense of commitment and buy-in regarding that mediator.

The stage at which client buy-in needs to be achieved may vary depending on the mediator selection mode the parties have selected (*see* Substep 2.2). For example, under any option where you submit a list of mediator candidates for possible acceptance by your opponent, you will need the client to be on board with all the candidates on that list. If the option involves your deciding among mediator candidates on your opponent's list, you may either get the client involved in making the choice among those candidates or go to the client for approval of the candidate that you recommend as the best. If you informally agree on a mediator during an informal back-and-forth conversation with opposing counsel (i.e., option 2), the best approach would be to make that informal agreement contingent upon approval by your client.

2.4 Execute a mediation agreement.

Once the parties have agreed on a mediator, the next step is usually to execute a retention contract. This document is often titled "Mediation Agreement," and the source may be the mediator herself or the alternative dispute organization for which she works.

As Prof. Golann notes (2009a, p.261), "Mediation agreements are usually form documents." His perspective is that "counsel rarely bargain over them in detail." However, another longtime mediator, Larry Watson (2002, p.6), cautions:

> There is often a natural tendency for the parties and counsel to transfer their disagreements and contentiousness on the central issues of the dispute to the simple agreement to mediate the dispute. Care should be taken to avoid prolix, overly detailed agreements that will serve as focal points for still more arguments.

In any event, you should be aware that despite typical commonalities, the terms of mediation agreements may vary from one to the next. You will want to check the form handed to you, not only to be aware of its provisions but also to determine whether there is anything you think needs to be changed or added. One or more provisions might spur you to make an early decision on some aspect of how you would like to see the mediation conducted.

Functionally, the mediation agreement becomes an additional governing document layered on top of whatever else applies, such as the procedural rules of a court-annexed mediation program or alternative dispute organization, statutes or mediators' professional-association rules regulating mediator conduct and confidentiality, state ethics-board opinions, and so forth. Some examples of mediation agreement forms can be found on the web, including those of JAMS (2005) and Bickerman Dispute Resolution, PLLC (BDR; undated).[7]

Larry Watson (2002, p.6) believes that the amount of detail needed in a mediation agreement should vary depending on the jurisdiction. Where detailed mediation rules are already in place, a mere "stipulation to mediate" may be

---

7. Excerpts from the BDR form are reprinted here by permission of John Bickerman on behalf of Bickerman Dispute Resolution, PLLC.

enough, while otherwise a "simple agreement to mediate" will be needed.

The process of entering into a mediation agreement overlaps somewhat with the next listed step in this book (Step Three): agreeing on tailored ground rules. In effect, some of the provisions that the mediation agreement is likely to include—such as who should attend the mediation session and how much time will be allotted for it—constitute some initial tailoring of the process.

A review for this book of three mediation agreement forms—for JAMS, BDR, and Global Intermediation, PLLC (GI; published as Appendices A and B[8] of Poon, 2010)—shows a number of commonalities along with some distinct variations. This review served as the basis for the following discussion of mediation agreement provisions (which is not intended to be exhaustive).

The following may serve as a checklist of provisions that you may encounter or want to include in a mediation agreement:

A. Who must (or may not) attend the mediation session

For reasons discussed later in this book, making sure the right parties attend the mediation session can be crucial for success. The JAMS, BDR, and GI mediation agreement forms take varying approaches to this issue. The BDR form makes it clear that at least one representative of each party with full settlement authority must attend the joint mediation session, as well as participate directly "in all phases of the mediation process." The GI form requires "an officer, partner, or other employee authorized to make decisions concerning the resolution of the dispute," but it does not specifically use the term "full settlement authority." The JAMS mediation agree-

8. Appendix A of Poon's book is a sample confidentiality agreement, also titled "Statement of Understanding," which functions as the mediation agreement (including such items as the mediator's fee). Appendix B contains the applicable mediation rules. Excerpts are reprinted here by permission of Gary P. Poon on behalf of Global InterMediation, PLLC.

ment does not expressly require such attendance, although this may be addressed elsewhere in the organization's rules.

Of course, even if the mediation agreement does not require parties with settlement authority to attend, this requirement might come through (for example) the procedural rules of the court-annexed mediation program or ADR organization. But you may want to see the parties expressly sign off on this point, or perhaps be even more specific as to who will attend.

The flip side is that a mediation agreement form (e.g., JAMS and GI) may specifically *exclude* from attendance anyone *other than* the parties and their representatives, *except* by consent of all parties and the mediator. If you believe from the outset that someone other than a party or representative—for example, an insurer or expert—should attend in person or by phone, you may want to build this consent into the mediation agreement.

There may be special considerations where one party to the mediation is a government entity. "In the case of public bodies requiring compliance with 'government in the sunshine' laws," Larry Watson writes (2002, pp.6–7), "an acknowledgement of the required approval process may be noted to avoid later surprises." Those sunshine laws may prohibit the decision-making group from attending confidential sessions. "In those cases, assurances should be generated confirming that individuals who have the position and rank to make an influential recommendation to the governing body will represent the public entity."

B. Payment of mediation fees and costs

Fees for the mediator are typically paid at an hourly rate. The mediator's actual costs for travel, lodging, and so on, may be charged in much the same way one might expect in connection with the services of a law firm.

Scheduling a certain number of hours for mediation may create a minimum fee obligation under some agreements. For example, the BDR form also provides: "If a mediation session is completed in less time than was budgeted, the actual time reserved but not used will be billed unless the time can be used for another matter."

In addition to the mediator's own fees and costs, the mediation firm may assess a surcharge. For example, GI charges an additional 30% of the mediator's fees and costs for the stated purpose of covering its own costs.

The BDR form may be typical in calling for each "party" to be responsible for its own share of mediation fees and expenses, which probably presumes a pro rata division. But according to Prof. Golann (2009a, p. 261), this can sometimes be a point of contention in multiparty disputes. For example, in a mediation involving one plaintiff and three defendants, the defendants might take the position that each *side* should pay its own costs, with the plaintiff's side paying half and the defendants' side paying the other half (by splitting it three ways).

Also, "a party with limited financial resources should not be shy about asking other parties to pay the fee," advises San Francisco commercial litigator David Grappo (2006, p.185). For example, if you are representing the plaintiff in a contingency case, Edna Epstein suggests that you might try for an arrangement where the defendant fronts the expense of mediation—subject to an agreement that your side will later pay half if the case settles as a result. She describes this type of conversation:

> The other side will say, "Well, no, I'm not going to pick up the tab, because then that leaves your person (meaning the plaintiff) free to bollix the whole thing up and stick me with the cost." You can then say—and that's often worked for me—"Well, you know, why don't you front the costs, and if we get to yes—because you are the person who will have to be paying the settlement—well, then we won't mind paying our half when there is money there to be paid."

As you read the agreement form, you may also want to note whether it imposes an extra fee in the event that the parties seek to cancel or reschedule a mediation session.

C. Confidentiality and privilege

Mediation agreements appear almost universally to contain clauses on the topic of confidentiality. Although Larry Watson acknowledges that "[o]bviously, provisions should be made to cover the confidentiality of the process" (2002, p.6), he (like some other mediators interviewed) does not see this as a major element for concern. In an article on preparing for civil trial mediation, he writes (2002, p.6):

> While some states impose a legal privilege on the process—excepting only any signed settlement agreement that may evolve—all that is really needed is an acknowledgment that any concessions, admissions or communications exchanged during the mediation process are inadmissible in any subsequent evidentiary proceedings. Most states already have appropriate evidential rules precluding the admission of settlement discussions that can be referenced.

In any mediation form presented, you are likely to find some or all of the following provisions related to confidentiality, privilege, and preservation of privacy.[9]

(1) Confidentiality and assertion of privilege for statements made and documents prepared in course of mediation

Although differently worded, the mediation agreement forms of JAMS, GI, and BDR are typical in seeking to prohibit disclosure to third parties, or use in judicial or other proceedings, of any communications made during mediation. JAMS and BDR specifically assert privilege "under Rule 408 of the Federal Rules of Evidence and any applicable federal or state statute, rule or common law provisions."

Of the three forms, only GI's contains a long paragraph setting forth multiple circumstances under which the mediator may disclose communications or documents exchanged or used during the mediation (Poon, 2010, pp.107–08):

> [T]he Mediator may disclose any communication, documents, or information in the following limited circumstances: (1) all parties consent in writing to the disclosure;

---

9. *Also note*: "If there is a protective order in the case, the mediator should also sign whatever declaration is requested by the order if there is any chance that confidential or highly confidential information will be communicated to the mediator" (Bowbeer, 2011, p.186).

(2) the highest court in a competent jurisdiction issues or affirms a final order compelling the Mediator to make the disclosure; (3) without necessarily assuming a duty to do so, the Mediator reasonably believes that there is a serious risk of harm to the life or safety of any natural person if the information in question is not disclosed; and/or (4) the Mediator reasonably believes that there is a serious risk that he/she may be subject to criminal proceedings unless the information in question is disclosed.

As distinct from asserting confidentiality obligations (and perhaps exemptions to them), confidentiality forms also may be likely to clarify that some items do not become confidential merely because they are used during a mediation. This clause from BDR is an example: "However, evidence previously disclosed or known to a party, or that is otherwise admissible or discoverable, shall not be rendered confidential, inadmissible, or not discoverable solely as a result of its use in the mediation." Along the same lines, a mediation agreement form (e.g., BDR's) may also expressly state that participation by a party's expert during mediation will not disqualify the expert from assisting that party in subsequent litigation of the dispute at hand.

As noted previously, the confidentiality provisions in a mediation agreement may be considered cumulative to protections already built in by statute or rule. Even so, you may want to be sure you are satisfied with their wording. A question: To the extent that statutory or rule-based privilege and confidentiality are waivable, could less stringent provisions in a mediation agreement covering the same points constitute a waiver?

(2) Prohibition on compelling the mediator's testimony in subsequent proceedings

You can expect to find a clause designed to prevent the mediator from being called as a witness in any subsequent arbitral or judicial proceeding related to the mediation or the underlying dispute. However, the language can vary a great deal.

(3) *Provision that the mediator will not disclose to other parties in the mediation any information that one party has requested her to keep private*

It is probably widely assumed that during the mediation proceedings, one party may privately communicate information or thoughts to the mediator that she does not want the mediator to disclose to the other parties. The privacy of such statements may be protected by a mediator's code of conduct or some other means, but it is not always addressed specifically in mediation agreements. Among the forms reviewed, GI is an exception, providing as follows (Poon, 2010, p.108):

> In any private communication with the Mediator . . . , a party may instruct the Mediator not to disclose certain information or documents to the opposing party or parties. Upon receiving such instruction, the Mediator shall not disclose the designated information or documents to the other party or parties, unless the instructing party subsequently authorizes such disclosure.

Note that this provision only applies where a party *expressly* requests nondisclosure, which may also reflect widespread mediator practice. This may be important to bear in mind during any ex parte communications you may have with the mediator during the course of the proceedings.

(4) *Provision for destruction of the mediator's records after mediation*

A mediation agreement may oblige the mediator to destroy all notes and other records regarding the mediation within a defined period after mediation. For example, the BDR form requires such destruction at 45 days, the JAMS form at 30 days "unless otherwise instructed by the parties."

(5) *Prohibition against future work by the mediator for one of the parties in relation to the dispute*

After a mediation, you probably would not want to see the mediator working in relation to the dispute in question on behalf of any of the other parties, in any capacity. The BDR form contains an example of such a prohibition. The GI form does not, but a prohibition to this effect is contained in the organization's procedural rules. Paul Lurie, a Chicago construction lawyer and mediator, recommends adding a provision that bars the mediator from providing professional services to any of the parties, in *any* matter, for a period of six months after the end of her services in the mediation (2006, p.260).

(6) Prohibition on recording of mediation proceedings

Probably most people take it for granted that mediation proceedings will not be recorded or stenographically transcribed, but the GI form is an example of an agreement that specifically bans it.

(7) Use of mediation discovery in underlying litigation

"Particularly in huge document cases, where a party puts forth the effort to respond to document requests during the mediation, it is inefficient and unnecessary to do it all over again during litigation, should the mediation fail," notes Janet Kole (Philadelphia, PA). She recommends dealing with this issue in the mediation agreement.

D. Scheduling

Mediation agreements may vary greatly in whether and how specifically they address scheduling. For example, the BDR form calls for the parties to comply with a mediation schedule appended as an attachment. On the other hand, the GI form does not address scheduling at all, and the organization's rules simply provide that the mediator will set a session date after consulting the parties (Poon, 2010, p.114). You may want to consider whether there is any advantage in your case to specifying a specific date in the mediation agreement.

E. Disclosure of mediator's relationships with parties to mediation

You are likely to see a clause affirming that the mediator has disclosed business, professional, or social relationships with any of the parties or their law firms (perhaps within a defined period) and putting a similar burden on the parties and their counsel. You may want to confirm that the wording is satisfactory to you.

F. Mediation procedure

Provisions regarding procedure in the mediation proceedings may be found in a separate set of mediation rules, but sometimes some are contained in the mediation agreement. For example, the BDR form covers a number of procedural points, including that the representatives of parties may be expected to present positions and respond at a joint initial session.

G. Odds and ends

Any particular mediation agreement form may contain its own particular wrinkles. For example, you may encounter clauses disclaiming liability on the part of the mediator "for any act or omission" related to the mediation (JAMS); giving the mediator the right to follow up with "individual discussions by telephone or in person" following an unsuccessful mediation session (BDR); or providing that the mediator "may be assisted by others as reasonably necessary" (BDR).

2.5 File a notice of mediator selection (if required).

If required, your final step in selecting and retaining the mediator may be to file a notice in the appropriate forum that you have done so. As noted previously, the rules of some court-annexed or other mediation programs may contain a deadline for this.

SIDEBAR 2-1

Facilitative Behaviors That Characterize an Effective Mediator

By P. Jean Baker

The best mediators "are able to employ multiple styles at different points during a mediation based on their assessment of what approach is most likely to move the participants toward resolution," writes Jean Baker (Washington, DC), a vice president at the American Arbitration Association (2011, p.24). As discussed in Substep 2.3B, these styles include facilitative, evaluative, transformative, and more. Baker believes that "regardless of which style is being used, facilitative skills enhance the effectiveness of the mediator." In this excerpt from an article (2007a, pp.5–6), she recommends the following types of behaviors as among those that characterize an effective mediator:

1. Is willing and able to coach the participants in the fundamentals of joint problem solving both before and during the mediation.
2. Ensures weeks before the mediation begins that all the necessary administrative arrangements have been made.
3. During mediation comfortably utilizes the following facilitative techniques to reduce the possibility of an impasse:
   (a) Treats stated positions like problems to be discussed rather than ultimate solutions;
   (b) Facilitates discussion of the specifics of the stated positions by eliciting significant disclosure of information either in joint sessions with the parties or during private caucuses;
   (c) Subordinates demands that might increase initial bargaining leverage for one party in favor of those demands that enhance mutual agreement;
   (d) Facilitates reduction of the number of demands to manageable proportions;

(e) Focuses efforts to unveil all possible alternative solutions and any attendant implementation difficulties;

(f) Facilitates the presentation of differing points of view by restating them as suggestions rather than as contentions, paying considerable attention to avoiding differences that involve abstract principles;

(g) Facilitates open and complete exchanges of information either jointly with the parties or in private caucus, including the accurate expression of the parties' intentions and expectations, as well as revelation of all the key facts.

4. Maintains active listening skills during the entire session to assure the participants of the benefits of continuing to engage in settlement discussions.
5. Recognizes differences in negotiation style and responses to conflict exhibited by the participants and shapes his or her behavior accordingly.
6. Displays sensitivity to psychological movements during the session and empathy for the parties' differing views of reality.

SIDEBAR 2-2

Should the Mediator Be a Former Judge?

In the late 1980s, it was all the rage for former judges to serve as mediators, and they remain important today. Still, there has been a growing recognition of their pluses and minuses, viewed as a group.

Among those with reservations is Hob Jordan, Executive Vice President and General Counsel of a privately held firm based in the Midwest: "I've been in front of the classic former judge who likes to rule as if he or she is still wearing the robes and doesn't really grasp the concept of the dialogue and all the listening that needs to take place in a mediation."

Edna Epstein (Chicago) says, "I'm not sure that judges have the best training for this, by and large, because judges are used to deciding and telling people what to do—and this is a process whereby people have to really figure out their own solutions much more." In her view, a mediator needs to be "much less bossy," and more "seemingly passive" in their techniques, than judges typically are trained to be.

Walter Stuart (New York) puts it this way:

> Mediator skills are frequently different from judge skills. Judges have to make a decision. Mediators have to make a deal. A mediator who gets actively involved in an understanding of the case, in all its complexities, and is able in separate sessions to present those articulately, is in a much better position to facilitate a settlement than is a judge who may just be acting like a judge and deciding on various points.

Michael Braun, who litigates employment law cases and other civil actions in Chicago, deliberately avoided selecting a former judge to mediate a dispute between a school administrator and the school district where the administrator used to work. Instead, the two sides chose as the mediator an attorney who also represents school districts, reasoning that his familiarity with this type of practice would be an asset. "It's been a great selection," Braun says. "I think that he has done more to get the matter resolved than any of the former judges we might have selected."

On the other hand, you may specifically want the mediator to be a former judge if you believe that an emphasis on evaluation will be crucial for success. That tactic is favored by Stuart, despite his general reservations. He is likely to seek a distinguished former judge to mediate "a particularly legalistic case, where for me to win in court, I need to have a judge rule my way on a particularly tricky legal argument." In that situation, Stuart wants the mediator to be able to say, "Look, I was a judge for a long time, and I have analyzed this and looked at the cases, and I would rule in favor of Walter's client" on the claim in question. Such an evaluation by an ex-judge carries even more weight if the issue would be settled in court by a judge rather than a jury, Stuart notes.

You may even want a former judge for the purpose of convincing your *own* client. That possibility was suggested by the late Andrew Berry, whose New Jersey–based practice concentrated on complex litigation such as mass torts and insurance coverage disputes. He used a hypothetical where a respected ex-judge says, "I have to tell you, if I had this case when I was on the bench, I would be very impressed by the point that the other side just made about 'alpha.'" Even though there is no way to be certain whether a ruling on "alpha" would actually be negative at trial, "sometimes it's nice for a client with unrealistic expectations to hear [the mediator] say that."

Of course, just because someone *used to be* a judge doesn't mean she can't possess—or learn—so-called facilitative or even transformative skills just like anyone else. At least one private ADR company arranged training programs specifically to teach such skills to former judges, and if you are considering an ex-judge as a candidate, it may be worth asking whether she has taken one, as well as asking other lawyers about their experience in mediation sessions with her.

SIDEBAR 2-3

A Federal Court Describes the Functions of a Mediator

The United States District Court for the Northern District of California is known as a leader in federal court-annexed ADR. One of the court's publications contains this description of the mediator's role:

> The mediator, who may meet with the parties in joint and separate sessions, works to:
>
> - improve communication across party lines
> - help parties clarify and communicate their interests and those of their opponent
> - probe the strengths and weaknesses of each party's legal positions

- identify areas of agreement and help generate options for a mutually agreeable resolution

The mediator generally does not give an overall evaluation of the case. Mediation can extend beyond traditional settlement discussion to broaden the range of resolution options, often by exploring litigants' needs and interests that may be independent of the legal issues in controversy.

Source: United States District Court, *Dispute Resolution Procedures in the Northern District of California* (2011), p.10.

SIDEBAR 2-4

The Power of Good Listening

David A. Hoffman (interview)

To some, the concept of transformative mediation—which attempts to address underlying emotional and personal barriers to resolving a dispute—can seem too New Age for hard-nosed civil litigation. But mediator David Hoffman (Boston) believes that in combination with other approaches, it can show real results. The story he tells here[10] demonstrates how important it can be for a mediator to have good listening skills, so that the parties "feel really heard and understood." It also illustrates the potential power of client venting (see Substep 9.4 and Sidebar 9-5: "The Power of Venting").

This is a story in which I was the mediator. It suggests the opportunity that lawyers have for clients to feel really heard and understood.

This was an employment case. The plaintiff was a midlevel manager who got fired for being—well, he thought he was being a whistle-blower, calling attention to ethical violations by the com-

10. After this interview, Hoffman recounted the story at greater length in a chapter of *Stories Mediators Tell* (2012, p.141). That fascinating book is filled solely with memorable mediation experiences told by experienced mediators.

pany. The company thought the guy was just a pain in the neck who thought that everything he saw in life was an ethical violation of some kind. When he first started complaining about ethics violations by the company, they would look into it. Sometimes they brought it to the attention of the board, the board convened a committee, the committee looked into it, said "No, this is not a problem, what we are doing is ethical."

After doing this over and over again, this fellow got a warning from the company that if he kept doing this they were going to let him go. He did keep doing it. They fired him, so he sued them for wrongful termination based on violation of public policy. The bargaining in the mediation went back and forth. He was looking for a very high number. The company thought the suit was ridiculous and offered very little money, but they offered some.

When I met with him—meeting with the plaintiff and his lawyer separately—I asked him about his career. I had a copy of his résumé; it was part of the mediation materials. I noticed he had been in the Army for 20 years, and I asked him what that was like. He told me he had felt really good about his Army service. He mentioned he had been in Vietnam. He had been in combat. I asked him about what he had seen there. He said, "You know, in the Army, you knew what the deal was. You knew that you could count on your fellow soldiers to watch your back. There was a code of honor and ethics there that people respected. And people turned square corners, there was a set of definite rules to follow."

He said, "When I left the Army after 20 years of service and retired, went into the private sector, I felt like I'd entered an arena where there are no rules—anything goes." And as he was talking about this I saw the light go on over his head. I just saw some insight and recognition that he was in the wrong place. You know, what he really wanted was a place more like the Army, where there were definite rules, boundaries, roles, and real clarity about what was expected and what was prohibited.

After that, the case settled very quickly. He said, "You know, let's make another offer, and see if we can wrap this up." So the plaintiff came out of that mediation with much greater insight about what his needs were and what were the things in life that really gave him meaning.

SIDEBAR 2-5

A Judo Maneuver: Opting for Your Opponent's Choice of Mediator

"It is important for lawyers to understand they do not necessarily want a mediator who would seem to be on their side," says Susan Yates (Chicago) of Resolution Systems Institute. "In fact, it is often more fruitful to have someone from the other point of view working with your opponent, speaking their language."

For litigators trained to battle their opponents' wishes at every turn, the idea might come as a shock. But since a mediator (unlike a judge) can't *force* the resolution of a dispute on any particular terms, sometimes your smartest move may be agreeing to one of the other side's preferred choices for that role. You might think of this as a judo maneuver, using your opponent's momentum to your own advantage.

The rationale is simple. In order to be successful at her job, a mediator has to get the parties to settle. That is what she wants to do, so she will employ all her mediation techniques to that end. And such techniques are most likely to be effective on the other side if the mediator is someone whom your opponents know, like, and trust. (Meanwhile, the mediator will also use the same techniques on you, but she cannot make you agree to any settlement you find unfair.)

Such reasoning is persuasive to Milwaukee litigator Nate Cade. "I always operate on the premise that if it is a mediator the other side wants, that is potentially someone who is more likely to convince the other side's client to settle."

The same point is underscored by Bowen Tucker, who (until retirement) was Associate General Counsel for a major corporation, responsible for directing all the company's litigation:

> I would listen to the other side as to whom they wanted as a mediator. If, let's say, it was a personal injury case, and the plaintiff's lawyer said he liked to have John Smith, we would usually say, "Fine. Have him!" Because John Smith would be much more persuasive with him than somebody I picked. So I

didn't have any problem with that. I was going to control what I offered anyway. What difference did it make?

This approach is also endorsed by Larry Watson, one of the first civil trial mediators certified by the Florida Supreme Court. He writes (2002, p.5): "Perhaps the most important consideration in selecting the right mediator . . . is the simple question, *'Who will the other side listen to?'* Many experienced trial lawyers will conscientiously defer to the other side's choice of mediators based on that fundamental concern."

Deferring in this way does not necessarily mean you have to accept your opponents' choice blindly. Consider asking opposing counsel for a short list of his preferred candidates, telling him that you will try to select one of them (*see* Goldberg & Sander, 2007, p.44; Watson, 2002, p.5). From that small group, you can do due diligence to decide which one offers the best match of qualities and abilities for this case.

SIDEBAR 2-6

How Sara Soto Selects

Sara Soto (interview)

Sara Soto (Miami) is an advocate with her feet in two worlds: arbitration (e.g., securities disputes) and litigation (general commercial and business disputes). Both worlds involve mediation, but she has found some differences when it comes to selecting a mediator. Her comments are included here not because they are unusual, but because they probably illustrate how many lawyers go through the process of picking mediators in real, everyday practice.

The securities disputes practice is a relatively small world. So even though we are not under any constraints as to whom we use as a mediator, we tend to pick the same mediators over and over. It's a small group, people who do this kind of work, where everybody knows who everybody is, or they have a friend that gossips. These guys build their reputation over time. There are three or four top mediators in the field, and generally speaking, people think of those.

In the commercial cases, there are many more mediators to choose from. The selection process takes a little longer because there are so many more possible candidates, so many more lawyers. It's not a relatively small world, it's a large world. So you suggest candidates, and generally there are a couple of conversations about who, and a couple of rejects, and then ultimately you agree on somebody. I will generally go by the people I know.

Sometimes the other side—there is still a percentage of folks in this world who have this thing that if I said, "I want Mr. X," they must say no to Mr. X. I have no idea why they feel that way about life, but there they are. So then they propose their Mr. X or Mrs. X, and if I've never heard them, I send an e-mail around. I ask around, or I look them up on the Internet. And I decide, "Yes, I'll go with that person," or I won't. To be more precise, I decide, "Yes, I should recommend this mediator to the client" or "No, I shouldn't."

When I'm trying to make a decision, most of the time what I will do is call up the person. I will ask them what their mediation style is, and how do they feel about being evaluative, and how strong—what is the meaning of that word to them—and what will they do and won't do. I mean, this may be completely incorrect on my part, but if you don't consider yourself an evaluative mediator, I probably don't want you.

Unfortunately, I find that any person of whom you ever ask that question will tell you that they are evaluative. Nobody wants to say, "No, I'm just a messenger." But when it comes down to actually doing it, it's a different story. I don't know why I bother to call and ask—but I feel I must.

I do try to match a mediator to the particular case. Obviously, this is something you can do effectively only when you've already had several prior experiences with the mediator, and you have an understanding of how that person thinks about things. Some mediators' styles are too weak or too strong for most people, but they could be just what is needed in a particular case.

STEP THREE

Agree on Tailored Ground Rules (As Needed)

Perhaps the most interesting [survey] finding about the preparation phase [of mediation] was that sophisticated repeat users wanted to have substantive input into the mediation process itself.

—ABA Section of Dispute Resolution Task Force on Improving Mediation Quality (2008a, p.7)

"I remember when I started in the mediation field," recalls Prof. John Lande (Columbia, MO), "I had a sense that, if you go to mediation and it doesn't work—big deal! It's just a little bit of time." But since then, Prof. Lande—former director of the LLM Program in Dispute Resolution at the University of Missouri School of Law—has come to a very different view:

> Well, it actually *is* a big deal. People invest a lot—in time and money, emotion, and opportunities for settlement. Sometimes if you have mediation and it doesn't settle, that can sour the relationship and actually reduce the chances of settlement.
>
> There is a cost to having a mediation that doesn't go well. If people are alienated from each other, they may be less willing to engage in negotiations after mediation. If you have a mediation process that is not well planned and designed, that's very frustrating for people, and it can inhibit the process.

After conducting a study involving experienced mediation participants (primarily advocates and mediators) from a number of U.S. cities, the ABA Section of Dispute Resolution's Task Force on Improving Mediation Quality (2008a, p.9) noted an increasing preference for tailoring the mediation process to suit the needs of each individual dispute. Such users' "desire for substantive and procedural pre-mediation discussions indicates a real evolution in the field," which "implies that a higher level of process design and substantive pre-mediation collaboration between mediators and users is a trend for the future."

John Lande was the among the Task Force's members. Recalling this study, he says:

> Part of the overall lesson I took from the Task Force's work is that lawyers and mediators should be thinking about their cases individually and tailoring the process to fit the needs of the parties and the circumstances of the case. That's part of what the value of doing the preparation before everyone gets to the mediation table is about: thinking about what the substantive issues are, thinking about the process and planning it. Because that's going to make it more successful.

The Task Force calls this work "customization" (2008a, p.12). Mediator and law professor Dwight Golann (2009a, p.258) calls it "structuring the process." In this chapter, it is called "tailoring the ground rules"—that is, all points regarding your particular mediation process that are not specifically covered in the rules governing your mediation, plus any customized variances in those rules that may be allowed by agreement of the parties. These rules may range in scope and importance from what documents and other information about the case will be exchanged between the parties to when and where the mediation session will take place.

There are two basic substeps to tailoring the ground rules in mediation:

1. Decide what specific aspects of the mediation process you need to tailor.
2. Use a pre-mediation conference or other communications with the mediator and your opponent to arrive at a mutually agreed-upon customization of the process.

3.1 Decide what specific aspects of the mediation process you need to tailor.

If you followed Step One, you already are familiar with the procedural rules that govern your mediation, so you know what the default process will be. You also know which aspects of that process the parties are allowed to modify if desired (for example, where rules of a court-annexed mediation program allow the parties to "otherwise agree"). In addition, you know what details are not addressed by the rules, such as the location at which the mediation session will be held. Beyond this, after executing a mediation agreement as described in Step Two, you know what details of the mediation process may already have been modified or filled in by that agreement.

The degree to which you involve your client in considering how the mediation process should be tailored may vary according to the client and the case. By this time, you presumably have a good sense of how actively the client wants to be involved in your handling of the case, as well as how committed she is to the mediation process. To give an obvious example of how this matters, if your client only wants the minimum amount of effort and expense required to "jump through the hoop," you probably will want to avoid having to take time-consuming steps such as submitting a written mediation statement (*see* Substep 3.1B). But you should also communicate sufficiently to understand how the client's goals may be advanced by some aspects of the mediation process. For example, even if the client is not committed to mediation per se, you might be able to further her goals by using the mediation process to obtain documents or information items that will be helpful for the underlying litigation.

In deciding what aspects of the mediation process you may still need to tailor for your individual case, you may want to consider the following possibilities. Even in a small case, it will be worth taking a few minutes to review them.

A. Presession exchange of information between the parties

"Information gaps often present barriers to resolution," writes Bennett Picker (2003, p.58). As mediator and former appellate judge Bruce Meyerson (Phoenix) points out (in Bickerman et al., 2002, p.8), an essential element of preparing for mediation is "to obtain adequate information on which to meaningfully negotiate." On that point, he says:

> Now, obviously, that doesn't mean you have to have *all* the information. If you did, then that would become very expensive. But I think it's important for lawyers and their clients to identify the important issues, the important information that they need, and then obtain that, either through formal discovery or through informal negotiation with the other side. That way, when they come into the mediation, they can really negotiate intelligently because they have adequate information upon which to base their negotiating position.

From his experience mediating cases across the United States, John Bickerman (Washington, DC) has the same view. "The first question is to intelligently think about the kind of information that both sides are going to need ahead of time," he says. "And if you don't have it, ask the mediator to get it before you ever get into a caucus or a mediation before the session."

Note that Bickerman refers to the information that *both* sides are going to need—not just you. Of course, you need enough information about your opponent's case to properly assess it for mediation purposes and negotiate intelligently. But it is also in your interest to make sure that your opponent has enough information to feel confident about her ability to assess *your* case—because this can be equally key in being able to arrive at a settlement. For litigators, this may require developing a different mind-set. For many of us, the general instinct is probably to seek as much information as possible about the other side's case while revealing as little as possible about our own (in order potentially to gain an advantage at trial).

In this context, the question frequently arises whether it would be better to hold back one or more key pieces of information, if possible, in case the dispute does not settle and you want to be able to spring it later in an adversary proceeding. For a discussion of this topic, read Sidebar 8-5: "'Should I Hold Something Back for Trial?'"

Among factual elements that are important for both parties to understand for a successful mediation, documentation of damages claims looms large, because (among other things) substantiated damages may define the theoretical upper limit for settlement. It is certainly a focus for Steven Brom (Birmingham, AL): "The most important thing for me to do as a defense attorney in preparation for mediation—and in consultation with the insurance adjuster or whoever the client is with the full and final settlement authority—is really to see how much of the alleged damages can actually be substantiated."

Susan Yates (Chicago) of Resolution Systems Institute observes, "We are seeing more sophistication in some jurisdictions as to what information is shared only with the mediator and what is shared with the other party as well. This is part of a growing sophistication in terms of preparation for mediation. Mediators and parties are refining the process by identifying what will be most productive in particular cases."

In making an assessment about tailoring the mediation process with regard to exchange of documents or other information, the logical way to begin is to take stock of what you already have and decide what more you reasonably need before the mediation session. If the governing rules already contain a provision for exchange of documents or information in other forms, you should make use of that. Regardless, you can (as Bruce Meyerson's quote implies) make some informal requests or agreements on the topic with your opponent.

In any event, prior to your pre-mediation conference or other communications with the mediator (*see* Substep 3.2), you should be prepared with a list of items that you still need to receive in advance of the mediation session. P. Jean Baker

(Washington, DC) of the American Arbitration Association (2007a) recommends obtaining a written agreement that the items will be shared by a specific date.[1]

B. Shared mediation memos

Mediation statements or memoranda are discussed in Step Four, including considerations as to whether they may be worthwhile in your case. Take a look at that discussion. If mediation statements are not required by the general rules governing your mediation, then you may want to tailor the process by pushing for a mediation statement requirement in Substep 3.2. If mediation statements are already required, you may have nothing more to do than agree on a due date. If the general rules require statements but you do not believe they are warranted in your case, you may want to tailor the process to "otherwise agree."

C. Confidential mediator briefs

Confidential briefs submitted from each side to the mediator (only) are discussed in Step Five, again including considerations as to whether they may be worthwhile in your case. In connection with tailoring the mediation process, much the same logic applies as discussed in Substep 3.1B. As noted in Step Five, you may also want to consider a confidential brief as a *supplement* to an exchanged memo.

If you opt against confidential mediation briefs (or mediation statements), you will still need to consider what *will* be needed (e.g., copies of the pleadings or other court papers) to bring the mediator fully up to speed on the case in advance of the mediation session. In a pre-mediation conference or other communication, the mediator will probably state what items he wants—but you should be prepared to make additional suggestions if warranted.

---

1. "Note the issue also of whether or not the discovery obtained in mediation can be used as if produced during the discovery phase of litigation," writes former litigator Janet Kole (Philadelphia, PA). "This issue should be dealt with in the mediation agreement" (*see* Substep 2.4C(7)). If it is not in the mediation agreement, consider dealing with it in an agreement related to the mediation conference.

D. Advance disclosure of the plaintiff's planned opening demand

In Sidebar 3-1 ("Requesting a Demand"), Steven Brom describes why he seeks advance disclosure of the dollar amount that the plaintiff will use as the starting point for negotiations at the mediation session. If you are representing the defendant, and the plaintiff has declined such a request, you may want to bring it up with the mediator in Substep 3.2.

E. Logistics of the mediation session

The term *logistics* is used here to mean the management of details of an operation—the operation being the mediation session. Aspects of internal procedure for the session (such as whether the parties will make opening presentations) are discussed separately in Substep 3.1F.

(1) Exactly who will attend the mediation session?

Mediator Lawrence Watson (Maitland, FL) advises, "Having the right players at the table is critical to the success of any mediation" (2002, pp.7–8). Getting specific commitments in advance as to who will attend the mediation session may go a long way in that direction.

(a) Parties

As discussed previously in this book, general mediation rules and mediation-agreement forms often require that each party be represented at the session by someone with "full settlement authority" (or similar language), but this is a point that you may well want to nail down more specifically. Where a party is an individual, presumably you want to make sure the individual herself attends. Where a party is a corporation—especially a large one—things can get more complicated. Larry Watson writes (2002, p.7):

> In the case of large corporations . . . a representative from the general counsel's office may suffice as a mediation representative of the company if the mediator is reasonably convinced that the legal department

> of the company has, as a matter of corporate policy, full authority to settle the case. If the corporate policy in such matters would require settlement proceeds to be taken from the operating funds of the division or department involved, however, it may be advisable for the mediator to suggest an appropriate representative of that department attend as well.

In Watson's view, authority problems most often raise their heads where the ultimate decision must be made by a claims committee, a board, or some other group effort.

A subtler problem can arise where a corporate representative was personally involved in the developments that gave rise to the controversy. As Watson puts it: "Often individuals directly involved in the underlying dispute carry an agenda that makes an objective evaluation of the issues problematical." So you may want to consider pushing to have a corporate representative with no personal involvement in addition to (or instead of) the one directly involved. For more on this, see Sidebar 6-4: "When the Alleged Wrongdoer Is on Your Mediation Team."

(b) Nonparties

Do you anticipate having experts giving input at the mediation session? Is the insurance adjuster a key decision maker? You will want these matters to be agreed upon in advance of the session. This is especially important given that the general mediation rules may prohibit nonparties such as experts from attending.

(2) Will one or more parties be allowed to participate by phone?

The general rules governing some mediation programs require that all parties attend the mediation session in person, and some programs specifically extend this requirement to nonparty insurance representatives. To arrange for phone attendance may require the consent of other parties or even specific waivers in advance. For example, in the Northern District of California, such phone attendance requires advance permission from a magistrate judge (ADR Local Rule 6-10(d)). In some other mediation contexts, the general rules may not speak to this issue at all.

Some fundamental problems with attendance by phone are that (a) the interpersonal dynamics are very different from when everyone is physically present in the same room, and (b) the person on the phone may not feel as much commitment as if she had to go to the trouble of traveling to the session and staying there for the duration. As Tampa mediator Peter Grilli notes, "It's very easy to sit on the other end of the phone and say 'no, no, no,' and not be invested in the process." For an anecdote illustrating the potential downside of phone attendance, see Sidebar 3-2: "Johnathan Bolton's Bad First Time."

In her Miami practice defending claims against brokerage firms, Sara Soto gives "overwhelming weight" to having the claimant physically present. "If the claimant is not going to be at the mediation, I am not interested," she says flatly. Her rationale: "I give a tremendous amount of weight to being able to communicate with the claimant without interference."

The question of attendance by phone often arises in cases involving relatively small damages claims, where it may simply not be reasonable to require a defendant's out-of-state insurance adjuster or corporate representative to incur travel expenses. Representing defendants in this type of case, Steven Brom has found many plaintiffs' lawyers to be flexible:

> Typically I'll talk about whether they're going to demand that the insurance adjuster or the person with full settlement authority is physically present if they are out of state. Frequently the plaintiff's counsel will not object. They'll say that's fine, just as long as they are available by phone.

In that situation, one may anticipate that the negotiation "on the ground" will be conducted by the attorneys, who will consult with their clients by phone as needed. Interestingly, Sara Soto "has not found any difficulties" with mediation sessions where her out-of-state corporate client (frequently the brokerage's inside counsel) attends by phone. "You know, 99.9

percent of the work you are going to do with your in-house counsel, you are going to do before you get there" to the session, she says. So during the session itself, "there shouldn't be any surprises."

(3) When will the mediation session be held?

If a date for the mediation session was not set in the mediation agreement (*see* Substep 2.4D), this will need to be done in Substep 3.2.

(4) How much time will be allotted for the mediation session?

Many mediation veterans understand that reserving a specific amount of time for the mediation session—and the *correct* amount for the dispute—can make a significant difference in how the mediation plays out. A survey conducted by the ABA Section of Dispute Resolution's Task Force for Improving Mediation Quality (2008a) found that "[f]ifty-two percent (52%) of the users and 66% of the mediators felt it was important, very important, or essential to confirm the beginning and end time" (p.7). Larry Watson (2002, pp. 5–6) warns against creating situations where the parties feel unduly rushed or end up forced into late-night marathons.

So what is the correct amount of time to reserve? Watson offers this general advice: "The decision-making temperament of the parties, their distance from an agreement when the mediation commences, and the time needed to think through the issues and make a decision are important factors in scheduling time for the caucus" (2002, p.5).

What this means in practice for your particular case may be harder to determine. For some simple disputes, a few hours might be enough. For intellectual property cases, inside counsel Hildy Bowbeer (St. Paul, MN) suggests that while most mediations of this type can be completed within a day, it is usually better to reserve a second day. She writes (2011, p.184):

> There are several advantages to scheduling the extra day. First, it ensures that none of the principals will expect to catch a late afternoon flight the first day,

which means the mediation can continue into the evening if necessary. Second, it allows some "breathing room" if progress is being made late in the first day but one or both parties need to gather additional information or consult with additional stakeholders, or the mediator concludes that the meeting would be more productive if the parties got some rest and could start fresh the next day.

In complex commercial cases, the norm might be two or three consecutive days (Picker, 2003, p.76; Watson, 2002, p.6). At the extreme end, mediating massive litigation such as mass tort class actions may require multiple sessions "over several weeks or even months" (Gary, 2004, p.3). Watson suggests asking your mediator for advice on this point.

(5) Where will the mediation session be held?

One obvious priority in considering where a mediation session will be held is for the location to be reasonably convenient for the parties from a travel standpoint. In disputes where all the parties are local, this may just mean somewhere easy to drive to. In huge cases where parties will fly in from around the country, the best location is sometimes an airport hotel.

A second requirement is that the facilities should be physically adequate for the task. At a minimum, this will usually mean enough rooms of sufficient size and privacy to accommodate the parties for a joint initial session plus break-out caucuses. In large cases, storage space for equipment or files might also be needed.

A more controversial question is whether choosing the location should be considered part of a party's negotiation strategy. Here is a range of input:

- "Ideally, the choice of location for a mediation session should be driven solely by the physical requirements necessary to stage the event. . . . Choice of location should never be allowed to become a positional issue involving a 'home court' advantage of one party or another." —*Larry Watson (2002, p.5)*

- "I don't think it matters much. The mediation session is usually held at one or another of the lawyers' offices, but I don't think it matters much." *—Edna Epstein (Chicago)*
- "The negotiation theory that I've read says that people are more likely to be effective as negotiators in their own office than in the opponent's office. And more effective in their own office than on neutral ground. So if we can, I want the location to be at my office, if the other side will agree." *—Thomas Dye (West Palm Beach, FL)*
- "[Focus group p]articipants expressed different views about where to conduct mediation, in particular whether it is appropriate to hold it in the office of one of the lawyers. Some said that it is fine to mediate in a lawyer's office if there is not an appearance of bias. Others expressed concern that the lawyer hosting the mediation may be distracted by other matters. Some expressed concern about taking certain clients to law firm offices, such as low-income clients and medical professionals." *—ABA Section of Dispute Resolution Task Force on Improving Mediation Quality (2008a, pp.33–34)*
- "Don't waste time arguing about the location of the mediation. Other than finding a comfortable place with amenities, it doesn't make any difference. There is no benefit or detriment in meeting in the offices of one of the lawyers. Objections to such a site because it is not 'neutral' are absurd and childish. Tell your client that if the client makes the objection." *—Timothy Corcoran (2007, § 3.a)*

To some extent, the customary location for mediation sessions may vary according to region or practice type. As several of these quotes imply, meeting at a law firm appears commonplace in at least some areas. On the other hand, a study of court-referred mediation for litigation in the U.S. District Court for the Eastern District of Missouri found that in 52 of 59 cases, the mediation sessions were conducted in the offices of the mediator (*see* "Court-Referred Mediation Survey," n.d., p.9).

(6) Are there any special logistical issues for the mediation session that need to be resolved (such as shared use of special equipment)?

An example of a logistical issue might be audiovisual equipment such as a computer projector or screen, in cases where the parties' presentations may require them (Bowbeer, 2011, p.183). Also, don't forget really basic points such as availability of high-speed Internet access.

(7) Will there be any shared meals?

Although this may seem a trivial point, having both sides around a table sharing a meal—before or during a mediation session—can make a constructive difference in attitudes. If the other side is arriving from out of town, Hildy Bowbeer even suggests volunteering to bring in lunch or to host a breakfast before the session or a dinner the previous night (2011, p.183). In her view, this gesture "can send a positive message that costs you very little and might yield big returns by helping to break the ice and build some trust between the parties." For more on shared meals, see Substep 10.8B.

F. Procedures for the mediation session

Some mediators like to meet with each side separately in person before the mediation begins—often on the day the session is scheduled. You will want to know if the mediator has this in mind.

As will be seen at length in Steps Eight through Eleven, the classic format for mediation involves a joint initial session with oral presentations by each side, followed by a series of separate caucuses between each side and the mediator, ideally culminating in an agreement to settle that is memorialized in a closing joint session. In that context, you should consider how much time you are likely to need for an effective presentation of your case and make sure this comports with the time the mediator is intending to allot. Also, will rebuttals be permitted? In complex cases, what will be the order of the parties' presentations?

A common departure from the classic model is to eliminate opening presentations. To help you decide whether opening statements are appropriate for your case, read the materials in Substep 8.4A, which describes the pros and cons. Also take a look at Sidebar 3-3: "When a Joint Opening Session May Be the Wrong Idea." Be aware that in any event, the mediator may likely want to start by giving an opening spiel of his own (*see* Substep 8.3).

Also consider whether you might want to use all or part of your allotted presentation time in less traditional ways. For example, you might want to follow the lead of Thomas Dye (West Palm Beach, FL), who likes to use such time as an opportunity to ask the other side questions about how they see the case. For more on this, see Sidebar 8-2: "Why Tom Dye Asks Lots of Questions." Another possibility is to bring in one or more experts to present their opinions on key issues, perhaps in the context of a presentation that practically amounts to a minitrial (*see* Substep 8.4).

The mediation procedure that probably departs most strikingly from the norm is found in the Understanding-based approach, alluded to in Substep 2.3B. For more on this model, read Sidebar 3-4: "A Noncaucus Model: 'Understanding-Based' Mediation."

You may want to consider such variations and push for their adoption in Substep 3.2. To avoid surprises and allow good preparation, you will want to be sure that everyone is clear on the exact procedure to be followed, well in advance of the mediation session, even if this means only an affirmation of the classic model.

G. Allocation of fees and costs

The allocation of fees and costs among the parties may have been specified in the mediation agreement (*see* Substep 2.4). But if not—or if any previously unforeseen costs have arisen (such as for facilities or equipment) that you believe should be handled differently—you will want to get these matters settled in Substep 3.2.

H. Some other possible points

In her article "Avoiding Impasse During Mediation" (2007a), Jean Baker includes a long, helpful list of issues she believes should be addressed in advance of the mediation session. Among items that have not been addressed elsewhere in Substep 3.1 are these (pp.4–5):

- "Discuss whether there is an added cost or risk if the mediation is unsuccessful and what, if any, steps should be taken to reduce these added costs or risks. (i.e., written agreement to stay legal proceedings, limited use of joint sessions to minimize the danger of unwanted disclosures, etc.)."
- "Determine whether there is any likelihood of damage (i.e., conversion of assets) if a person voluntarily agrees to mediate and the other party ultimately refuses to participate or participates in bad faith."
- With regard to the agreed-upon allocation of fees and costs among the parties, "determine what will happen if a party does not pay in accordance with the agreement."
- "[O]btain agreement of all participants that there will be no interruptions during the time period allocated [for the mediation session] because important concessions tend to occur as the established deadline approaches."
- "To avoid creating the appearance of an unbalanced playing field, establish the ground rules for who can and cannot participate." (Presumably, Baker is referring here to situations where the number of attendees for one side may greatly outnumber those for the other side. Under those circumstances, perhaps only certain attendees for the larger side might be designated to speak.)
- "Determine whether a party contemplates use of a standard settlement document and ensure that all participants are provided an ample opportunity to review and approve use of such a document prior to its introduction during mediation."

- "Ascertain whether there are any enforcement concerns (potential bankruptcy[2]) or impediments to enforcement (i.e., involvement of an international party) that need to be addressed. (Currently there is no mechanism for enforcement of a cross-border mediation settlement agreement. Such a mediation settlement, however, could be converted to an arbitral consent award that would be enforceable in countries that are signatories of the New York Convention.)"

You may want to consider whether to raise any of these issues in Substep 3.2, and if so, how you think they should be handled in your case.

3.2 Use a pre-mediation conference or other communications with the mediator and your opponent to arrive at a mutually agreed-upon customization of the process.

As noted by the ABA Section of Dispute Resolution's Task Force on Improving Mediation Quality (2008a), "[m]any mediation training programs have traditionally not paid substantial attention to the content of pre-mediation discussions" (p.6). This is a significant lack, because (as the Task Force found) many mediators of business disputes regularly use them, and they were rated positively in focus groups of experienced mediation participants.

However, the practice is not universal. In some court-annexed mediation programs (though perhaps not many), mediators are actually barred from communicating with any participant before the mediation session itself (Task Force, 2008a, p.6)

The classic format for pre-mediation discussions is the pre-mediation conference, which convenes all parties for a discussion in person or (perhaps more often) by telephone. Some mediators may follow up with more joint teleconferences afterward. Another possibility is for the mediator to talk separately with each side (Corcoran, 2007, § 3.k.iii).

2. For more on what do when one or more parties to a dispute may be in danger of bankruptcy, see Callahan (2010).

A. The pre-mediation conference

"The goal of pre-mediation conferences is to formalize the preparation for mediation by the parties and the mediator so that the mediation [session] itself will be more efficient and go more smoothly," writes former bankruptcy judge and Florida mediator Timothy Corcoran (2007, § 3.k.i). Such conferences can be instrumental in helping to customize the mediation process for your specific case, as well as in helping bring the mediator up to speed.

Pre-mediation conferences are standard operating procedure for Louise LaMothe, whose mediation practice is based in Southern California. She has developed an extensive checklist of topics to cover, which is included as Appendix A to this book. Information exchange between the parties is a major emphasis (2010, p.65–66):

> During the pre-mediation conference with counsel, I frequently find that no information exchange has occurred. My first step then is to help the lawyers manage that exchange so that adequate information has been shared in advance of the mediation to help the parties prepare. Usually that includes an exchange of core documents and sometimes, they even agree to a single deposition.

The use of pre-mediation conferences seems to vary by jurisdiction (and possibly by practice area). They are actually mandatory by rule in some court-annexed programs. For example, ADR Rule 6-6 of the District Court for the Northern District of California provides: "The mediator shall schedule a brief joint telephone conference before the mediation session with counsel who will attend the mediation session to discuss matters such as the scheduling of the mediation, the procedures to be followed, the nature of the case, the content of the written mediation statements, and which client representatives will attend."[3] For more on the Northern District's

---

3. A commentary to this rule adds: "If more than one pre-session phone conference is conducted, all counsel do not necessarily need to participate in every call but the lead counsel who will attend the mediation session must participate in at least one pre-session phone conference. *See* ADR L.R. 6-10(b)."

rationale, read Sidebar 3-5: "Why Pre-mediation Conferences Are Mandatory in the Northern District of California."

By contrast, Kansas City, MO lawyer John Phillips told an audience in 2003, "My experience has been that not very many mediators are requiring that at this point in time" (in Bickerman et al., 2003, p. 10). He added: "[I]f it is not a mediator's custom and practice to require a pre-mediation conference, then I, as an advocate, often suggest it."

In a pamphlet for mediators, the Task Force on Improving Mediation Quality (2008b) offers this advice (p.2):

> At a minimum, communications with counsel before the mediation should address issues such as who will attend, when, where, for how long, fees, who has settlement authority, possible conflicts of interest, what documents will be helpful, and whether confidential pre-mediation memos are needed. Lawyers and mediators often find it helpful to have more extensive pre-mediation conversations when the case warrants investing the time and expense.

A more extensive list of possible topics suggested by the Task Force for discussion during pre-mediation conferences is reproduced in Sidebar 3-6: "The Mediator's Goals for Pre-mediation Communications With the Parties."

Notwithstanding the Task Force's reference to "time and expense" as a limiting factor in what to cover in a pre-mediation conference, it should only take you a few minutes to consider for yourself the issues raised in Substep 3.1. If you choose what you believe are the most important points to nail down in tailoring the ground rules for your particular dispute, you may be able to cover a great deal of important territory while expending time only in proportion to what the size of the case will justify. A modest amount of time and effort at this stage may go a long way toward helping to ensure a positive result at the mediation session.

It must be acknowledged, however, that in the real world, when pre-mediation conferences are used, they are not always well utilized by the parties—sometimes, far from it. This may be a particular problem in mandatory mediation programs where one or more parties may not really be interested and are really just "punching their ticket" (*see* Sidebar 1-4: "'Punching Your Ticket' and Good-Faith Requirements").

Paul Sandars has encountered this problem in pre-mediation conferences while functioning as a mediator in New Jersey's mandatory program. For example, he says, "I've had situations where the lawyer for one side 'wasn't available.' Instead, you've got a paralegal on the phone who knows nothing about the case. When something like that happens, I say, 'Look, we are going to adjourn this conference until I get somebody who knows the file.'" Under those circumstances, pre-mediation conferences may at least provide an early indicator of a party's level of seriousness about mediation.

B. Follow-up joint phone conferences

Magistrate Judge Mary Pat Thynge (Wilmington, DE) is an example of someone who uses "serial teleconferences" to set up ground rules in advance of a mediation session when she serves as a court-appointed mediator (2011, p.150). The first is a joint teleconference covering some of the main topics described in Substep 3.2A, such as major issues in the case and how much time should be scheduled for the mediation session. But that is just the beginning (p.152):

> I use follow-up teleconferences to: confirm that necessary information is being exchanged; discuss the mechanics of the mediation (e.g., use of presentations, joint submissions where there are multiple plaintiffs or defendants, or the date when a particular defendant will mediate in the case of multiple defendants); confirm the attendance of business participants; and address any other problems that may affect the mediation process.

In addition, she may make some calls on an ex parte basis.

C. Ex parte phone calls

For a discussion of the propriety of ex parte communications between one side and the mediator, see Sidebar 3-7: "Ex

Parte Communications With the Mediator." Where permitted, they sometimes serve as a substitute for a pre-mediation conference in addressing the points discussed in Substep 3.1. In a survey by the ABA Section of Dispute Resolution's Task Force on Improving Mediation Quality (2008a), "survey participants were about evenly divided between preferring private, individual calls with a mediator as opposed to joint calls" (p.7). There was also a marked preference for counsel-only calls (i.e., without the client), although the Task Force includes the caveat that "the survey participants almost all were counsel to parties and not parties themselves."

Although ex parte calls for presession planning purposes have the advantage of allowing more frank communication with the mediator, their disadvantage is that representatives of each side are not able to communicate and coordinate with each other during the call in addition to the mediator. On the other hand, ex parte calls might serve well as a supplement to a pre-mediation conference that includes both sides.

For example, Judge Thynge (2011) sometimes makes ex parte calls when following up after an initial joint teleconference. Her reason for this is that "without an audience, the parties will more frankly discuss their concerns related to mediation as well as the potential goals of the process (i.e., approaches to resolution)" (p.152).

In this context, such calls are perhaps less likely to be used in tailoring the mediation than in confidentially briefing the mediator on each party's view of the case. The use of ex parte calls to confidentially brief the mediator is discussed further in Sidebar 3-7 and in Step Five.

SIDEBAR 3-1

Requesting a Demand

Steven M. Brom (interview)

Steven Brom practices law in Birmingham, AL, where he often represents defendants in cases where input from insurance adjusters plays a major role. Here he talks about asking plaintiffs in advance for the opening figure for negotiation ("demand") they intend to use at the mediation session.

As to the monetary damages, I'll say, "What is going to be your opening figure at the mediation?" Very frequently they'll give that number to me, because they understand I've got to get settlement authority prior to that mediation. If I'm having to guess what their demand is, and I guess low, the plaintiffs understand that I'm going to have a low authority at that mediation.

If they refuse to tell me what their demand is, I just guess based on my review of the case. I speak to my folks and say, "Well, I think the case is possibly evaluated at $50,000. I think that may be what their demand is." Then that's how our settlement authority is going to be based when we go into the mediation.

If the plaintiff's attorney has not given me their number, and all of a sudden we walk into the mediation and they demand a million dollars—well then, immediately the mediation is in trouble. Because I'm going to tell them, "That's just completely out of line with anything that we were thinking. We don't have the ability to come anywhere close to that number. So unless you're going to drop your demand dramatically, we are not going to accomplish much in this mediation."

Most plaintiff's attorneys understand that. So when I speak to them ahead of time prior to the mediation, I'll tell them, "You've got to give me your starting number so that I can speak to my folks about it." And if they say, "Our starting number is going to be a million dollars," well then, that allows me as a defense attorney to look at the case and think, is there anything here that would substantiate that, to justify that amount?—as opposed to being surprised by such a high demand at mediation.

SIDEBAR 3-2

Johnathan C. Bolton's Bad First Time

When Johnathan Bolton got his first chance to represent a client in mediation, he was still "fresh green out of law school," in his first year at the Houston office of an international law firm. He had taken a course on alternative dispute resolution and was full of idealistic enthusiasm. Unfortunately, his initiation into the real world "put a really bad taste about mediation" in his mouth, "right out of the box."

Bolton represented the plaintiff in a breach of contract case where the amount in dispute was about $50,000. He suggested trying mediation, and the defendant's counsel agreed. Bolton took the right next steps: He got input from senior lawyers at his firm on mediator names, consulted with the other side, and got everyone to agree on a local mediator with a good reputation for pragmatism.

On the day of the mediation session, however, Bolton got two unpleasant surprises. One was that the defendant, who lived in another city, did not show up with his lawyer. Bolton had assumed that both sides would appear at the mediation in person, but instead the defense lawyer simply called his client on the phone from time to time. "I think he was on a jobsite," Bolton says. "I remember hearing a helicopter flying by in the background."

The second surprise was that the negotiations did not proceed the way Bolton had envisioned. Although he knew that the defendant had asserted a counterclaim for $50,000, he viewed the claim as clearly "bordering on frivolous." So he was not prepared for the defense's unrelenting tactic: Every time Bolton's client offered to settle for receipt of a given amount—say $32,000—the defendant's lawyer responded by demanding payment of exactly the same amount on the counterclaim.

And that was how it went all day long, from about 9 to 5, until the session ended in complete failure. "In my view, that mediation was really a complete waste of time and money," Bolton says.

In those days, Bolton did yet not know he had the option of simply leaving the mediation once it became clear that absolutely no progress could be made. With the benefit of hindsight and experience, he thinks he and his client "should have been out of there by 11:30 or noon."

Also, Bolton says he should have obtained a commitment in advance that the defendant would attend the session personally. He believes the process works a lot better if both parties have to suffer the inconvenience of being physically present in the place where both parties are expected to make sacrifices.

Ultimately, Bolton's story had a happy ending—but not through settlement. His firm took the case to trial and won a full judgment of $50,000 plus $500,000 in attorneys' fees, and successfully defended the judgment on appeal.

That first mediation fiasco took place in 2000. "Subsequently," Bolton says, "I've been involved in much larger cases where mediation has worked greatly." So today, despite his bad first experience, he is still very much a believer in the mediation process for the right cases.

SIDEBAR 3-3

When a Joint Opening Session May Be the Wrong Idea

John Bickerman (interview)

In his Washington, DC–based national mediation practice, John Bickerman is a big believer in tailoring mediation sessions to the individual case. Here he talks about when the classic joint initial session may not be the best way to go. (For a thorough discussion of the pros and cons of opening statements, see Substep 8.4A.)

It is not always necessary to have a joint session with presentations by the parties. A joint session has value when we think principals aren't fully aware or engaged, and we want a direct communication between principal to principal, or we want the principals to hear the case in a way that they might not have heard it before. But if everybody is up to speed and we have a highly emotional case, it doesn't make sense.

In two recent cases, I didn't have a joint session. I didn't need a joint session. The parties had more or less gotten pretty far down the path negotiating, and they were stuck on something. They really knew the issues. I didn't need to go into the issues. What I needed to do was focus on the things that were holding them up. I put the parties in separate rooms, and I went to talk to them.

I'll give you another example. I did a big insurance coverage case several years ago, where I had met with the parties ahead of time. They all had like 30 pages of defenses and affirmative defenses and arguments. I went through their legal points, and it turned out that two were important issues; 28 were unimportant. So I got the parties together, and I went through the issues. I said, "These are the two that matter, right?" They said "Yeah." So I said, "So let's talk about these two." Then I separated the parties for further discussion.

We settled the case in four hours, although they had booked two days, because they figured they had to go through all 28 issues. There was some familiarity on my part with insurance coverage law in the particular state in which this dispute occurred, and thus the ability to say to the parties, "You know, 28 of these issues don't matter." If I hadn't said it, they would have argued 28 issues. We would have been there for two days just arguing the issues.

SIDEBAR 3-4

A Noncaucus Model: "Understanding-Based" Mediation

In *Challenging Conflict: Mediation Through Understanding* (2008), authors Gary Friedman (Mill Valley, CA) and Jack Himmelstein (New York) advocate a model for mediation sessions that completely rejects the use of private caucuses between each side and the mediator. They write (pp.xxxv–vi):

> Many other approaches to mediation recommend that the mediator shuttle back and forth between the parties (caucusing), gaining information that he or she holds confidential. Our central problem with caucusing is that the mediator ends up with the fullest picture of the problem and is therefore in the best position to solve it. The mediator, armed with that fuller view, can readily urge or manipulate the parties to the end he or she shapes.

For more on Friedman and Himmelstein's critique of private caucuses, read Sidebar 9-3: "The Problems With Caucusing."

Their preferred alternative, as noted in Substep 2.3B, is to keep the parties talking together at the same table throughout the mediation session:[4] "[I]f the mediator is motivated and prepared to help the parties *work through their conflict together* and the parties are willing to do so, staying together has many more advantages than risks" (pp.188–89).[5]

Friedman and Himmelstein name their mode of mediation an "Understanding-based model" (pp.xxvii). "[W]e work with the parties to understand what *underlies their conflict* in terms of how it may have them trapped in their dynamic," the authors write (p.xxxiii)—delving into "psychological, emotional, and value-laden issues that may lie beneath the stated conflict" (p.xiii, from preface by Robert Mnookin). Proceeding in that way, "[r]epeatedly, we find that *the basis for resolution comes from discovering together with the parties what lies at the very heart of their dispute,* which is often a surprise, and which often has a profound effect on our work together" (p.xxxv).

The authors are affiliated with Harvard Law School's Program on Negotiation—part of the same organization that produced *Getting to Yes* (Fisher & Ury, 1981)[6] a generation earlier. "Understanding

---

4. Keeping the parties together in a continuous joint session rather than breaking into caucuses is typical in family and community mediation, although it is rare in commercial mediation (Golann, 2009a, p.22).

5. All italics in quotations from *Challenging Conflict* are in the original.

6. For more on *Getting to Yes*, read Substep 7.4A.

the parties' interests in helping resolve their disputes is hardly unique to our understanding-based approach," they acknowledge. "Indeed, it is a mainstay of what is termed 'interest-based negotiation,' and a central theme in Roger Fisher's and William Ury's groundbreaking *Getting to Yes*" (p.131). In Friedman's and Himmelstein's view, "[w]here we likely differ from many mediators is that we work hard with the parties to help them find and articulate what is important to them, rather than the mediator concluding it for them, and we stress the importance of including the emotional significance to the parties more than many mediators might."

Both Friedman and Himmelstein are former litigators (p.xvii). They are conscious of "a common perception and challenge that working in this way is simply not realistic for most conflicts and most people," but respond strongly that "many parties in conflict, if given the opportunity, can and want to do it" (p.xxxvii). In their book, they describe a dispute between two major corporations involving hundreds of millions of dollars where the parties opted for Understanding-based mediation in preference to a more traditional mediation style, which they also considered (pp.17–40, 231–244).

Challenging Conflict made a splash in the mediation world, and training for mediators in the Understanding-based model is offered both across the United States and internationally. So it seems likely that this type of mediation will become increasingly available for parties who want to pursue it.

Playing devil's advocate, however, at least two points can be made. First, as one book reviewer noted, "understanding-based mediation will likely consume more time than other mediation approaches" (Oberman, 2009). In the case of the corporate dispute referred to previously, the process required four two-day mediation sessions over a period of almost six months (Friedman & Himmelstein, 2008, p.30).

The second point concerns the types of disputes described in Friedman and Himmelstein's book. Most of that volume consists of narratives describing the course of 10 mediations of "commercial conflicts" mediated using the Understanding-based model (p.xxiii).[7] What most of these narratives have in common is that they involve disputes where the parties had a long ongoing relationship, with a high incentive to reach a solution that would facilitate this relationship going forward.

Here are some examples:

- A multiyear conflict between an adult brother and sister over proper commercial management of a ranch they inherited from their parents (pp. 3–16, 95–114).
- A dispute between two major corporations (noted previously), where the companies had been clashing in their business relationship over almost 30 years and management wanted to stop this from continuing indefinitely (pp.17–40, 231–244).
- Tensions between an elderly Holocaust survivor and the writer she hired to write her life story, which threatened to prevent the parties from ever finishing the book (pp.41–58, 115–135).
- A labor contract dispute between musicians and management at a major orchestra (pp.81–94).
- A multiyear, multifaceted conflict between an elderly environmentalist and her neighbor, a real estate developer, which culminated in an alleged assault (pp.199–228).

In a couple of other narratives in *Challenging Conflict*, the incentive to keep working together after mediation was not as obvious, but the relational aspect was still strong (albeit hostile):

- Strife between a book author and her longtime publisher over whether a contract gave the publisher the right of first refusal on future books (pp.137–170).
- A dispute between the sister and life partner of a deceased gay man, which grew out of the parties' caregiving

---

7. It is impossible to know exactly which details in these narratives may have been fictionalized, because in eight of the 10 cases, "all names, identifying characteristics, and circumstances have been changed to thoroughly protect the parties' privacy and the confidentiality of the mediations in which they participated" (p.xxiii).

> at the end of the man's life and the disposition of the man's financial estate thereafter (pp.171–198).

Still, at least a couple of the 10 narratives involved a situation where there was no ongoing relationship between the disputing parties (and no desire for one). In one, a mother sued the school her mentally ill daughter had formerly attended, alleging that "the school had conspired to make her daughter a pariah after she had suffered a psychotic episode there" (pp.275–304).

The narrative that most plainly supports a view that Understanding-based mediation is a practical option for relatively run-of-the-mill transactional conflicts involved a construction dispute (pp.245–274). In that case, the mediation-session participants (besides lawyers and experts) consisted of a homeowner, a building contractor, and the contractor's insurance representative. The contractor had retired since the construction of the home, so further work by him was not contemplated, and the ultimate settlement consisted solely of monetary payments. From the description, the dispute was apparently resolved in a single mediation session, and the disputants shook hands and wished each other good luck in a moment that "felt genuine" (p.267). At the end, the authors quote the following exchange between the insurance representative ("John") and the mediator:

> John: You haven't made me a believer, but I must admit I'm a little less skeptical about this idea of staying together [without private caucuses]. There aren't many cases it could work for, because most of the cases I handle are just about the money.
>
> Mediator: I thought you felt that way about this case in the beginning.
>
> John: I guess I did. I'll have to think about that some more. But I've got to run to another case, and let me assure you—that one's really all about the money.

Summing up, it is probably fair to say that parties are least likely to pursue an Understanding-based model of mediation when they expect to go their separate ways after settlement is achieved. They may be most motivated to pursue the possibility of Understanding-based mediation where a resolution that is not only fair but amicable is a major goal. At least to judge from examples in Friedman and Himmelstein's book, the parties seem to complete the process feeling much more positively disposed toward one another than one would ordinarily expect.

Before leaving this topic, we should note that no-caucus sessions can sometimes also occur outside the context of Understanding-based mediation. For an example, read Sidebar 8-7: "The Initial Joint Session That Swallowed a Mediation." In addition, bear in mind that at a regular mediation session, if developments in the parties' separate caucusing seem to warrant further direct discussion between the two sides, you always have the option of asking the mediator to hold a joint caucus (*see* Allen, 2009, p.13; Little, 2007, p.22).

SIDEBAR 3-5

Why Pre-mediation Conferences Are Mandatory in the Northern District of California

Howard A. Herman (interview)

The ADR Program of the District Court for the Northern District of California takes a multioption approach, offering arbitration and other ADR methods in addition to mediation. As Program Director, Howard Herman has an intimate knowledge of the mediation process there. I asked him why pre-mediation conferences are considered so important as to be mandatory in his district. This is his response:

The court has had an attitude from the very beginning of the mediation program that each case is unique. It grows out of the whole multioption approach. The idea is not just to pick the ADR process that is going to be right for the case, but within that process to make sure that we are crafting a procedure that meets the needs of the lawyers and the parties. It's not one size fits all.

The pre-mediation phone conference is not intended to be just a scheduling call. It really is about making sure that the mediation procedure to be used is the right procedure, and that everybody understands what it's going to look like. It allows the lawyers and the parties essentially to customize the process.

If the lawyers and the mediator don't have some mechanism by which they can actually explore what's going to happen, no one is going to be adequately prepared to have that event be not just some hoop that people jump through, but something that's real—that really is going to matter. So it's an absolutely core piece of what we do.

It doesn't have to take very long. It might be as simple as the mediator saying, "Here is how I usually do things. Is this what you are looking for? Is this right?" It's an opportunity to make sure that the statements that are exchanged between the parties are going to adequately address the problem. It also allows the mediator an opportunity to work with the lawyers on how to be more effective in preparing and in working with the clients in advance.

SIDEBAR 3-6

The Mediator's Goals for Pre-mediation Communications With the Parties

ABA Section of Dispute Resolution Task Force on Improving Mediation Quality

Based on a study conducted in cities across the United States, the ABA Section of Dispute Resolution's Task Force on Improving Mediation Quality (2008a) observed that "[m]ediators who confer with counsel/parties either privately or jointly [in advance of the mediation session] may appropriately pursue a variety of goals in their communications" (p.8). Here are bullet points from the Task Force's report (pp.8–9) listing some such goals:[8]

- [T]o discuss the overall procedure of the mediation in order to be certain that all participants have similar un-

8. For a checklist of items to cover at a pre-mediation conference, see Appendix B to this book.

derstandings of the process and to avoid surprises at the mediation;

- to discuss the mediator's approach to mediation, especially with regard to offering analysis and opinions, and including discussion of whether the mediator needs permission to offer analysis or opinions;
- to discuss who will attend the mediation and who will have authority to settle and possible rescheduling if the "necessary" people will not attend (Settlement authority was a repeated theme of the parties interviewed. Several were blunt in their assessment that this was a part of mediator preparation. One party suggested that the mediator should include an agreement that specifically dealt with settlement authority that all participants had to sign in advance.);
- to gain insight into party interests that might not otherwise become apparent to a mediator until much later, if at all;
- to allow the mediator to begin to understand how the dispute might be settled and get ideas from participants about possible settlement approaches (e.g., will the disabled tort plaintiff consider a structured settlement, will the employer consider taking back the terminated employee, or will the plaintiff on the contaminated property consider conveying the property as part of a settlement and will someone at the table buy it?);
- to seek process input by discussing with participants whether "opening statements" by participants are desirable, to discuss or "coach" them on the content and tone of such statements, and to plan alternative approaches if such statements are not desirable;
- to seek process input by discussing which issues might best be handled in caucus and which in joint session;
- to determine whether further exchange of documents or other information, either before or at the mediation, might be productive;
- to understand any previous settlement discussions;

- to learn about the procedural posture of any litigation;
- to understand potential impediments to settlement such as personality or emotional issues or hardened attitudes parties might have about the "merits" of a case or settlement approaches; and,
- to identify anything about the case that might call for an atypical process for the mediation.

SIDEBAR 3-7

Ex Parte Communications With the Mediator

Generally speaking, ex parte communications between one side and the mediator before the mediation session appear to be a common practice in mediation. This applies both to the types of procedural issues often associated with joint pre-mediation conferences (*see* Substep 3.2) and to verbal confidential briefings during the period leading up to the mediation session (*see* Step Five).

Such ex parte communications are expressly authorized in some jurisdictions. For instance, Rule 1.720(i) of Florida's Rules of Civil Procedure provides that "[t]he mediator may meet and consult privately with any party or parties or their counsel." Likewise, the mediation agreement form (*see* Substep 2.4) of at least one private mediation firm (Bickerman Dispute Resolution, PLLC, n.d.) specifically states that the mediator may "communicate *ex parte* with mediation participants" (p.1).

In the context of communications to help design the mediation process for an individual case, Philadelphia mediator Bennett Picker (2003) expresses this view: "While *ex parte* contacts [with the mediator] are entirely appropriate, it is important that they be disclosed in a general way and balanced overall in order that the mediator be perceived by the parties as absolutely impartial" (p.75).

Attitudes in the legal community may be evolving toward fuller acceptance of presession ex parte communications with mediators, even on substantive matters. Around 2003, John Phillips (Kansas City, MO) described ex parte communications in mediation as still "perhaps controversial," and he noted that a local rule in the District Court for the Eastern District of Missouri restricted the parties from ex parte communications with the mediator except for issues relating to process (Bickerman et al., 2003, pp.10–11). In 2005, however, the court amended that rule to state: "The neutral designated in a case may communicate privately and ex parte with counsel and unrepresented parties prior to the commencement of the formal dispute resolution process" (Local Rule 16-6.04(B)).

Even so, as noted in Substep 2.3G, some people—in at least some locales—continue to see such ex parte contacts as improper. Although a small survey of experienced mediation participants conducted by the ABA Section of Dispute Resolution's Task Force on Improving Mediation Quality (2008a) found that more than three quarters of them approved of private calls between one party even for "substantive matters," and a full 85% approved of ex parte calls "at least for procedural matters," this means that 15% still objected to such calls for any purpose whatsoever (p.7).

Edna Epstein (Chicago) is an example of a lawyer with strong reservations about ex parte communications. "I think ex parte communications with anybody who is supposed to play any kind of role as a neutral is not a good idea," she says. She recommends that presession communication take the form of joint conference calls or letters with copies sent to the other side, because "people will get very queasy about any ex parte communications."

There may be a difference between perceptions of presession ex parte communications that a party privately initiates and ex parte discussions that a mediator explicitly builds into the presession process. For more on this, see the discussion in Substep 5.2.

Bottom line: You may want to proceed with awareness that acceptance is not universal, unless ex parte communications with the mediator are expressly authorized by the governing rules. The Task Force (2008a) recommends: "If pre-mediation conversations address substantive issues, mediators should make sure that everyone is aware that these conversations are taking place" (p.32).

STEP FOUR

Exchange Information With Your Opponent, Including an Exchanged Memo for the Mediator (As Warranted)

> Q: *Do you, as inside counsel, always or typically read the mediation memos from the other side?*
>
> A: *I do.*
>
> Q: *And have there been times when those have affected your view of a case?*
>
> A: *Yes.*
>
> —From an interview with John DeGroote while he was serving as Chief Litigation Counsel for a global consulting firm

In Substep 3.1A, we described the importance of figuring out what documents and related materials need to be exchanged between the parties to enable a productive mediation session. In Substep 3.1B, we noted that you also need to decide whether, in your judgment, the information exchange in a particular case should include a mediation memorandum (when optional). In Substep 3.2, we pointed out that exchanges of documents and memoranda are frequently discussed and decided upon at a pre-mediation conference with the mediator.

Although mediation memoranda are primarily seen as a method of briefing the mediator, they are included in Step Four because they are also an important means of communicating directly with the *opposing party* (as further discussed later). This chapter will start by talking a bit about document exchanges, then deal with mediation memoranda at some length. The latter discussion should help you decide whether a mediation memorandum would be useful for your case (if it is not mandatory).

Step Four has two substeps:

1. Exchange documents and related materials.
2. Exchange mediation memos (where required or useful).

4.1 Exchange documents and related materials.

It is probably safe to make a general statement that rules of court-annexed mediation programs, as well as those of private mediation programs, do not include provisions for formal discovery. Documents or other discovery items must be obtained either by mutual agreement (often in conjunction with the mediator) or through the discovery rules of the underlying litigation or arbitration. As noted in Step Three, in the case of voluntary exchange there is wisdom in getting a written commitment from the parties, perhaps as a follow-up to a pre-mediation conference.

Daniel Terrell is now inside counsel in Baton Rouge, Louisiana. In an interview while he was practicing law at a firm in New Orleans several years ago, he underscored the importance of document exchange in a then-ongoing construction dispute:

> We have a complex construction matter—a $25 million dispute—going to mediation in September. We, as counsel for the owner, are right now exchanging project documents with the architect and general contractor. We believe in this case that this information exchange will be valuable to all sides in determining the strengths and weaknesses of each party's case, such that all parties can be fully prepared for the mediation and together maximize the chances of a successful resolution.
>
> Preparation is key. If you want to have a good likelihood that the case will settle in mediation, you

> have to be able to see the landscape. In other words, you need to see what your exposure is and what your strengths are, so that you can appropriately argue your positions and discuss them at the mediation—and also just to have the ability to correctly analyze proposals from opposing parties and the suggested courses of action by the mediator.

In Sidebar 4-1, Richard Shusterman (Berwyn, PA) talks at length about how document exchange may typically be handled in complex multiparty construction disputes.

A. Timing of document exchange

In the context of medical records in personal injury cases, mediator J. Anderson Little (Chapel Hill, NC) stresses how important it can be for plaintiffs' counsel to make these records available well in advance of a mediation. He writes (2007, pp. 40–41):

> The plaintiff's bar typically views medical records and medical expenses as a given in the case. The defense does not. The defense scrutinizes medical records and medical expenses carefully. They discover things in the record that plaintiffs have not bothered to review. The defense frequently will refer records to consulting doctors and nurses for help in analyzing medical treatment and expenses.
>
> . . . Thus, [defendants] need time to process the information that plaintiffs provide through discovery before deciding what value they will give the case. If they don't get basic claims information well in advance of the settlement conference, they will not be able to make informed decisions and negotiate a settlement. Plaintiffs' lawyers often fail to take this need into consideration as they approach settlement discussions and, unwittingly, thwart their hopes of reaching settlement.

Similar considerations can apply in any type of case. For more discussion on the importance of timing, see Substep 4.2D.

B. Mechanics

Whether your case is large or small, the actual mechanics of the exchange will probably be basically the same as for formal discovery in litigation. That is, you will make sure the documents are logged, numbered, and—where a large volume of documents is involved—entered in a database. Instead of (or in addition to) a separate exchange, key documents may be appended to an exchanged mediation memo.

4.2 Exchange mediation memos (where required or useful).

"The reason I want memoranda sent to me before a mediation in cases where lawyers are going to participate actively is to give me a sense of the situation, including their legal perspectives," explain mediators Gary Friedman (Mill Valley, CA) and Jack Himmelstein in their jointly written book (2008, p.246). They go on to observe (pp.246–47):

> Usually this necessitates a 5- to 10-page memo from each side, which allows me to get enough of a feel of the situation that I can hit the ground running when we begin. It also makes the lawyers more comfortable to be able to provide the mediator with information about the case in their role as advocates for their clients. I learn a lot from these memos not only about the facts of the case and the law, but also about the attitudes of the lawyers toward seeking resolution.

The mediation memorandum is also known by a variety of other names, including *mediation statement* (Allen, 2009, p.13), *premediation submission* (Cooley, 2002, p.127), *mediation letter*, *mediation package*, and *mediation brief* (Poon, 2010, p.67). Confusingly, similar or identical terms are sometimes used for a different type of submission: a confidential written brief for the mediator that is *not* exchanged between the parties and may be used either instead of or in addition to an exchanged memorandum. For clarity, in this book the exchanged version will usually be called a *mediation memo*, with the confidential version called a *mediator brief*.

Use of exchanged mediation memos appears to vary widely in jurisdictions across the United States. In some places, they are required. For example, in the U.S. District Court for the Northern District of California, each party to a mediation must serve a written mediation statement on all other parties in addition to the mediator (ADR Local Rule 6-7). At the other extreme, the ADR rules of the Commercial Division of New York County call for a memorandum that "shall not be served on the adversary" unless otherwise agreed (Rule 8(c))—that is, a confidential mediator brief (*see* Step Five). However, even where an exchanged mediation memo is mandatory, you may want to consider also sending a confidential brief to the mediator. Likewise, where a confidential brief is required or customary, you may want to consider also sending a nonconfidential memo to your opponents. (For more discussion about deciding to send both types, see Step Five.)

The remainder of this chapter will cover the following topics related to exchanged mediation memos: (a) functions, (b) contents, (c) style and tone, (d) timing, (e) how much time to put into a mediation memo, and (f) replies.

A. Functions

A mediation memo has a built-in dual function. Because of its exchanged nature, it provides a means of direct communication not only with the mediator but with the opposing *party*. The memo's dual function is emphasized by Walter Stuart (New York):

> Number one, it needs to speak to the other side's client. Number two, you want it to be meaningful to the mediator and make sure that the mediator understands the case. So it's first to the opposing client, second to the mediator, and maybe third to the lawyer on the other side.

The function of communication with the opposing client is part of the rationale for why exchanged mediation memos are required in the mediation program of the District Court for the Northern District of California (where they are called *mediation statements*). Here is what the program's director, Howard Herman, has to say on the topic:

> We start with the idea that statements are exchanged because mediation as we practice it in this district is about opening up the lines of communication from one side to the other. The rules acknowledge that the exchanged statement may be supplemented by a confidential submission to the mediator. But as a general proposition, if the idea is to open the lines of communication, it's more helpful for the parties to exchange statements.
>
> The audience is the client on the other side. We can't force it, but the presumption is that you should be writing a statement, as the lawyer, that the other side's client is going to read. The case only resolves if the decision makers on each side are willing to accept a settlement. We are trying, at least, to move mediation into being a client-centered event.

In some circumstances, the person who will read a mediation memorandum on behalf of a corporate client is the corporation's inside counsel. As indicated by the quote that begins this chapter, John DeGroote (Dallas) regularly read the opposing side's mediation memos during his years as Chief Litigation Counsel at a global consulting firm. He explains why:

> If I don't read that stuff, or if I don't have a good understanding of the other side's case, I think it borders on a fiduciary-duty problem. I mean, that's why we are doing what we are doing, right? The whole point of the mediation exercise is to figure out the positions and the interests of the other side and determine if common ground can be reached. I do nobody any good if I don't listen to what the other side has to say.

As noted, the other main function of the exchanged mediation memo is to communicate with the mediator. This involves both bringing the mediator up to speed and (one hopes), in doing so, presenting a positive view of your case.

As to presenting a positive view of your case, of course that is built in anyway because of the persuasion directed at your opponent. But insofar as you have the mediator specifically in mind, you may ask: Since the mediator does not have authority to make an adjudication, why should you care how she assesses your case? True, the mediator is not acting as a judge. But if she is good at her job, she will probably be strategizing how the parties might achieve a settlement, before the session begins. Part of her analysis undoubtedly will involve a calculation or instinct as to what a reasonable settlement amount would be—which obviously depends on the relative strengths of each side's case.

Richard Spencer (Los Angeles) puts it this way, from his experience both as a litigator and as a mediator in the personal injury arena:

> Even a mediator who is primarily a facilitator is going to be influenced by the mediator's view of the probable outcome of the ultimate trial if the case doesn't settle. The mediator knows that in order to settle the case, he or she has to account for the fact that you believe you have a strong position. If the mediator agrees, that's going to affect the focal point of the potential outcomes, or potential settlements. In order words, the mediator will have a view of what ultimately might happen if this case goes to trial, and that's going to influence how he is going to talk to the parties.

But quite aside from potentially engendering a favorable view, it is important simply to make sure the mediator understands in advance what the dispute is all about. This applies both to the underlying facts (and allegations) and to the applicable law.

B. Contents

In some court-annexed mediation programs, the required contents for exchanged mediation memos are set forth by rule. For example, here are the contents required by ADR Local Rule 6-7(c) of the District Court for the Northern District of California:

> **Content of Statement.** The statements must be concise, may include any information that may be useful to the mediator, and must, unless otherwise directed by the mediator:

(1) Identify, by name and title or status:

(A) The person(s) with decision-making authority, who, in addition to counsel, will at-tend the mediation as representative(s) of the party, and

(B) Persons connected with a party opponent (including an insurer representative) whose presence might substantially improve the utility of the mediation or the prospects for settlement;

(2) Describe briefly the substance of the suit, addressing the party's views of the key liability issues and damages and discussing the key evidence;

(3) Identify the discovery or motions that promise to contribute most to equipping the parties for meaningful settlement negotiations;

(4) Except to the extent prohibited by applicable laws of privilege or by these rules, describe the history and current status of any settlement negotiations;

(5) Provide additional information about any needs, interests or other considerations not described elsewhere in the statement that might be pertinent to settlement; and

(6) Include copies of documents likely to make the mediation more productive or to materially advance settlement prospects.

If you do a mediation memo, this would be a useful template to follow regardless of whether you are required to do so by rule.

Exchanged mediation memoranda are also required in the mediation programs of some private ADR firms. For example, Rule 6.1 in the mediation rules of Global InterMediation, PLLC states: "The parties shall exchange a mediation brief setting forth at least the following information: (a) the procedural history and status of the case; (b) the factual background of the dispute; (c) the applicable jurisdiction and law governing the dispute; and (d) the issues that need to be resolved" (Poon, 2010, p.114).

Mediator Peter Grilli (Tampa, FL) gives this example of what he likes to see:

> What I'll say to a plaintiff's lawyer, for example, is, if you want that adjuster to pay you a million dollars, then three weeks or a month before the mediation you send a settlement package over that shows why they should be concerned about paying three million. You know, here is liability, here is damages—here is out-of-pocket, some specials, here's the information about noneconomic damages, here are comparable jury verdicts. I have seen some really good packages put together for people and it really does two things. It lets them know that the other side is prepared, but it also gives them some reason to compromise.
>
> Unless you have a bet-the-company case—and especially if there is insurance involved—people are pretty willing to face the risk of a trial. What you've got to do is give them enough information that they are worried about—enough exposure that they'll settle in some reasonable range. That's really the key to it, I think: giving the other side documentation enough for their file so that they won't get in trouble when they give you the compromise that you want them to give you. I think that goes for both the plaintiff and defendant.

Obviously, an exchanged memo will *not* include any information that you want the mediator to know but not reveal to other parties. That type of information is the province of confidential mediator briefs, discussed in Step Five.

(1) Should you include a settlement proposal?

"Unless you are required to do so in a court-mandated mediation, there is a tactical decision to be made as to whether or not you set forth your settlement proposal in the [exchanged] mediation brief," writes Gary Poon (2010, p.68). "Many mediators would caution against staking out your position, especially so early in the mediation."

(2) Cooperating on a joint set of pleadings

To facilitate references by all parties later, as well as to help the mediator, consider working cooperatively with all parties to submit a single joint set of relevant pleadings. As mediator Jay Cohen (Winter Park, FL) puts it, he would rather not receive multiple copies of the same motions or pleadings sent by the various parties individually: "It's wonderful when they get organized about that."

C. Style and tone of the exchanged mediation memo

As to style and tone, Gary Poon notes that two very different approaches are found (2010, p.67):

> There are generally two schools of thought on the approach that a party should take in drafting the [exchanged] mediation brief. One school says that the mediation brief should advocate the positions of the party, similar to a legal brief, since each party's objective in the mediation is to achieve the most optimal settlement for its side. The other school believes that the mediation brief should simply set forth the factual and legal issues in as objective a manner as possible, since the mediator is not in a position to render a decision in the case.

Poon's view is that good mediators find both approaches acceptable, because they can "look beyond the stated positions of the parties to ascertain their underlying interests" (p.68). The question of which approach may be more effective in carrying out both of the exchanged memo's two main functions—speaking directly to the opposing client and bringing the mediator up to speed—is a separate issue.

For the tone effective with mediators, see also the discussion of this topic in Step Five. One may generalize that what works best in this context is a relatively dispassionate approach that conveys your side's strong points without much adversarial language. Nate Cade (Milwaukee) advises:

> Lay out your case—"here are the bare-bone facts that you need to know"—and don't shade them. Don't try

> to say everything is for your client as opposed to the other side. You want to be objective in the facts. After being objective in the facts is where you say, "Here is the law." Don't hide adverse precedent, because if the mediator finds out that you are hiding law or the other side points it out, you have lost all credibility.

Also stressing a modulated approach is Laura Kennedy, a Phoenix-based litigator (2010, p.160):

> In your exchanged brief, tell a compelling story that helps both the mediator and the opposition understand the claims, defenses, damages and the parties' respective positions. Consider attaching key documents, but do not substitute documents for thoughtful, well-written presentation of the case. And, do not attach so much material that the significance of the key data is diluted.
>
> The exchanged brief should not be polarizing but should impart information on your position, giving the mediator tools to effectively express to the opposition its downside and weaknesses. And, it should convey your position to your opponent's decision-maker(s) to give them much to think about as they consider what a third party decision-maker might do with the case.

As to the mediation memo's function of speaking directly to the opposing client, obviously you want to be persuasive (though again, without shading the law or facts). The late Andrew Berry said that in his drafting, an exchanged mediation memo would read more like a trial brief or summary judgment brief than would a confidential mediator brief: "It will have some adverbs and adjectives in it. It will read a little more 'hot' than a simple exposition of what the case really is."

The trick is to convey a powerful message—which may call for more forceful expression than you need for the mediator—without the type of bombast that will backfire. If your choice of language and expression ticks the opposing client off and causes him to close his ears, your opportunity to have an impact on his view of the case is lost.

Beyond the mediator and opposing client (and counsel), your mediation memo has a third important audience: *your own client*. In fact, presumably your client will be the first person outside your firm to read it, reviewing your draft for critique or approval purposes. The danger of drafting a mediation memo that seems *too* nonadversarial is that your client may feel you are unwilling or unable to be a strong enough advocate for his position—which could undermine your professional relationship. Sometimes, these competing considerations may require a careful balance.

D. Timing

"Timing is critical" for mediation memos, advise members of one Florida mediation firm (Upchurch, Sands, & Orfinger, 2011, p.2). They point out that "it will take several days, at a minimum, for the 'claims committee' [of a corporate defendant] to meet, compare notes, and set an appropriate reserve on the file."

Where exchanged mediation memoranda are required by rule, the rules may also contain a deadline for submission. For example, the rules of the District Court for the Northern District of California provide that such memos must be submitted at least 10 days before the first mediation session (Local ADR Rule 6-7(a)); the rules of the private ADR firm Global InterMediation, PLLC also require 10 days (Poon, 2010, p.114). Similarly, if the parties voluntarily agree on mediation memos at a premediation conference, they may also agree on a deadline.

However, you should consider whether for strategic reasons it would be better to submit your mediation memo earlier. Recall that Peter Grilli spoke of urging plaintiffs to send the defendant a mediation package "three weeks or a month" in advance of the mediation session. In Sidebar 8-5 ("'Should I Hold Something Back for Trial?'"), Grilli makes a point that helps explain his reasoning, especially where corporate defendants are involved. He notes that decision making at corporations may require input from multiple executives or committees. So if you want such a defendant to be prepared to settle within the range you think is justified, you need to give the corporation plenty of time to absorb and adjust to the supporting information you provide in a mediation memo. The same reasoning applies to corporate plaintiffs—and even to individuals, if you want the mediation memo to help encourage an attitude adjustment in advance of the mediation session.

On the subject of timing, also don't forget the time it will take to send your draft to your client and get feedback before submitting it to the mediator and parties. "You should allow enough time for your client to reflect on the matter so that your offer for suggestions is perceived as sincere," advises John Bates Jr., a mediator based in San Francisco (2009, p.64). "In that way, you may even obtain some useful information."

E. Deciding how much time to put into a mediation memo

Legal memos or briefs of any kind are time consuming to produce. In the real world, how much effort should you realistically put into a mediation memo? "There are many variables," says Richard Spencer. "You're not going to put 100 hours in on doing a mediation brief for an injury that you hope to collect $5,000 or $10,000 for." But legal complexity is another factor, he notes; you may need to spend more time than you would otherwise if there are complicated legal points to deal with. In addition, there are instances where a relatively small case may merit intensive treatment because of larger implications for similar cases coming down the line. Ultimately, the calculus is essentially what you would use in deciding how much time to devote to other aspects of your case during the litigation process.

That said, at least some mediators probably feel that mediation participants too often fail to put enough thought into their mediation memos, undercutting their potential contribution to a good ultimate result. Southern California mediator Louise LaMothe observes (2010, p.66):

> Frequently the mediation statements I receive are disappointing. Perhaps the lawyers don't want to do the extra work, or they delegate the job to someone too inexperienced. Frequently, the statement is just a

> condensed litany of the allegations in the pleadings. Sometimes, the lawyers dump on me the documents they have already prepared for a court filing—usually a motion for summary judgment. Sometimes I get two banker's boxes—an MSJ from each side—before the session.

To say that mediation counsel should put thought into mediation memoranda does not mean that the memos have to be long—or *should* be. Note Gary Friedman's reference to a "5- to 10-page memo." Page length is discussed more in the context of confidential briefs in Substep 5.1C. Much of the same reasoning applies to the length of exchanged memoranda.

F. Replies

Replies to a mediation memo are rare but not unheard of. For example, Walter Stuart says he occasionally has drafted a reply to an opponent's memorandum, although he emphasizes that the memos alone are usually sufficient.

SIDEBAR 4-1

Information Exchange in a Complex Multiparty Mediation

By Richard M. Shusterman

Before launching an independent ADR practice, Richard Shusterman chaired the ADR group of a long-established law firm in the Northeast. He also founded and chaired the firm's insurance coverage and reinsurance practice groups. In this sidebar, which he wrote for this book, Shusterman describes the typical process of information exchange in the mediation of complex, multiparty insurance disputes. Similar approaches may be used in other types of complex multiparty commercial mediations.

Comparing information exchange in mediation to formal discovery, I have found that mediation is often a better and more efficient way of quickly getting the essential information. The party decision makers who attend the mediation are in the best position to assess what information they consider essential to their decision-making process. Once they identify the essential information, the mediator is a very strong asset in defining, and focusing the parties on, the exchange of that essential information.

The mediator serves to focus the parties on what is essential and to facilitate the exchange of that information. By focusing the parties on the essential data, he can keep the parties from being overwhelmed with broadly worded discovery requests for nonessential, peripheral, and overly detailed information that will rarely be seen—let alone reviewed—by the decision makers. Such broad discovery demands are expensive, time consuming, and frustrating to the parties, and divert them from the task at hand of resolving their dispute.

Talk to corporate executives and you will find they all share the same frustration with the scope, cost, and nonessential nature of much of the formal discovery that they are confronted with in their litigation. Whereas in mediation, a party can go in and say, "This is what I need to make a decision, and I may need some kind of an explanation from your standpoint to help me understand the information that you are providing. I do not need a deposition of your people. Just help walk me through what I am looking at, so I have a better grasp on the essential facts." Businesspeople understand that they would never be able to operate in a business setting if, before they made a decision, they had to review the type of information that is frequently requested in formal discovery.

The mediation agreement can provide protections that make it easier for the parties to exchange information in the mediation and not be concerned about triggering the many troublesome issues that can come up in litigation, such as waiver of attorney–client privilege and disclosure of confidential business information. In addition to generally providing for the confidentiality of the entire process, the mediation agreement can provide that some or all of information that is being shared shall be returned to the party that provided it, and cannot be used in the underlying litigation. Other issues of concern to the parties can also be addressed in the mediation agreement.

Presession initial meeting

Particularly in complex multiparty mediations, the first step in information exchange is almost always a face-to-face meeting, so the mediator can look people in the eye and see who he is dealing with. Frequently this happens with only the lawyers and the mediator, but it can be greatly facilitated by having the party representatives present as well. That way, the mediator can encourage the parties to separate the information that the businesspeople really need from the information that the lawyers are requesting. This often simplifies the initial exchange and gets the mediation moving forward.

Usually the information flow and access to the information is unequal at this initial point. Frequently there hasn't been a lot of discovery. So one of the first things the mediator will say is, "What information do you need in order to understand the issues and go to the next phase of decision making?"

In a complex insurance coverage dispute, frequently the insured has been involved in the underlying litigation for quite a while and has more information than many of the insurance carriers. If the underlying litigation is still pending, the insured may have important information about what it would take to settle (or defend) the underlying litigation based on knowledge gained in that litigation, including meetings he may have had with the claimants and their counsel.

There may also be some important information that the insured needs from the carriers. For example, sometimes you're dealing with historical policies, and the insured may not have copies of all the policies and endorsements in its own possession.

After the initial sharing, often no further exchange is required before the mediation session. If it is required, the scope of needed information can be narrowed and focused based on how the mediation is progressing.

Written memoranda

Memoranda exchanged by the parties serve as a way of further educating the parties and the mediator on the issues to be resolved and the legal (and business or other) issues that need to be resolved or otherwise addressed during the mediation. The mediator may also give each party the option of preparing a separate private statement for the mediator's eyes only, which will address such issues as obstacles to resolution (e.g., absence of a key decision maker), hidden (nonlegal) business concerns, personality conflicts, prior efforts to settle and what went wrong, limits on authority, etc.[1] Both types of submissions are helpful to the mediator in preparing for and deciding how to approach the mediation.

Particularly in multicarrier insurance coverage litigation involving many years and layers of coverage, some of the parties may want to make a joint submission on some or all of their common issues. With multiple parties, you will frequently break it down between common issues and issues that are unique to particular parties.

A common issue might be how you allocate a loss that occurred over many years to the various insurance policies that were in effect over those years or between the insured and the

1. Note: Private mediator statements are covered in Step Five of this book.

insurers. Would the insured have to bear the allocation for gaps in coverage? Is there a dispute about the number of years during which the loss occurred? Would the loss be allocated equally to each year? Would it be allocated based on when the loss was discovered or when the loss occurred and remained undiscovered? Would the limits of coverage or gaps in coverage in particular years affect the result? How would you break it down in terms of allocating that loss over many years between the insured, primary, and different layers of excess coverage? What is the magnitude of the loss? What has been paid to settle the loss? Are there both covered and noncovered components to the settlement of the underlying loss? Has there been a settlement? Is a settlement contemplated? At what amount?

A unique or individual issue might be whether there is a particular provision in some of the policies that would exclude the particular loss or some portion of the particular loss from that policy. How would that exclusion apply? Another frequent unique issue is that some insurance policies provide for recalculating the premium based on the losses so that it is retrospectively evaluated—so that issue is unique to a particular policy and how that policy works.

Multiparty mediations are complex. You do not want the mediation itself to be overrun by individual issues. You want to deal with as many of the common issues as you can to move the group forward toward more global resolution. Then, down the road, you will need to have what I would call submediations of issues that are unique to particular parties.

Oral presentation by the insured at the mediation session

After the parties have exchanged written memoranda—and perhaps also submitted private statements to the mediator—a formal mediation session will be scheduled. At this session, attended by counsel and the party representatives, the parties or their counsel will make an oral presentation setting forth their position, what they are seeking to achieve in the mediation, and what they are willing to do to achieve that result.

Often, the session where the oral presentation is made will be the first time that many of the party representatives—preferably the actual decision makers—will be there and have an opportunity to evaluate the issues as presented by their adversary and to meet and interact with their counterpart from the other company. This may open an opportunity for early-stage party-to-party talks facilitated by the mediator. Such talks can help the people doing the negotiations get to know each other and dispel myths and misconceptions that may have arisen during the course of litigation or earlier discussions. Getting the parties to talk to each other and feel comfortable and nonthreatened in discussing their respective wants and needs with each other is a very important role for the mediator.

Follow-up information requests

In complex mediations, more than one session may be needed to resolve all the issues. During the mediation process, one or more of the parties may reach a point where additional information may be needed for that party to understand or clarify one or more of the issues that affect it. The information may be requested in writing, or orally in one of the sessions, along with an explanation of why it is needed. The mediator will then be actively involved in clarifying the request in a phone conference or a breakout session during the course of a mediation session. He will help the parties resolve any issues that the request raises.

Planning of future sessions

Where a number of mediation sessions are required, it is frequently helpful at the end of each session to prepare a summary of what was resolved, narrowed, or clarified at that session. At the same time, it is important to make a checklist of the matters that are going to be addressed in the next sessions and the people who will be taking the lead in addressing them.

Throughout the mediation, the mediator is continually trying to understand the issues, the parties' needs and wants, the limits to their respective authority, and the facts and documents that will be needed to clarify issues and positions (and the reasons this information is important). The mediator is also using the presentations of the parties to help the parties test the strength and weaknesses of their positions and come up with ideas for moving the process forward toward resolution. Useful exchanges of information during the mediation process can greatly facilitate a good result.

Particularly in complex mediations, there are instances where the process results in a resolution of some but not all outstanding issues. Even if the mediation is not successful in resolving all the issues, the process can help narrow and streamline the remaining litigation (including the formal discovery that will be pursued) going forward.

SIDEBAR 4-2

Helping a Senior Lawyer With Document and Memo Exchange

"The mediation is something where frequently a young lawyer can really assist, in terms of working through the presentation, the PowerPoints, the accumulation of documents and deposition excerpts, etc.," says Walter Stuart (New York). Stuart's perspective is that of a senior litigation partner at a huge global law firm. His practice is focused on big-ticket commercial cases, which are "very document driven; that is, there will be a lot of documents to review." Here is more of his view:

> Younger lawyers who are involved in the document-gathering stage of a case are usually the best resource that a lead lawyer has in uncovering the most important evidence. At this very granular level of examination of the facts through the documents and the depositions, the young lawyer is able to assist better than anyone else in deciding what evidence is going to be most impactful. If they do it well and are always looking to understand how a document fits in, lawyers who feel they have only a minor role in the

> case because they are just doing document reviews could find themselves a critical part of the team when it comes time to have a mediation or a trial.

As a partner at a Sacramento, California, law firm with fewer than 50 lawyers, Maralee Eriksen also sees younger lawyers' potential contribution in mediation as important. Although she is a partner now, she recalls the proactive preparation role she used to play as an associate:

> Usually what I would do is have a meeting with the lead attorney at least a couple of weeks before our mediation briefs were due—even if it was just a very short 10- or 15-minute meeting, because the lead counsel are almost always very busy people. I would go in with a list and say, "Okay, are there any discovery responses you want me to have ready? Are there any key documents that you want me to make sure we get or attach to our brief or have with us? Do you want me to research any legal points? Do I need to go back and look through our case investigation or our legal research from the outset of the case and pull any key cases to come with us?"
>
> Oftentimes as I got more advanced, as a second chair I was taking a first draft at the brief. I would still have that meeting, just to assess anything that the lead lawyer wanted to be sure that we brought out.

Like Eriksen, Daniel Terrell—when he was an associate in the New Orleans office of a regional law firm—found that lead attorneys were open to letting him tackle the first draft of mediation briefs. He was given guidance on the purpose of such papers, along with samples from mediations in prior cases. The type of feedback he received on his drafts was "similar to what you would expect from other work product," he says. "When you work with a senior lawyer for a while, you understand the style and tone which are generally used and so forth. But to the extent that you don't, those are areas of comment—and then, your arguments are often commented upon to strengthen the overall presentation of the case to the mediator."

SIDEBAR 4-3

Don't Sound Like a "Freshman"

Jay M. Cohen (interview)

Mediator Jay Cohen (Winter Park, FL) offers this heads-up that an overly adversarial tone can mark the writer as inexperienced or inept in mediation:

Your experience as a lawyer in prepping or preparing a mediator is clear within the first couple of paragraphs of what you send. First, there are the freshmen. You know, they're kids. They'll use expressions that make folks like me chuckle:

"It is obvious that . . ."

"The facts are clear that . . ."

"It is without dispute that . . ."

There's a lot of that stuff. Immaturity, that's what it displays. To me, what it means is, "Uh-oh, if I've got somebody who hasn't got this figured out, God knows what they're going to do when it comes to handling people!"—which is what's coming up next.

STEP FIVE

Confidentially Brief the Mediator (As Allowed or Required)

> *[T]he more information the parties can share with the mediator on a confidential basis, the better he is able to help both sides reach a settlement.*
>
> —Gary P. Poon, mediator (2010, p.69)

In every mediation, you are likely to have information that would be helpful to the mediator in working toward a potential settlement but that you would not want to communicate to the other side. Richard Spencer (Los Angeles) offers these common examples: "Settlement position. Specific objectives or problems that a party has. Things they definitely do not want to do, or they think are critical to do. Opinions they may have of the other side's objectives or motivations."

Other possibilities include the existence of evidence one party does not want an opponent to know about yet—but would like the *mediator* to know about because it affects the terms on which the party would be willing to settle. For example, as Nate Cade (Milwaukee) notes, a party may want to keep secret the existence of a video recording that undermines an opponent's position. For a long list of sensitive issues that an advocate may want to consider communicating to the mediator, see Sidebar 5-1: "Confidential Topics for Confidential Communications."

Failure to disclose important confidential information to the mediator can have a destructive impact on a mediation session. As an "extreme example" from his insurance practice, Christopher Carroll (New York and New Jersey) cites a dispute between an owner and an insured where the owner had secretly negotiated an advance cap on damages with some (but not all) of the defendants. This important fact—which naturally influenced the negotiating positions of the parties to the side deal—was not disclosed to the mediator. The result was that in a multiday mediation session, negotiations "went nowhere" for several days. "The mediator was just apoplectic," Carroll recalls—"didn't understand the dynamics, didn't understand what was going on." On the final day, Carroll was able to convince the parties to the side deal to disclose it to the mediator. But before that happened, they "wasted four days of haggling back and forth over numbers that were unreal because there was already an agreed-to cap."

Carroll's example is indeed extreme—and unusual. But just as the mediator's efforts in that dispute would have been much more effective with the benefit of confidential information, any mediation is likely to benefit if the mediator's knowledge is as complete as reasonably possible.

Confidential briefing of the mediator in advance of a mediation session may occur in one of two ways: in writing (Substep 5.1) or orally (Substep 5.2). Depending on the circumstances of your case and the rules in your jurisdiction, you may want to engage in one or both.

5.1 Submit a confidential mediator brief (if required or warranted).

The term *confidential mediator brief* is used in this book to refer to a written submission about your case that is sent confidentially to the mediator only, and not exchanged between the parties. As with the exchanged mediation memorandum, confidential mediator briefs are also known by a variety of other names. In fact, some of the same names (e.g., *mediation letter*) are used for both types of submissions—a confusing overlap.

The use of confidential mediator briefs appears to vary widely across the United States. For example, in New York County, the Commercial Division's alternate dispute resolution rules require parties to send the mediator a memo that "shall not be filed in court nor, unless otherwise agreed by the parties, served on the adversary" (Rule 8(c)). In Florida, one veteran mediator (Jay Cohen) estimates that about 90% of the briefs he receives from parties before a session are marked "confidential"—which he describes as the "default position" there. By contrast, the mediation rules of the District Court for the Northern District of California require an *exchanged* memo, although they give mediators the option of submitting a "confidential written statement" as a supplement (Local ADR Rule 6-9).

It is easy to find litigators who express positive views about confidential mediator briefs, either as stand-alones or as supplements to an exchanged memo:

- Confidential briefs are "critical for a successful mediation." —*Steven Brom, (Birmingham, AL)*
- "The private memo makes a huge difference." —*John DeGroote (Dallas)*
- "I also like the idea of a private letter—anything that you might want to add separate and apart from what you've publicly stated to the mediator. And that could be anything from: Here's the politics of this discussion. Here are some of the personal issues that need to be considered and factored in. Here are some of the more sensitive considerations. Things of that nature that are not going to be coming out in the more formal mediation submission because it's just not the appropriate place to do so, but give the mediator a flavor." —*Christopher Carroll (New York and New Jersey)*
- "If there is an issue that we view as confidential, we will ask the mediator for permission to submit something confidential and we will instruct him to keep it confidential until such time as we want it revealed in the mediation, if ever." —*Walter Stuart (New York)*

For the perspective of one experienced mediator, see Sidebar 5-2: "Q & A on Mediation Briefs." Another mediator (and the author of a book on mediation for corporate counsel), Gary Poon (Washington, DC) believes it is a good idea to submit a confidential mediator brief even when it is not required. "Indeed, the more information the parties can share with the mediator on a confidential basis, the better he is able to help both sides reach a settlement," he writes (2010, p.69).

Still, this view is not universal. "In my own mediation practice, sometimes I want confidential statements and sometimes I don't," says Howard Herman, who directs the ADR program for the U.S. District Court for the Northern District of California. As an example of the latter, he points to disputes where "there is a lot of mistrust." In such situations, the parties may "do better feeling like they know what's being put on the table, and they want to work jointly before they work privately. They want to get a feel for it." Under those circumstances, "maybe it's not a good idea to have people telling me things privately—at least until we've all had a chance to gather and meet and establish some trust." Herman prefers an ADR rule that makes confidential briefs optional rather than mandatory.[1]

The rest of this treatment of confidential mediation briefs will cover: (a) matters to include; (b) style and tone; (c) length, degree of effort, and timing; and (d) confidential briefs as a supplement to exchanged memos.

A. Matters to include in the confidential mediator brief

If a confidential brief is submitted without an exchanged mediation memorandum, it needs to include every element an exchanged memo would have, plus the confidential matters. Those elements were discussed in detail in Step Four. If the confidential brief is a supplement to an exchanged memorandum, obviously it will contain only the confidential matters.

From his experience as a mediator in the bankruptcy arena, Timothy Corcoran (Tampa, FL) developed a list of 10 elements that should be included in stand-alone confidential briefs. To see that list and some related advice, read Sidebar 5-3: "What the Mediator Needs From You." Laura Kennedy (Phoenix) has provided a very detailed list of confidential matters to consider, in Sidebar 5-1: "Confidential Topics for

1. Also, proponents of Understanding-based mediation do not accept confidential mediator briefs, as part of their general insistence that the mediator must never at any time have a communication with one side that is not also shared with the other side (*see* Friedman & Himmelstein, 2008, pp.245–246). The unusual approach of Understanding-based mediation was discussed earlier in this text, in Substep 2.3B and Sidebar 3-4: "A Noncaucus Model: 'Understanding-Based' Mediation."

Confidential Communications." Also, be sure to read Sidebar 5-7: "Your Ex Parte Statement: Practices and Strategies."

In some jurisdictions, matters that must be addressed in the confidential mediator brief are established by rule or judicial order. For example, in her mediation work as a federal magistrate judge, Mary Pat Thynge (Wilmington, DE) issues a standard order that requires parties to address seven topics (*see* Sidebar 5-8: "Mediator Brief Topics: A Sample Order").

Judge Thynge (2011) laments the fact that when drafting confidential mediator briefs, "parties often fail to strike the balance between the legal issues part and business interests/solutions portion of the submission. *The latter frequently receives little, if any, attention*" (p.156, italics added). You should not make the same mistake.

B. Style and tone of the confidential mediator brief

As with content, considerations of style and tone were earlier discussed for exchanged mediation memos in Step Four. The obvious difference for confidential mediator briefs is that the audience for them does *not* include the opposing side. For that reason, there is even less rationale for a bombastic, adversarial tone, although you will still need to keep your own client confident that you are representing his interests with strength.

Many lawyers probably agree with Maralee Eriksen that the most effective confidential briefs are "very concise" and "very candid" about their case's strengths and weaknesses. For more of Eriksen's observations on this topic, drawn from experience clerking for a federal magistrate judge at the outset of her legal career, see Sidebar 5-4: "A Clerk's-Eye View of Confidential Mediation Briefs."

In Jay Cohen's mediation practice, he is most impressed by briefs that "present a relatively reasonable description of what the fight's all about from both sides." You will gain detailed insights into the structure and content of a great confidential brief from reading his observations in Sidebar 5-5: "Why Jay Cohen Reads Tom's Mediation Brief First."

The perspective of mediator John Bickerman (Washington, DC) is very compatible with both Eriksen's and Cohen's. Bickerman emphasizes the importance of being up-front about your cases' weaknesses, as well as avoiding a harsh, adversarial tone:

> Just as the mediator has to get credibility with the parties, the lawyers need to get credibility with the mediator. The mediator has to be able to trust the reliability of what the lawyer said. So I think it is really important that a lawyer play it straight and help the mediator. I don't believe that strong advocacy requires you to be harsh and hard. I think a more effective approach is to be honest and say, "Look, these are the strengths"—and then acknowledge some of the weaknesses as well. Because if the case was a slam-dunk, the parties would not be there. It is obvious there are some weaknesses.

Tamping down on rhetoric was also stressed (in a 2008 interview) by the late Andrew Berry, whose Newark, New Jersey, legal practice spanned 40 years and included substantial experience with mediation:

> [In the confidential statement], I'm not going to use [language like] "unbelievably, the other side has contended . . ." or "without a shred of support, the other side suggests. . . ." I'm just going to say, "Here's our position, [and] here's their position. Here's why on the facts or on the law their case isn't worth very much, or my case is worth a great deal." And I don't need to shout and yell and use names about it. It's a document that operates at a much lower temperature [than an adversarial brief in litigation]. Because you're not going to impress an experienced mediator by adjectives and adverbs.
>
> Any time you tell your story in a lucid and persuasive way, you're advantaged. At the margin, mediators are human! They prefer to be dealing with people who are relatively candid and relatively intelligent and relatively open about their needs and their willingness to make compromise. Don't come in with a statement that says, "We don't owe a nickel." Come in with a mediation statement that says, "On the law and the facts, we don't think we really face exposure

beyond zero if we were to try this case, but recognizing some value in certainty and yada yada yada, here's a nickel."

In a confidential brief, where a party theoretically could disclose anything, there is always a question of just how much to reveal. "Some advocates take the position that the particular case will probably not settle without being completely candid, and expose all weaknesses to the mediator in the paper," notes Daniel Terrell (Baton Rouge, LA). "Others are more guarded in their approach, choosing to style the paper as a persuasive brief without sharing everything with the mediator. The degree to which weaknesses and other confidential information are disclosed in the paper is often driven by a host of factors, including any past experience with the particular mediator." The question of how much to disclose in confidential communications with the mediator will be discussed at more length later in this book in Step Nine, in the context of private caucuses during the mediation session.

C. Length, degree of effort, and timing for confidential mediator brief

"It's interesting to see what you get," says Paul Sandars (Roseland, NJ), referring to the briefs he receives when serving as a mediator. "Sometimes you get a whole 20-page thing with exhibits and everything else. Sometimes you get a two-page thing—and obviously it was done on the way to work in the car."

As with exchanged mediation memoranda (*see* Step Four), the maximum length for confidential mediator memoranda may be set by the applicable rules. But you may want to shoot for something shorter than the max—not because you tossed it off on your way to work, but because a well-crafted shorter memo can be more effective.

Here are a few quotes from mediation advocates and mediators on the topic of length, assuming that the confidential mediator brief will be submitted as a stand-alone rather than as a private supplement to an exchanged mediation memo:

- "The busiest mediators are not always the best mediators—but the best are very busy. If you give them a really good 10 pages with some attachments, they're going to be happy about that." —*Andrew Berry*
- "The written document—if you separately supply things like the pleadings and summary judgment motions and the like—shouldn't be more than 15 or 20 pages." —*John DeGroote (Dallas)*
- "It's a rare lawsuit that takes more than six or seven pages. And most of them can be done in five—I would say five or less. What would make them longer would be either the number of parties or the number of different lawsuits that are being combined in one single attempt to resolve everything between these folks." —*Jay Cohen (Winter Park, FL)*

See also Sidebar 5-4 ("A Clerk's-Eye View of Confidential Mediation Briefs"), where Maralee Eriksen observes that one of the best confidential mediator briefs she saw while clerking for a federal magistrate judge (in his role as a mediator) was only six pages long.

(1) Timing

In deciding when to submit your confidential mediator brief, many of the same considerations apply as for an exchanged mediation brief (discussed in detail in Step Four). The short answer might be: as early as you might reasonably expect the mediator to start focusing on your case in advance of the mediation session. In the view of Andrew Berry, "most good mediators want to see a mediation statement—depending on how busy they are—a week [or] 10 days in advance." (*See also* Sidebar 5-6: "A Mediation Pioneer on Confidential Briefs.")

(2) Degree of effort

The amount of time and effort you should reasonably expend was also discussed in the context of exchanged mediation memos in Step Four. The same basic considerations apply, such as how much time you can afford to put into the file (often determined by the litigation budget and the stakes), how hard the case is to understand; and how pivotal supplying confidential information or perspectives might be in helping the mediator spur the parties to settlement.

D. Confidential briefs as a supplement to exchanged memos

The downside of using a confidential mediator brief as the only written submission before a mediation is that you lose your opportunity to educate the client on the other side, which is possible with the exchanged mediation memo (*see* discussion in Step Four). On the other hand, if you submit only an exchanged memo, you lose a useful opportunity to inform the mediator on matters that should not be disclosed to your opponent.

Therefore, if the size of the case permits, you may want to consider submitting both an exchanged mediation memo and a confidential mediator brief. If so, of course, the confidential brief would be much shorter than otherwise, because its contents would consist solely of the confidential points you want to communicate.

This dual approach is endorsed by some experienced advocates, including John DeGroote:

> To me, the best approach is the one taken by a magistrate in the Eastern District of Virginia for mediated settlement conferences. He says, "Give me a letter that you copy the other side on, and give me a letter that's just to me, and say whatever you want—whatever you think advances the ball."
>
> So you have one submission that's an advocacy piece that says, "I'm going to rip their ears off, this is why." And then there is a separate letter that says something like, "We fully acknowledge that some particular witness may testify against us—but this is why we think that's going to be okay. And note that we've offered to settle for 100 grand, and they've offered to take 103, and we just can't bridge that last $3,000 gap." So that the mediator has a better sense of really where he is starting.

5.2 Engage in confidential oral communications with the mediator in advance of the session (as allowed and appropriate).

Confidential oral communications with a mediator may take forms ranging from an informal phone call to a scheduled in-person meeting. One major difference between oral communications and a mediator brief is that oral communications allow for back-and-forth between the participants, so a mediator can easily ask follow-up questions in response to what she hears. Ex parte phone calls may be especially valuable in cases where the budget simply does not afford the cost of a written confidential brief.

Gary Poon, of Global InterMediation, PLLC, considers ex parte calls a typical part of follow-up by the mediator. He writes: "[T]he mediator will likely call each of the parties separately to discuss any issues raised by the party's submissions or to gather more information about the dispute" (2010, p.69).

Scheduled in-person ex parte meetings—in addition to or instead of a written confidential brief—may be supported by the budget of only larger, more complex cases. As the result of such meetings, in the view of Bennett Picker (Philadelphia), "the mediator will learn more about the business operations of the parties, obtain necessary confidential information, develop a better understanding of the parties' rights and interests, begin the process of building trust and develop a structure for the mediation best suited to the particular dispute" (2003, p.30).

John Bickerman, whose mediation practice focuses on large, high-stakes disputes, sees such ex parte discussions as an integral part of the presession mediation process:

> What more and more parties expect—and more and more successful commercial mediators are doing—is meeting with parties in advance of the process. And they are learning the things that are not on the written page, because frequently the most important information isn't put in a brief or statement. They

> are learning about the interpersonal dynamics, both intraparty, within one side—you know, how is everybody interacting, who is getting what pressure, what incentives are there that may or may not be related to the claims—and then interparty. Can we put these people in the same room [at the upcoming mediation session] until they talk constructively, or is somebody just a real burr under the saddle of the other side? And based on that information, we'll formulate a process for when we get together.

Participants in presession oral ex parte communications may include the client as well as the mediator and counsel, but not necessarily. Direct input from the client can contribute by adding an additional dimension. On the negative side, you as counsel may feel more constrained in your discussion of the case, because you are aware of how your client may be judging your performance.

Sometimes ex parte oral communications can serve as a supplement to a confidential mediator brief for the purpose of conveying information that a party would rather not write. Walter Stuart provides an example:

> We might say confidentially to the mediator, "We want you to take a look at the other side's client, because we think that he's a pretty shady character, and will not come across as a good witness. And besides that he has a former conviction." Something that you might not want to put in the actual written statement itself but would be an important fact for somebody to take notice of.

In the case of ex parte calls between the mediator and a lawyer where the lawyer's client is not on the line, a lawyer may also be inclined to offer private observations about his *own* client in relation to the underlying dispute or the mediation process. In that context, do not lose sight of ethical obligations inherent in the lawyer–client relationship, even if you feel certain insights could help the mediator's approach to the mediation session.

SIDEBAR 5-1

Confidential Topics for Confidential Communications

By Laura H. Kennedy

"Certain sensitive issues, if raised in an exchanged brief, may further polarize the parties and inflame passions," writes litigator Laura Kennedy (Phoenix). With regard to the types of issues raised in this sidebar, this is probably an understatement—yet addressing them may be very helpful to a mediator in considering how best to move the parties toward settlement. Kennedy points to confidential, nonexchanged briefs as a vehicle to discuss such issues. In this excerpt from an article on preparing for a mediation session (2010, pp.160–162), Kennedy suggests topics that you may want to consider covering in this type of brief. Some topics—such as the mind-set of your client—may best be handled orally instead (see Substep 5.2), to the extent you discuss them at all.

The Opposing Parties and Their Negotiators. Introduce the mediator to the parties and their expected negotiators. How does your opponent view him or herself? What is his or her reputation in your community? What is their relevant historical background? If they are high profile, you may wish to include newspaper or web articles that capture others' views of their personalities. What drives that person? Are they smart? Charming? Glib? Socially awkward? Clever? Cunning? Practical? Low-key? Self-[r]ighteous? Proud? Loyal to other players? What do others say about him or her? Competitive? Control freak? Hot-tempered? Even-keeled? A deal junkie? Give examples where particularly compelling.

What is the relationship with their counsel? Will they be relying upon their counsel or will a decision be made with little guidance from their counsel?

What might the mediator first experience with that person that you have found to convey a false impression? What is their past relationship with your client(s)? Do they have real authority to settle or do they need to look to someone else? Who is the real decision-maker?

What are their attitudes? How do they view their exposure and thus the mediation? Do they have an unfair sense of entitlement? What are their incentives to settle? What are their disincentives to settle? What is the culture of the corporate client? What is their negotiating style? Attenuated negotiations? Come close to making a deal, but fails to finalize? Renegotiates points already agreed upon?

Opposing Counsel. Introduce the mediator to counsel with whom he or she will be dealing. What is your experience with counsel? What is counsel's legal/trial experience? What is their style? Prepared? Smart? Charming? Endearing? Sanctimonious? Sincere/[i]nsincere? Willing to try cases? Capable? Strategic? Should the mediator look to opposing counsel for help in settling the case? Influence over the decision-makers?

Your Clients. Take this opportunity to educate the mediator about your client(s), his or her experience, successes, values and personality. Share with the mediator the emotions your client(s) experience about the dispute. Are they angry and why? Are they embarrassed by the advantage taken of them? Are they practical? Thoughtful? Decisive? No-nonsense? Good judgment? Are there reasons a settlement for your client now is wise? Will a mediation in the future be less likely to succeed for whatever reason? For example, do you know that historically your client gets wed to the litigation process once involved?

Your Background. If you are new to the mediator, you may wish to share your background, the nature of your practice and your relationship with your client.

The Case and Legal Climate in Your Community. If you are working with a mediator who is from out of town, you may wish to share nuances about your court system. Are your juries pro-plaintiff? Pro-defendant? Does your court see high dollar verdicts? Are there nuances to the system that could impact the litigation? What are the unique rules that govern? Disclosure obligations? Limits on depositions? Who is your judge? Who are your arbitrators? When are you set for trial? If particularly significant, share with the mediator your impressions of the effectiveness of witnesses—both lay and expert.

Historical Settlement Efforts. If you do not share historical settlement efforts in the exchanged brief, do so in the confidential brief. The mediator should know where you have been, and when in the process it occurred. The mediator should know why this time the settlement terms will be significantly different or why this time the case has a better chance of settling.

Settlement Concepts. Many cases are just about payment of money. Others have different currencies. Can you settle with a business deal? Should there be a complete divorce? Will an apology help? A joint press release?

Mediation Dynamics. What are the dynamics of the dispute that make resolving the dispute a challenge? Personalities? Is ego involved? What are the dynamics that impair the chance to settle? Is one party willing to take substantially less than the stated claim in order to fulfill an unrelated need? Share what you believe might lead to a resolution. Does the mediator need to show one side that it has real risk?

SIDEBAR 5-2

Q & A on Mediation Briefs

Peter J. Grilli (interview)

Peter Grilli (Tampa, FL) has been a full-time mediator since 1993, with more than 3,000 cases under his belt. Here is part of our discussion about mediator briefs.

Q: Do you typically ask the parties to exchange memoranda with each other, or to give a confidential memorandum to you?

A: I ask them to give something to me. I like to hear what people have to say. I like to hear what they like about the case. If they have some insight into the psychology on the other side, or if they want to tell me something privately about their own clients, that can help too.

Q: How important is that confidential memorandum to you in the mediation process?

A: Sometimes it's really important; sometimes it's not much help at all.

Q: When would it be important?

A: It's helpful when it's giving me some information about the strengths and weaknesses of the case, or when it's giving me some information that I might not otherwise have about some legal peculiarity. I've mediated 3,000 cases now, so when it comes to civil cases, I've done a little bit of almost everything. I know a little bit about a lot of areas of law. There's always more to be learned. If there's some turning point to the case that exists in some obscure area of the law, it's really great to have an explanation of that somewhere.

Q: A young lawyer just getting into this might think, "You know, a mediator can't just force the parties to do anything. Why should I put much client time into preparing a confidential memorandum?" What would you say to that?

A: There's a lot of reasons to do that preparation. One of them is to sharpen your own thought processes. When you sit down to write down the explanation of why you think the case is strong, you might get some insight that you didn't have otherwise. You might be able to anticipate a question the mediator is going to ask. One of the worst things that can happen is to have the mediator ask a question that you haven't thought of the answer for.

SIDEBAR 5-3

What the Mediator Needs From You

By C. Timothy Corcoran, III

Before studying for the Roman Catholic priesthood, Timothy Corcoran pursued a long legal career that included years as a federal bankruptcy judge in central Florida and a subsequent private practice in which he often served as a mediator. While speaking on the topic of mediation at a bankruptcy seminar some years ago, he offered the following perspective and advice on confidential mediation briefs.

I see mediations in which the lawyers just show up with their clients. The lawyers provide absolutely no information to the mediator beforehand. I guess they expect that the mediator will pick up information about the dispute on the fly and do all the work. Sometimes the lawyers will just provide the mediator with the pleadings. None of this is very helpful.

What you want to do is help the mediator by feeding the mediator before [the session] insightful information that the mediator can use to help get the case resolved. The mediator needs to know (1) the dynamic of the case, (2) what is really going on in the dispute, and (3) why that is going on. The pleadings and a mere statement of the claims and defenses never reveal this key information. The mediator wants—and needs—your analysis more than your pleadings.

[Here is] a checklist [of] what the mediator needs from you:

1. A brief review of the procedural status of the litigation.
2. A brief factual overview.
3. Identification of the key factual and legal issues in the litigation, including a detailed "damages" analysis.
4. A bullet-style list of your factual and legal strengths.
5. A candid, bullet-style list of the other party's factual and legal strengths, along with your responses.
6. Your view of the underlying business or personal needs of each party from a nonmonetary perspective.
7. A history of settlement discussions, including the last proposals and whose court you think the ball is in now.
8. Your view as to the past and current barriers to settlement, including your thoughts as to the other side's realistic view of the case.
9. Highlighted copies of the key documents and pleadings.
10. A summary of any other information that will assist [the mediator] in working with you.

Sit down and think about the case beforehand. Use that checklist in preparing a pre-mediation submission for the mediator. Mark your pre-mediation statement as confidential, and send it to the mediator for his eyes only. Share it with your client.

SIDEBAR 5-4

A Clerk's-Eye View of Confidential Mediation Briefs

Maralee Eriksen (interview)

While Maralee Eriksen was clerking for a federal magistrate judge in Wyoming, she had the opportunity to read confidential briefs submitted in advance of at least 40 "mediated settlement conferences," where the judge served as the neutral. Here are her observations about the characteristics of mediation briefs that she found effective or ineffective.

There was certainly a range of quality in the briefs. There were papers where you could tell someone just did not put a lot of thought or attention.

Sometimes, the attorney would be so "married to the case," if you will—so close to it—that he or she would not start at the beginning to explain the factual underpinnings. They would just kind of jump in the middle somewhere, and it would leave the reader a bit confused as to the underpinnings of the case. I think was the most common ineffective thing that I saw.

There were some attorneys that just would not acknowledge weakness in their papers. In effect, what they did was communicate—whether the attorney intended or not—that the attorney had not made a reasonable assessment of the case. It was ineffective, particularly with the judge, to not acknowledge their weaknesses in the case.

Part of the settlement statement brief was also a calculation of damages. Sometimes claimants would hide the ball about what their damages are because they're not quite sure.

In the converse, most effective briefs I saw were very concise. They were also very candid about what their strengths and weaknesses were.

A mediation brief doesn't need to be the size of a novel in order to get the gist of the case across. It's kind of like an opening statement in trial: If you want to talk for two hours, the jury may fall asleep on you or may not remember what you say. One of the best ones I ever saw was six pages. It was a business case. The writing was very succinct. It wasn't flowery at all. The author was just very efficient in communicating the points that needed to be communicated.

One thing that I found fascinating about the process—being a new attorney—was that the judge, after he read the confidential mediation briefs, formulated in his mind a range that he thought would be an appropriate settlement. He never disclosed that figure to the parties, but he did formulate that. He had a fabulous settlement record—I want to say 98% or 99%. And I think the vast majority of their cases settled within the range that he had already estimated before the parties walked in.

SIDEBAR 5-5

Why Jay Cohen Reads Tom's Mediation Brief First

Jay M. Cohen (interview)

In the course of conducting more than 4,000 mediations since 1990, Jay Cohen (Winter Park, FL) has read more than his share of mediation briefs. I asked him: "Think about the best pre-mediation memorandum or e-mail in whatever form you've gotten. What made it so good and so helpful?" Here is part of his response.

There's a young man by the name of Tom [surname withheld]. I take him as an example because I'm going to be at a mediation with him tomorrow. There are several other folks like him. When I get into a case, especially if there are three or four lawyers in it and Tom's one of them, I always grab his mediation brief first.

The reason is, in the first few paragraphs he explains to me in a comfortable and relaxed tone what the case is all about—not as an advocate from one side, but a reasonably fair reading of all the sides. I never find that part to be an exaggerated advocate's position. For example, he'll tell me they don't agree on who said what at a factually important conversation. "My guy says this, his guy says that." He's never far off. He doesn't come to the conclusions just yet.

The next thing, he explains to me what the case is about from a legal standpoint—again in a relaxed tone. He's not advocating anything. "So here's where we are in the case. They filed a complaint, here's the counts, here's my defense," he'll say, as though we were having a beer. That's what I mean by a relaxed tone. Not "whereas," "wherefore," and "obviously," and "without a doubt." Not that stuff.

I always go to his brief, because those first four or five paragraphs—or page and a half, or however long it takes him to get through what I just told you—sets the stage for me in a reasonable, fair fashion. I will get a reasonable summary of where we are. I like that. And that's what's helpful about the opening.

Then he starts with advocacy, and he cranks up the tone. About the argument—I understand that the client is getting a copy of the letter. And I understand that the lawyer has to satisfy that master. I understand that it has to appear somewhere, and it's fine if it appears here, so you can make up for having been reasonable earlier in the memo about your opponent, that liar.

The next thing is—and again I'll go back to Tom—he will never leave me without a concise outline at the end of what the money is all about, from both sides. "Today, here's where we are. This is what they want and why. Here's how they got to that number. This is what we think we owe them and why, and here's how we got to that number."

So again, the best to me are the ones that present a relatively reasonable description of what the fight is all about from both sides. I'll grab Tom's mediation brief first tonight when I sit down to read them.

SIDEBAR 5-6

A Mediation Pioneer on Confidential Briefs

Linda R. Singer (interview)

Linda Singer (Washington, DC) received the D'Alemberte-Raven Award from the ABA Section of Dispute Resolution in 2012, honoring her contributions to the dispute-resolution field. She published a book on conflict resolution more than two decades ago (1990) and continues actively mediating today.

Q: When serving as a mediator, what do you tell your lawyers about confidential briefs?

A: I tell them that the most useful thing for me is the story of what happened, and then confidentially anything that they think I ought to know about sensitive information or settlement possibilities going forward. Don't just write me a brief about your great case.

Q: How do you characterize the quality of what you usually get?

A: Uneven.

Q: Not surprising. How long do you think such a statement—

A: Short.

Q: Meaning what?

A: It depends on how complicated a dispute is, but I think you can usually tell the story in 10 pages or less. You may want to include attachments. If you want the mediator to be familiar with documents or court decisions, send them. But then expect us to read them and spend the time reading them. So send them in time to have them read. Don't send them the night before.

Q: Which I'm sure happens sometimes.

A: Oh, yes!

SIDEBAR 5-7

Your Ex Parte Statement: Practices and Strategies

By Hildy Bowbeer

Hildy Bowbeer (St. Paul, MN) is Chief Intellectual Property Counsel at a major manufacturing firm. In this excerpt from a book chapter (Bowbeer, 2011, pp.202–203),[2] she offers advice on drafting confidential mediator briefs. Although her advice is geared to intellectual property lawyers in a plaintiff's position, it is equally applicable to mediator briefs in any type of dispute.

1. **Prepare the ex parte submission with the same seriousness you would exercise for any other key briefing.** Do not throw the submission together at the last minute or guess at the answers to the mediator's questions.[3] Do not relegate it to a junior person on the litigation team.
2. **Your mediation strategy should be reflected in your mediation statement.** The very topics you will be discussing with your team in preparation for the mediation—strengths and weaknesses, business objectives, BATNAs and WATNAs,[4] and perceived obstacles to settlement—are the topics the mediator will want you to address in your mediation statement. Therefore, preparation of the statement should not be decoupled from the rest of your preparation, but rather an integral part of that preparation and reflective of it.

---

2. Bowbeer's chapter appears in *ADR Advocacy, Strategies, and Practice for Intellectual Property Cases*, edited by Harrie Samaras and published by the ABA Section of Intellectual Property Law (2011).

3. Bowbeer is referring here to topics that a mediator may require parties to address in the confidential brief. (*See, e.g.*, Sidebar 5-8: "Mediator Brief Topics: A Sample Order.")

4. For a discussion of BATNA and WATNA, read Substep 7.4A.

3. **Help the mediator understand why certain objectives are important to your client.** Some objectives are self-evident. Others may not be, or may seem overreaching or overkill. Take the opportunity to explain why they are necessary and reasonable when viewed in the context of your client's "big picture." For example, you can explain that this defendant is only one of a number of suspected trademark infringers, and therefore the resolution of this case will have "ripple effects" on your credibility in enforcing your marks against those other parties. Or, you may want to let the mediator know that you have "most favored nations" clauses in other licensing agreements that limit your flexibility with regard to the royalty rate you can accept from this defendant. You should also be able to articulate why a resolution on unacceptable terms could be worse than losing the case after trial.
4. **Do not avoid discussing the weaknesses in your case and the strength's of your opponent's case.**This does not mean that you have to brand them as "weaknesses" in your position, but you can set forth your understanding of the arguments you believe the other side will be emphasizing in its statement or at the mediation, and then discuss how you intend to respond to them if the litigation proceeds. That will show the mediator that he can count on you to be realistic and straightforward in your approach. Credibility with the mediator is just as important as credibility with the judge or jury.
5. **Include a firm offer.** This will avoid wasting time at the outset of the mediation determining what your opening offer should be.
6. **Do not include your bottom line.** Just because the mediator is there to help you does not mean you want him to know how low you would be willing to go. If you do, you can virtually guarantee you will not do any better than that. Keep your options open.

SIDEBAR 5-8

Mediator Brief Topics: A Sample Order

By Magistrate Judge Mary Pat Thynge

As a federal magistrate judge in Wilmington, Delaware, Mary Pat Thynge often serves as a mediator in court-assisted mediation. In this excerpt adapted from a book chapter (Thynge, 2011, pp.151–152, n.27),[5] she reproduces a portion of her standard order that sets forth requirements for confidential mediator briefs.

My standard order governing mediation conferences and mediation statements identifies seven topics to be addressed in the confidential mediation statement. My order has evolved over time, and the requirements I set forth therein are included with a purpose.

Those topics are:

a) "*The Parties*": provide a description of who the parties are, their relationship, if any, to each other, and by whom each party is represented, including the identity of all individuals who will be participating on behalf of a party in the mediation conference.

b) "*Factual Background*": provide a brief factual background, clearly indicating which material facts are not in dispute and which remain in dispute.

c) "*Summary of Applicable Law*": provide a brief summary of the law, including applicable statutes, cases, and standards. Copies of any unreported decisions (including decisions from this jurisdiction) that counsel believes are particularly relevant should be included as exhibits.

---

5. Judge Thynge's chapter appears in *ADR Advocacy, Strategies, and Practice for Intellectual Property Cases*, edited by Harrie Samaras and published by the ABA Section of Intellectual Property Law (2011).

d) "*Honest Discussion of Strengths and Weaknesses*": provide an *honest* discussion of the strengths *and* weaknesses of the party's claims and/or defenses.

e) "*Settlement Efforts*": provide a brief description of prior settlement negotiations and discussions, including the most recent offers or demands exchanged between the parties and the reasons for rejection, and the party's assessment as to why settlement has not been reached.

f) "*Settlement Proposal*": describe the party's proposed term(s) for a resolution. Identify any interests or issues not directly involved in this matter that may frustrate or further settlement. If the party has any suggestions as to how the Court may be helpful in reaching a resolution, such suggestions should also be described.

g) "*Fees and Costs*": list separately each of the following: (i) attorneys' fees and costs incurred to date; (ii) other fees and costs incurred to date; (iii) good faith estimate of additional attorneys' fees and costs to be incurred if this matter is not settled; and (iv) good faith estimate of additional other fees and costs to be incurred if this matter is not settled.

STEP SIX

Prepare Yourself for the Mediation Session

A common complaint of mediators is that advocates come to mediations only partially prepared, and sometimes fully unprepared.

—John W. Cooley (1943–2009)
magistrate judge and mediator (2002, p.50)

Preparing adequately for a mediation session is critically important, says Timothy Corcoran (Tampa, FL), a former mediator and bankruptcy judge (2007, § 3.d). While he was actively mediating cases as a former bankruptcy judge, Corcoran too often saw situations where participating lawyers had not prepared enough for good results.

There are at least three reasons to prepare to the extent justified by the size of your case:

- Skillful preparation can maximize the likelihood of a favorable outcome for your client. Well-considered communications during the session may lower your opponents' appraisal of their own position, and a well-considered negotiating strategy could aid your success in the game. Although a mediation is not an adjudication, the mediator's own internal estimate of what a reasonable settlement would look like can also be affected by your efforts.
- Your opponents will be judging your performance, gauging not only the strength of your case but your competence as a lawyer. Even if you don't settle now, this could affect attitudes during the future course of the litigation. It could also affect what your opponents might ultimately be willing to settle for on the eve of trial.
- Your own client will also be judging you. If you come off as ill prepared or fumbling during the mediation session, your client may wonder about your general

conduct of the litigation as well as your likely performance at trial.

As with every other step in the mediation process, how much preparation work is reasonable under the circumstances will vary widely. But even for small cases, you should address each possible substep—at least in the most minimal way—to make sure you have covered the bases.

In this book, Steps Six and Seven are highly intertwined. You will not be ready to prepare your client for the mediation session until you have done some important work yourself—but insights gained and decisions made during the process of preparing your client will probably be vital to your own final preparations.

As discussed later in this book, where inside counsel is also involved on your side, your degree of centrality as outside counsel at the mediation session may vary widely (*see* Sidebar 9-1: "Roles of Inside Versus Outside Counsel in the Caucus Room"). The same is true of your role in preparing for the mediation session. Typically, you will have major responsibility for preparing an opening presentation for the initial joint session (if one will be given), since outside counsel may usually deliver that presentation even in mediation sessions where inside counsel will later play a dominant or coequal role. For similar reasons, outside counsel is likely to take the lead in preparing "zingers" and white papers (*see* Substep 6.6). On the other hand, as noted in Substep 6.1, your role in preparing a financial evaluation of the case may be limited to filling in a form to aid inside counsel in her work. Thus, you will need to make sure you understand what your expected role will be and adapt the guidance in Steps Six and Seven accordingly.

Step Six has seven substeps:

1. Move toward calculating a financial value for your case.
2. Start assembling your mediation team.
3. Start developing a negotiation plan.
4. Prepare an agenda of matters to cover in your client prep meeting.

5. Prepare your opening presentation (if applicable).
6. Prepare zingers and white papers as appropriate.
7. Prepare a skeleton settlement memorandum.

6.1 Move toward calculating a financial value for your case.

It would not make sense to sell your house to someone without a good sense of what it was worth on the market. It would be equally foolish to buy a house without confidence that it was worth the price. In the same way, it is essential for you and your client to figure out what your case is worth in order to make intelligent decisions about possible settlement in a mediation process.

Albert Watkins (St. Louis, MO) makes this point from his experience with securities industry disputes. In that specialized arena—where claims that are not settled in mediation go to binding arbitration—the situation is aggravated by the fact that lawyers representing securities claimants may not necessarily have the needed background to make a knowledgeable appraisal. As a result, he believes such lawyers may not recognize a good settlement when they see one:

> I think the mistake that most often is made by beginners who participate in mediation on behalf of investors is a wholly inappropriate assessment of the value of the claim. Because they're unfamiliar with the protocol that's followed in these securities claims and in arbitration in general—and because they're unfamiliar with the way an arbitration panel actually assesses a claim from a damages standpoint—they are without capacity to really embrace a bona fide offer.

Calculations about a case's value are relevant not only to your own client's decisions about settlement but also to figuring out the other side's likely mind-set. Bill Garcia (Washington, DC) stresses the latter element from the standpoint of a lawyer on the defense side:

> Doing your homework means finding out what the likely jury award in the jurisdiction is for a case of this

> type. You have to figure that if it's a personal injury case at the low end of sophistication, the lawyer who is representing the claimant is going to have a couple of hundred cases like this on their docket. They are going to sort of intuitively know the value of the case. At the other end of the sophistication spectrum, where there's enough money at issue, the claimant is going to have done enough research on what claims have been like, and what jury awards have been like—and maybe even done some jury research on their own case—to have a sense of what the value is.

At the mediation session, the value of the case will probably dominate the conversation during the initial joint session and private caucuses (Little, 2007, p.22).

As outside counsel, the degree and type of responsibility you will have in calculating a financial value for your case may vary from one client to another. In some instances or types of practice, the primary responsibility may be on you to arrive at an approximate figure or range, which you then explain to the client for acceptance or modification. "In preparing for the mediation, generally we would have outside counsel prepare an evaluation memo containing a settlement recommendation," recalls Tracey Salmon-Smith (New Jersey and New York), who used to work as inside counsel for a large securities firm. "That memo would get filtered through the legal department for necessary approvals, and the settlement recommendation is also approved by the corporate representative who is sitting in on the mediation."

In other situations, your input may be strictly subsidiary to an appraisal performed by inside counsel. The client corporation may even have a standardized form for you to fill out on the topic of value.

In relatively simple cases, a common approach to valuation is through comparable verdicts or rules of thumb (e.g., for some types of personal injury suits). In many other instances, lawyers are turning to some version of decision trees. This can vary from hugely detailed, expensive analyses performed by outside consultants to back-of-the-envelope calculations.

A. Decision trees and Litigation Risk Analysis

Decision trees are often used as part of Litigation Risk Analysis (LRA)—a technique associated with Marc Victor, a Stanford JD and MBA who asserts a trademark for the term. Law professors Stephen Goldberg (Chicago) and Frank Sander (Cambridge, MA) describe LRA like this: "Litigation risk analysis uses decision theory, commonly employed by businesspeople to model business decisions, as a tool for legal decision making. Stated simply, litigation risk analysis estimates the probabilities of different litigation outcomes and of various damages awards as well" (2007, p.41).

This book is not the place for a thorough treatment of how to develop decision trees. To view a graphic showing a sample decision tree, however, see Sidebar 6-1: "Decision Trees: A Basic Illustration." To read a former inside counsel's view of decision trees and Litigation Risk Analysis, see Sidebar 6-2: "A Corporate Counsel on Case Evaluations." Some articles on LRA cowritten by Marc Victor are available for free download from the web, such as "Evaluating Legal Risks and Costs with Decision Tree Analysis" (Victor, Glidden, Lea, & Whitworth, 2000) and "The Role of Risk Analysis in Dispute and Resolution Management" (Calihan, Dent, & Victor, 2004).

One potential risk of LRA and decision trees is that they can convey an overstated sense of accuracy. For one thing, they are only as good the probabilities that are estimated for all the key decision points. In addition, they tend to assume that each variable is independent, whereas in the real world the adjudication of seemingly separate and independent issues may be affected by the adjudicator's overall view of the case.

John Buchanan (Washington, DC) makes the latter point from his experience in dispute resolution and insurance coverage litigation:

> There's a certain mathematical fallacy built into those models: that each variable is analytically independent, and that you can simply multiply out the percentage discounts on each of the branches of the decision tree.

> At least in my type of litigation, however, some courts or fact finders tend to be somewhat result oriented. That is, they're going to be inclined either to find coverage, or not to find coverage, for a loss. And that sort of result orientation as a practical matter affects their analysis of each of the theoretically separate issues.

One way to compensate, Buchanan says, is "to *group* the issues in the decision tree in a way that at least partly overcomes that inherent fallacy."

Unlike many lawyers, Buchanan typically does not use decision trees as a *starting point* for valuation:

> Although I don't put too much stock in the decision trees, I find them to be a useful test against my gut feelings as to how much the settlement value of a claim is, or how much I should discount it for likelihood of losing. So, I frankly start out with a gut sense, based on my experience, about how much my opening settlement demand should be discounted from a 100 percent recovery; and then I often either confirm it or adjust it in light of a more detailed decision-tree analysis.

Buchanan is by no means alone in continuing to give weight to his gut. Discussing evaluations of cases for mediation of disputes within an arbitration (not litigation) process, Michael Braun (Chicago) observes: "There is a fair amount of 'This is my gut based on what I have seen arbitrators do in other cases'" (*see* Sidebar 6-3: "Evaluating a Case in the Context of Mediation Within an Arbitration Process").

By the same token, it is probably not a coincidence that Buchanan has had several decades of experience in his field through which to develop a "gut feeling" about his cases' worth. In any event, many others take a different view, as illustrated by the comments of Bowen Tucker (Arlington Heights, IL) in Sidebar 6-2: "A Corporate Counsel on Case Evaluation."

B. Substantiating plaintiff's damages

When representing a defendant, consider a special focus on how much of the plaintiff's alleged damages have demonstrable substance. Steven Brom (Birmingham, AL) puts it this way:

> The most important thing for me to do as a defense attorney in preparation for mediation—and in consultation with the insurance adjuster or whoever the client is with the full and final settlement authority—is to see how much of the alleged damages can actually be substantiated. If we're getting a demand for a million dollars, but all of the evidence we have is indicating that the actual damages are in the range of $25,000, that disconnect is what we're focusing on. Our work is making sure that we are not missing something, if we have a disconnect that's that significant.

Dubious, nebulous, or speculative damages elements may predictably lead to impasse in mediation if there is a disconnect of the type Brom describes between the parties. For example, as mediator Jean Baker (Washington, DC) has observed: "It is extremely difficult for parties to reach agreement concerning lost profits or pain and suffering in the absence of a mutually agreed upon objective method for assessing value" (2007a, p.4).

6.2 Start assembling your mediation team.

Your mediation team consists of you plus anyone else who will be present along with you at the mediation session, or available by phone (or otherwise) for consultation at a remote location during the session. In a larger sense, your team includes anyone (such as an executive at a client corporation) who has a role in planning and decision making in advance of the mediation session.

The size and composition of your mediation team will vary widely with the size and complexity of the case in dispute. The central (and sometimes only) figure may be your client (or corporate representative), perhaps joined by inside counsel. Or it may just be an insurance adjuster attending by phone.

A. Choosing the corporate representative

Where the client is a corporation, the corporate representative typically serves as the client's main voice during a mediation session, including making decisions in negotiations. However, as outside counsel you may have little or no role in selecting this person. Instead, that choice may typically be made within the client corporation, such as by the inside counsel with whom you are working.

That was the case for Tracey Salmon-Smith when she worked as inside counsel for a brokerage: "Generally, I liked to have someone there who wasn't just a body—someone who didn't really understand the case. I preferred to have someone who was from the particular branch office, or who knew the broker, so that they understood the situation better—because they were better able to contribute during the session."

Still, to the extent that input is possible, you may want to exert some influence. Bennett Picker (Philadelphia) advises (2003): "[I]t is more important to encourage the participation of a decision maker with full authority to make resolution decisions, including the impact any such decision may have on a division's budget or the company's reported earnings" (p.78).

In particular, you may need to be proactive if you are concerned that the planned corporate representative may be unsuitable. A major example would be where the planned rep was closely involved in the events underlying the dispute. For more on this, see Sidebar 6-4: "When the Alleged Wrongdoer Is on Your Mediation Team." Sometimes you may still want to see the executive there, but supplemented by someone else from the corporation (like a higher-up).

For more opinions from a former inside counsel on some ideal personal qualities in a corporate rep, see Sidebar 6-5: "The Value of Empathy in a Corporate Representative."

B. Insured defendants in negligence suits

Claims against an insured defendant on a negligence theory—such as personal injury suits—may constitute the majority of cases in civil mediation at the trial court level (Little, 2007, p.9). In such cases, "quite often neither the defendant nor the plaintiff understands that the defendant's insurance company has the deciding vote as to what is offered in the case"—making the insurer in effect "the 'real party in interest' on the defense side" (Little, 2007, p.14).

In this context, mediator J. Anderson Little has received requests from the defense side in auto personal injury cases to excuse the defendant from attending the mediation conference, and he often does not object (2007, p.15). However, he has observed that many defense lawyers insist that insured clients must be part of the team, despite their lack of decision-making power:

> Many of the defense lawyers I work with . . . require that their insured clients attend the settlement conference even though the plaintiff might agree to excuse them. They know the plaintiff may be provoked by the absence of the defendant; they know that the defendant may supply useful information that others did not anticipate would be needed or supply an apology or work of sympathy that may soften the plaintiff's position; and they know that the defendant may be excused after the opening session if that seems appropriate.

C. Filling out the mediation team

"There are three basic functions mediation team members can provide to the process—participating in the opening presentations, providing services as an information source, and participating in the final decision-making," writes mediator Lawrence Watson (Maitland, FL). For more considerations regarding each of these functions, read Watson's discussion in Sidebar 6-6: "A Mediator's Advice on Assembling Your Mediation Team." His discussion is geared to big-ticket cases, but it can give you ideas for handling smaller ones.

Watson's discussion notes that in some types of big cases, expert witnesses can potentially be effective in presenting certain complex aspects of liability or damages. But be aware that experts can also bring a potential for harm. In her experience as a mediator, Magistrate Judge Mary Pat Thynge (Wilmington, DE) has come to believe that "bringing experts—particularly damages experts—to mediation is generally not helpful. It tars the process with an adversarial brush and telescopes a 'trial win' starting point for negotiations" (2011, p.155). As an alternative, she suggests "providing a summary of experts' reasoning as part of the analysis in the mediation statement" (p.155).

A typical defense team in mediations of securities claims filed by brokerage clients is described by Tracey Salmon-Smith. She says that in addition to outside counsel, a team at a mediation session is likely to include a corporate representative and inside counsel, plus the "financial advisor—the person who was in direct contact with the claimant, and who is the person that has the factual knowledge of the relationship."

As noted previously, in negligence-based claims against insured defendants, the insurance company plays an all-important role on the defense side. But in other types of cases, input from insurance carriers can sometimes also be very important in relation to a mediation session. Bill Garcia makes this point:

> Sometimes the preparation has to include getting your carrier on board. If you're going to settle something within the limits of the Self-Insured Retention, then the carrier won't likely worry about it, but if your carrier is on notice and at risk, that's another level of complexity. And sometimes you need to have that carrier on the phone with you during the mediation session. If the carrier is involved, you need to make sure that they've bought into your negotiating strategy—your nonconfrontational strategy—because sometimes the carrier's representative can create confrontations that are not productive to "getting to yes."[1]
>
> I've been in mediations where they are physically there, where they are in a different conference room, and where they are available by phone. It depends on the case, on the coverage, on the carrier, and the car-

1. This is a reference to the highly influential book on negotiation *Getting to Yes* (Fisher & Ury, 1981).

rier's representative that you are dealing with. Some are more hands-on than others.

6.3 Start developing a negotiation plan.

"Texts often speak of mediation 'advocacy,'" writes law professor and mediator Dwight Golann (2009a, p.264), "but as you know, mediation consists primarily of negotiation. Lawyers usually make presentations at the outset, but the rest of the process consists of discussions and bargaining. You should plan for mediation in much the same way you would for a direct negotiation, while looking for ways to incorporate the mediator in your strategy."

For much of this planning, close consultation with your client will be essential. For that reason, you will find the primary discussion of this topic in Step Seven.

6.4 Prepare an agenda of matters to cover in your client prep meeting.

"In preparing your client, use a written agenda," advises Phoenix-based litigator Laura Kennedy (2010, p.158). "Much of the information you will impart to the client will be new and perhaps overwhelming. Your client will then have something to reference when focusing and preparing for the mediation." For sophisticated clients, what you impart during the presession preparation meeting may not be overwhelming, but at a minimum, using an agenda will help keep your meeting focused and on track.

Before preparing an agenda, read Step Seven to remind yourself of or familiarize yourself with key elements to be covered during the client prep meeting. Also, note that this book's appendix includes a sample agenda that was drafted by Kennedy.

6.5 Prepare your opening presentation (if applicable).

Opening presentations are covered in detail in Step Eight—including the issue of whether to make one. If that decision was not already made earlier in the process, you and your client will need to confer on the topic in Step Seven.

6.6 Prepare zingers and white papers as appropriate.

Law professor Charles Craver (Washington, DC) is among those who advise you to "[a]nticipate [your] opponents' arguments and prepare effective counter-arguments" in advance of the mediation session (2011, p.9). His rationale is that this will bolster your confidence while undermining your opponents'.

An effective approach in this context is to prepare what Larry Watson calls zingers and white papers. In his terminology, a zinger is a compelling point in support of your contentions that you can present to the mediator during a caucus, for the mediator's potential uses in "fulfilling his or her reality check function with the opposition" (2002, p.11). Watson describes zingers at greater length in Sidebar 6-7: "Creating Positional Vulnerabilities With Zingers."

White papers involve a greater investment of time. Watson recommends that for each contention you expect your opponent to raise during the mediation session, you put together a one-page, bullet-point list of rebuttal points. He gives more advice about the creation and use of white papers in Sidebar 6-8: "Preparing White Papers in Advance of a Mediation Session."

During his years as Deputy General Counsel in charge of litigation for a global consulting firm, John DeGroote (Dallas) independently started using a similar technique. "In our first caucus, I often give the mediator a piece of paper with our primary points," he says. "It's typed out with the points highlighted and any subpoints, in a big font." DeGroote knows that mediators typically like to soften up each side's appraisal of its own case by privately pointing out weaknesses. In that sense, he thinks of the mediator as "the only advocate I have in my opponent's caucus room." For that reason, DeGroote wants to make sure the mediator has his side's strong points readily at hand when caucusing with his opponents. For example, in an intellectual property dispute, "when the other side says, 'there are no damages here,' he or she can look down at the paper and say, 'Well, damages are one thing, but I want to get back to the patent itself. You're having problems with the '814 patent, aren't you?' Otherwise, a very lucrative point may just be forgotten."

As with Watson's advice on mediation teams, his recommendations for zingers and white papers are geared toward big-ticket cases. But even in a very small case, your morning drive to the office might be productively used to think up some zingers for use in the mediation session. And even just one or two single-page white papers, which might reasonably be prepared on a small budget, could come in handy.

6.7 Prepare a skeleton settlement memorandum.

"Do not wait until the day of the mediation expecting the mediator to be in a position to recommend all the magic language that needs to be incorporated to effectuate an enforceable settlement agreement," advises Jean Baker. She and others recommend preparing at least a skeleton form of agreement in advance of the mediation session. The reasons for this, and the types of elements to include, are discussed in Step Eleven.

SIDEBAR 6-1

Decision Trees: A Basic Illustration

By Lawrence D. Rosenberg

Decision trees are an integral part of Litigation Risk Assessments (see Sidebar 6-2)—a useful approach to case valuation for mediation purposes. In this excerpt from an article on winning high-stakes corporate litigation (2011, pp.2–3), Lawrence Rosenberg (Washington, DC) offers a basic illustration, creating decision trees from a hypothetical.

Perhaps the most effective way to perform a case value analysis is to develop a decision tree that articulates the primary issues in the case, the critical decision points that could affect the disposition of those issues, and assign probabilities (even if very rough) for each of the critical decision points. For example, in a product liability case, the key issues could be a possible breach of a duty of care, causation, and damages. If the plaintiff seeks $10 million in damages, and the assessment is that there is a 50% chance of an ultimate finding of breach, and a 60% chance of a finding of causation, the chance of a liability finding would be 0.5 × 0.6 = 0.30 or 30%.

Lose or Win on Causation

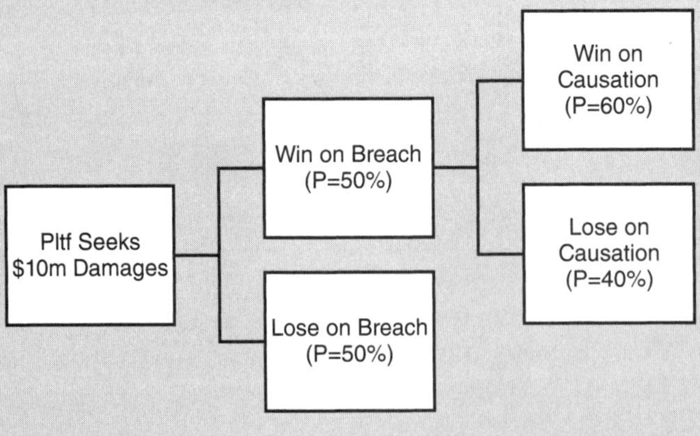

If one were to determine that the median amount of damages that would likely be awarded would be $5 million (meaning that it is 50% likely that $5 million or more would be awarded and 50% likely that $5 million or less would be awarded, and there is no basis to believe that there is a significantly better chance of a higher result than a lower result), then the value of the case would be $5 million × 0.30 = $1.5 million.

Plaintiff's Median Expected Value
(0.5) × (0.6) × ($5M) = $1.5M

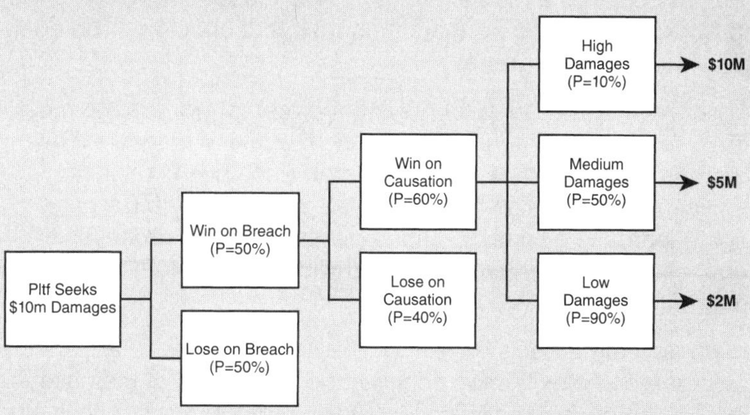

Far more comprehensive and statistical case value analyses can be performed usefully. Going through with such an exercise is likely to help the corporation and its counsel make better and more informed judgments about litigation and its progress.

SIDEBAR 6-2

A Corporate Counsel on Case Evaluation

Bowen H. Tucker (interview)

Bowen Tucker (Arlington Heights, IL), now retired, formerly was responsible for directing all litigation at a global corporation. Here he describes case evaluation in the mediation context from his perspective as inside litigation counsel—including his frustration with outside lawyers whose idea of evaluating a case was to say "you have a good chance of winning it."

One of the things I think is critical to corporate counsel in managing litigation is to make certain you have a realistic understanding of the value of the case. Every case is worth something. It could be only a dollar, or five dollars, or it may be a million dollars, but every case has a value. There's no such thing as one that doesn't. Learning how to assess that value and doing it accurately is critical to getting a fair resolution—particularly when you're going into a mediation. It really is the responsibility of the corporate counsel to do that. It's a task that should not be abdicated to outside counsel.

While there are a variety of ways of doing that, for me the most effective way of doing it was through the use of Litigation Risk Analysis, developed by Marc B. Victor, Esq. This is really an application of decision-tree analysis—which every MBA candidate learns in business school—to the litigation process. It requires some judgment. We could wish it were statistically perfect, but it isn't.

If you develop a decision tree with as many issues as are important—the complexity may depend upon the value of the case—you can get a very realistic view of both your chances of winning and losing, and the real value of the case. If you don't have that information, it's not very meaningful to go into a mediation and expect to come out with a resolution that reflects what the company ought to have happen.

Although I'll emphasize these are the responsibilities of corporate counsel, I certainly believe in working with outside counsel. That person is critical to the evaluation process, especially when you're managing cases across the country.

Did I find that outside lawyers were generally accustomed to the Litigation Risk Analysis concept? Generally not. I encouraged some of them to go to a course. But other times, it wasn't as important that they learn it as it was that I sit down with them and go through the issues and what they thought was the probability of winning or losing a particular issue, as well as what I thought.

If you don't do this at all, the problem you have with outside counsel—all too often—is they would say, "Well, I think we have a good chance of winning it." Well, what do you mean by a good chance? Do you mean better than 50 percent? "Oh no, no,

I don't think it would be better than 50 percent. But it may be 30 or 40 percent." There is a tendency to just use garbage talk about chances of winning or losing cases, unless you pin people down. You're not communicating when you don't know what the person means by a "good chance."

SIDEBAR 6-3

Evaluating a Case in the Context of Mediation Within an Arbitration Process

Michael F. Braun (interview)

The Financial Industry Regulatory Authority (FINRA) "operates the largest dispute resolution forum in the securities industry to assist in the resolution of monetary and business disputes between and among investors, securities firms and individual registered representatives."[2] Under FINRA's system, disputes that cannot be settled through their mediation process go to binding arbitration. Michael Braun (Chicago) maintains a practice that includes securities disputes as well as business, employment, and intellectual property litigation. In this sidebar, he talks about evaluating cases in advance of a mediation session, with special reference to work for a major brokerage client in FINRA's dispute resolution system.

Once that decision is made to mediate, the businesspeople, in-house counsel, and outside counsel have to work together and come up with their strategy. "What's our authority—what are we willing to pay? Where we are we going to start our financial settlement discussions with the mediator?" At least with my brokerage client, that has been a three-part discussion, in terms of the businesspeople weighing in and the legal people giving some guidance as to what they think the matter's value is. Or the potential risk, if we're acting as the defendant. Everyone is getting some comfort that our evaluation of the case—in-house

2. Retrieved from http://www.finra.org/ArbitrationAndMediation/index.htm (accessed July 15, 2011).

and outside counsels' joint evaluation of the case—is consistent with the businesspeople's comfort level in evaluating the risk and exposure on the case. Also, perhaps noneconomic matters—such as bad publicity, inconvenience, things along those lines—that the businesspeople may value differently than the lawyers do.

Q: At your brokerage client, you are asked to evaluate the case using a form they have for that. Have you ever done similar things with other clients?

A: Not quite so formulaic, I guess. Typically there is some evaluation, often in the form of a written memo. But with the clients that I work with, our brokerage client probably has the most formalized procedure for that type of pre-mediation evaluation.

Q: What is it exactly that you are trying to evaluate when you typically do so before a mediation?

A: In the broadest terms, the likelihood of an adverse decision if I am representing the defendant, and the range of exposure if that adverse decision takes place. On a more basic level, it's an evaluation of the strengths and weaknesses of the evidence as we know it. In the brokerage context, we are doing this based on written discovery—primarily document production. In FINRA arbitration and mediation, you don't really have interrogatories, and you don't have depositions by and large. So you are really basing it on whatever paper has been produced by your side, and by the other side, and your interviews of nonparties who are willing to be interviewed.

Q: What would be an example of an outside nonparty that you might talk to?

A: You may talk to a former employee who is cooperative and friendly—former employees or former managers who may have had some managerial responsibility at the time of the incident, but who retired or moved on to a different firm or a different capacity. That's probably the primary nonparty that you would have an opportunity to have some discussion with in evaluating the case for mediation or arbitration.

Q: While you are evaluating the case trying to put a monetary value on it, do you use any kind of a formal analytical method or decision tree? Or is it more your gut as you are looking through the various issues?

A: I have used decision trees. I have had some clients who have wanted decision trees. In the context of the recruiting litigation or recruiting arbitrations that go off to mediation—where you are involved in the hiring of financial advisors from another firm and the claim is a breach of contract or violation of restrictive covenants—there is certainly case law and other arbitral awards that can be analyzed. A comparison could be made between your facts and the facts of those other cases to give you something a little more formal than what your gut is. But ultimately, you may have a better handle on what the law is in the judicial system as opposed to what three arbitrators—two of whom may not be lawyers—may think is the right result.

There is a fair amount of "This is my gut based on what I have seen arbitrators do in other cases. These are facts that are particularly helpful or these are facts that are particularly troublesome, that if I were an arbitrator, based on what I have seen arbitrators react to in the past, I think help us or hurt us in evaluating what the case is worth."

SIDEBAR 6-4

When the Alleged Wrongdoer Is on Your Mediation Team

"Is the client representative sitting in the room the one who is alleged to have done the wrong?" John DeGroote (Dallas) raises this scenario when discussing the dynamics of mediation when one of the members of your team is an executive who was actively involved in the transaction or incident that led the plaintiff to sue your client. He gives the examples of a CIO who allegedly misappropriated the plaintiff's source code or a human-resources head who made the decision that has resulted in a wrongful termination suit.

"If the person who is allegedly at fault is the decision maker on how much to pay on the claim, it's much, much, much, much more difficult to get him or her to pay," DeGroote says, "because they are going to have to admit wrong." In DeGroote's view, it is rare for such a person to acknowledge that there were problems with their past actions or to decide to pay enough just to get the case out of the way.

An executive who was personally involved in the underlying dispute may find it difficult to keep perspective, evaluate the case dispassionately, or see the big picture. The executive may also feel that if the corporation pays a substantial sum to settle a dispute in which he or she was involved, this may have negative repercussions for his or her career.

"If the client representative is the one who is going to have to admit fault before a real number is paid, then the client really ought to be sending somebody else to the mediation," DeGroote says, speaking from his prior experience as inside counsel in charge of all litigation matters for a global consulting firm.

So what should you do if you realize that this type of scenario is shaping up, and your corporate client is planning to send the "wrong" person to make decisions at an upcoming mediation session?

"It could be a fairly dicey situation," DeGroote acknowledges:

> Under those circumstances, the outside lawyer should go to somebody else in the company and say: "I don't think so-and-so should attend this mediation without somebody else from the company there, because she was actively involved in the events that gave rise to this dispute. It would make the discussions too personal, and she'll be more focused on defending herself than finding the best way to get this resolved. Although we'll need her perspective early on, I recommend that you send someone else as the primary client rep."

Broaching the problem to this other individual in the organization must necessarily be done with diplomacy and discretion. But from DeGroote's perspective, the individual you talk to is still likely to get the message and "realize that the person who allegedly harmed the other side can't really be the decision maker on how much to pay."

SIDEBAR 6-5

The Value of Empathy in a Corporate Representative

William T. Garcia (interview)

Over the course of decades as a commercial litigator, Bill Garcia (Washington, DC) has worked both as a law firm partner and as inside counsel for major corporations. He talks here about some of the qualities he looks for in choosing the company executive who will represent a defendant corporation in a mediation where the plaintiff is an individual.

As counsel for a corporate defendant, part of what you're trying to accomplish during the mediation session is just letting the plaintiffs tell their story—venting their story—so that the mediation can get past the emotion of what underlies the lawsuit to the dollars, to try to get it resolved. You want to have the other side feel as if they have been heard—that their complaint, whatever it is, has been heard by the corporation.

You need to have an executive who is perceived to be sufficiently senior, who is in a position to do something about this person's complaint. So you should try to avoid walking in with the lowest level sales manager. If somebody has a highfalutin title, that is attractive, because that helps the other side understand that yes, the corporation is listening. Individual plaintiffs are often as motivated by the concern that no other family should have to suffer as they did as they are by financial compensation. If process changes are part of your strategy, your corporate representative needs to be perceived as having sufficient power to make the changes happen and to make them stick.

At the same time, you are looking for a representative who can understand that the game plan here is to let the other side tell their story. So you need somebody who can be empathetic and won't be confrontational—an active listener, who can engage the other side without conceding the validity of the other side's perspective. You know, it's sort of like the nonapology apology: "I'm sorry you feel the way that you feel." That doesn't concede the accuracy of the feeling—it's just "I regret that you feel that way," because even at this point you will want to be cautious about admissions of wrongdoing. That may sound disingenuous, but it isn't meant to be. Plaintiffs feel they have been wronged, and part of the settlement process is for them to be able to tell that to the other side. You have to be prepared to let them do that. This is "their day in court," and they want to tell their story. And you should let them, because (1) it is part of the healing process (which is good for them), and (2) it makes coming to a resolution possible (which is good for them and for the corporation).

You want somebody who in the course of the mediation can get across to the other side some sort of empathy, asking the right kinds of questions: "How did you feel when that happened?" "How did you feel when the district manager told you that you were a jerk?" Again, let them get it all out on the table to "make the corporation understand." Sometimes that means you have to sit back and take a lot, whether you agree with it or not.

Then, when it comes time for the company to make its points, the client representative ought to be in the position of saying, "I understand that this is the way that you feel. Let me tell you our perspective on that. We might have to agree to disagree on the significance of some of these facts. You say that the light was green. We might have to agree to disagree on whether the light was green. We think the light was red, because we've got a busload of nuns who were at the intersection, and they will all say that the light was red. But I understand that you feel the way that you do, and we feel the way the way that we do. We need to get past that to see what sort of resolution we can have."

SIDEBAR 6-6

A Mediator's Advice on Assembling Your Mediation Team

By Lawrence M. Watson Jr.

In 1988, when the movement for mediation of lawsuits was still in its early stages, Larry Watson (Maitland, FL) became one of the first civil trial mediators certified by the Florida Supreme Court. His mediation practice focuses on complex, multiparty disputes. In this excerpt from an article on preparing for mediation sessions (2002, pp.8–9), he describes the components of a strong mediation team. His discussion is geared to big-ticket litigation that warrants a big expense for mediation sessions, but it also bears review to consider what particular types of capabilities might also be useful and justified in smaller disputes.

The people selected to serve as party representatives in a mediation proceeding are obviously a critical component of a successful outcome to the process. An effective mediation team consists of carefully selected and prepared individuals who understand both the overall process and their specific roles. Rather than choosing a mediation team based on titles, seniority, or simple relationships to the parties, mediation team members should be selected on the basis of their ability to make a meaningful contribution in one or more specific phases of the process.

There are three basic functions mediation team members can provide to the process: participating in the opening presentations, providing services as an information source, and participating in the final decision-making.

A. The Opening Presentation Players

The opening presentations in a mediation are designed to both present the best case for each party's day in court, and to give each party some opportunity to "vent" stored-up emotional feelings about the dispute that would otherwise serve to block fair consideration of settlement options. The people selected to make the opening presentations should be capable of meeting each goal.

Clearly, lead trial counsel (along with any special counsel to be utilized) is primarily responsible for making the opening presentations in a mediation session. Depending on the nature of the case, however, key expert witnesses can be effective in giving short samples of their proposed trial testimony as well as taking the parties through some of the more complex aspects of liability or damage positions. Another potentially effective participant might be a key lay witness who would be willing to either directly participate to offer a preview of their trial testimony, or indirectly appear through affidavits, letters, or a video taped appearance.

The opening presentations in mediations are basically condensed versions of the complete trial position each party will present should the dispute be adjudicated. Within the overall duration of an average mediation session, however, there is a relatively limited amount of time available to present a fair representation of what would be a lengthy, complex trial. Quite apart from the time available, the audience in a mediation has limits on what it can or will effectively absorb. To maximize use of the time available for these abbreviated presentations, more and more trial lawyers are turning to specially created graphics to quickly and effectively illustrate their points. Computerized power point illustrations, videotape segments, overhead view graphics, slides, and simple board charts have all become integral tools for effective opening presentations in mediation sessions.

B. The Information Sources

One principal factor that leads parties in a mediation to a settlement agreement is the discovery of new or different information during the mediation process. Whether the "new" information consists of a previously unknown fact, or simply another slant to a previously known fact, the data learned serves to give the parties a "safe" reason to change their minds without loss of face. New data prompting a reason to change that doesn't require an admission of fault, direct recognition of wrongdoing, or acknowledging an error in judgment.

In many cases, a post presentation dialogue will inevitably raise issues concerning one or more of the specific matters in controversy. In the midst of settlement options being discussed in caucus, it is quite common for new questions to be raised concerning critical elements of one or more of the sub-issues in the case. Answering these questions promptly and forcefully can be critical to the outcome of the mediation. Verifying asserted contract balances, change orders, the content of meeting minutes, confirming test reports, notices, and existing testimony are but a few of the endless stream of underlying challenges that can emerge in this respect. A well-prepared mediation team will be ready to respond to those instances with prompt access to the documents, testimony, or other information relevant to the issues raised.

Portable computers can obviously simplify this task. Deposition records can be indexed, key documents can be scanned, and both can be electronically stored for prompt and accurate retrieval during the mediation session. Alternatively, documentation control personnel can be charged to stand by remote file storage centers with cellular telephones and telefax machines in hand to promptly respond to requests for key documents required.

In some cases, key employees with direct knowledge of the underlying facts can serve as extremely helpful information sources during a mediation session. Their simple presence at the mediation can serve to quash temptations to wander too far afield from the facts during the case analysis phase. Assuming their memories are sound, and their deliveries convincing, they might even be given a speaking part in the joint-session presentations. Whether "information source" representatives should stay with the process and take an ongoing role in decision-making, however, bears careful thought. Often individuals directly involved in the underlying dispute carry an agenda that makes an objective evaluation of the issues problematical.

Other information sources that might be kept available on or off-site include home office staff, employees, or administrators who might help deal with settlement scenarios—sales, marketing, service, or administrative personnel for example.

Finally, the information source component of the mediation team should also consider arranging for access to key non-party witnesses. Many times, it will become helpful for parties to a mediation to place a joint telephone conference call to a critical non-party witness to clarify or resolve an issue under consideration.

C. The Decision-Makers

The people who will ultimately decide upon settlement terms are obviously critical components of any mediation team. In addition to someone with complete and full authority to both define and bind a party to an agreement, the decision-making components of a team may also include the financial, administrative or executive advisors appropriate to reach an agreement. While care should be taken to insure that the decision-maker's support group doesn't ultimately take over the decision making process, the people who are to decide should be given ample resources to enable them to decide intelligently.

Some care should be taken in advance of a mediation to make sure everyone participating in the process has a clear understanding of who will be making the ultimate decision. Mediation is a relatively unstructured process. Absent clear instructions, strong personalities found in experts, relatively low level employees, and even trial counsel can rise and dominate the group in the decision making process. Decide who is to decide, then let them decide.

SIDEBAR 6-7

Creating Positional Vulnerabilities With Zingers

By Lawrence M. Watson Jr.

In addition to white papers (see Sidebar 6-8: "Preparing White Papers in Advance of a Mediation Session"), zingers can be a handy and effective part of your arsenal at a mediation session. In this excerpt from an article, Larry Watson (2002, p.11) describes what zingers are and how to prepare and use them.

During the caucus sessions, it is helpful to provide the mediator with what you consider strong or compelling points supporting your contentions in the case—"zingers"—that the mediator can raise in fulfilling his or her reality check function with the opposition.

Prior to the mediation session, prepare a list of the ten most compelling points you feel the opposition should fairly consider in making its own "trial or settlement" analysis. The list may include not only perceived weaknesses in the opposition's case at trial, but political, economic, or pragmatic reasons to settle as well. Prepare a short briefing statement to support each—again, on a single sheet of paper.

The "zinger" list may and should include points favoring your side of the positional debate to be resolved at trial. Include on the list major credibility issues, positional inconsistencies, procedural obstacles, prior jury verdict ranges, and any other aspects of litigation that the opposition will have to meet and overcome to achieve a successful outcome at trial.

The list might also contain a series of practical reasons not to try the case no matter who wins or loses. Examples might include an analysis of the cost of litigation (in time and money), the market impact and benefit to competition of the debate going public, disruption of business activities, corruption of future business relationships, and potential adverse precedents created.

In short, the "zingers" list should include any considerations that speak for a settlement over litigation. The zinger list should serve to provide the mediator compelling points to raise with the opposition that will favor settlement.

SIDEBAR 6-8

Preparing White Papers in Advance of a Mediation Session

By Lawrence M. Watson Jr.

One-page white papers, to rebut the contentions your opponent may make at an upcoming mediation session, can be a very effective tool when the size of your case will support the expense. Even in smaller cases, some of the steps recommended here—such as prioritizing a list of likely arguments—could help sharpen your preparedness for the session. In this excerpt from an article, mediator Larry Watson (2002, p.11) describes in greater detail what white papers are and how to prepare them.

Prior to mediation, an effort should be made to research objectively the pleadings, correspondence, discovery documents, notes of oral arguments, and any "table talk" comments recorded to prepare a detailed list of the opposition's principal contentions and defenses regarding the case. Locate and record what the opposition has actually been saying, don't be led astray by what you believe the arguments against your case should be. Focus then on the opposition's most frequently raised arguments.

Prioritize a list of their arguments. These same arguments will become a central part of the mediation discussions. Odds are, the opposition will be raising the same themes in mediation that they have been raising during the life of the litigation process.

After listing each contention raised against your case, research the law and facts which balance or rebut each of those points you can expect the opposition to assert at mediation. Think through and succinctly record your response along with the sources for your response.

On a single sheet of paper, then combine each contention you can expect the opposition to raise, followed by your response. Using an abbreviated "bullet" format set forth in simple language and plain terms both their contention and your points rebutting that contention. The final product should be a tool that can be given to the mediator as a guide in quickly and succinctly responding to the opposition arguments as they are raised during mediation caucuses. Attempt to limit each to one or two pages with footnoted references to supporting documents, testimony, etc. that can be retrieved if necessary.

Organize the total number of white papers in a simple, easily retrievable manner—perhaps an indexed notebook or file folder. Be ready to get to the points analyzed quickly and efficiently in the heat of battle. Have back up data accessible, but don't make it part of the main package. The benefit of the white paper work is in its simplicity and brevity.

When your vulnerabilities are then probed during the caucus sessions, you will be ready to meet the mediator's inquiries with a comment like, "Good point—and we are glad you asked that question. Here is a brief analysis of that issue which presents both sides, or better balances the problem we have." The mediator will then have a single sheet of paper to refer to in the event the point arises again, or when he returns to caucus further with the opposition.

No case is perfect. It is inevitable that there will be anticipated or unanticipated contentions raised by the opposition that simply have no pat answer or convincing rebuttal. Part of the mediation caucusing process is to flush out these issues and provide a confidential, "safe" environment to give them fair consideration with a neutral. In analyzing the "trial or settlement" decisions that must be made in the course of a mediation, it is critical that both good and bad points of the trial option are fully presented. That analysis cannot be intelligently made without all points of view getting the full and fair credit they deserve. Once again, clouding that fair consideration with overly enthusiastic advocacy is a misuse of the mediation process.

STEP SEVEN

Prepare With Your Client for the Mediation Session

> Q: *What do you find are the most common mistakes that beginners make in representing clients during the course of a mediation?*
>
> A: *Lack of preparation of their client, number one. In other words, they made a mistake before we got here to the mediation session. They didn't prepare their clients for what was about to happen. They didn't prepare their clients for the process, and they didn't prepare their clients to compromise the claim. Inexperienced lawyers don't do that as well as experienced lawyers.*
>
> —From an interview with Jay Cohen, mediator

This step is titled "Prepare *With* Your Client"—rather than "Prepare Your Client"—because preparing for the mediation session is very much a two-way street. It is not just a matter of you preparing the client. The process requires discussion and joint decisionmaking with your client on matters that are essential for your own self-preparation. That is one of the reasons that, as noted in Step Six, there is a high degree of overlap and interplay between Steps Six and Seven.

As the quote at the beginning of this chapter indicates, failing to prepare your client adequately for mediation is a rookie mistake. Even so, such failure is apparently still quite common. "It's surprising how many attorneys don't really have a meeting with the client or substantive discussion in preparation for the mediation," observes mediator and mediation advocate John Phillips (Kansas City, MO) (speaking in Bickerman et al., 2003, p.11).

Big cases offer much more elbowroom than small ones in terms of the amount of time you can devote to such preparation. But regardless of whether your client prep session consumes 15 minutes in a very small, simple case, or a full working day for a large one, essentially the same bases need to be touched, with the amount of time for each adjusted proportionately.

Bennett Picker, a Philadelphia mediator, offers some general perspectives on client preparation in his *Mediation Practice Guide* (2003). Read Sidebar 7-1 ("Checklist of Questions for Client") for his checklist of questions to ask your client in preparing for a mediation session.

If effectively done, a client prep session can have an additional benefit: solidifying and potentially expanding your professional relationship with your client. For more on this, read Sidebar 7-2: "Using Mediation Prep to Connect With Your Client."

Advice from the ABA Task Force. Some research-based guidance on what clients want in mediation prep comes from the ABA Section of Dispute Resolution Section Task Force on Improving Mediation Quality. As part of a larger study, Task Force members interviewed 13 parties (i.e., clients or client representatives) with past experience in two or more mediations (2008a, p.36). Five of the interviewees participated on the plaintiff's side of the mediation process; seven participated on the defense side; one had participated on both sides. The disputes involved a wide range of civil cases, including employment, contract, and commercial disputes—mostly complex. This excerpt (2008a, p.37) summarizes the Task Force's findings on the topic of how these sophisticated mediation clients prepare, and what they said they want from presession preparation.

> The interviewees provided a rich and multi-layered perspective on the role they expected their attorneys to play before and during the mediation. These experienced professionals want their lawyers to play a variety of roles in the mediation. The roles were often specifically discussed and agreed to during preparation.

From the parties' points of view, prior to the mediation, their lawyers should:

- Discuss weaknesses of the case with the party and assess the risks involved if the case is not resolved in mediation;
- Provide a realistic view of the likely outcome of the case and discuss valuation;
- Ensure that the client is aware of all the facts and do what is necessary to prevent the client from being blindsided in mediation;
- Provide the party with the political lay of the land (how the other side will react to the high and low offer, and a description of the personalities of the other parties, opposing counsel, and the mediator); and
- Provide a perspective on how that type of litigation usually fares in the jurisdiction where it is filed.

Timing of client prep session. Client preparation needs to be far enough in advance to allow further preparation before the session, but near enough for memories of the prep session to stay fresh. For cases that support the time, litigator Laura Kennedy (Phoenix) suggests holding two prep sessions (2010, p.158):

> The first preparation session should occur as far in advance of the mediation as is necessary for your client to absorb the information and complete any "homework" assignments you may make. Ideally, this first meeting should occur at least two weeks before the scheduled mediation. Conduct a second preparation session the day before the mediation, and not only reemphasize the critical aspects of the client role and expectations, but cover any new developments, e.g. issues that have arisen in communications with opposing counsel, issues that have been raised in briefs, etc.

Working with inside counsel. For purposes of client preparation, as with many other elements of mediation, the term *client* includes inside counsel if you are working with one on the case. Miami lawyer Sara Soto advises that "99.9% of the work you are going to do with your in-house counsel, you are going to do before you get to the mediation session." As a result of this groundwork, "when you get there, there shouldn't be many surprises." The same principle—good preparation now will prevent glitches or unpleasant surprises later—applies across the board.

Keep in mind that where you are representing a corporation, it is also quite possible that inside counsel will play a primary role in preparing the business executive who serves as client representative. John DeGroote (Dallas), for example, used to prep business people for the client-rep function when he was inside counsel for a global consulting firm. He describes the points he would typically cover in Sidebar 7-3: "Prepping Business Executives for Mediation."

Beyond this, there is a wide variety in how central a role you will be expected to play both in preparation for the mediation session and in the session itself, as noted at the beginning of Step Six. As stated in that step, you will need to adapt the guidance of this chapter accordingly.

Substeps for preparing with client. Step Seven involves seven basic substeps:

1. Fill in any additional factual information you may need from your client.
2. Brief your client on the basics of the scheduled mediation session.
3. Jointly evaluate your case.
4. Agree on a negotiation plan.
5. Strategize on how best to show the strength of your client's case during the opening session.
6. Finalize a mediation team (as applicable).
7. Encourage a productive attitude for negotiations.

As noted in Step Six, it is a good idea to use a written agenda of items to cover during the prep session. The discussion in this step should be helpful in developing such an agenda.

7.1 Fill in any additional factual information you may need from your client.

If you have been following the steps in this book, by now you already should have in hand most or all of the factual information you need about the case for mediation purposes. However, in the course of Step Six you may have realized there may be some ways in which you need to fine-tune your understanding of the facts.

Many mediators lament that too often—perhaps especially in court-ordered mediation—lawyers arrive at the session with huge gaps in knowledge. In the words of one mediator: "I go to mediations, and I sit down in a private caucus, and I have their clients telling me things that the attorneys have never heard before." She attributes this phenomenon in part to lawyers who view mandatory mediation as "just another rubber-stamp procedural hurdle that they have to jump through" in the litigation process. She has seen that such lawyers arrive totally unequipped to get the best deal for their client—which leaves the client ill served if the case actually ends up settling at the mediation session.

7.2 Brief your client on the basics of the scheduled mediation session.

In every case, you of course will need to inform your client about the who, what, when, and where of the upcoming mediation session. Another basic function of client prep is to make sure that your client fully understands the basics regarding both mediation as a concept and the procedures to be followed at the upcoming session.

A previous section of this chapter referred to Sidebar 7-3 ("Prepping Business Executives for Mediation"), in which a longtime inside counsel walks you through some of the basic points he makes when talking to corporate representatives or other executives who will participate in an upcoming mediation session. You will also want to read Sidebar 7-4 ("Telling Clients How Mediation Sessions Work"), where outside counsel Walter Stuart (New York) describes what he sometimes tells clients about the basics of such sessions.

Depending on your client's legal knowledge and depth of previous experience with mediation, in this portion of your client preparation you will want to cover topics including (a) the who, what, when, and where; (b) how mediation differs from arbitration and litigation; (c) the nature and purpose of mediation; (d) session procedure; (e) the roles to be played by each type of session participant; and (f) the style and tone of conduct that you and your clients need to maintain at the session. After discussing what you may want to tell your client about those roles, this section will point you to some other knowledgeable first-person advice on briefing the client.

A. Who, what, when, and where

Laura Kennedy's sample presession prep agenda (Appendix B) includes a section regarding such information as the scheduled mediation date, place, and time; the identity of the mediator; and the names of everyone who is expected to attend on behalf of each side, along with your side's travel and accommodation plans. Don't forget to make it clear how long you anticipate the session may possibly last.

To the extent that your client is not already familiar with the mediator, you will also want to describe her background and what you know of her style as a mediator. If your client does not know everyone expected to attend on your opponent's side, including opposing counsel, you will want to supply available details about them.

B. How mediation differs from arbitration and litigation

First-timers "will tend to confuse mediation with arbitration or some sort of administrative adjudication" (Watson, 2002, p.2). For example, Steven Brom (Birmingham, AL) has found this to be true when representing insured defendants. "A lot of times, people just don't know what mediation is," Brom says. "They confuse it, I guess, with arbitration. They're afraid that we're going to get a verdict and be stuck with it." For that reason, part of Brom's prep of such clients conveys assurances like this:

> Mediation is not binding. Don't panic about mediation. Just because we are going to mediation, that does not

> mean that something bad is going to happen. We're not going to get a verdict. We're not going to get a judgment against anyone. It's a purely 100% voluntary process. Nothing can happen at the mediation that we all don't agree to.

C. Nature and purpose of mediation

Lawrence Watson (Maitland, FL) notes that clients without much previous experience in mediation tend to think that their goal for a "successful" mediation should be for settlement terms that would be about equal to the results of a court judgment in their favor. This misconception "needs immediate and forceful readjustment" (2002, p.3). In preparing for the mediation session, you need to define the true goal of mediation and convey a clear understanding that the definitions of *success*, *winner*, and *loser* in the mediation context are very different from in litigation.

Watson offers a good example of what you might tell your client about this (2002, p.3):

> "Winning" in the mediation process does not mean successfully convincing the other side to buy into a settlement agreement that would mirror a victory in court conceived without their input. . . . The goal of mediation is to develop and present the best settlement option available and thus create the opportunity to accept (or reject) a viable option to the lawsuit. The "winner" in mediation, therefore, is the party who conducts themselves in such a manner that the other side is persuaded to offer up their very last and best option to litigation before any decision to accept or reject is made. The "loser" in mediation is the party who causes the termination of the process without getting the best alternative available from the other side extended.

D. Session procedure, including "downtime"

Clients with limited experience in mediation also need to be briefed on the procedure that will be followed at your upcoming session. In suggesting what to say to a client on that topic,

Watson assumes the "classic" procedure that includes an opening joint session followed by caucuses (2002, pp. 2–3):

> The client should be informed . . . that the first part of mediation, the opening presentations, seeks only to define and explore the complete aspect of the adjudicatory process—not to decide the case. At the end of the opening presentations, both parties should have a realistic and balanced concept of their adjudication option. The second phase of the mediation[] then utilizes a private caucus process to face the problem-solving task of creating a reconciliation option that deals with both parties' interests in an acceptable manner. At that point, a choice is made [to settle or not].

(1) Breaks and downtime

Discussions of mediation session procedure may sometimes neglect telling clients about the role of downtime and breaks. Some lawyers might be surprised to hear mediator John Bickerman describe the "need to take breaks" as one of the most important things to explain to clients about the session process (Bickerman et al., 2003, p.7). One example of such a need may come during a caucus with the mediator, when a lawyer and client decide they should talk together privately before continuing the discussion. For more on this, read Sidebar 7-5: "Prepping on 'Special Aspects' of the Mediation Structure."

Anyone who has been through a mediation session knows there is typically "a whole lot of downtime," as John DeGroote puts it (*see* Sidebar 7-3, "Prepping Business Executives for Mediation"). For example, during the caucus phase, each party has to wait while the mediator is in private caucus with the other side. But waiting is a built-in part of the process. Laura Kennedy recommends making this clear in advance (2010, pp.154–155):

> Many clients want to see "action" at the very beginning. In some cases, the client may be an impatient executive accustomed to having full control, and must be prepared (and have the trust) to give up some of that control to the mediator and for long periods of

> time. The client should be assured that mediation is a process—"a marathon, not a sprint" and that frequently the "action" occurs in the last few hours of the scheduled mediation. The client should be prepared for massive shifts of momentum. The mediation process can be an emotional roller coaster as the client tries to read cues from the mediator, makes difficult concessions that are not accepted, believes a deal is imminent, only to learn of a new barrier. The client should remain patient, but vigilant.

In this context, Kennedy believes clients should also be specifically told that they should not use the downtime "for anything other than continued internal dialogue on the dispute you are mediating" (p.155).

E. Roles of the session participants

For clients not already well versed in mediation, consider discussing the distinct roles that the various types of session participants will play. Essentially, the basic roles are: mediator; client (or corporate representative); counsel; insurance-company representative (for personal injury and some other types of cases); and sometimes experts or others.

(1) Role of the mediator

Mediator and law professor Homer LaRue (Columbia, MD) suggests the following type of explanation about the mediator's role (speaking in Bickerman et al., 2003, p.16):

> [Y]ou need to explain to the client that the mediator's role is not to be the ally of the client or you. The mediator's role is there to assist us, assist you and the client, in reaching a resolution. The mediator is not a neutral fact finder. The mediator is not interested in finding blame. The mediator is there to facilitate a negotiation between you and the other side. And that is the purpose. And the client needs to understand that so that the client doesn't go into the process believing somehow that the mediator's role is that of assisting the client to reach what the client wants.

Bowen Tucker (Arlington Heights, IL), a retired Associate General Counsel, drives home the mediator's primary goal even more bluntly:

> The mediator's objective is to settle the case. He or she doesn't care whether it's fair or unfair. I have no problem with that, either—and I don't say that critically. The job of the mediator is to get the case settled. It's not the mediator's job to decide whether it's fair or unfair to either side.

In keeping with this reality, you may specifically want to counsel your client against revealing too much—such as thoughts about your side's bottom line—without privately consulting with you first. *See* Sidebar 7-5 ("Prepping on 'Special Aspects' of the Mediation Structure") and Sidebar 10-8 ("Should You Ever Tell the Mediator Your Bottom Line?").

(2) Role of the client or corporate representative

Law professor and mediator Dwight Golann (Boston) offers a list of things you should advise the client to say—and not say—in mediation (speaking in Bickerman et al., 2003, p.9):

> I would tell a client there are things you will always be able to say, things you should never say, and things that you should follow my lead about saying. In the "never" category, the bottom line; legal arguments, because the lawyer can handle those; and what I might call "silver bullets," that key piece of case information that you're not even sure you want to disclose to anyone. In the "always" category, I'd put anything that makes you a more attractive person or a better plaintiff or someone who's more likely to get damages or less likely to give them up as a defendant.
>
> And in the "maybe" category I guess that depends on the signals that the lawyer wants to send about, for example, whether they want to play good cop/bad cop, where the client is being the tough cop, and the lawyer is trying to hold him in, or vice versa, because we know that that can be effective; whether one of them wants to be the tough negotiator and one wants to be the idea person; whether one wants to have authority

> and one doesn't—there are all sorts of ways to play it. But I think that you can get advantages, just as you can in direct negotiation, by doing that.

Also in the "never" category, John Bickerman (in Bickerman et al., 2003, p.7) says lawyers should remind clients: "One should not make concessions or make statements that are adverse to your position unless they are well considered."

When Sara Soto preps corporate representatives, she typically asks them to be closemouthed much of the time:

> Usually I instruct these people that there is to be no talking while the other people, i.e., the other side, are in the room. You are to say nothing. You are to not give dirty looks; you are to do nothing. If the mediator comes in, if he asks you any questions, answer his questions, answer them truthfully and to the point. If he asks you nothing, say nothing.

In Soto's experience, "most people are happy to take that advice—they really don't have any desire to put themselves out there."

John DeGroote agrees that the businessperson generally should not be doing much of the talking. However, he adds, "there are things that are going to be in their sweet spot, that you want them to talk about." For example, you may want the client to express emotion on a particular topic, or provide facts in an area you know he or she feels comfortable with, or demonstrate that he or she is strongly on board with a point you have just made.

Of course, it would be too complicated to try to predict before a session exactly when you would like a client to speak up. So in preparation, you might advise your client to be alert for cues on your part. DeGroote provides these examples of cues: "I would say, 'You know, Bob why don't you tell Fred here [i.e., the mediator] just how bad this is?' Or, 'Why don't you tell Fred here the impact of the other side's failure to do what they are supposed to do on your business?' Whatever point you want to get across."

Somewhat related to DeGroote's sweet spots is the role of client venting. Many experienced mediation players endorse allowing a client the opportunity—during a private caucus, for example—to express strongly held views and feelings about the case directly to the mediator. The idea is that getting things off the client's chest can psychologically facilitate the mediation process. Client venting is discussed in Substep 9.4, Sidebar 9-5 ("The Power of Venting"), and Sidebar 2-4 ("The Power of Good Listening"). Although you may not necessarily want to discuss the theory of venting with your client, you could alert him in advance that he will have the opportunity to speak freely if he watches for your cue.

While Sara Soto's instructions include speaking truthfully to the mediator, Laura Kennedy goes so far as to call that a "golden rule" (2010, p.157):

> You must counsel your client to avoid "fooling" the mediator. If your client is successful in "fooling the mediator," for example, "x dollars is my bottom line," the mediation could well fail based upon an artificial and false construct. Time, expense and most importantly, an opportunity, will have been wasted. . . .
>
> Be resolved, but follow the golden rule: Never Fool the Mediator.

At a more general level, Kennedy believes clients should be advised to convey an attitude of firm resolve during the mediation session (p. 157):

> The client must be prepared to demonstrate her sincere and steeled resolve for fairness. The key message to send to the mediator (and thus to the opposition) is your client's (truthful) resolve to see the case through in the absence of a reasonable and fair settlement as defined by your client. Thus, you must counsel your client on the importance of resolve.
>
> Equally critical, however, is an explanation that there exists some natural tension between being resolved/emoting resolve and obtaining a settlement.

In *Mediation Advocacy* (2002, pp.91–106), the late John Cooley provides detailed guidance for the behavior of clients during a session. Among other things, he advises that clients should never argue but only state facts; listen with care when the other side speaks—without interrupting; and avoid showing any visible reaction to settlement offers.

Beyond this type of advice, there is the possibility that you and your client will agree to play specific roles in a performance sense at the mediation session, such as good-guy and bad-guy roles. Prof. Dwight Golann refers to this as a "strategy choice" (speaking in Bickerman et al., 2003, p.15, italics added):

> One of the dirty little secrets of mediation is that it allows people to be tougher than they could be in a direct negotiation. If you want to offer someone $10 to settle a $100,000 case, if you offer it in a direct negotiation, they'll walk out. In a mediation, you've got the mediator there to scrape the other side off the ceiling and to keep them in. And you know by agreeing to mediation they've made a multi-hundred- or thousand-dollar commitment to the process. So therefore they're not going to walk out. So you can be tougher. So, there's a strategy choice. *Do you want to have your client be the tough guy, or tough gal, while you either play along with that or you try to be this quasi-conciliator, sort of the deputy mediator?* Knowing that the mediator's job is going to be to take that unpalatable, insulting offer, or demand, to the other side and keep them in the room, which they will. That adds a strategy component.

Lastly, you may want to address the topic of general tone and demeanor that you recommend your client should maintain during the joint parts of the mediation session. For more on this, see Substep 8.1.

(3) Roles of counsel

On the topic of your roles, the most important thing you need your client to understand is that you will be playing two very different ones during the mediation session: advocate (in public) and counselor (in private). For a discussion of this—and the tensions that can arise—read Sidebar 7-6: "The 'Two Eds' of Mediation."

You may also need the client to understand that even in your public role, you will be less combative at the mediation session than might be appropriate in a litigation setting. This is also discussed in Substep 8.1.

One other point: If you think that it might be beneficial during the mediation session for you to express some empathy for the opposing client, you should make sure that your own client is prepared for this possibility and understands it. Mediator David Hoffman (Boston) has this to say about this type of expression:

> It can be a very powerful moment when the lawyer across the table expresses genuine concern for the party on the other side. And one very powerful way to be involved in mediation is to express that kind of empathy and concern, because the party on the other side generally won't expect it. Of course it has to be genuine, or else it will seem condescending or smarmy.
>
> If a lawyer is going to do something like that and express that kind of empathy or concern for the party on the other side of the table, it's very important for the lawyer to prepare his or her client for that moment. In other words, part of the preparation for mediation is telling your client that he or she is going to see a different style of legal representation as compared with courtroom advocacy, because otherwise the client might be appalled.

For more on the role of empathy or apologies in mediation sessions, see Substep 8.4.

(4) Role of the insurance company representative

Specifically in the realm of insurance defense work, there is an additional point to make while prepping the insured defendant: The insurance company—not the defendant—has the right to decide whether to accept a settlement offer within the policy limits. Steven Brom (Birmingham, AL) describes this element of preparation:

> I explain to the insureds ahead of time to let them know that the insurance companies get to make that

decision for themselves. They're not necessarily bound by what the insured says, whether it is to settle or not to settle. That burden really falls on the insurance company. And most insureds understand that. They understand that it's the insurance company's money. As long as it is not going to cost them anything out of pocket, they really are okay with it—or at least they understand how it works.

(5) Role of experts or others

If your mediation team will include experts or any other type of personnel of this nature, of course you will also want everyone to be clear about what each player is supposed to do and how this will relate to the whole endeavor.

F. Style and tone of conduct that you and your clients need to maintain at the mediation session

Presession preparation is your opportunity to explain to your client both how you intend to conduct yourself at the session vis-à-vis your opponent and the mediator and what the rationale is for that approach. It is also the time to discuss and agree on the style and tone that your client and other team members (if any) will maintain. For a discussion of style and tone in relation to the conduct of the mediation team, read Step Eight—especially Substep 8.1.

7.3 Jointly evaluate your case.

This substep includes three closely intertwined joint evaluation activities with your client: (a) Review together the strengths and weaknesses of your side's case; (b) agree on your case's financial worth; and (c) discuss your client's goals, including objectives that may be advanced even if the case does not settle at the session.

A. Review together the strengths and weaknesses of your side's case

"You want the client to know what you know," says Sara Soto. "Obviously not in excruciating detail—but you want to get the person a thorough report of what this case is about. This is what the evidence shows, these are the pros and cons."

The briefing process will inevitably elicit questions and comments from your client. Sometimes this can include relevant additional information that for some reason did not come out earlier. It is important to listen well, so that "when you get to the mediation there will not be that many new things you are going to hear," as Soto puts it.

If your client is an individual, she is likely to feel that she knows all the relevant facts, but her focus may naturally be on what she perceives as the strength of her own position rather than its weaknesses or the other side's possible strengths. If your client is a corporation, inside counsel may be very conversant with the facts and possess some objectivity, but an executive who was personally involved in the underlying dispute may have essentially the same attitudes as an individual client. Meanwhile, if the corporate representative is a higher-up who had no personal involvement, his knowledge of the facts may be slight (except to the degree that he has been brought up to speed by inside counsel).

By this time, you or your corporate client may have undertaken a Litigation Risk Analysis or other decision-tree approach to financial evaluation (*see* Step Six). If so, the various decision points in the decision tree can provide a natural focus and guide to discussing the strengths and weaknesses of your case.

In analyzing your case with your client, it may not be easy to discuss weaknesses as well as strengths without appearing to be a weak advocate for your client's position—but it is very important. Former mediator and bankruptcy judge Timothy Corcoran (Tampa) has described the need for balance like this (2007, § 3.c.ii):

> My observation is that the best lawyers—from the beginning of their representation—strike a healthy balance between taking their client's side and strongly advocating for their client, and also ensuring their clients understand that (a) there are always two sides to every dispute, (b) the client is focusing only on the client's side, (c) one challenge in the case will be to

> understand the opponent's side, and (d) only when that additional understanding is obtained can the lawyer and client make a proper evaluation of the situation. In other words, a lawyer does not want to create from the beginning of the representation unrealistic expectations that cannot be met at the end.

In the specific context of preparing a client for the mediation session, Laura Kennedy stresses the importance of including a discussion of the case from your opponent's likely perspective (2010, p.158):

> Your client should not hear the opposition's position for the first time at the mediation. Let your client know what she should expect to hear about your case from the other side. While you may not need to explore every nuance of every claim and defense, you should globally explain the claim or defense and the basis for each and, if applicable, any settlement themes that your opponent is likely to present. This aspect of the pre-preparation process will not only allow the client time to consider and develop a response, but will give her confidence to project genuine and thoughtful resolve.

For more on exploring the possible downsides of your case, see Sidebar 7-7: "Probing Liability Risks With Inside Counsel."

B. Agree on your case's financial worth

Various approaches to financial evaluation of your case were discussed in Substep 6.1. As noted in that step, depending on the type of client and practice you have, the degree to which you lead in this analysis may vary. In some instances, your client may depend completely on you to estimate the case's probable worth, and your role will be to explain how you arrived at your conclusions, respond to questions, and try to bring the client on board. At the other extreme—especially with some large corporate clients—inside counsel may take the lead in financial evaluation, and your role will be limited to input and discussion. The use you will make of the financial evaluation in client prep is discussed in Substep 7.4.

C. Discuss your client's goals, including objectives that may be advanced even if the case does not settle at the session

What are the easiest mistakes for a rookie lawyer to make in negotiations in a mediation session? "Not knowing what the client wants—and believing his client when his client says what he wants!" That is a view expressed by John DeGroote. He is in a good position to speak, since he worked for years with outside lawyers of varying experience levels in his role as inside counsel directing litigation for a global consulting firm.

On the first point—not understanding what the client wants—DeGroote says: "Most younger, less experienced lawyers presume that their client genuinely wants to just pay as little as possible. And that's not always the case. There can be other terms that could drive the deal as much as a monetary settlement."

The ABA Section of Dispute Resolution's Task Force on Improving Mediation Quality (2008a) echoes this view: "Counsel should be certain to ask their clients, 'What is really important to you about this dispute, and why?' This question helps counsel develop additional settlement options based on the client's interests, instead of solely focusing on getting or giving a certain dollar amount" (p.11).

True, for a defendant the most obvious goal might be simply to make a lawsuit go away as cheaply as possible. Likewise, many plaintiffs may simply want to extract as much money as they can to help make up for their grievance. But even in simple cases, a client's goals may not really be that straightforward. To give a few offhand possibilities:

- An aggrieved plaintiff's major goals might include an acknowledgment of wrongdoing rather than solely receiving dollars.
- In addition to concern about the *amount* of money, the decision maker for a defendant corporation may be concerned about the *timing*—such as not paying until after the end of a fiscal period.

- A corporate defendant may be very concerned that settling this case on terms acceptable to the plaintiff might encourage other similarly situated people to sue the company. In the same vein, the nature and strength of any confidentiality provisions may be an important issue for the corporation.

As Gary Poon (Washington, DC) has observed, sometimes a corporate defendant's interests may be inconsistent or conflicting—especially "when there are several constituencies or factions within a corporation that have a stake in the dispute and its ultimate resolution" (2010, p.64). Because the real world can be complicated, John Bickerman says "trying to figure out what your client's goal is" is one of a lawyer's biggest potential challenges in preparing for a mediation session (Bickerman et al., 2003, p.7). After making this point, he continues:

> [S]ometimes the client's goal may not be entirely obvious to the client himself. Sometimes the client will have other parties that he has to respond to and react to. So sitting down with your client and clearly defining what the goals are [is essential], both in terms of the issues that might be present in the suit, but also issues that might affect the company that he works for, the relationship that they may have or want to have with the party on the other side. There are a whole slew of factors that one has to consider.

The second point John DeGroote makes—don't automatically believe what the client says about his goals—relates primarily to issues of the amount of money a defendant client is really willing to pay for settlement. Those issues are discussed in Substep 7.4B(3).

As you explore your client's goals, bear in mind that sometimes you can make use of the mediation to serve other objectives besides the narrow goal of settlement. For more on this, read Sidebar 7-8: "Mediation Objectives Besides Full Settlement."

Finally, it is not enough just to know your client's goals; for strategic purposes, you need to work out how those rank in importance. "The client is going to spell out to you a number of things that he or she wants," says Prof. LaRue (Bickerman et al., 2003, p.12). "It's necessary for you to understand that those need to be prioritized."

7.4 Agree on a negotiation plan.

On the topic of advance plans for negotiating at a mediation session, John Bickerman advises (in Bickerman et al, 2003, p.16):

> [Y]ou need to have a strategy going in. Don't wing it. What do I mean by a strategy? I mean . . . sit down with your client. Figure out where your bottom line is. And then figure out how you're going to get there. . . . [T]hink of how you're going to parcel out your concessions over time to signal the other side where your bottom line is.

From his experience as an advocate in mediation, Thomas Dye (West Palm Beach, FL), agrees. "Everything should be thought through, including your initial offer, your fallback points, and your bottom line, to when you walk out the door," he says. "I would want to have all that talked about with my client beforehand." Bennett Picker underscores the point: "All too often, parties lose significant advantages in mediation as the result of having planned only initial offers and demands and tentative final positions" (2003, p.81).

J. Anderson Little (Chapel Hill, NC) defines the concept of a negotiation plan in language that is both succinct and unusually detailed (2007, p.77):

> What do I mean by having a plan for negotiations? I mean first of all answering the following questions:
>
> After I have reviewed my case,
>
> After I have decided what I get on a good day and on a bad day in court,
>
> After I have factored in all of the costs and contingencies,

After I have conducted a thorough case analysis,
After all of that,
At what number will I start the negotiation?
At what number will I walk away from it? and
How will I move from number to number in between?

This sounds simple, and it is. Surprisingly, the majority of negotiators I work with give little thought to this kind of planning.

Agreeing on a negotiation plan with your client is a substep with several substeps of its own. Before proceeding to deal with those substeps, however, let's first step back to discuss some basic negotiation theory and key concepts.

A. *Getting to Yes* versus *Making Money Talk*

In 1981, two leaders of the Harvard Negotiation Project[1]—Roger Fisher and William Ury—revolutionized the field by publishing *Getting to Yes: Negotiating Agreement Without Giving In*.[2] The creative problem-solving approach recommended in that enormously influential book—closely associated with "interest-based" negotiation—soon became the standard doctrine on how to negotiate successfully. For many years, it provided the foundation for virtually all mediator training programs. Every mediation advocate needs to know the basic concepts of *Getting to Yes*, not just for their intrinsic merit, but because you need to recognize the terminology when you hear it and because you need to understand the training background of many mediators.

In 2007, *Getting to Yes*'s applicability to the mediation of civil court cases was directly challenged by J. Anderson Little in *Making Money Talk: How to Mediate Insured Claims and Other Monetary Disputes*. Little's basic point is that in cases where the fundamental question is how much the defendant will pay the plaintiff in order to settle a claim, there is usually

1. The Harvard Negotiation Project is a founding member of the Program on Negotiation at Harvard Law School.

2. In later editions, Bruce M. Patton was also credited as one of the authors.

little room for creative problem solving of the type that *Getting to Yes* espouses. Instead, he recommends facing the fact that in this context, the process of negotiating at a mediation session is mostly what he calls "traditional bargaining"—essentially the same as negotiating at a used-car lot. The approach that Little advocates for facilitating settlement in civil-court mediation is based on this recognition.

This part of this substep will provide a brief overview of (1) *Getting to Yes*; (2) Little's alternative viewpoint; and (3) some harmonization of views.

(1) Key concepts in Getting to Yes

It is impossible to do justice to Fisher and Ury's brilliant book (1981) in the space of a few paragraphs. However, for the purposes of this discussion, their central advice is to "focus on interests, not positions" (p.41). Another key concept that Fisher and Ury introduced is *BATNA*—an acronym for *best alternative to a negotiated agreement*. This is a term that every lawyer hears frequently in mediation.

(a) Interest-based negotiation

Consider a hypothetical dispute over ownership of an orange. In position-based negotiations, each disputing party may take the position that she wants the entire orange. By contrast, an interest-based approach would instead focus on each party's reason for wanting the orange. Theoretically, this could result in both parties getting what they really want (Goldberg & Sander, 2007, p.42):

> The classic illustration of the interest-based approach to mediation is found in the story of two sisters who had only one orange. Each wanted the orange; neither was willing to share it. The mediator asked the older sister why she wanted the orange. Her response was "I want the rind to flavor a cake." The mediator then asked the younger sister why she wanted the orange. "To make orange juice" was her response. At that point an agreement was apparent: The younger sister used the orange to make juice, the older sister used the rind to flavor her cake. By determining the

interests underlying each sister's position, the mediator was able to assist the sisters to find a mutually beneficial outcome.

The idea that both parties can come out ahead in resolving their dispute has given rise to another well-known buzzword: win-win negotiation.

(b) Best alternative to a negotiated agreement (BATNA)

Fisher and Ury present BATNA as a tool for evaluating possible settlement agreements "that will protect you against both accepting an agreement you should reject and rejecting an agreement you should accept" (1981, p.104).

As an example, they apply a BATNA analysis to a family that wants to sell their home. Many sellers might start by asking how much money they should be able to obtain from the sale. But Fisher and Ury suggest that this is the wrong question when trying to decide on the minimum price for which they would be willing to sell. Instead, they should ask themselves what they will do if they are unable to sell the house within a certain period of time.

For the purposes of this hypothetical, Fisher and Ury say the family may consider a range of alternatives, such as leasing out the house to receive rent or even tearing it down to open a money-making parking lot. After exploring their alternatives to sale, the family members are in a position to decide whether the best such alternative is worth more to them than accepting an offer to sell for, say, $80,000. Or it may be that selling for as little as $62,000 would be preferable to keeping the property unsold for an indefinite period.

Closely related to BATNA is another very common acronym, *WATNA*—the worst alternative to a negotiated agreement. It is certainly worth considering the worst thing that might happen to you if you fail to arrive at an agreement.

(2) *Little's critique of* Getting to Yes

As noted previously, mediator J. Anderson Little has written a book (2007) contending that the *Getting to Yes* model of interest-based, problem-solving negotiation is ill adapted to the reality that legal claims for money in civil lawsuits can typically be resolved only through position-based bargaining. However, Little does agree that there are certain types of civil court disputes where there is sometimes room for creative problem solving, albeit within a larger framework of traditional bargaining. In addition, Little strongly supports Fisher and Ury's concept of BATNA in the context of good case evaluation. This section will address each of those points in turn.

(a) The realities of position-based bargaining

Little's experience as a mediator dates back to 1992, when he convened the first settlement conference in North Carolina held under that state's newly created program for court-ordered mediation (2007, p.xi). By that time, he had completed 180 hours of formal mediation training in the *Getting to Yes* tradition, learning "to help [the disputing parties] define their needs and interests and create elegant solutions for mutual gain, and to help them reframe positional bargaining into joint problem solving" (p.xii).

Despite this training, Little experienced great frustration trying to apply those elegant techniques to a claim for the proceeds of a double-indemnity accidental-death insurance policy (p.xi). After mediating that case and others, he eventually concluded that Fisher and Ury's interest-based approach was ill adapted to the realities of mediating legal claims for money. Little writes (p.xii):

> From my experience in mediating the settlement of civil litigation over the past 15 years, I have come to believe that disputes about money are fundamentally different from other types of disputes. Claims for money start with positional bargaining, end with positional bargaining, and resist our efforts to reframe them into problem-solving experiences. Settlement negotiations in claims for money are difficult, indeed, because they are dominated by traditional bargaining. . . .
>
> They are usually settled with prolonged bargaining consisting of numerous rounds of painful concessions.

By "traditional" bargaining, Little means position-based bargaining—exactly the type of negotiation that Fisher and Ury advise against.

Little does not contend that position-based bargaining is easy or elegant—just that in the real world of mediating legal claims, it is mostly how the job has to get done (pp.24-–25):

> [E]verything you have heard about position-based bargaining is true. It's hard to reach settlement by arguing over positions. It's hard to get the process started; it's hard to keep making concessions; it's easy to get mad or discouraged along the way and want to stop; and it's hard to reach settlement if it appears that a gap will exist between the parties' positions at the end of the process.
>
> Mediators who are schooled solely in a problem-solving orientation to the mediation process may experience a great deal of frustration with this type of process. They may try, as I did at first, to convert this bargaining to a problem-solving exercise. They will rarely succeed.

Little is by no means alone in pointing out that position-based bargaining is the primary practical model for negotiating the settlement of legal claims. For example, Prof. Dwight Golann writes (2009a, p.51):

> In legal disputes, parties typically arrive at mediation expecting to exchange money offers in a gradual "dance" toward agreement—so-called positional bargaining. If bargainers are experienced, have a good working relationship, or have strong reasons to reach a deal, they can usually accomplish this dance successfully. Often however, positional negotiations degenerate into impasse.

Little's book *Making Money Talk* teaches techniques intended to help mediators facilitate settlement of claims for money using a position-based model of negotiation. One such technique—encouraging parties to plan for movement—is covered later in this chapter. Some other techniques are described in Step Ten. For more, mediation advocates will find it very useful to read Little's book.

(b) The (limited) role of creative problem solving

In Little's view, Fisher and Ury's interest-based approach is least applicable to insured claims based on a theory of negligence (such as auto-accident cases), which comprise a large part of civil litigation (2007, p.9). However, he agrees that some other types of business cases, construction disputes, or employment claims can sometimes offer more opportunities for creative problem solving.

In particular, Little suggests that the problem-solving model may be useful "in business disputes in which the parties have had [lengthy] working relationships in the past or wish to have such relationships in the future" (p.201). In such cases, settlement may include devising a way for the parties to resume or continue their ongoing relationship. Nevertheless, as a general matter, Little stresses that most civil suits for damages share with negligence cases the fundamental characteristic that their settlement is typically achieved "through the negotiation of an amount of money that is paid by one side to the other" (p.9).

John Bickerman agrees that room for creative problem solving is often quite limited in mediating litigated disputes. "There are some cases where one can really do some creative problem solving," he says (Bickerman et al., 2003, p.16). "But the sad story I have to share with you as a mediator is that quite a few cases are just win/lose situations: one side's going to take, and the other side's going to get."

Dwight Golann (2009a) once informally interviewed professional mediators from around the United States in an attempt to see how often disputants are actually able to reach interest-based, win-win settlements in commercial cases (p.70). According to the mediators, they were able to repair a preexisting business relationship between parties up to 20 percent of the time—almost always in so-called "too expensive to get divorced" situations. (Some mediators might think that estimate is high.) Prof. Golann provides an example of this type of situation (p.71):

> In one case, for instance, a landlord sued a commercial tenant who had not paid its rent. The landlord would

> have preferred to evict the tenant, but doing so would have driven the tenant into bankruptcy and made it impossible to recover the arrearage. The landlord therefore agreed to restructure the lease, allowing the tenant to stay at a higher rent and repay the arrearage over time.

For an example of a bitter business dispute that was completely resolved by an interest-based approach in mediation, see Sidebar 10-10: "An Example of Creative Settlement."

(c) The importance of BATNA and case evaluation

Even while downplaying the importance of Fisher and Ury's interest-based, creative problem-solving model for negotiating in the context of mediating legal claims for money, Little reinforces the importance of BATNA in this type of mediation. He writes (2007, p.13, footnote removed):

> A negotiator's BATNA is what he or she will do if agreement is not reached in a negotiation. Fisher and Ury suggest that negotiators clearly define their BATNA in order to provide a foundation for their negotiations. This insight has not received as much attention in the literature of mediation as their insight about "needs and interests," but it is an especially useful one in the negotiation of claims for money.
>
> What lawyers do positively for their clients in mediation is to help them analyze their BATNA and negotiate on the basis of it. They help their clients understand the value of their case and use that value as a benchmark for their negotiations.

For the purposes of evaluating claims for money in civil court, Little provides a more focused definition of BATNA than is found in *Getting to Yes*. He reduces it to "a series of questions that form the basis of an adequate case analysis" (p.49):

> What do you get if you go to court? That is, what is the likely result in monetary terms?

What are your chances of obtaining that outcome?

What does it cost you to get that outcome?

What are your chances of collecting a judgment if you obtain one as a result of trial?

The fourth question is phrased as though asked to a plaintiff. Presumably, for a defendant, it could be rephrased as "What are your opponent's chances of collecting a judgment from you if one is entered as the result of trial?"

(3) Some harmonization of views

Prof. John Lande (Columbia, MO) notes that the interest-based negotiation model may have greater applicability in cases where "there are multiple issues, some shared interests, and/or the potential for an ongoing relationship in the future" whereas "the classic case for positional negotiation is a personal injury case involving a plaintiff and insurance company to agree on a monetary settlement and have no further relationship" (2011a, p.66). Also, he observes that "[i]n practice, negotiation is much more complex than is suggested by either of these conceptions, and many negotiations blend elements of both approaches" (p.71).[3]

Dwight Golann has observed that in some cases, creative, interest-based opportunities may exist for some *part* of a settlement that is primarily accomplished through the payment of money using a bargaining model (2011, p.26). For more on this, see Substep 10.3B.

---

3. In a law-review article, "Teaching Students to Negotiate Like a Lawyer" (2012), Prof. Lande advances the concept of "ordinary legal negotiation" (OLN). He describes OLN as distinct from both interest-based and positional negotiation models (p.118). For example, while the positional model views negotiation as a zero-sum game, and interest-based negotiation seeks "optimal, positive-sum results" through a joint analysis of interests and options, OLN focuses on "legal norms" of what is considered a reasonable outcome in the relevant practice community, aiming for "good results" that "help preserve lawyers' and parties' relationships" (p.120). The OLN model reflects Prof. Lande's "perception of what a lot of lawyers—perhaps most—generally do" in the negotiating process (personal communication, May 3, 2012). The types of negotiation he is talking about span the entire range of lawyers' activities—not just settling lawsuits, but everything from agreeing with opposing counsel on a filing deadline to helping a client form a business partnership to adjusting the client's bill for legal services (2012, pp.122–24).

B. Steps toward agreeing on a negotiation plan

As noted earlier, the substep of agreeing on a negotiation plan includes several substeps of its own. These are: (1) Get consensus on your client's best alternative to a negotiated agreement (BATNA); (2) agree on—or at least discuss—your client's opening number; (3) get a sense of your client's bottom line; (4) discuss possible creative options for settlement; and (5) agree on a plan for movement.

(1) Get consensus on your client's best alternative to a negotiated agreement (BATNA)

In the previous section, we quoted J. Anderson Little's four questions to arrive at an understanding of a party's BATNA. The first and second of those questions can be answered with help from the financial evaluation you performed as part of your preparation (discussed in Step Six and earlier in this step). The fourth question—regarding collectability of a potential judgment—probably applies only where there is a possibility that the defending party may be (or may become) insolvent or somehow beyond the practical reach of the law. Only the third question will be discussed further here.

Little's third question probably most often refers to the expense of taking a case to trial, which may be mostly attorney fees. At least in the context of corporate defendants, John DeGroote cautions against pushing the attorney-fees part of the equation too early and too hard in talks with business executives. This perspective comes from his years as inside counsel for a global consulting firm. In that role, DeGroote was very familiar with the resistance and resentment that many businesspeople are inclined to feel when asked to include the cost of taking a case to trial in deciding how much the company should be willing to pay in order to settle the case at mediation.

Given that sensitivity, DeGroote recommends introducing the attorney fees gently. For example, when he first introduces the executives to outside counsel in connection with a planned mediation, he might say something like the following:

> We've got John Doe here from whatever important law firm, and he filed our answer to the complaint.

> Yes, we have spent $50,000 in fees to date, and we frankly haven't really done anything much, so far. Understand, you know, that we have done three of these cases in the past, and they cost an average of $1.2 million each. I'm not asking you today to pony up the $1.15 million left to spend—but understand, I want that in the back of your mind.

DeGroote recommends that sort of approach because "if in that initial meeting you start pushing that concept on business executives too quickly—the concept of throwing fees on top—people tend to revolt." For that reason (which is probably applicable to other types of paying clients as well), introducing a figure for attorney fees by simply plugging it in while discussing BATNA—separately and preceding any discussion of a bottom line or walk-away number for the upcoming mediation session—may be a diplomatic strategy.

(2) Discuss an opening number with your client

The most familiar type of number in settlement negotiations is the plaintiff's demand. If advice offered earlier in this book is followed, the demand will be disclosed to the defendant well in advance of the mediation session, so that the defendant (often in the person of corporate executives or insurers) will have time to mull it over—which may have an impact, among other things, on the settlement authority the defendant's representative is able to bring to the table.

Assuming that negotiations begin with a plaintiff's demand, the defendant's starting number will be a response. If the plaintiff's demand is not learned until the mediation session, the defendant may not decide on its starting number before that time. However, as will be discussed later, at least one prominent mediator recommends that the defendant formulate its expected starting number independent of whatever demand the plaintiff makes.

Following is some advice on how to arrive at a starting number from three experienced observers: a law professor (Charles Craver), a mediator (J. Anderson Little), and a former litigation counsel (John DeGroote). Two more viewpoints on starting numbers are briefly presented in Substep 9.8.

(a) Insights from Craver

Charles Craver is the Freda H. Alverson Professor of Law at The George Washington University Law School in Washington, DC He is the author of many legal books, including *Effective Legal Negotiation and Settlement* (2009) and *Alternative Dispute Resolution: The Advocate's Perspective* (2011). The insights here are from his short guide *Legal Negotiation: Process and Techniques* (2011; italics in original):

- "Establish '*principled opening positions*' that can be defended 'objectively' when presented to adversaries" (p.11). You should choose your starting number "as far from actual objectives as you can while still being able to rationally defend your proposals"—that is, quite high on the plaintiff's side and low on the defendant's side—while still seeming reasonable enough that your opponents will not lose all interest in the negotiation (p.10).[4]
- Along with the starting number, you should "[prepare logical rationales to explain each component of [your] positions" (p.11). In Craver's view, the value of this approach is that it (a) "[b]olsters [your] own confidence and undermines that of uncertain opponents"; (b) "[e]xplains [your] reasons for choosing overall positions selected, rather than less beneficial starting points"; and (c) "[f]requently allows [the proposing] person to control [the] agenda, by causing opponents to directly focus upon each segment of stated positions" (p.11).

---

4. Thomas Dye, while generally advocating a hard-line negotiating approach, acknowledges that extreme initial offers have inherent risks. "There are generally three choices: (a) a fair opening offer, (b) a moderately unreasonable opening offer, and (c) an absolutely unreasonable opening offer," he writes (2010, pp.7–8). "Studies reveal that for cases that are settled, the 'absolutely unreasonable opening offer' is likely to bring the best result for the offering party. However, there is a caveat. The 'absolutely unreasonable opening offer' is also more likely to result in an impasse." In mediations where you sense that "your opponent is very motivated to resolve the dispute and avoid the alternative to a negotiated settlement," Dye suggests "your client may benefit most by starting with an absolutely unreasonable opening offer." However, "if an impasse is a significant possibility, a modestly unreasonable offer may be best."

- "Lawyers should try to offer opponents terms that seem like *gains* rather than *losses* because of *gain-loss framing*" (p.10). Craver explains the phenomenon of "gain-loss framing" like this: "People offered sure *gain* and possibility of greater gain or no gain tend to be *risk averse* while persons offered sure *loss* and possibility of greater loss or no loss tend to be risk takers trying to avoid any loss."
- "Negotiators should also be aware of impact of the *endowment effect*" (p.10). Because of this effect, "[persons who own something tend to *over-value* those items while people who are thinking of buying the same items tend to *under-value* those goods."

The downside of a too-generous opening is what Craver calls the anchoring effect. "Due to '*anchoring*,'" he writes, "people who begin with generous opening offers embolden opponents who think they'll do better than they thought while those who begin with less generous offers undermine opponents who think they'll not do as well as they hoped."

(b) Insights from Little

J. Anderson Little played a major role in helping to establish civil trial mediation programs in his home state of North Carolina. The insights on starting numbers here are from his book *Making Money Talk* (2007).

"The greatest motivation of the parties to settle is the perception that the case can settle," Little writes (p.83). Conversely, "the greatest impediment to settlement is the perception that the case will not settle." From Little's perspective, that is a reason why plaintiffs should not make their initial offer too unreasonably high and defendants should not lowball their first numbers. He believes mediation participants too often shoot themselves in the foot with extreme openings (p.77):

> Plaintiffs typically start much higher than their own case analysis supports. Defendants often have a best number in mind, but start low in reaction to the plaintiff's high starting number. Neither has a plan for what happens next and the rest is predictable.

> Left to their own devices, the parties typically quit the process after swapping a few proposals, believing that their best numbers are very far apart and that the case won't settle.

To help avoid this danger, Little advises defendants to opt for an initial offer that does not exceed their own highest possible evaluation of their case (p.78):[5]

> A number at the top of the plaintiff's verdict range may be no more acceptable to the defense than one that is 150 percent higher. However, the defense's reaction to it and their willingness to negotiate in realistic ranges themselves is much more different and more positive. Thus, I frequently ask one side or the other to consider how their starting number relates to their case analysis and how the other side, as a consequence of that relation, will react to it.
>
> Based on those thoughts, I believe that plaintiffs should not start their negotiations with a number higher than their own case analysis.

As to the defendant's opening number, Little advises against simply reacting to the plaintiff's opener. This is especially true where the plaintiff's demand is unreasonably high, so the reactive temptation is to respond with a lowball. Instead, he urges defendants to arrive at a starting offer by asking themselves two questions: "What would have been a reasonable number for the plaintiff to begin with?" and "Where would you have started if they had been reasonable?" (p.79).

(c) Insights from DeGroote

As a former head of litigation for a global consulting firm, John DeGroote speaks from many years of participation in mediation sessions as inside counsel (and sometimes as the corporate representative). He did not apply any particular

---

5. Little acknowledges, however, that a special problem is presented for plaintiffs in catastrophic, high-dollar personal-injury cases, where the value can be unusually difficult to gauge (p.78).

rule of thumb to arrive at an opening number, but in an interview he offered some observations and advice on the topic.

To defendants' counsel, he says:

> Your starting number is a number that gives you enough runway to work with for the rest of the day and that gives the beginnings of an indication of your value for the case. It sets the outer marker. You will never, in the history of the planet, pay less than that number to settle the case. Even if the case does not settle during mediation, your opening number becomes the floor for any future settlement at a later point in the litigation process, barring a verdict or some other truly dramatic development in your favor.

DeGroote also notes that where plaintiffs' lawyers are working on contingency, they will be subtracting their contingency fees from the settlement amount. Such fees may amount to two thirds of the total. Thus, if the plaintiffs need to get $30,000 in order to feel satisfied with the settlement, the total settlement amount would need to be $90,000. "When you are a defendant, you need to think about how much money the plaintiffs want to have in the case, because your settlement is usually going to be 3 times that, at the very least," DeGroote says. "And no fancy footwork on your part is ever going to change that, barring a case where you have gotten summary judgment or they found that they don't really have any legal claim to damages or some other problems."

To plaintiffs' counsel, DeGroote advises:

> When you are a plaintiff, don't factor in punitive damages, unless punitives are so clear that you are really going to get them at trial. You are probably not going to get punitives in mediation anyway, so let's take a look at your credible damages and ask for a subset of those. But understand the same thing I said to defense lawyers—this opening number is going to be a bracket for the case, for the rest of eternity.

(3) Get a sense of your client's bottom line

Inside counsel Hildy Bowbeer (St. Paul, MN) defines the term *bottom line* as "the least you would be willing to accept, or the most you would be willing to give, to resolve the case based on your current analysis" (2010, p.199). She notes that this is not necessarily the same as the number that would cause you to "walk (i.e., close the discussions for the time being)." Bowbeer's advice is to identify both numbers in preparing with your mediation team. In her view, at a mediation session it is sometimes best to walk before reaching your bottom line, if you become convinced that the other side's series of offers has not demonstrated enough willingness to move toward a settlement that would be acceptable to you. For more advice from Bowbeer on preparing your team for mediation, read Sidebar 7-11: "Prepping Your Business Team."

The bottom line concept is not necessarily such a bright line as it may sound, because it is not uncommon for parties to reach a settlement even after there is a gap between their bottom lines. For a mediator like Anderson Little, the crucial factor at that late point in a session is the size of the gap, which determines whether it is bridgeable or not. This point will be discussed further in Step Ten.

This section is headed "*get a sense* of the client's bottom line"—rather than simply "learn" or "agree on" a bottom line—for a reason: Experienced mediation players disagree on whether pinning the client down to an exact numeric bottom line in advance of a mediation session is really advisable—or even possible. Indeed, there are reasons why a certain degree of ambiguity in the parties' bottom lines may increase a mediation's chances of success.

In addition, as counsel (either outside or inside), you need to be aware that the bottom line a client tells you is not necessarily what he privately sees as his true bottom line, and the amount of settlement authority granted to a defendant corporation's representative in advance of a mediation session does not necessarily represent the maximum authority that the representative may ultimately receive before the session ends. Moreover, it is always possible that the client will end up settling at a number at least somewhat higher (for a defendant) or lower (for a plaintiff) than he ever believed beforehand he would be willing to accept.

For these reasons, your client's bottom line is potentially as elusive as it is important in the mediation process. Nevertheless, you will need to use some stand-in for the bottom line in order to do any useful negotiation planning in advance of the mediation session (or even during the session itself).

This section will discuss the role of the bottom line in negotiation planning; the reasons why a true bottom line may be unobtainable by counsel; the importance of flexibility in the bottom line; and the role of projected attorneys' fees in bottom-line discussions.

(a) The role of the bottom line in negotiation planning

You can't do any negotiation planning—and can't provide any meaningful input to your client during the actual negotiations during the mediation session—unless you have some concept of what the client's bottom line is.

In the context of defendants, Jay Cohen uses the term *budget* in referring to the client's bottom line. From his perspective as a mediator, he says:

> Lawyers need to know what their budget is, as realistically as possible. Because until they understand what their budget is, they can't set a goal for this event [i.e., the mediation]. And without doing that they can't possibly plan how much to give up on each of the iterations. If you don't know how much money you have in your pocket to start with, how do you know how much to add to the initial offer each time? You're not sure when you're going to run out. What are you going to do? Reach in all of a sudden and say, "Oh my God, I don't have any more"?

Christopher Carroll (New York and New Jersey) has represented many clients in mediation of insurance coverage disputes and other business matters. He refers to the client's bottom line as the *endgame*.

"I am a lawyer that really would like to know the endgame," Carroll says. "I know a lot of clients aren't comfortable with giving their counsel the endgame, because their thought process is that we'll work a little harder if we don't know. I am of the exact opposite mind-set."

Carroll explains his need to know the client's endgame this way: "Every move that you are making in negotiation is intended to get you to that point. So for me, knowing where I need to get is as important as knowing how I am going to get there, and the earlier I can find that out, the better."

(b) The reasons why a true bottom line may be unobtainable by counsel

From his experience as inside counsel, John DeGroote cautions that it can be a mistake to take as gospel what the client (meaning here a business executive within a corporation) says about the bottom line. Some clients, he says, prefer to give a "false bottom" to their own outside lawyer. For example, the client might tell the lawyer, "I'll never pay more than $10,000 in this case" when in reality, the client is willing to pay up to $15,000.

DeGroote does not believe in taking this approach himself, but he says some businesspeople "do that as a management technique with their outside counsel, so that their outside counsel are working toward that lower number."

An already strong attorney–client relationship may increase your chances of getting an accurate reading on the bottom line. It is useful to "have a good understanding with your client built up over time through this case, or otherwise, so that your client is more likely to be straight with you," DeGroote says.

On some occasions, Christopher Carroll has been direct in explaining to a client exactly why it is important for him to understand the client's endgame. He agrees with DeGroote that the trust level is key.

"You need to earn their trust and earn their respect," Carroll says. "Really show them that you are committed to them, that you're committed to the process, that you're in it as much as they're in it, that this is your money as much as their money." Asking directly to be told the endgame does not guarantee that a client will tell you, but Carroll would rather try "than not give it a shot at all."

Getting an accurate fix on your clients' endgame—"what their stopping point is"—may typically be a challenge in dealing with new clients, the late Andrew Berry once noted. Given the lack of a previously established relationship, such clients are perhaps especially likely to give you a bottom line that is "some distance away from their real stopping-point."

Lack of candor on the bottom line can get even more complicated in situations where several people participate in a mediation session on behalf of a corporation. DeGroote warns of the possibility that even one of your corporate attendees may have been given a false bottom line.

> "I have also seen mediations where a client representative is given a certain amount of authority, and an in-house counsel is privately given a little more authority—or perhaps vice versa," DeGroote says. "So the one on the frontline driving the communications in the mediation is working toward a hard number, not realizing that there is a fallback position held by somebody else."

(c) The importance of flexibility in the bottom line

When you do get a bottom line number from your client, you have something to plug in for negotiation-planning purposes. However, a downside is that the existence of such a number—if too inflexible—may become an impediment to actual settlement during the mediation session.

John DeGroote's concern about precise bottom lines is that they can take on a life of their own. Once articulated, a maximum dollar amount for a defendant may become a line in the sand, which can prevent further compromise even if new factors emerge that might warrant it. For that reason—while acknowledging that his viewpoint may be controversial—he is "a big believer in *not* having [the] client articulate a bottom line prior to mediation." DeGroote gives this hypothetical illustrating the problem, before moving to his proposed solution:

> I know many clients like to sit in a conference room discussing an upcoming mediation and say, "You know, I will never pay more than $10,000 in this case." So all of a sudden there is a line in the sand. And then the vice president for claims, say, goes off to the mediation, with the CEO and COO back in the home office. And in the mediation session, new facts, new circumstances, new situations are revealed that indicate that a result of $15,000 might be an excellent

> result. I mean, the reason that you have a mediation is because it helps you to arrive at a better understanding of the case.
>
> It's not fair to have the vice president of claims sit there and have a $10,000 cap on what he or she can offer, and all of a sudden the plaintiff reveals the "photo of the CEO at spring break"—which is a shorthand way of saying some smoking-gun document or other matter that you don't ever want to have published. In that kind of situation, I guarantee the vice president of claims, if they pay $15,000, is going to go back to the home office, and somebody is going to question his or her judgment even though that higher figure is fully justified.

A more responsible and effective approach, in DeGroote's view, is to sit down before mediation with a group of company executives that includes the real decision makers, and use decision trees or other techniques to arrive at a consensus on the approximate value or general range of values of the case for settlement purposes. Then make sure the person who will serve as corporate representative at the session is granted leeway to make decisions based on her best judgment regarding what emerges during the mediation. DeGroote says:

> I think everybody needs to understand *generally* where the client's perspective on the case is, so that you have a *general* view of what the case is worth, and what the client's willing to pay. But I don't like bright lines among people who are not going to be at the mediation. It sort of takes away a lot of the reasons for having the mediation. The information mix is going to change the instant the mediation starts. That's why the bright line doesn't do anybody any good.

DeGroote acknowledges that under no circumstances is a corporate representative likely to have unlimited authority to settle above the general range agreed on before the session. He also acknowledges that sometimes a corporation will simply insist on giving a specific dollar cap, even if the executives do not reveal this number to you as outside counsel.

If there is a specific number, DeGroote suggests making sure there is an advance arrangement whereby the corporate representative can easily phone a higher-up during the session if a settlement figure that exceeds the amount of the representative's authority has become justified.

That is the approach Tracey Salmon-Smith used to take when she worked as inside counsel in mediations where her employer (a large brokerage firm) was the defendant in securities disputes. Settlement authority was typically given in the form of a specific number, not a range. But she recalls that this number could be subject to later change if circumstances warranted:

> If during the course of the mediation something comes up that's unexpected that may drive that number higher, I would first obtain approval from the appropriate person in the legal department. Then we would have to contact another businessperson—usually the regional director—in order to get the additional authority.
>
> I usually tried to make a point, ahead of time, of figuring out where everyone is who I might need to contact—whether they are only going to be reachable by cell phone, by BlackBerry, or whatever—to make sure that they know that we are doing this mediation and that at some point we may need to speak in the afternoon. Just keep them on standby, to at least expect that we may call.

Some lawyers prefer to have their clients express a bottom line to them as a specific number rather than a range. Christopher Carroll is an example. In his view, ranges do not make much sense, because when a defendant gives a range, in effect only the highest number in the range really counts as the endgame (even though a lower number would obviously be preferred). Likewise for a plaintiff, only the lowest number is really operative as that client's endgame.

However, Carroll agrees strongly on the importance of flexibility in a preplanned bottom line to account for new information or perspectives during the mediation session:

If there is a rigidity going in, you're less likely to get to a settlement. Flexibility means, "Maybe I haven't seen everything right. Maybe there is something that I missed. Maybe there is something that I didn't know, and that will change or alter or somehow adjust my evaluation." In that respect, I often am hopeful that the client doesn't necessarily have a locked-in bottom line. You do want some flexibility.

(d) The role of projected attorneys' fees in bottom line discussions

In pure economic theory, a defendant should be willing to settle at mediation for an amount consisting of the financial value he has calculated for the case, plus the transaction costs (mostly attorneys' fees) that he would have to pay if the case went to trial. But in the real world, "nobody is excited to turn over those transaction costs to the other side," John DeGroote observes (echoing many lawyers' experience).

As noted earlier in this chapter in the context of case evaluations, DeGroote prefers not to bring up attorneys' fees too early in his discussions with company executives before a mediation session, because businesspeople often resent and resist the concept of having to pay all or part of their projected attorneys' fees as part of a mediation settlement.

For the same reason, DeGroote prefers not to focus on projected attorneys' fees when discussing the client's endgame in presession planning. Instead, he sees the projected attorneys' fees as a figure that is often useful at a much later stage. During the caucusing phase at the mediation session, if both parties have reached their bottom lines—and there is (as often occurs) a gap between them—"the transaction costs very often are used as the way to get parties to bridge the gap." DeGroote will also bring up attorneys' fees during presession discussions about a settlement authority limit, "if people are trying to get sticky with just the underlying case value."

(4) Discuss possible creative options for settlement

"If you have effectively understood what you're trying to accomplish and what the other side's trying to accomplish," says John Bickerman (in Bickerman et al., 2003, p.7), "[mediation prep] is an excellent opportunity for you to sit down with your client and explore some creative solutions, to brainstorm, and brainstorm with your client ideas that you might be able to share during the mediation process."

As discussed earlier in this chapter, creative, interest-based possibilities for settlement are frequently limited in the context of civil court litigation and similar legal disputes, but they do sometimes exist. This topic of creative settlements will also be raised further in Step Ten.

Meanwhile, here is some advice on preparing for the possibility from Larry Watson (a full-time mediator) and Laura Kennedy (a commercial litigator):

- "Reconciliation offers far more choices [than litigation] to craft a customized settlement of the conflict that can look forward to the future relationship as well as dealing with past offenses. Thinking through and developing contingent plans to utilize these options in advance, doing feasibility research on settlement alternatives before the mediation starts, can dramatically increase the potential for a successful outcome. Structured annuities, future work, letters of apology, product discount programs, bartered services, use of equipment, joint undertakings to raise settlement dollars, introductions and bid invitations—the realm of possible settlement tools is limited only by . . . the creativity of the mediator, the parties and counsel. That creativity should never be chained with fixed dollar concepts." (Watson, 2002, p.3)
- "Ask your client not to wait until the mediation to consider settlement scenarios, but to creatively think about potential solutions well in advance of the mediation. Push your client to raise the level, to reach out to others within the organization and think outside the box. . . . Identify the settlement 'currency.' It is not just the amount of money, but the timing and characterization of it. Think about tax consequences—both positive and negative. Ask your

client to consider whether there are viable alternatives to money. For example, is future busi-ness worthy of consideration? What motivates the claim or defense? Is there a personal offense? Is business reputation at stake? Are there options that address those concerns—an apology, a press release, confidentiality?" (Kennedy, 2010, pp.157–158)

- "A good method for getting clients off 'bottom line' thinking is to explore what constructive steps must be taken to resolve the damage done. Rather than focus a pre-mediation client on dollar amounts, focus instead on how the dollars would be used to remedy the damage done. Define the interests that have been directly impacted by the dispute and look at the widest range of possibilities for accommodating those interests." (Watson, 2002, p.3)

(5) Agree on a plan for movement

"[M]ost negotiators never get beyond case analysis to develop any plan for movement during the negotiation," writes J. Anderson Little (2007, p.76). Instead of doing such planning in advance, at the mediation session "negotiators react reflexively to the other side's movement by walking way, demanding that the other side bid against themselves, and throwing low- and high-ball proposals. More often than not, they react in ways that impede the progress of negotiation and make settlement impossible" (p.62).

To maximize the probability of a positive outcome at the session, it is not enough to have figured out your side's planned starting-point and goals before you walk into the room. You also need to have some kind of plan for how you will move along the way.

This section will start with advice on planning movement from Prof. Charles Craver and add some thoughts from John Bickerman. Then we will look in depth at an unusual suggestion from Little. Under his proposed approach, you can map out your entire series of moves in advance without knowing what your opponent's offers along the way will be.

(a) Craver: Design alternate routes to your destination

"Carefully plan your desired methodology as if you were choreographing the movement from your opening offer to your desired objective," Craver advises (2011, p.11). Of course, you face limits on what you can know in advance. For example, at the session, an opponent may make an opening offer that is more generous that you anticipated, or at some later point your adversary my make an unexpectedly large concession. For that reason, Craver believes it is not enough to plan a single course of movement. Rather, you need to think about the various types of scenarios that may develop, and plan how you would move under those changed circumstances.[6]

"Imagine a road map with various routes from opening position to ultimate objective," Craver writes. "You must be prepared to change routes in response to opponent tactics."

Your series of offers moving closer to your opponent's position—as your opponent makes offers moving closer to yours—forms what Craver calls a concession pattern. In thinking out your concession pattern in advance, "[y]ou may use *bracketing* to keep [your] own goal between current positions of the parties, making equal concessions until you end up in [the] area you hoped to achieve" (p.18).

As with the proverb that all roads lead to Rome, the various offer-and-concession routes you plan for the mediation will all lead to your final offer (unless your opponent accepts one of the offers you make before reaching your end point). Your planned final offer should be "sufficiently tempting to

6. Representing his clients in mediation, Thomas Dye applies the multiple-scenario concept to include his own initial offer—depending not just on his opponent's first move (if made yet) but on his assessment of his adversary. He may go so far as to consider in advance making several different initial offers—fair, moderately unreasonable, or completely unreasonable. "I would have a strategy figured out for why I am going to choose one of those three," Dye says. For example, "if at the mediation session I sense fear in the other side at going to trial, then I'm going to start with a more unreasonable opening offer, because I know I'm likely to get a better result than if I was more reasonable in my opening offer." On the other hand, "if I know that they are ready to walk out, and if I'm afraid of going to trial because of what's going to come out and I think we're going to lose, I would be more reasonable in my opening offer. But I would have all that planned out."

risk-averse opponents vis-a-vis [the] consequence of non-settlements that opponents will be afraid to reject the proposed terms" (p.11).

John Bickerman agrees with Craver that "[u]nderstanding how to make concessions in a mediation, and having a plan of how to do that, is very important" (Bickerman et al, 2003, p.7). In that context, he stresses an incremental approach: "Don't get there all at once. Research shows that, if you make too big a concession and close too fast, you're not going to get a deal. So rather than closing too fast, think of how you're going to parcel out your concessions over time to signal the other side where your bottom line is" (p.16).

In addition to dollar figures, the "parceling" approach also may apply to any interest-based, creative ideas for resolution you may have developed in your brainstorming before the session. "One doesn't come out and put the best ideas on the table right away," Bickerman says (p.7).

(b) Little: Consider a plan for movement that does not depend on your opponent's series of offers

"Many negotiators have never thought of developing a plan and need help with the concept of a plan itself," J. Anderson Little observes (2007, p.80). In an unusual twist, he advises negotiators to "develop a plan that *does not depend on the other side's proposals*" (p.83, italics added).

Little's premise is the widely accepted concept that numbers are a major form of communication in the negotiating process. In his view, when parties merely react to their opponent's numbers rather than proceeding according to their own plan, the result can be an emotion-based series of moves that may easily derail the mediation process. For more on the topic of communication through numbers—and a hypothetical illustrating how reactivity can scuttle a negotiation—read Sidebar 10-12: "How Parties Can (Mis)communicate Through Numbers."

To explain what he means by a plan that does not depend on your opponent's proposals, Little offers a couple of possible options. Here is my description of the hypothetical he uses to illustrate the option he prefers (pp.80–82):

A plaintiff has arrived at the conclusion that its highest evaluation of the case in dispute is $100,000, and it will walk away from the mediation rather than accept any settlement below $50,000.

Step 1 in constructing the negotiating plan is to determine what Little calls the "available range for negotiations," or more simply put, "negotiating range." In Little's hypothetical, the negotiating range is $50,000, calculated by subtracting the plaintiff's walk-away number from its highest evaluation of the case.

Step 2 is to decide how many negotiating moves to plug in for purposes of the plan. In his hypothetical plan, Little uses a total of 16, including both the highest valuation and the walk-away number. He notes that there is no magic in the number of moves he chose for his hypothetical; a planner is free to choose any number that seems suitable for a particular negotiation.

In Step 3, Little divides the available negotiating range by half of the planned total number of moves. In the hypothetical, this means dividing $50,000 by 8, resulting in equal increments of $6,250.

Step 4 is to create a column in which numbers representing those increments are listed in descending order below the highest evaluation, stopping at a number two increments above the walk-away number. Here, this results in the following list: $100,000, $93,750, $87,500, $81,250, $75,000, $68,750, and $62,500.

The remaining gap between your walk-away point and the number two increments above it is your remaining negotiating range. For Step 5, divide that remaining negotiating range by the other half of the planned total number of moves. In Little's hypothetical, the remaining negotiating range is $12,500, and half of the planned total number of moves is 8, resulting in equal increments of $1,562. If negotiations get this far in mediation, the shift to smaller increments will signal to the party that you are getting close to your walk-away number.

Step 6 is to list the numbers related to these increments directly beneath your previous column. In this hypothetical, that means $60,938, $58,356, $56,508, $55,242, $53,680, $52,118, $50,546, and $50,000. So now you have a single column of descending numbers, from your highest valuation to your walk-away number.

Applying your plan at the session

Remember, in the example we are using, you are in the shoes of the plaintiff. At the mediation session, your first move is your demand, which according to Little's recommendations should be your highest evaluation of your case—in this hypothetical, $100,000. After private caucuses, the defendant eventually will respond with a counteroffer.

In Little's model, regardless of the amount of the defendant's counteroffer, your second move is the next number in your descending list—in this hypothetical, $93,750. You follow the same pattern in response to each successive move by the defendant. In this way, you are not actually moving in reaction to whatever number the defendant throws out; you are proceeding according to your own plan.

As the defendant continues to offer numbers in response to yours, you will be able to perceive whether the defendant is likely to end up in a range that will allow the parties to reach a settlement. If the defendant accepts one of your offers before you reach your walk-away number, you have finished ahead of the game. At the other extreme, if the defendant's offers continue to be so unrealistically low that settlement is clearly unachievable at the mediation session, you can always stop negotiating at some point rather than keep proceeding with a sequence that would eventually reveal your walk-away number.

A third possibility is that you will perceive that although there will ultimately be a gap between your walk-away number and the defendant's likely final offer, it will probably be narrow enough that it will be worthwhile for you and the defendant to stretch beyond your walk-away numbers and bridge the gap in order to settle the case.

Under Little's approach, a defendant can construct a negotiation plan using exactly the same approach. The most obvious difference is that in the defendant's format, the first number would be the smallest in the column, and the last number (the walk-away) would be the largest.

In line with the discussion of opening numbers (*see* Substep 7.4B(2)), the defendant would need to choose a starting number (i.e., its counteroffer to the plaintiff's demand) that can be objectively justified according to defensible criteria—not so outrageously low as to appear to communicate that settlement within a reasonable range will be impossible.

Customizing mediation plans

As noted previously, Little makes it clear that his discussion of designing a mediation plan is intended to explain the principles rather than to impose one particular format. The most obvious variation would result from changing the number of planned moves, but other possibilities clearly present themselves. For example, instead of a two-phase plan, where the increments in the second phase are smaller than in the first, one might try a three-phase plan.

Pros and cons of this type of plan for movement

Among Little's listed advantages to this type of format (p.82) are that it:

- Creates a "sense of movement" while effectively concealing the walk-away number until the smaller increments (Step 5) kick in.
- Provides a clear signal that the party is reaching the end of its range when the smaller increments *do* kick in—a useful form of communication by numbers.
- Allows a party to proceed through the negotiations in an efficient manner while avoiding "the many agonizing discussions that occur" when a party tries to "create proposals solely in reaction to the other's movement."

Little does not list any disadvantages for using plans for movement rather than waiting until the mediation session and deciding one-by-one on numbers in reaction to each individual proposal that the other side actually makes during the course of the negotiation. One possible critique might be that when the parties are simply following their own predetermined plans for movement rather than truly responding to their opponents' offers, they are not engaging in a dialogue through numbers—they are just each following a script.

However, even in following their own scripts, the parties are at least communicating their intentions as the moves progress. And if following their plans for movement allows the parties to advance to their walk-away ranges, it might be said that at that point the true negotiation can begin in earnest.

Another possible objection might arise from the advice of Prof. Craver (*see* Substep 7.4B(2)) and other experienced players that it is important to accompany your early offers with a rationale to justify your number. Generating numbers in a plan for movement of the type Little recommends does not require rationales. However, once you have generated the numbers, you can arrive at rationales to support the first few numbers in the series on an ex post facto basis. In some instances, providing a reasonable rationale for your first two or three offers might spur you to modify those numbers slightly.

In the absence of empirical data one way or the other, the lengthy discussion just concluded is for informational purposes rather than implying an endorsement. As far as I know, no one has tried experimental simulations to test the planning format described by Little against other approaches. It would be very interesting to do so.

7.5 Strategize on how best to show the strength of your client's case during the opening session.

Now that you and your client together have evaluated your case and agreed on a negotiation plan, you are in a good position to make some firm decisions as to how best to convey your strengths to your opponent and the mediator at the upcoming session. If the mediation participants have followed the steps recommended in this book, the question of whether to include presentations from each side in a joint opening session has already been decided earlier in the process. If no such decision was made, you and your client will need to decide as part of your session preparations now. For a discussion of the various considerations and possibilities, see Step Eight.

If you have decided in favor of a presentation, you will need to agree on how best to do it, with regard to both form and content. For example, on content, what should be your major themes? What are the most important points to get across? On form, will you as counsel make the entire presentation yourself, or will the client undertake part or all of it? In cases where the stakes and issues support it, should an expert assist in presenting some special aspect of liability or damages?

On the topic of damages, Gilda Turitz (San Francisco, CA) writes (2010, p.13):

> Counsel should consider how much of the company's damages analysis they want to share with the opposing party in mediation. Counsel should also consider how to best present this information. Charts and graphs can readily be prepared on common computer programs without much expense and can have a powerful impact. For example, these figures may be overlaid with timelines and other factual information to demonstrate a failure to mitigate by the opposing party or to justify the corporation's actions that had an economic impact.

7.6 Finalize a mediation team (as applicable).

The topic of mediation teams is covered in Substep 6.2 and Sidebar 6-6: "A Mediator's Advice on Assembling Your Mediation Team."

7.7 Encourage a productive attitude for negotiations.

Many mediators lament that too often, parties come into mediation with inflated expectations of what kind of "victory" they can achieve through the process. At the other end of the spectrum, some parties arrive at a session believing the whole thing is a waste of their time.

Obviously, both of these attitudes are detrimental to the prospect of attaining a settlement through mediation. For that reason, it is essential for you to encourage your client to approach the upcoming session in a productive way. To do this, (a) convey a sense of realism—not pessimism—to your client, (b) dampen unrealistic expectations and encourage a mind-set of flexibility, and (c) give a little pep talk as needed to help put clients in a proper mind to settle.

A. Convey a sense of realism—not pessimism—to your client

"Many lawyers preface a mediation experience with their clients with the statement, 'This isn't going to get us anywhere, this is not likely to work,'" observes Walter Stuart. "I think you are far better off telling your clients that many cases, if not a majority, settle through mediation. I would make sure that my client understands that the process is important, and that while he or she might be disappointed, he or she should be prepared to make a deal, and should enter into negotiations with an open mind and in good faith."

B. Dampen unrealistic expectations and encourage a mind-set of flexibility

The importance of adjusting expectations and encouraging flexibility is a point that comes up time after time from experienced mediation players. The following bullet points provide a sample:

- "Make sure the client's attitude is properly adjusted to accept compromise. If the client has developed unrealistic expectations, work on getting them adjusted downward. I see cases in which one party comes into the mediation thinking that the purpose of mediation is to obtain victory and to vanquish the opponent. Those are difficult mediations." *—Timothy Corcoran (Tampa; 2007, § 3.d.i.1.b)*
- "[O]ftentimes clients' expectations about the outcome of the dispute may be somewhat inflated, maybe inadvertently from the lawyer, maybe from what they've read in the paper about other judgments, from what they've seen on TV. So clients sometimes may not have realistic expectations about the

process of litigation. . . . In preparing for mediation, it's important to address those expectations and explain to the client what is possible to achieve in the mediation. Because it's probably going to be different than what might happen in the litigation." —*Bruce Meyerson (Phoenix; Bickerman et al., 2003, p.5)*

- "Clients can't have an expectation as a plaintiff they are going to walk away with some gigantic amount, you know? That's TV. What you don't want is for clients to have set in their mind, 'It's this number or nothing,' because they miss out on potentially a lot." —*Nate Cade (Milwaukee)*
- "If defendants go into a mediation session saying, 'I'm not paying a dime,' the case is not going to settle in mediation. I don't care how good you are as a mediator. If the client's attitude is 'I'm going to get my day in court and I don't care—I didn't do anything wrong,' that's not the right attitude. It's going to be a frustrating day for the mediator, and everyone is going to leave unhappy. If the client is not on the right page, you're wasting your time." —*Paul Sandars (Roseland, NJ)*
- "[D]iscussions about settlement options can be counterproductive if they leave a party with inflexible and unmanageable expectations about settlement outcomes that turn out to be unrealistic. Throughout the representation of a client, and especially in the context of preparation for mediation or another negotiation session, counsel should avoid unintentionally leading their clients to unrealistic expectations, through what may seem like ordinary, zealous representation." —*ABA Section of Dispute Resolution Task Force on Improving Mediation Quality (2008a, p.11)*

See also Sidebar 7-9: "Don't Let Insecurity Keep You From Preparing Your Client to Compromise."

(1) Built-in tension with your role as advocate

As a lawyer, your challenge in trying to temper unrealistic expectations on your client's part presages a difficult balancing act you may have to perform during the mediation session itself: encouraging realism in your role as counselor without making the client think you're weak in your role as advocate. J. Anderson Little writes of this in the context of plaintiffs (2007, p.207):

> The dilemma that plaintiffs' lawyers face is very interesting. They work hard to bring the client's expectations into a realistic framework. However, if they do so too strenuously, the plaintiff begins to wonder whether the lawyer is "really on my side." In other words, plaintiffs' lawyers walk a fine line between educating and working with a client to develop realistic expectations and losing the confidence of their clients.

In many cases, this same type of dilemma is also faced by lawyers on the defense side. For more on the counselor/advocate role dilemma, read Sidebar 7-6: "The 'Two Eds' of Mediation."

C. Give a little pep talk as needed to help put clients in a proper mind to settle

Every coach knows the value of a pep talk before the game. In mediation, consider giving your client a pep talk at some point in advance of the session—maybe just beforehand, or as part of your earlier prep, if your client's attitude seems to warrant it.

The content of your pep talk will depend on all the circumstances, including the particulars of the dispute and the client's previous familiarity with the mediation process. Maralee Eriksen (Sacramento, CA) describes giving her client something like a pep talk in Sidebar 7-10: "The Value of a Heart-to-Heart." Edna Epstein (Chicago) offers this sample of the type of pep talk she might give to a client who is entering her first mediation:

> Look, this is not litigation. It isn't "winner take all." It's your ability and the other side's ability to cut a deal together in an environment where you can air what the concerns are, without fear, and without any risk.

You've got a problem we've got to solve here, and litigation is long and costly—and it's very, very rare that people get what they want out of it. The only thing that's for sure is I'm going to get very rich from it as your lawyer.

You know if you go in front of the judge you can win it all or you can lose it all. And even if you win it all, it can be a Pyrrhic victory.

Do you want this resolved? This is going to give you an opportunity to talk directly to your adversary and tell your adversary what you need and what you want—but also to find out what your adversary needs and wants. This is your opportunity to come to closure with the other side—not through me, not through the lawyers, not through the mediator. If you hear each other, maybe you two can come up with a solution that the lawyers won't necessarily be able to do for you, and certainly no judge can do for you.

SIDEBAR 7-1

Checklist of Questions for Client

By Bennett G. Picker

This checklist of "questions to review with the client in preparing for a mediation" is one of many bullet-point lists in Bennett Picker's succinct and useful book Mediation Practice Guide: A Handbook for Resolving Business Disputes *(2003, pp.84–87). Since the list is oriented toward business disputes, some questions do not necessarily apply to other types of cases. Also, some questions might already have been dealt with earlier in the mediation process than Step Seven.*

- What was the sequence of events—facts?
- What business interests are involved in this dispute?
- How do you feel about this dispute? How does the other side feel about the dispute?
- What do you want/need?
- What is most important?
- What is least important?
- What do you believe are the strengths and weaknesses of your case?
- What do you believe are the strengths and weaknesses of your opponent's case?
- What alternatives would you consider if agreement cannot be reached?
- What is the most attractive alternative?
- What is the least attractive alternative?
- How would you prioritize the alternatives?
- What are your bottom-line monetary recovery needs?
- What are your settlement expectations?
- What compromises will you consider to reach a negotiated agreement?

- What are you unwilling to compromise under any circumstances?
- What do you believe are the opposing party's interests, goals and objectives in the dispute?
- Can you prioritize the opposing party's interests?
- What is the opposing party's interest in a negotiated settlement?
- Are you interested in privacy or do you prefer a public forum?
- Are you interested in a speedy resolution?
- Do you have an interest in preserving a continuing relationship with the opposing party?
- Do you have any contracts or relationships with the opposing party that are not the subject of this dispute?
- What are the barriers to settlement?
- Do you believe that emotions or hostilities will be a barrier to settlement?
- Who are the decision makers for the other side?
- How would you describe the personalities of the other side's decision makers?
- Are there any other potential parties with an interest, who, if notified, would increase the likelihood of serious negotiations taking place?
- Who should be participating directly in the presentation of the case? The negotiations?
- What particular concerns do you have about mediating this dispute?

SIDEBAR 7-2

Using Mediation Prep to Connect With Your Client

By John Bates Jr.

In an article titled "Mediation: An Effective Way to Connect With Clients" (2009), John Bates (San Francisco) discusses how lawyers can use the mediation process as an opportunity to "create a lasting bond" that will strengthen your lawyer–client relationship. This excerpt (pp.62–63) focuses on preparation in advance of the mediation session.

Most legal professionals think of mediation merely as a process to settle cases, but it also presents incredible marketing opportunities. The process allows you to work collaboratively with your client and to showcase your skills for preparation, advocacy, and negotiation. Managed properly, mediation can solidify your relationship with your client and help you to develop future business. . . .

Most clients like to be involved, and want to have input, in getting ready for and participating in the mediation session. By seeking your client's collaboration, not only will you gain the client's appreciation but you will also frequently gain invaluable insights from him or her. If nothing else, having relayed the information and knowing that it has been received will raise your client's confidence in you. Solicit ideas from your client and get his or her reaction to your plan to manage the process. This back-and-forth will unify you as a team and give your client tremendous comfort. He or she will learn just how important you are to achieving a satisfactory result. At the very least, you should establish with your client the strategy (goals) and the tactics (approach) for the mediation. Keep in mind that your client may well have more experience in negotiations than you do, so you will want to acknowledge his or her skill and take full advantage of it.

During these discussions, remind your client that what you need to do to maximize your leverage at the negotiating table is far less than what you would have to do to win at trial. You and your client must decide what you will need for the mediation and then, if the matter does not settle, what you need to do to get ready for trial. Equipped with a budget, you can demonstrate to your client how you are using mediation as a cost-effective way to manage the litigation. If the case does not settle, no doubt your client will blame the other side, enabling you to do whatever is necessary to win at trial.

SIDEBAR 7-3

Prepping Business Executives for Mediation

John DeGroote (interview)

During his years as Chief Litigation Counsel at a global consulting firm, John DeGroote (Dallas) participated in mediation of more than a few big-ticket cases. In that capacity, he often prepped the executives of the firm to serve as corporate representative at the mediation session. DeGroote describes here how he approaches the task.[7]

Before the mediation, I walk through the case with my business client, the positives and the negatives. I have a good sense of where they want to go, what they want to spend, and the risks they want to assume.

Then I explain the mediation process. I explain the role of the outside counsel, my role, and their role. I tell them how many mediations I have done. I tell them there will be an uncomfortable opening statement, and there will be a whole lot of downtime where it looks really, really unproductive. Then 10 minutes before the mediation is supposed to end, things will get very,

7. For a lengthier discussion of prepping business executives, read Sidebar 7-11: "Prepping Your Business Team."

very productive. The case will either settle or not, based on the last few moves.

I tell the executive, "So now you know more about what it's going to be like. It is unlike anything you've ever seen. You are going to be fantastically upset at the inefficiency of the process. But understand that's a micro view. By midafternoon you are going to think to yourself, 'I wasted an entire day!' But this is a dance, and the dance has to play out. So the day will look inefficient, but if you resolve the matter by killing one day, that's a whole lot better than resolving the matter over the next four years with a little bit here and there."

Now that I've been through mediation with a lot of my senior execs, I say to them, "Call your buddy so-and-so who has been through this. They will tell you it is the weirdest process in the world. Our people have been through it a lot. Just follow my lead and you will be in good shape."

I tell them, "The big problem is that mediation looks easy and it's really not. It's not intuitive. It's not easy. You can't shortcut the process. So follow my lead."

Set the executive's expectations that this is going to last well into the night, and it's a bizarre process, but ultimately it's more efficient than the alternative. It's just going to take a while.

SIDEBAR 7-4

Telling Clients How Mediation Sessions Work

Walter B. Stuart (interview)

Although the clients of Walter Stuart (New York) tend to be large companies, he never takes for granted that the client representative is familiar with the mediation process. Here Stuart talks more about this and paraphrases how he brings clients up to speed on how sessions work.

While lawyers go to mediation all the time, clients don't. Frequently for the client, it's a whole new experience. So I really try and take time to explain how mediation works: what they can expect; why I'm going to be making a presentation; why the other side is likely to say what it will say; the structure of it.

I tell clients, "You need to set aside all day" if that's the case. "We'll start off, and the other side will start off. We'll talk for 20 or 30 minutes, and the other side will respond. Then the mediator is likely to say something, and then we'll break into separate groups. You probably won't come into direct contact with the other side throughout the rest of the day. The mediator will meet with the plaintiffs and say, 'Okay, I need a number—I need a settlement number from you.' And there is some discussion around that before the number goes back to the other side.

"The defendant, while that's going on, will have some serious downtime—there won't be much to do except to wait for the number." I always warn clients of that. "Then the mediator comes out and says for example, 'Well, here is the number: $20 million. What's your reaction?' At that point, the client has got to be ready. He's got to be doing nothing else and ready to tune in to this issue. When he's needed, and when the lawyers are needed, they're really needed. They can't dally."

So I talk to clients a little bit about the structure of the session. I also tell them that while the mediation is expected to end at 5:00 or so, it's not unusual for these things to go late into the evening. They should be well rested the day before, and they should make no plans for that night. Because frequently, successful mediations resolve after hours.

The other thing I tell clients is: "Don't despair during this process." They should expect in the early stages numbers that are very, very far apart—and that the most movement is likely to occur toward the end of the mediation.

SIDEBAR 7-5

Prepping on "Special Aspects" of the Mediation Structure

Dwight Golann (CLE panel discussion)

In this excerpt from a CLE panel discussion on mediation sponsored by the ABA Section of Dispute Resolution and the ABA Center for Continuing Legal Education (Bickerman et al., 2003, p.9), law professor and mediator Dwight Golann (Boston) talks about the importance of two items of client prep in advance of a mediation session: the possibility of arranging a subtle lawyer–client signal, and a critical time to call for a break.

What you should cover [in presession client prep]? Apart from your regular negotiation goals, what you intend, there are some special aspects of the structure. I would warn a client that many mediators, like me, will ask a client if he or she wants to say anything, even if the lawyer has given the presentation in the opening session. And the lawyer and client should talk out what, if anything, the client should say while the other side is in the room. They should be aware that many mediators view the opening session as a time to exchange information. And the good news is you can find out things that you need to know about settlement; but the bad news is somebody may ask you a question. Again, if you want the client to look to you, the lawyer, before answering, better have a signal system set up.

Even when you're not in front of the other side, when you're in caucus with the mediator, there are two levels of caucusing. Because the mediator is not on your team, there'll be a period of time in the caucus. But often, before you formulate your next move, your concession, or your offer, it's perfectly reasonable for you, the lawyer, to confer with the client while the mediator's outside the room. And you should explain to the client that that should happen before the client starts explaining their bottom line in front of the mediator. I mean, you can reveal the bottom line, but that should be a choice you make. It shouldn't be something blurted out by the client who thinks that the mediator's a therapist, because they're not.

SIDEBAR 7-6

The "Two Eds" of Mediation

Edward M. Mullins (interview)

As a lawyer in a mediation session, you must play two distinct, contradictory roles that inevitably create some degree of tension in the client's mind. Wearing your advocate hat, you forcefully convey the strengths of your client's case (and the weaknesses of your opponent's) to your opponents and the mediator. But then, wearing your settlement hat, you must privately point out to your client the weaknesses in your case and the strengths of your opponent's position. There is always a danger that your client will wonder at some point whether you are really "on his side" or sufficiently aggressive as a litigator.

Edward Mullins (Miami) is very aware of this built-in danger. He has learned to deal with it by specifically addressing the issue when he prepares his clients for a mediation session—especially with clients who have not been through the process before. He talks here about the problem and his prepping approach.

You need to be up-front with the client. I say, "Okay, look. I want to tell you there are two 'Eds' going into this mediation session—the Ed that is going to be the advocate, and the Ed that's going to be your counselor. In the opening session, I am going to tell the other side we are going to win and they don't have a chance. When you listen to this, remember I'm sending a message to the other side and to educate the mediator. It's not a message to you alone, although you should consider all of the factors so you make the right decision. All I told you before about why you need to think about settling this case still holds. I haven't backed off of that. But I also want you to remember when we are in caucus alone and thinking about the other side's offer that all the reasons I told you and the other side that we are going to win, still hold true as well. Remember there are many reasons why you might consider settling today, including the aggravation of having a case pending. In short, you have to remember in the opening session my job is to tell the other side the weaknesses in their case and to educate the mediator; their lawyer might even have told them some of these things. In caucus, my job is to counsel you on why there may be reasons to settle, maybe even beyond the merits. But don't think I don't believe in your case or, to the contrary, I don't think you should not settle if you can get a great deal, because both are true."

You have to have that speech with the client. Because what happens is, you go into this opening session, and you go through this whole spiel about how you are definitely going to win—and the client starts believing it to such an extent [as to] forget the other reasons that settlement might be preferable—including nuisance or even the ability to craft an agreement better than the client could get in trial [on] his or her best day in court. Then you go into caucus, and the plaintiffs come back with their first offer. You say to your client, "Okay, now we need to come in at blank dollars" or "We need to think about an innovative way to structure this deal." And they'll look at you and say, "Wait a minute! Why should we be giving them anything? Why should I settle at all? Didn't I just hear you saying we should win?"

Then you have to say, "Well, I have on my counselor hat now. Remember, I told you, you weren't supposed to get caught up in what I was saying at [the] opening. That was for the other side to know the weaknesses in their case and so we could educate the mediator. Now, I was not bluffing there; we believe it. But that does not mean we should not settle, because a jury could come out the other way. Or we might be able to get a deal today better for you in terms you could not get at trial. All the stuff I told you before about how it would be good to settle is still true. Now we need to go on with the offer." This is always a concern in these mediations, when you're putting on your counselor settlement hat. It is not that you are being duplicitous—you are going to lose credibility if you do bluffing in opening session—you should be forthright and show why you will [win].

Often the mediator, through questions or conveying the other side's thoughts, will show the weaknesses in your case so you can get beyond wearing two hats and positions and start focusing on resolutions.

If you have an in-house counsel who's been to a thousand mediations, they understand your dual roles. But a lot of times you've got a private individual—or in our firm's case, people from foreign countries who have never gone to mediation—and they're just not experienced with it or misunderstand that it is not a court proceeding. They become concerned that you are not the person they thought you were—not this tough litigator as they thought. And it's really not that. The point is, you are switching over to being a counselor, and sometimes they don't realize that they need that role in that situation. It becomes an issue more so when the mediator does not help you out by showing the other side.

But as I said, if you start out with the client in the beginning—before you are in the mediation session—and say, "Okay, this is how this is going to go," you should be all right and can meet the client's expectations.

SIDEBAR 7-7

Probing Liability Risks With Inside Counsel

By Gilda R. Turitz

In this excerpt from an article on how inside and outside counsel can collaborate to maximize results in mediation (2010, p.13), Gilda Turitz (San Francisco) focuses on calculating a defendant client's liability risks as part of preparations for the mediation session.

In preparing for the mediation, collaboration between in-house and outside counsel is essential to realistically assess the risk of prevailing in the prosecution or defense of the claims at issue. In-house counsel should be direct with outside counsel about the type of evaluative report and level of detail the corporation's decision makers will need on the liability issues to make an informed decision about settlement. Some tough questions counsel should discuss include the following:

- What are the chances of prevailing on or defeating summary judgment?
- Will our key witnesses be believed, or are they vulnerable to impeachment on material issues because of

incriminating documents, inconsistent statements, poor demeanor in general or at deposition, or other bad behavior that might adversely impact the fact finder at trial?

- Are the corporation's defenses highly technical and not likely to be favored by a jury?
- Is the adverse party very sympathetic even if his or her liability case against the corporation is weak?

No case is perfect, and a good mediator will probe these areas vigorously, so advance consideration of such questions is essential. Well-thought-out and appropriate responses to these tough questions can only increase the mediator's confidence in the company's position and therefore improve the company's chances for a reasonable settlement as well.

SIDEBAR 7-8

Mediation Objectives Besides Full Settlement

By Lawrence M. Watson Jr.

Of course, full settlement of all claims is in most cases the ideal mediation goal. But in this excerpt from an article (2002, p.4),[8] mediator Larry Watson (Maitland, FL) advises counsel also to discuss with their clients some of the other objectives that can be accomplished through the mediation process.

The first step of any journey is to decide where you want to go. In mediations, the destination of choice is obviously a full settlement of the case. As noted, preparation for that step is initially taken by simply sitting down with the client and mutually agreeing, in concept, on a range of acceptable outcomes to the mediation process without fixating on "bottom line" dollar amount absolutes. There are also, however, other equally important objectives that can be obtained through mediations that do

8. The final paragraph of this sidebar appeared only in an unpublished version of the article.

not include a full settlement of the dispute. Such objectives may include:

A. Partial Settlement of Peripheral Issues.

One reality of litigation is that all claims and all defenses arising out of the same facts and circumstances must be asserted in the same lawsuit. The judicial goal here—to avoid multiplicity of suits—is important to the judicial system and must be met.

An unfortunate consequence of the rule, however, is that many lawsuits end up filled with peripheral arguments that really aren't determinative of the central issues between the parties. This tends to expand, rather than narrow, the focus of the trial and drives up the time and cost of an adjudicated resolution. Mediation can serve to eliminate those peripheral disputes by final or interim partial settlement agreements, stipulations to abate certain portions of the trial, or agreements to informally set certain issues aside pending the resolution of the main claims.

B. Process to Move Toward Final Settlement.

Many times, despite the best efforts to prepare for every contingency in advance, mediations become stalemated because of insufficient information or lack of agreement on what the facilitated negotiations reveal to be core or pivotal issues of fact or law. Rather than calling an impasse and returning to the litigation path, the mediation process can be used to facilitate an agreed "downstream" program defining and scheduling further steps aimed at breaking those logjams and continuing steps toward reconciliation. The variety of downstream programs available is discussed in detail below.

C. Better Understanding of the Opposition's Case.

Plan to listen to everything said during a mediation. Despite the considerable discovery skills developed by practitioners within the trial bar, it is seldom that the opposition's full story—complete with intended themes, nuances and emphasis—is flushed out during discovery. More often than not, discovery will only reluctantly yield what we ask—not what we need to know. More importantly, mediation can provide the critical opportunity to see both sides of the story contrasted against each other. A unique opportunity to hear both sides of the issues presented in their best light side by side which is never available through traditional discovery tools. Finally, with the consent of the party and with the right mediator, a neutral third party's reaction to the issues is also available through mediation.

Obviously, any preparation for mediation should be undertaken with a full understanding of the complete set of goals that are available through the dispute resolution process.

SIDEBAR 7-9

Don't Let Insecurity Keep You From Preparing Your Client to Compromise

Jay M. Cohen (interview)

In his decades as a mediator, Jay Cohen (Winter Park, FL) has seen it all, including countless mistakes made by rookies. Here he talks about how inexperienced lawyers' insecurities can impede them in the performance of the "simple basics" of client prep in advance of a mediation session.

Your inexperienced people are usually insecure around their clients, and that insecurity makes them hang onto their client's view of the case a lot longer than they should. The first time that client's view of the case gets challenged is at the mediation, and the lawyer has to sort of sheepishly admit, "Yeah, well I guess that could happen." Like lose the case. "Of course you can lose the case!" "I thought we had the greatest case!" "Well, I never exactly told you that."

Another example: A guy says to me privately, "I told my client we shouldn't take less than $100,000." I say, "Idiot! What did you do that for? The case isn't worth that much." He says, "I know." You get stuff like that!

Younger, inexperienced lawyers are much more likely to be pushed around by their clients. Even with malleable clients, they don't understand to prepare them for the process of "Listen, this is an opportunity to compromise. Here's why they would, here's why we should."

They don't know enough to do the simple basics. "We're going to make an offer, they're going to hate it. They're going to make an offer back, we're going to hate it. We're going to try to reach some kind of deal like you do in a car lot. It's ugly, but it's the best way to do it. Trust me. And at least we've got a guy who's experienced, who's come to help us as mediator." It's kind of the basics, and people don't do that.

SIDEBAR 7-10

The Value of a Heart-to-Heart

Maralee Eriksen (interview)

In this sidebar, Maralee Eriksen (Sacramento, CA) recounts an actual example of how good communication with her client made a difference while preparing for a mediation session.

It's important to bring your clients to a mediation with an attitude in which they are ready to settle, and not to count on the mediator to convince them to settle. It's part of the attorney's job to get the client prepared for that.

I just had one within the last 90 days—a multimillion-dollar dispute. I didn't think there was any way we were going to get these parties to agree. I just was not sure it was going to happen. But I did my part. I thought, well, I am just going to do my part, to get us to where we can get in there.

I had a very, very serious heart-to-heart with my client. I told her this was the chance to get some certainty back into her life. It's not about who is right or wrong. It's about making a decision about what the rest of her time and life is worth.

What lawyers forget is how emotionally and physically tolling and just how stressing it is on clients to be involved in litigation. It's very, very stressful. I don't think lawyers fully grip what it is to be a witness and how stressful that can be just at a deposition. Until they have been deposed, they don't have any clue. And not many lawyers get deposed, so what opportunity would they have?

But understanding from a human perspective—and then explaining that to the client—can make a difference. You say, "Look, this is a long process. And even if the jury likes you and likes our case, they may award $300,000 and think they are giving you the sun, the moon, and the stars—when what you are really asking for is two or three million dollars."

Clients seem to understand that. They need to understand that there are not going to be many times during a litigation process where they can stop the fees and get some certainty and move on with life and not be a litigant any more. A mediation is an opportunity for them to do that.

SIDEBAR 7-11

Prepping Your Business Team

By Hildy Bowbeer

As Assistant Chief Intellectual Property Counsel at a major corporation, Hildy Bowbeer (St. Paul, MN) manages the company's intellectual property litigation. In this highly abridged excerpt from a book chapter (2011, pp.191–201),[9] Bowbeer outlines the topics that she believes a lawyer should cover in advance with the businesspeople who will participate as part of a company's mediation team. Given the typical nature of intellectual property disputes, this advice is geared to big-ticket cases that justify expending substantial time and resources.[10] Also note that where both inside and outside counsel are involved in a case, much

9. Bowbeer's chapter appears in *ADR Advocacy, Strategies, and Practice for Intellectual Property Cases*, edited by Harrie Samaras and published by the ABA Section of Intellectual Property Law (2011).

10. Even in small cases, however, you should try to cover the same points in a more summary fashion—perhaps spending a few minutes on a topic that might consume many hours of preparation in a big case.

of the preparation described might typically be handled by the inside counsel.

Time, energy, homework, role-playing, and most of all, *planning* are all mission-critical before a mediation. Counsel and the business representatives will need to meet several times in advance, with an agenda for each meeting. The participants at these meetings would, at a minimum, include those who will actually attend the mediation, but should also include others who can aid in preparation. The discussion at these meetings must include, at a minimum, the following topics:

1. Describe the mediator and the mediation process.

As a result of your "due diligence" in selecting the mediator, you know what your mediator's style and typical approach are, and you have reached or are in the process of negotiating the necessary agreements with the mediator and the other side on the mediation format and structure. Share that with your team, and walk through the anticipated process with them so they know what to expect.

2. Review the stage of the dispute and the possible outcomes if the dispute is not resolved.

If you have not done so already, bring the team up to date on what has happened in the case. Depending on the stage of the litigation, this might include the results of your internal document review and interviews with key players, a high-level summary of what has been learned in discovery (to the extent you can share it without violating a protective order), a review of how your own witnesses have done in deposition, and any important rulings that may affect your own or the other side's assessment of the case.

At the same time, you should update your clients on the costs incurred thus far and the likely costs ahead, including your estimate of anticipated fees and expenses through the upcoming phases, and the intangible costs (e.g., client time and distraction during discovery, disruption of customer relationships, and potential intrusion into proprietary information). Then, discuss with your client what success, or failure, would look like if you are not able to resolve the matter at this stage on acceptable terms. The mediator will expect you and your client to be able to articulate your Best Alternative To a Negotiated Agreement (BATNA) and Worst Alternative To a Negotiated Agreement (WATNA).[11] Essentially, you want to analyze fully the "return on litigation investment," taking into account the costs and risks of litigation at various points along its lifespan, as well as the value that would be derived if the case proceeds to trial and you achieve the verdict/award/order you believe is most likely.

3. Evaluate your opponent's case and its likely objectives.

To the extent possible, put yourself in the position of your opponent. Think through their likely strengths, weaknesses, interests, and concerns as if you were in their shoes or representing them. In addition, work with your client to assess and discuss what your client's BATNA and WATNA are likely to be. In this discussion it is important that you do not, and that you do not encourage your clients to, demonize the other side, either in preparation or at the mediation. Such ad hominem discussion will not only alienate your opponent and undermine the mediation, but also distract you and your client from an objective and productive analysis of how the two sides might be able to find a mutually acceptable resolution.

4. Assess and discuss the emotional "hooks" on both sides.

While the underlying disputes in an IP case may be business- and technology-driven, the obstacles to resolution are often extant emotional or relationship issues between the parties. There may be, for example, long-running or recently ignited competition between the companies, a history of acrimony between the principals, a sense of betrayal about the move of the plaintiff's key employee to work for the defendant, anger that litigation was filed before settlement was attempted, or a past history of a failed or aborted transaction. Confront such issues internally and prepare for how they will be addressed during the mediation. Challenge everyone on the team to think about what role emotion may be playing in the other party's view of the

11. For definitions of BATNA and WATNA, see Substep 7.4A.

case, and consider how best to defuse those emotions so they do not get in the way of resolution.

If your business decision maker is volatile or tends to "rise to the bait," you may want to limit his/her speaking role, or even look for an alternative representative at the mediation. Negative emotions that are not properly channeled can undermine your client's interests at the mediation.

5. Clarify your business objectives and authority to settle, and identify and vet a range of solutions to meet those objectives and your client's interests.

You should have identified your business objectives at or before the commencement of the dispute, but this is the time to re-examine and update them in light of developments in the matter itself and developments in the business and the marketplace that may affect your client's interests and needs. Then, identify and write out the range of acceptable negotiated outcomes and make sure you have the necessary authority in advance or at the mediation to agree to those outcomes. Explore with your client whether there are creative alternative business relationships that could be proposed beyond just a monetary settlement.

You will need to reach an understanding with your team about the relative importance or priority of various terms and options, including those that you would be willing to forego to secure the others. If there is a variety of "moving parts" in your settlement position, it can be very helpful to prepare a settlement matrix that sets out the various terms and identifies which are the "must haves," the "nice to haves," and the ones that are relatively unimportant to you but may be of value to the other side (and therefore can serve as bargaining chips).

6. Review the case themes and the key messages.

Review the themes you will communicate throughout the mediation and make sure the business executives are familiar with and agree with those themes. Have whoever will be giving the "opening statement" rehearse it in front of the entire negotiation team so they can make suggestions on the content and the graphics. Consider what messages you want to deliver to the other side, and who is best equipped to deliver them effectively.

7. Get ready for your breakout caucuses with the mediator.

Prepare for what you will communicate to the mediator outside your opponent's presence. Think about what materials (e.g., documents, deposition excerpts, sample products) to bring to the mediation to educate, illustrate, or corroborate for the mediator and your opponent the key points of your case.

You will also want to think through with your team how the "bidding" is likely to progress—your opening offer/demand and anticipated subsequent moves. You will then be better prepared to explain those moves to the mediator so he can in turn explain them to your opponent in a way that demonstrates a rational, well-supported approach.

Preparing with your team should also include not only identifying your bottom line (i.e., the least you would be willing to accept, or the most you would be willing to give, to resolve the case based on your current analysis), but also the point at which you would "walk" (i.e., close the discussions for the time being). Note that these two positions are not necessarily the same.

8. Practice with the business representatives.

Role-play with team members not only the points you would like them to make in the joint session or in caucus with the mediator, but also how they will respond if the mediator directs questions to them. In this regard, one important matter on which you should prepare is what you will do if the mediator asks to speak with one or more of the business representatives without counsel present, or suggests that they meet and negotiate directly with the business representatives from the other side.

9. Be ready to present the principal terms of your proposal/s in writing.

Nothing can unravel apparent progress in a mediation faster than springing new terms on the other side and claiming you had intended them to be part of your offers all along. If there are important terms that are part of the foundation of any proposal you make, even if they concern "legal language" (e.g., jurisdiction and venue, mutual releases, admissions of validity, agreement to a consent injunction) rather than money and grants of IP rights,[12] make sure those are explicit in your proposal. That ordinarily means you should provide the mediator with a bullet-point list of your key terms for the other side so that you can be sure they were communicated throughout.

---

12. Remember, Bowbeer originally wrote this advice for lawyers in the intellectual property (IP) arena.

STEP EIGHT

Start the Mediation Session Strategically

A good beginning makes a good end.

—English proverb

Anyone who has read articles or taken a course on mediation already knows the drill for a classic initial joint session: First, everybody sits down in a conference room to hear the mediator give an introductory spiel. Then the plaintiff's lawyer gives an opening presentation of his client's case, followed by the defendant's lawyer. After that, the mediator might ask a few questions before bringing the joint session to a close.

In practice, the only element that always follows the drill is the mediator's introduction. Although many lawyers favor giving opening presentations, others prefer to skip them as counterproductive. In this chapter, you will hear from one lawyer who always prepares an opening presentation, but sometimes decides not to give it, based on how he sizes up the other side across the conference table. You will also read about an initial joint session where a top mediator interrupted the lawyers' presentations almost before they began—turning the proceeding into something entirely unexpected.

Assuming that you and the other participants agreed on tailored ground rules as recommended in Step Three, uncertainties about the initial joint session will be reduced. Nevertheless, you should be prepared for anything.

Whatever happens, the following seven substeps should get you through:

1. Establish and keep the right tone, starting with the meet and greet.
2. Observe your opponents and the mediator closely.
3. Keep watching during the mediator's introduction.
4. Use your allotted opening time strategically.
5. Listen to your opponent's opening (and other comments) with fresh ears.

6. Be prepared for questions and discussion.
7. End the initial joint session on a productive note.

8.1 Establish and keep the right tone, starting with the meet and greet.

In litigation, you win by convincing a judge or jury to decide in your favor; it doesn't really matter what the other side thinks about you. In mediation, obviously you can only achieve success if you get your opponent to agree on a suitable settlement. And that will be a much harder job if you needlessly come across as—to quote a federal magistrate judge in Wyoming—a "horse's patoot."

Mediator Lee Jay Berman (Los Angeles) observes (2004, para. 6):

> Seasoned advocates understand that they are negotiating from the very outset. They are setting the tone for the negotiations from the time they set foot into the room. Little things like standing to shake the oppositions' hands and commenting that it is nice to see them again, or thanking them for coming all start winning points—points that will go a long way toward getting a client what they want.

A. The value of civility

As a general matter, John DeGroote is quite comfortable with legal head butting. As inside counsel, he managed all litigation for a big consulting firm, and he used to do trial work on the plaintiff's side. But he stresses that it is a bad idea to bring too much of this mind-set into the mediation room.

"I think the first mistake a lot of lawyers make is that they focus on what they *think* lawyers are supposed to do, which is akin to trial advocacy," he says. "Rather than trying to get the matter resolved in a way that is advantageous to their client, they are trying to show their client that they are tough and beat up the other side."

DeGroote thinks this is a particular problem in the initial joint session, where some lawyers make an effort "to rub the other side's nose in whatever warts they may have" instead of "focusing on what the interests of the other side may be and how to get the matter resolved." Although he believes there may be times when a harsh display is more important than cooperation, "in a majority of instances it's the wrong strategy."

Edna Epstein (Chicago) says excessive confrontation in mediation is often a mark of inexperience:

> I think the biggest way to spot a rookie—or maybe a better way of putting it is someone who doesn't understand the mediation process—is if he's acting like a jerk lawyer. Being very adversarial. Showing off for the client. Not recognizing that mediation is very different than the straight adversarial courtroom process.

Unfortunately, this type of behavior is by no means confined to "rookies." Maralee Eriksen (Sacramento, CA) observed the phenomenon many times during her judicial clerkship, when she had the chance to watch a federal magistrate judge conduct more than 40 mediated settlement conferences. In those proceedings, she often saw attorneys who acted like what the judge/mediator privately called a "horse's patoot"—behaving "with arrogance and 'demandingness' and just kind of in an obnoxious fashion, as if that was how they were conveying their value to their client," Eriksen says. But she also observed a different type of conduct that impressed her deeply:

> For me, it was important to see people who were entirely effective advocates, in front of their clients, who didn't behave that way. They were always respectful to everyone in the proceeding. That's not to say they were chummy with the opposing side—not at all. But they were at least respectful and civil.

For more of Eriksen's observations, see Sidebar 10-7: "What Maralee Eriksen Learned From Watching 40 Mediated Settlement Conferences."

This demeanor also seems most effective to mediator Peter Grilli (Tampa, FL). Asked to describe what distinguishes the lawyers who have impressed him most as mediation advocates, he highlights "their ability to maintain a firm position with regard to the strength of their case without making it personal. And they're able somehow to walk the line between expressing a willingness to negotiate and not giving anything away about where they're headed."

There definitely are lines to walk. If you are hostile and combative, you add an extra barrier to settlement. On the other hand, if you are too chatty and accommodating, your opponent may take this as a sign of weakness. Worse, your own client may indeed feel that you are not representing his interests vigorously enough.

The key concept is probably Eriksen's: civility. This implies conduct that is formal and correct in an old-school sense of the word—a cool, alert politeness.

Your client will be less likely to misinterpret your civil attitude if you deal with the issue in advance, as mentioned previously in Substep 7.2. He needs to buy in to the notion that this is the best approach, or at least understand your reasoning. If he insists on greater hostility (within the bounds of your professionalism)—well, he *is* the client. But make sure he understands the downside risk.

B. Playing a part?

In any event, your demeanor and your client's (and that of anyone else attending on your side) should be coordinated. As discussed elsewhere in this chapter, that does not mean you all have to act the same. For example, your side may agree that you as the lawyer will be the one to emphasize potential cooperation, while the client shows more grievance and emotion. Or you may take the part of the warhorse champing at the bit for trial, while inside counsel is the dollars-and-sense negotiator and the corporate representative is a sphinx.

Closely related to style and tone is the question of whether you or your client will play the more active role. On this topic, mediator Bennett Picker (Philadelphia) writes (2003, p.89):

> Because a mediator often will involve the representatives of a party directly from the outset of the mediation session, some attorneys assume a passive role and are almost non-participants in the process. At

> the other extreme, some attorneys argue their clients' positions relentlessly and fail to advance their clients' interests by failing to take a more collaborative approach to the negotiations or permitting the client representative to be actively involved in the process.

By implication, Picker clearly recommends a balanced approach, where the client is an active participant but you as counsel do not simply fade into the woodwork. Exactly where this balance lies in an individual case will depend in part on your client's preferences and personality.

Whatever approaches you agree upon, you need to be consistent over time. Beyond the initial joint session, there is a danger that game faces may slip as hours pass and the players on your side start to feel more at ease (or tired, or careless). Your hardball negotiator might be overheard on a phone call making kissy noises to his baby daughter. Your corporate rep might tell an off-color joke. Depending on the circumstances, such things can alter your opponents' image of your team in ways you do not want.

Of course, it is true that humanizing your side can sometimes be of benefit in a conflict situation. But to make such a calculated departure requires great perceptiveness and self-awareness. It is safer to maintain disciplined civility.

C. Addressing the mediator

In an interview near the end of his long career as a litigator, the late Andrew Berry advised: "Start out by being more respectful to the mediator than he or she might expect"[1]—for example, by addressing retired judge Charles Jones as Judge Jones rather than Charlie. Berry explained that he had two reasons for this. One reason is that—like accomplished individuals in many fields—some mediators may have high opinions of themselves and dislike your assumption of familiarity. Let the mediator be the one to strike a more informal note, if he wishes. "If Charlie says, 'That's Judge Jones,' you started out on the wrong foot," Berry commented. "If Judge Jones

1. This is rule seven of "Andrew Berry's Rules for Success in Mediation."

says, 'Please, call me Charlie,' everybody's going to get along just fine."

The second reason to err on the side of formality applies when you are tempted to be informal because you have a long acquaintance with the mediator—perhaps someone with whom you have mediated many previous cases. Your assumption of familiarity in greeting and address may not go over well if the other side does not share this familiarity:

> [Suppose] your adversary is Mr. New Guy in Town [or] Ms. New Woman in Town. If you go in and say, "Hi, Charlie," in the presence of the other side, that could be read as suggesting a level of familiarity with the mediator—and either an accurate or a false suggestion that your friendship with the mediator will be to your advantage and to their disadvantage. Because the mediator understands that it could be read that way, the mediator will be angry at you for saying, "Hi, Charlie."

Litigator Laura Kennedy (Phoenix) offers this advice on the topic: "The client (and counsel) should understand that they must have complete intellectual sobriety while in session and exhibit no familiarity or jocularity with the mediator" (2010, p.157).

D. Always being on stage

When John DeGroote flies somewhere for a mediation, he tells whoever is with him, "When we get to the mediator's zip code, you're 'on.' You watch what you say, you watch how you act. You should assume that the opposing party is with you for the entire day in terms of discussions, joking around on the way to the bathroom, or out in the lobby, or whatever else. That includes the Starbucks downstairs, the parking garage—everything. You know you are on stage."

8.2 Observe your opponents and the mediator closely.

Just as your opponents will be sizing you up, you need to be assessing them. A sample of things you might like to know:

- *What is the nature of the relationship between the opposing client and his lawyer?* Do they seem to know each other well—is this a position of established trust? Which of the two seems likely to be dominant and "drive the bus" behind the scenes during negotiations?
- *What is the character, attitude, and competence of the opposing lawyer?* Is she showboating to impress her client? How strong an adversary will she likely be if the dispute fails to settle and goes to trial (or other adjudication proceeding)?
- *Do your opponents seem to be taking this session seriously, or are they just here to jump through a hoop?* This can be a major question in instances where mediation is court ordered rather than voluntary.
- *What is the opposing client's attitude toward the mediator?* Does the client seem to see her as an authority figure, or just a go-between?
- *What is the opposing client's attitude toward you and your client?* Businesslike? Openly hostile or resentful? Nonchalant?

Some things you can learn directly through informal questions, like "Is this your first case working together?" But most information you have to glean by implication. For example, when you address a question to the opposing lawyer and client, which one usually answers first? Who does most of the talking? Do the two tend to stand and sit close to one another? (For more on possible types of questions and observations, see Sidebar 8-2: "Why Tom Dye Asks Lots of Questions.")

It has become a cliché that nonverbal cues—such things as stance, eye contact, and sitting position (among many other aspects of nonverbal behavior)—can reveal useful information. But speaking as someone who once studied with one of the pioneers in that field of study,[2] I urge you not to put much stock in advice of the "X nonverbal behavior means Y" variety—for example, that interlaced fingers indicate self-control or that

2. The anthropologist Edward T. Hall (1914–2009). In addition to professional literature, Hall wrote several popular books, including *The Silent Language* (1959), *The Hidden Dimension* (1966), and *Beyond Culture* (1976).

sitting on the edge of a chair means that a person is ready for something. The realities tend to be far more complicated, with the significance of any nonverbal element heavily dependent on context. Most people who are good at reading others probably can't say exactly what clues they have picked up on; the process is usually intuitive.

Meanwhile, you will also want to observe as much as possible about the mediator's personality and style in her interactions with you and your opponent. This is important because, among other reasons, she will become the principal means of communication between you and the other side during negotiations after the initial joint session ends.

8.3 Keep watching during the mediator's introduction.

The formal start of the session is normally marked by an opening statement from the mediator. The content usually has little to do with the substance of the dispute being mediated. Major goals for the statement include explaining the mediation process, establishing rapport with the parties, and fostering an atmosphere conducive to mediation.

The Mediator's Handbook (2006), by the late John Cooley, offers a nine-page checklist of items to cover in the opening statement (*see* pp.395–404). In an exhaustive statement, the mediator may introduce herself and talk a bit about her background; identify and introduce the parties (as needed); explain her role as mediator and affirm her neutrality; summarize the steps she has taken to prepare for this session; describe the goals of the mediation process; stress the risks that would flow from a failure to settle; ask the parties for a commitment to make a good-faith effort; explain procedural elements (caucuses, etc.); and lay down house rules on subjects like smoking and calling for breaks. However, some mediators' opening statements are much more cursory (*see, e.g.*, Goodman, 2004, pp.52–53).

This may be the first time you have seen the mediator perform in person. Obviously, you need to pay enough attention to the substance of her statement to absorb anything you didn't already know. And in any event, you want to look attentive, to help establish rapport. But beyond that, you will want to pick up any further clues you can about her and her approach to mediation that may aid you in dealing with her during negotiations. For example, is her statement incisive and to the point? Pompous? Meandering and long-winded? Are her instructions delivered in an authoritarian mode, or do you sense a desire to be liked? Of course, if you get any initial hints about her view of the case, so much the better.

During the mediator's statement, you can continue watching your opponents at a time when they are focused on something other than their interaction with you. Are the opposing lawyer and client both paying attention? Neither? Have they reacted to something the mediator said? Do they exchange looks like old pals, or are they sitting like strangers to one another? You never know what you might notice.

8.4 Use your allotted opening time strategically.

Needless to say, whether you or your opponent's opening goes first depends on which of you is the plaintiff. The listing of steps here assumes that you are in the first position.

You have several possible options for using your opening time: (a) Give an opening presentation, (b) ask the other side some questions in lieu of a presentation, (c) ask questions in addition to your presentation, or (d) skip your opening time completely and move on.

This discussion of the opening-time substep will begin with views on the pros and cons of opening presentations. Then, assuming you opt in favor of an opening presentation, you will hear opinions on who should give it (you, your client, or a combination). After that, you will find detailed advice on what your opening presentation should include and what the most effective delivery is. In Sidebar 8-2 ("Why Tom Dye Asks Lots of Questions"), Tom Dye (West Palm Beach, FL) pitches his preferred approach: asking your opponents informal questions, often (but not always) coupled with a presentation.

A. Pros and cons of opening presentations

In the ABA Section of Dispute Resolution's Task Force on Improving Mediation Quality's 2008 study, mediation players expressed "a range of views" as to the usefulness of opening presentations (2008a, p.12): "[A]bout two-thirds of lawyer participants in our survey agreed that opening statements are useful in all, almost all or most cases; a substantial minority thought they were effective in half or fewer cases." Despite the minority view, the Task Force noted that "in most jurisdictions, opening statements are expected" (p.13).

(1) Pros

Supporters of opening presentations praise them as (among other things) a rare opportunity to (a) present your case directly to the opposing client, rather than through the filter of his lawyer; (b) make sure the mediator is up to speed on the facts and relevant law; and (c) in particular, highlight talking points—strengths of your case (and weaknesses of your opponent's) that the mediator can use during private caucuses with your opponent.

Here are some examples of what supporters have to say:

- "I've gone into mediations where the other side really just expects to swap numbers, but I always believe in taking the opportunity to present the case. The key is that you're trying to impress the opposing client, not your opposing counsel. Once the initial joint session is over and the lawyer is alone with his client, he will be extremely dismissive of your arguments. But if the opposing client has had a way to experience them first-hand—in a way that's powerful to the client—it will, in my view, aid mediation." —*Walter Stuart (New York)*[3]

---

3. Litigator Edward Mullins expands on this point:

> Sometimes the lawyers on the other side have been feeding their client all kinds of—you know, pumping them up and telling them, "You are definitely going to win" and all these things. So you need to shake their foundation a little bit.
>
> And it's not just the legal arguments. It's also things like, "How much is this going to cost you?" and "Have you thought about going to trial? Have you thought about the ramifications if there is a public trial? Do you really want to have all your employees dragged in here waiting for a trial on a calendar call?" It depends on what the issues are, but there are a lot of reasons to settle besides whether you may win or lose. And you don't know if that's being talked about with the lawyer on the other side.

- "Many times lawyers filter what the other side is saying as it goes to their clients. It's a whole lot better to have an opponent's lawyer (or better yet, an opponent) articulate their position on a given issue, because as those filters are removed, you get closer and closer to a party's actual position." —*John DeGroote (Dallas)*
- "What happens is that [the opening presentation] gives the mediator talking points when he goes into caucus with the other side. Because he will say, 'Well, she said *this*, how do you feel about that?'—and that gets the discussion going in the other room." —*Tracey Salmon-Smith (New Jersey and New York)*
- "At that opening session, it tends to be very important for the client to feel, 'OK, the whole story is told, and I got to hear my story being told.' This is even more important in these days when trials are becoming few and far between." —*Edward Mullins (Miami)*[4]

Also, a well-done opening presentation can be an opportunity for you to shine in the eyes of your client, which can be significant if he has not really seen you perform before. This benefit may not be strictly selfish, if it gives you increased credibility with him during the rest of the mediation (and beyond).

Of course, the opposing lawyer will also be watching, sizing you up as an opponent in a future trial just as you will assess her (*see* Sidebar 8-3: "'What If I Don't Have Trial Experience?'"). If your presentation is disorganized or otherwise incompetent, it will be clear that she has little to fear. If your performance is impressive, this could affect how she views the prospect of a trial and make settlement more attractive. Or at least, that is the argument.

4. An opening presentation where your client's side of the story is told can offer some psychic or emotional satisfaction as a partial substitute for his "day in court" at trial (*see* Picker, 2003, p. 31). Of course, this consideration does not have much weight if your client is accustomed to disputes as part of doing business (or is otherwise not emotionally invested).

(2) Cons

Nevertheless, "more and more lawyers are afraid now that a joint session might be too emotional or raise the anger level and would just as soon skip it," observes mediator Linda Singer (Washington, DC). There is no shortage of experienced lawyers with a negative view of opening presentations in mediation. The gist of their criticism is this: Such presentations simply tend to antagonize your opponent, raising the adversarial pitch and hardening the parties' response.[5] Moreover, they are unnecessary, because your opponents and the mediator already know the facts before they enter the conference room. At best, they are a waste of valuable time, delaying the start of negotiations.

A few typical comments:

- "I can't stand doing opening statements at a mediation, because it causes people to get entrenched in their positions. When everyone is in the same room, and you start telling the other side why you think their case is without merit, people tend to get offended. They get their feelings hurt. By the time you begin the negotiation phase, people are upset, and they are not quite as willing to compromise. At the start of a mediation, we [already] know the strengths and weaknesses of our case and the opponent's case. My attitude is, 'Let's just get going. We'll start the negotiation phase. We don't need any opening statements.'" —*Steven Brom (Birmingham, AL)*
- "I have certainly seen enough people who come in and want to do their opening statement for an hour and lecture my client as to why their case is terrific and we are wasting our time by not writing a big check. That's off-putting and gets the mediation off to a bad start. Anything you are going to say, I have probably already heard—and if I'm doing my job, told

5. *See* Task Force on Improving Mediation Quality (2008a, p.12): "In the focus groups, some felt that in high conflict cases with angry clients, explosive opening statements can generate more hostility, and grind the opposing parties more firmly into their opposing views, thus impeding settlement."

my client about. Conversely, anything I'm about to tell you, you probably have told your client why my position is frivolous or not sufficiently credible." *—Michael Braun (Chicago)*

- "My gut reaction often is those opening presentations can be more polarizing than anything else. They can kind of spiral a mediation and take people off track. It could do more damage than good. I prefer to start a mediation session with questions from the mediator—any issues that he or she has from reviewing the submissions, any outstanding issues." *—Christopher Carroll (New York and New Jersey)*
- "My experience has shown that formal presentations by counsel in the presence of all parties are unproductive. In that setting, attorneys cannot avoid the temptation to perform, a.k.a. posture—especially in the presence of their client. They frequently grandstand or become argumentative, and by such behavior set a negative tone for the mediation." *—Magistrate Judge Mary Pat Thynge (Wilmington, DE; 2011, p.160)*[6]

This dissenting view of opening presentations also surfaced during focus groups conducted by the ABA Section of Dispute Resolution's Task Force on Improving Mediation Quality (*see* Lande & Wohl, 2007, p.20). The focus groups were held in nine major cities, with a total of about 90 qualified lawyers. Task Force member John Lande (Columbia, MO) was surprised to find that a significant number of people really did not want to have opening statements. Their objections were that such presentations "would be inflammatory and counterproductive, and that rather than bringing people together, they would alienate and polarize folks."

Even some supporters of opening presentations have seen them go wrong. Although Tracey Salmon-Smith (New Jersey and New York) generally favors openings, she warns: "You

---

6. Judge Thynge continues: "Opening presentations may be helpful, however, when mediation occurs very early in the case, when the parties have exchanged relatively little, if any, information, through discovery."

want to highlight your strengths without being too aggressive and over the top with it, because otherwise the opposing clients will get their back up against the wall and feel like they are being attacked."

Salmon-Smith recalls a case where a lawyer for the other side had already made a demand before the mediation. At that time, Salmon-Smith was working as inside counsel for a securities broker. After outside counsel for her company made a very aggressive opening presentation in the initial joint session, her opponent's demand actually went *up*. It took the mediator a couple of hours to get the parties back to where they had started out.

Where there are no opening presentations, the parties may still gather in a brief joint session to discuss procedural issues for the session, such as who will use which conference room and when to break for lunch, says John Buchanan (Washington, DC). "The mediator then relatively quickly goes to the shuttle-diplomacy mode, speaking with the parties separately and privately."

(3) Harmonizing views?

John Lande's involvement with mediation goes way beyond the ABA focus groups discussed earlier in this chapter. For a number of years, he directed the LLM Program in Dispute Resolution at the University of Missouri School of Law. Personally, he tends to support the practice of giving opening presentations. Like Salmon-Smith, he believes "you can be a very effective advocate and take a strong position without being insulting." But he recognizes the dangers.

To some degree, lawyers' bad reactions to opening presentations may reflect the strident way they are too often performed. Lande recalls that "one of the folks in a focus group was advising advocates to 'explain, don't argue.' If they can explain what their thinking and reasoning is, then it's less likely to alienate the other side than if they are making an argument which is more adversarial and perhaps making people more upset and defensive." (We will discuss proper tone in more detail later in this chapter.)

Former bankruptcy judge and mediator Timothy Corcoran (Tampa, FL) makes a similar point (2007, § 3.e.i.3):

> What can you say to the opposing party that will best incline that party to see the case through your client's eyes, and make him more conducive to a favorable settlement? It is probably *not* that your client's case is great, and his case is bad. It's probably *not* that you are the toughest dude and meanest lawyer on the planet. Yet these are the kinds of opening statements I too often [hear as a mediator].

From experience with her own mediation practice in Southern California, Louise LaMothe believes the primary reason many lawyers are increasingly "leery" of opening presentations is that "litigators have misused the joint session and we mediators have let them" (2010, p.67):

> Rather than preparing their clients to talk, and using the opportunity to hear the other side's position from the client, the advocate shuts down the client, does all the talking, and scurries into caucus as quickly as possible.
>
> Perhaps by eliminating the joint session, the lawyer is trying to conceal a lack of adequate preparation. I do think that fear is motivating most of this reluctance. Yet, the value of a joint session for all participants is significant in most cases. It is not meant to be a contest at which lawyers make oral arguments as if to the court or to a jury. It is an opportunity to speak, then to listen to the other side speak.

Regardless of tone, opening presentations may be contraindicated where tensions between the parties are simply running too high already. Prof. Lande says,

> In the focus groups, people referred to situations where the personal relationships between the parties were so hostile that just being in the same room together got the emotional temperature and anxiety and tension up to a point that was counterproductive.

> And this was not necessarily just the parties—it could be the lawyers as well, if they've gotten personally invested. If that's a dynamic between the parties, and coaching by the mediator is not likely to change it, then that might be a situation where avoiding an opening statement might make sense.

Other factors in an individual case might weigh for or against an opening presentation. As noted earlier, some lawyers object to presentations on grounds that the parties already know the facts. This is most likely true where mediation occurs near the end of discovery. But the situation may be quite different for a case that is mediated soon after suit is filed. Also, where mediation occurs outside of litigation—such as before a lawsuit is filed or under the ADR clause of a contract—each side may have a great deal to learn about the other's contentions. Moreover, much may depend on how much information the parties exchange (through memos or otherwise) before the mediation session.

Although retired judge and mediator Herbert Stettin (Coral Gables, FL) believes that "in many instances," opening statements are not the best approach, he also believes there are instances where opening statements could be important:

> An example would be where the client has not really been involved—has not heard very much, has not been deposed—or where it's simply a large corporation. Then, you've got a decision maker who maybe has not been fed enough information to fully apprise him of the risks involved. Then an opening statement definitely would be useful. Especially when you've got a talented lawyer on the other side. It's good to let them hear this.
>
> Now, it doesn't mean a presentation where the lawyer gets up and pounds his chest. That's a mistake, in my opinion, in mediation. It's a meaningless thing to do that.

Linda Singer sums up her view of the pluses and minuses like this: An opening presentation is "your opportunity to speak directly to the decision-maker on the other side. On the other hand, if you've done that already, and if everybody knows everything everybody has to say, and if you've seen the client on the other side in anything other than a deposition, maybe you don't want to do it."

All in all, Prof. Lande believes it is best to avoid a blanket policy with regard to opening presentations: "It should be a case-by-case analysis."

B. Lawyer-only, client-only, and blended presentations

Assuming you decide in favor of an opening presentation, theoretically you have three basic options as to who will make it: you (the lawyer), your client, or a combination of both. Although at least one expert (*see* Cooley, 2002, pp.131–132) has contemplated that a client might make the presentation alone, in practice this seems quite rare in disputes where lawyers are involved. Indeed, many lawyers seem very wary of having the client participate at all.

"Mediators report that some of the very best—and some of the very worst—presentations made at mediations are made by parties," according to a study by the Task Force on Improving Mediation Quality (2008a, p.10). "Careful preparation can allow for the former and, where possible, avoid the latter."

Perceived possible advantages of client involvement include these:

- The client may have more detailed knowledge of the underlying facts—especially in the early stages of litigation.[7]
- If the client makes a good witness, his performance in the opening can drive that point home to the other side.
- Giving the parties a voice in the presentation can help them feel "engaged and not 'left on the sidelines'"

7. Although not a fan of opening presentations per se, John Bickerman advises from his many years as a mediator: "Use your client intelligently. The client almost always knows the facts much better than the lawyer. What is more, the client can talk to the other client across the table and is more likely to be heard than the lawyer—so that's significant."

(Task Force on Improving Mediation Quality, 2008a, p.34).

- Empowering clients to "speak directly to and hear directly from the other side . . . can help them understand each other and the risks of continue[d] litigation" (Task Force on Improving Mediation Quality, 2008a, p.34).
- Giving the client his say in the opening can put him in a better frame of mind to negotiate and settle afterward, as well as increase his subjective satisfaction with the mediation process.

The arguments against client participation in the opening presentation mostly boil down to a concern that it is simply too dangerous:

- The client may vent too much. If the client feels that need, it may be better for him to get it off his chest with the mediator during a private caucus (*see* Substep 9.4).
- Unduly aggressive or insulting behavior in an opening may provoke a similar response from the other side and poison the atmosphere for negotiation.
- It is too hard for the lawyer to control the content of what the client will say—and if the client goes off the rails, it will be awkward and difficult for the lawyer to get him back on track.

Horace "Hob" Jordan (Lake Forest, IL) is among those who believe that client participation in the opening can sometimes work. Jordan is a founder and general counsel of a privately held company that assists in the financing and acquisition of large equipment assets. He speaks in the context of someone who always tries to mediate as soon as possible after a dispute arises. He says,

> If you do mediation in an early time period, the client representative probably knows the facts best. He or she is the most intimate about the dispute, and can relay his or her understanding of the facts and how he or she has been wronged probably better than

> anybody else. If you mediate within the first couple of months of this dispute arising, the outside lawyer just won't have the facts at his or her fingertips to the same degree. So I think having client representatives talk might be an advantage, as long as they keep it to a short presentation.

But Jordan acknowledges this can only work if you have the right individual. "You can't put out a person whose wounds are so open they are just going to be mad the whole way through," he says. The role requires someone who can be "eloquent and a little dispassionate. Otherwise let the lawyer do it. Just keep it short and sweet, and we'll get the devil in the details when we go to caucus."

Mediator Lawrence Watson (Maitland, FL) raises the option of allowing the client to participate within the lawyer's opening. "In that event," Watson writes, the lawyer "would prepare and execute an opening presentation geared toward communicating the reality of the dispute to the opposition in a tone and manner best suited to complete the task. The client could then add the emotive element to the presentation while satisfying his or her need to vent" (2002, p.9).

Walter Stuart almost always avoids using client representatives in his opening presentations, because he worries about "opening the door to some kind of colloquy between the clients that gets heated." But even he has made exceptions at least a couple of times in his career. An example was when his firm represented bank directors being sued by a government entity in connection with the failure of a financial institution. The directors in question were both eloquent and highly accomplished. Stuart decided that it would be useful in that case for the government "to understand that these people were going to be highly articulate witnesses." He told the other side that he wanted each director to make a brief statement, without implying that they were available for cross-examination. The statements had an impact. After the litigation settled, the government lawyers "said that they were greatly moved by the apparent integrity and credentials of the people who spoke. So it really can be very instructive to the other side."

Despite the possible upsides of such client involvement, however, a probably common view is expressed by Tracey Salmon-Smith: "I don't have enough control over what they may say or not say, so I would rather that they just not say anything."

(1) "Coda" by inside counsel

A somewhat different twist is offered for your consideration by John DeGroote: a very specific sort of kicker or coda delivered by *inside counsel* (or, if emotionally removed enough, a businessperson).

In this twist, after the outside lawyer gives his presentation, DeGroote as the inside counsel will highlight a limited number of points from his own perspective: "Every place that I have checkmate on the other side, I am going to highlight that." He begins by saying that he agrees with much of his outside lawyer's presentation but has a slightly different take. Then he will say something like: "You know, there are four questions you cannot answer (or ten questions or two, or whatever else), that to me are what I perceive the case is really about."

For example, in a software dispute, DeGroote might say, "At the end of the day, the manufacturer of that software is not in this room, and the question that you can't answer is, 'Why aren't they here?'" Or in a traffic-accident dispute: "It all boils down to, 'You can't prove the light was green.' We all know there were four people in the intersection and all of them were looking at their toes. My guy said it was red, and he was the only guy looking at the light."

The advantages of such a coda, in DeGroote's view, are that it may make a distinct impression on the other side because it "has the imprimatur of the client," and because it offers a chance to highlight your side's themes or major points in a slightly different way.

C. Content and delivery of an effective opening presentation

You will not be surprised that there is substantial variation in approach among lawyers who opt for opening presentations (*see* Wilk & Blum, 2004, p.18). Such variations can depend on the personality of the lawyer, the nature of the opposing side, the type of case, the amount at issue, and perhaps the customs of the jurisdiction.[8]

For the same reason, the length of an opening can vary enormously. In some mediations, the opening presentation may be expected to take only 5 or 10 minutes.[9] The late John Cooley, a well-known mediator, advised that a lawyer's opening in the average case might take between 15 minutes and half an hour, but it could extend beyond an hour in "complex, high-stakes" disputes (2002, p.130).

After another look at the purpose or goal of opening presentations, this section will describe both a full-blown "mini-trial" approach and less extensive alternatives. It will end by discussing some issues that can apply to all types of presentations, including the possibility of an apology, as well as inherent limitations. (*See also* Sidebar 8-4: "Conflicting Needs for Opening Presentations.")

(1) Purpose or goals

There is a great deal of natural overlap between the purposes and goals of opening presentations and the advantages or pros already discussed. Here are some statements about presentation goals made by various interview participants and writers on mediation:

- "[T]he party's opening statement is a one-of-a-kind opportunity in mediation to make your most complete, persuasive settlement pitch to the mediator and to the opponents on behalf of your client." —*John Cooley (2002, p.131)*
- "The purpose of the presentation is to raise issues or questions within the mind-set of the other side that

8. *See* Bickerman, 2007, p.2: "[T]here are strong regional differences. What parties expect mediation to be in Florida and Texas is vastly different than what parties in New York or California expect."

9. For example, that was the expectation in the mediated settlement conferences attended by interview participant Maralee Eriksen (*see* Sidebar 10-7: "What Maralee Eriksen Learned by Observing 40 Mediated Settlement Conferences").

will be the cracks that the mediator can use to forge a mediation settlement." —*Robert Craig (Houston)*[10]

- "What you're trying to do is to give the other side a preview of how this case is going to unfold in court." —*Walter Stuart (New York)*
- "The lawyer's job is to make the other party aware that the lawyer's client can win the case and that the other party has risks in proceeding with the litigation. Although a party will probably not be convinced that he will lose, such party may fear that a judge or jury may be persuaded by what the party has just heard." —*Michael Wilk and Henry Blum (2004, p.18)*
- "An opening statement in a joint session is an opportunity for the client to tell its story." —*Bennett Picker (2003, p.90)*
- "The presentation of the client's case in the opening phase of a mediation is a task that must meet two often-conflicting needs. First, the client must feel his or her story has been told. . . . Secondly, there is a need for the opening presentations to clearly and objectively communicate the 'other side of the story' to the opposition." —*Larry Watson (2002, p.7)*
- In the opening presentation, seasoned lawyers "walk the narrow line between trying to sketch out for the decision maker on the other side what could happen if the case isn't settled and trying to make the initial overtures towards a negotiation." —*Linda Singer (Washington, DC)*

At a secondary level, you may need to show your adversary that you would be a strong opponent in court if the case does not settle; *see* Sidebar 8-2 ("Why Tom Dye Asks Lots of

10. Laura Kennedy (Phoenix) elaborates: "[T]he opening plenary session may be the first time that the decision-maker(s) for your opponent will actually hear the substance of your client's viewpoints unencumbered by her lawyer's re-packaging of your client's position. Like a game of 'telephone,' sometimes messages are lost in the translation" (2010, p.162).

Questions") and Sidebar 8-3 ("'What If I Don't Have Trial Experience?'").

(2) Full-blown minitrial

An interesting thing about Walter Stuart's participation in an interview for this book is that he was recommended by one of his former *opponents*—a prominent inside counsel who was been impressed by Stuart's performance (and results) in mediation as viewed from across the table. Stuart is a partner in the litigation group of a global law firm. He urges counsel to consider making their opening presentation "as if it were a minitrial"—combining elements of a trial opening statement, closing argument, and presentation of evidence.

The idea, Stuart says, is to show not just the merits of your case, "but also the way it will be presented"—to "almost take them into the courtroom." In effect, you address the opposing client as if he were sitting in the jury box, so he can "see what the jury will see in terms of documentary evidence and testimony."

Stuart believes that this type of presentation has "infinitely more impact" on the opposing client than other approaches. And the opposing client really is functioning as a juror, in the sense that his vote will be critical in deciding the outcome of the mediation.

One obvious element of the presentation is to lay out the most important documents, deposition excerpts, and so forth. Like many lawyers, Stuart likes to incorporate these into a PowerPoint sequence. "We make the point, we illustrate it with the evidence, then we reiterate the point and move on through an argument that's like an analytical treatment of the case."

By *argument*, Stuart does *not* mean anything legalistic. "It's very important that you not get distracted by technical, legal arguments in a mediation," he says. "You need to make sure you're clearly communicating with the opposing client, and if the client is not a lawyer, that you speak in layman's terms." For example, in a securities fraud case, if part of your argument is that Rule 10b-5 does not apply, "you've got to either minimize the argument or explain it in a way that a layman would understand it."

Another aspect of seeing the opposing client as a juror is "to stress underlying emotional themes or relative size of the parties—that sort of thing" if it's to your advantage. In Stuart's view, this is all part of the mix that encourages the opposing client "to actually envision the case as it's likely to unfold before the ultimate trier of fact."

Among other reasons Stuart believes so strongly in this approach is that he has seen it used effectively on *his own* clients: "I've had clients that I've represented faced with a very powerful presentation by the other side that is essentially nonlegal. And I've watched the effect of it on them. There is no question that they are really moved by the same thing that other laymen would be moved by in the opening mediation statements."

Stuart's minitrial approach to opening presentations may be similar to what is envisioned by mediator Larry Watson (2002, pp.8–9). As Watson describes them, "[t]he opening presentations in mediations are basically condensed versions of the complete trial position each party will present should the dispute be adjudicated." But he cautions that the presenter should generally stick to the big picture, going into "specific instances only to demonstrate a point" or when challenged.

(3) Something less

A full-blown minitrial approach is at the most elaborate end of the presentation continuum. As Michael Wilk and Henry Blum (2004, p.18) observe, "[t]he lawyers' presentations can take various forms, from a detailed PowerPoint presentation to a general overview similar to a summation in trial."

One common-sense factor in deciding the elaborateness of your approach will be cost. Something Walter Stuart and Larry Watson have in common is that they both tend to be involved in mediation of big, high-stakes, complex lawsuits—disputes that would warrant the expense of preparing, practicing for, and delivering an extensive presentation. (On the other hand, a supporter of the minitrial approach will likely point out that many smaller cases are also less complicated, so the cost of a full-blown treatment would naturally be less.)

In his former posts as inside counsel, Robert Craig saw (and did not always like) the bills his outside lawyers presented. You may recall his statement earlier in this chapter that the purpose of a presentation is to create specific "cracks"—issues or doubts in the opposing client's mind—for the mediator to use. Craig's next words: "So there is no need to present the whole case." He explains further:

> I don't think a mediation requires the attorneys to prepare as though they were preparing for trial. It's something they should be able to do almost off the top of their head. They should come in prepared, and they should be able to tell their story in a matter-of-fact way that hopefully will open the door to settlement. It's not a theater that requires lots of extra time getting ready for. You give the mediator enough to understand your side and your perception of the other side.

That is Craig's general attitude, but he acknowledges exceptions. He starts to say that he "really get[s] upset" when his outside lawyer comes into a mediation session "with a huge PowerPoint" after doing "three practice runs"—but then he pulls back. "I can always think of big cases where it makes a difference," he says.

As a practical matter, if your client has experience with mediation, you really need to make sure that his vision of the opening presentation meshes with yours. And for any client, obviously you can't spend more time (money) putting the presentation together than the client can reasonably be expected to pay.

Even when Tracey Salmon-Smith worked for a huge investment-services company, she did not generally believe in elaborate presentations. Based on her experience in mediation of disputes with investment customers (which will go to an arbitration hearing if unresolved), she advises: "You want to highlight what could happen at a hearing, and how you see it playing out, along with a discussion of your strengths, while keeping it short and to the point."

(4) Handling weak points

Whatever approach to an initial presentation you choose, Walter Stuart urges you to handle the weak points in your case directly. "It's no use putting your head in the sand," he says, because they will eventually come up one way or another. It's better to take the initiative "in the context of your overall positive presentation of the case, where as you're doing it you address these obstacles that you may have."

With regard to the other side's anticipated defenses, Larry Watson (2002, p.10) advises a different approach: Just focus on the affirmative elements in your initial presentation. Then, "[i]f and when the anticipated defenses are raised during the opposition's presentation, deal with them in a systematic, 'bullet point' manner in a short rebuttal." If such a rebuttal is likely to be needed, Watson suggests that you plan for rebuttal time in advance, while you are still working out the ground rules for the session with the mediator and your opponent.

(5) Strategic apology?

Nate Cade (Milwaukee) reflects a commonly accepted bit of wisdom when he says, "Some people need mediation just to clear the air—to hear someone say they're sorry, or to feel like they were somehow vindicated, if you will." If you are representing the defendant, and the plaintiff is carrying a strong sense of grievance, the right kind of apology might lower a barrier that is impeding settlement negotiations.

"One of the things that I have noticed as a mediator is how often the parties are looking for something deeper than just money," says David Hoffman (Boston):

> The parties may come in to a mediation thinking this is going to be a negotiation about money. But I have seen over and over again, after people get into the substance of what brought them to the table, that there is something else. That might be an apology, or some acknowledgement, or some recognition, or some

> understanding, or some empathy. And I've found that very often those elements are just as important as—and sometimes, even more important than—the financial terms of settlement.
>
> It can be a very powerful moment when the lawyer across the table expresses genuine concern for the party on the other side. One very powerful way to be involved in mediation is to express that kind of empathy and concern, because the party on the other side generally won't expect it. Of course, it has to be genuine, or else it will seem condescending or smarmy.

As an inside lawyer, Hob Jordan has been involved in mediation of employment disputes (among other things). He likes to mediate as soon as possible—preferably before the dispute becomes a lawsuit. He also considers strategic apologies useful:

> In negotiating, outside counsel shouldn't be afraid to apologize or advocate that the party representative apologize—to say, "I am sorry that this resulted. I don't feel totally responsible, but I am sorry for it." That can make a world of difference. I don't think you would see that in a court of law, but in mediation you can do that as long as everyone understands that the statements are made in the context of settlement discussions.

In this context, Susan Yates points to a Chicago-area hospital "where the representative from the hospital often finds an opportunity where it's appropriate in medical malpractice cases to apologize on behalf of the hospital when there has been a mistake that's been made." She hastens to add that this happens "only if it's appropriate, and only at the time that's appropriate in the mediation." Nevertheless, "that particular institution has taken a position that if an error was made, then it's only right to make that apology. That's part of what's so positive about this mediation program—they have the opportunity to actually sit with members of a family and say that."

Of course, caution is in order. Even while favoring apologies where appropriate, Hob Jordan urges that you should be careful what you say, and weigh the likelihood that your apology will make a difference: "If it looks like the dispute is going to litigation, an acknowledgment that 'I was wrong' can come back to haunt you."

In his *Mediation Practice Guide* (2002), John Cooley points out that it is possible to "acknowledge the basis for the plaintiff's negative feelings toward the defendant" and be empathetic without a legal admission of wrongdoing on your client's part (p.165). Where appropriate, that would be the kind of apology to strive for.

(6) Holding something back

A recurring question for lawyers in mediation is whether to hold back some piece of information or evidence in case the dispute ends up going to trial. For a discussion of this, see Sidebar 8-5: "'Should I Hold Something Back for Trial?'"

(7) Audiovisual aids

"People learn in multiple ways," says David Hoffman. "We learn from what we see, what we hear, what we experience in a variety of ways. Good mediation advocates need to be teachers. So being creative about all the various tools that can be used in a mediation setting is an important quality for skilled mediation advocates."

For that reason, advises John Bickerman, "if you are going to spend the money for demonstrative exhibits that you would spend in a trial, then you should spend it in a mediation as well." In his position as a mediator, Bickerman has seen that "they can be extremely persuasive."

In his practice as a mediator, Larry Watson (2002, p.8) noticed early that "more and more trial lawyers are turning to specially created graphics to quickly and effectively illustrate their points. Computerized PowerPoint illustrations, videotape segments, overhead view graphics, slides, and simple feather board charts have all become integral tools for effective opening presentations in mediation sessions."

People interviewed for this book often mentioned PowerPoint slide presentations, usually in a positive context. But when you use graphics, there is a common temptation you need to avoid. Too many lawyers throw loads of verbiage onto their computer slides or overheads, then proceed to read them verbatim in presentations. Using too many words robs a graphic of its impact, and reading them all out loud will make your presentation stilted and boring. "A good use of graphics summarizes key points rather than advances the entire argument" (Watson, 2002, p.10). A few well-chosen words and phrases on the screen will go a long way. Use them solely as headlines for your oral presentation.

In big-ticket cases, such as some major personal injury claims, the potential effectiveness of a well-produced video or other elaborate exhibit may justify the large expense. In Sidebar 8-6 ("A Humanizing Video That Stunned the Defendants"), David Hoffman tells the story of a memorable video in a nursing-home case.

Generally, however, "you don't need to spend a fortune on preparation for mediation," Hoffman says. In some disputes, a large blowup of a photograph can make a big impact. For example, Hoffman remembers a case involving a construction worker who suffered a paralyzing injury while on the job. Plaintiff's counsel brought in big photos of the construction site "showing how various safety measures weren't in place." In another case, involving an injury at an amusement park, "plaintiff's counsel brought in some big photographs of the amusement-park ride to give a more three-dimensional sense."

In the smallest cases, even PowerPoint slides or large photos may be more time consuming or expensive to prepare than the budget allows. Sometimes an old-fashioned easel pad—or even just a few key photocopied documents or excerpts—can still do the job perfectly well, for a big case or small.

"I remember one party who made some boards up that had quotes of what somebody said, or key statutory language, or key contractual language," John Bickerman recalls. "They put it up, and it stayed up in the room the entire mediation session. You could not avoid looking at it. And it was extraordinarily persuasive and helpful."

(8) Don't read!

"As a general rule, presentation notes should stay in outline form—avoid reading a scripted narrative" (Watson, 2002, p.9). This is golden advice. Unless you are a professional from the broadcast media (or an actor), if you read from a script you will sound stilted and probably boring. On top of that, trying to write every word down on paper will take you 10 times as long.

Instead, just make a list of the points you want to make (possibly including a few key phrases to say verbatim). Then go through your talk in your head and at least once out loud. The same advice applies to opening statements at trial, so if you haven't gotten used to the technique yet, it's time to start.

(9) Balancing of tone

"I've gotten less confrontational now than I used to be," says Sara Soto (Miami). "I have tried to present my opening statements in mediation the way I think a fact finder is going to look at it. I am going to say, 'evidence of such-and-such, which the arbitrators will not interpret favorably to you,' as opposed to my old methodology, which was, 'Based on such-and-such, obviously your case is worthless.'"

The question of tone has already come up twice before in this chapter, but it is worth discussing a bit more because of a built-in conflict related to your opening presentation. This arises from the fact that if your client is emotionally invested in the dispute—and this can be true even in the most sophisticated corporate litigation—the tone that would often be most satisfying to the client runs directly contrary to what best promotes the success of the mediation.

Previous sections have already quoted lawyers saying that chest-beating aggressiveness is predictably counterproductive. In the same vein, Michael Wilk and Henry Blum write: "The opening presentations by the lawyers should be civil and polite and name calling and inflammatory statements should be avoided" (2004, p.18). Similarly, Bennett Picker stresses: "While it is appropriate to show anger or other feelings about the dispute, an opening statement should not use emotionally charged words which might simply antagonize the other side" (2003, p.90).

Peter Grilli elaborates:

> Sometimes people feel it's so important to be tough that they alienate the decision maker on the other side. So you're there in an opening session, and you're giving an opening statement. There is somebody on the other side who either has a checkbook—and you want them to write a very large check—or they have a claim that they think is very large, and you want them to compromise it significantly. You've got to consider: What's the most persuasive way to reach them?
>
> Often, it's *not* to accuse your opponent of criminal or fraudulent behavior. Even if there is criminal or fraudulent behavior, you have a way to express that without making it personal and without alienating the person on the other side.
>
> Also, you're not really going to scare somebody by telling them that they're going to lose the case. It's a lot less likely that somebody is going to be fired for losing a case than it is for them to be fired for paying too much or getting too little in a settlement.

Nevertheless, as Larry Watson observes, "Many clients to a dispute might be quite pleased with a lawyer [who] relieves built up feelings and relates their position in ominous, scolding, or even threatening terms." (2002, p.9) It may be tempting to take this tone simply because you sense (or believe) that it will make your client happy. The fact is, you have a balancing act to perform—making your client feel that you are always in his corner, while at the same time keeping that same civil tone with which you commenced the initial joint session.

Watson recommends erring in favor of presenting your case in the objective-sounding manner necessary to communicate well to the other side. His reasoning is that a client's need for emotional release can be met in other ways at the session, but the opening presentation is your only opportunity to "bring the opposition to understand and fully appreciate all dimensions of the dispute" (2002, p.9).

There is also, potentially, a second (though related) balancing act. You will recall Walter Stuart saying that where his case has elements such as "underlying emotional themes or relative size of the parties—that sort of thing," he does not hesitate to stress them to the opposing client. And you have just read a quote from Bennett Picker that it "is appropriate to show anger or other feelings about the dispute." How on earth is it possible to stress such emotional elements while—as Picker also instructs—avoiding "emotionally charged words which might simply antagonize the other side"? Probably the best answer is simply to keep asking yourself that question as you are framing your presentation in advance.

(10) Inherent limitations

There are inherent limits on what even the most effective opening presentation can accomplish. If the other side is prepared, they already will have done the same thing you did: evaluated the case beforehand to come up with a target range for possible settlement. If your presentation is particularly damning, the result might be to push your opponents more easily toward the top of their predefined range (or below it, if your opponent is the plaintiff).

But what if, during the opening presentation (or some other time in the session), you introduce facts (or something) that would strongly justify a settlement far outside your opponents' target range? By the nature of human psychology (not to mention the need of authority for corporate parties), the effect might be to stretch beyond what they can bring themselves to accept (or offer) during the mediation. In that case, the best outcome might be settlement on your hoped-for terms at some later point, based on a change in your opponents' expectations that began during the mediation.

This serves to underscore the importance of doing all you can to bring your opponents' settlement expectations in line with yours *in advance* of the mediation session. Even the best opening presentation is unlikely to work miracles.

Even so, under at least certain circumstances, a good opening can definitely have an impact. One example comes from

Paul Sandars (Roseland, NJ), a prominent construction lawyer (as well as a certified mediator). In general, Sandars says, he is not a fan of lengthy presentations. "But in some situations it's appropriate," he allows, "because you've got to talk to the adjusters if it's insurance money. Especially in construction, where there's always a room full of adjusters who are spending not-their-money. If they see a very good PowerPoint presentation on liability, you've hit them over the head."

(11) Responding to your opponent's opening presentations

"If the opposing party makes an opening statement by throwing gasoline on the fire, don't make the mistake of taking the bait," advises former mediator Timothy Corcoran (2007, § 3.e.iii). "It will not help the resolution process by getting into a verbal fight. It will not help the resolution process by allowing lawyers' personalities to take over. Lawyers are to assist their clients—not themselves become obstacles to resolution. Yet I sometimes [saw] this happen."

D. An alternative (or supplement): Asking questions

No law saws you have to spend your presentation time actually making a presentation. If you decide not to give a presentation, you may find it useful to spend your allotted time asking questions instead. Or you may give a short presentation that leaves room for you to ask questions also. For one lawyer's approach to these alternatives, see Sidebar 8-2: "Why Tom Dye Asks Lots of Questions." See also Substep 8.6.

8.5 Listen to your opponent's opening (and other comments) with fresh ears.

Don't let yourself be so focused on your own performance duties that you forget to listen. Pay special attention to any conflicts with your understanding of the facts and law, any "new" facts, significant areas of factual or legal agreement between the parties, and everything to do with the financial evaluation of the dispute.

Obviously, your opponent's opening statement will improve your understanding of how the other side currently views the case. Beyond this, if your opponent is the plaintiff (and thus presents first), the presentation may bring up items that you will want to address in your own opening. If you went first, your opponent's opening may raise items that you will want to address in rebuttal (assuming you arranged for this). Also, the presentation may point to questions you will want to ask (or need to be ready to answer) during a subsequent discussion period (if applicable). In addition, your opponent's presentation may bring to mind more "talking points" for the mediator that you will want to communicate when the opportunity arises. Finally, it may help you think of some alternative settlement possibility in lieu of (or in addition to) payment of money. For a discussion of creative settlements, see Step Nine.

"I don't think there's any mediation where listening hasn't provided me with significant guidance," says Christopher Carroll (New York and New Jersey), whose law practice largely involves insurance coverage disputes. "Listening and sort of 'reading'—seeing what the important points are from the viewpoint of your adversary. Hear what they are saying, hear how they are saying it, and respond accordingly."

Carroll gives the example of an insurance case where an evaluation of the claim involved a series of potential discounts from the full claimed value. Such discounts included the viability of the claim itself, as well as the total amount of damages alleged. A third potential discount was for the claim's net present value. Listening to his opponents talk, Carroll noticed that the present-value discount seemed particularly important to them. From Carroll's perspective, this was not a major factor. However, "even though that number really wasn't the one that drove the significant discounts, what *was* important to me was to let the other side understand that I recognized the sensitivity of that issue. So, when I continued to negotiate, that was the one that I recognized or offered the most flexibility concerning, because it was most important to them." Carroll finishes the story like this:

> The case ultimately settled. I'm not saying it settled because of that. But I will say this: At the close of the

> mediation, both sides said, "You know, it's pretty rare in a negotiation where you can go through a three- or four-hour process of fairly confrontational and difficult discussions—and feel comforted that you're talking to someone that you respect and that has respected you."

David Hoffman offers one more interesting reason for listening carefully to your opponent: The other side may be more receptive to your arguments if they perceive that you are genuinely and receptively listening to *them*. Here is how he explains the point:

> Each side has gone over their story and their arguments to the point where those ideas and that way of looking at things is pretty well engraved in the mind—pretty deeply etched. So the task in mediation is not so much to cause the other side to doubt their vision of reality and their vision of what is legally appropriate, but rather to understand *how the other side could view it differently*—how the other side's experiences or perspectives, legitimately, and in good faith, could simply be different. Not necessarily better, just different.
>
> In order to get the other side to open their minds to that possibility, the very first step has to be letting the other side know that they've been heard. Because *until people feel heard, they won't listen*. So it's kind of paradoxical that if you want your perspective to be understood, you have to first seek to understand the other side.

Mediator Eric Galton (Austin, TX) emphasizes that not only should you listen, you should use body language that *shows* you are doing so. "[M]ake sure by nodding your head, making eye contact, that the other party understands that you are seriously listening to what they have to say," he advises (speaking in Bickerman et al., 2003, p.12). He also urges "a few 'do not's'" (p.13):

> Do not look in a book or put your head down when the other side is speaking. Do not have a private

> conversation with your client and whisper when the other side is speaking. And today, for heaven's sake, do not have your cell phone on so that it rings and interrupts when the other side is making their important presentation.

8.6 Be prepared for questions and discussion.

You never know when questions might pop up, either from the mediator or your opponent, during the initial joint session. Your opponent might ask you something informally before the opening presentations begin. Although the mediator is unlikely to interrupt your opening to ask a question, it has been known to happen. More rare, but still possible, is a question from your opponent during your opening. More likely, if your presentation goes first, the mediator may ask questions before your opponent's opening. Perhaps most often, questions or discussion from the mediator or parties may arise after the parties' presentations have concluded (*see* Picker, 2003, p.32; Watson, 2002, p.10).

John DeGroote is unusual in that he explicitly welcomes questions from his opponents even while his side is in the midst of their opening presentation:

> Most people can't stand give-and-take in their opening. My perspective is, "Stop me at any time. I am happy to. If you've got a question, that means that there is an issue that's important to you, and I want to get to the bottom of it. Because at the end of the day, I don't want to bet on a bad case. I run risk management for my company, and I've got to go back and tell my CEO, 'This is what this case is worth and this is what it's *not* worth'—and I can't do that without your input."

If you ask questions of the opposing lawyer or client during the initial joint session, your opponents are probably more likely to ask your side questions as well. Since Tom Dye likes to ask questions, he says he also makes a point of "woodshedding" with his own client in advance of the mediation session, "in the same way I would with a deposition. I would prepare him for every contingency I could think of." If there is a question he absolutely does not want his client to answer, he will try to craft some diplomatic response that does not sound like a point-blank refusal.

Larry Watson urges caution, warning that direct questioning from one side to another during the joint session can become counterproductive (2002, p.10):

> While interactive exchanges during the opening presentations can be helpful, they should be carefully monitored and controlled. Be prepared for and encourage clarifying questions by the mediator or the opposition, but avoid debate. With some clients (as well as overly assertive experts, advisors, and other support personnel) there will be a compulsion to "play lawyer" during interactive sessions. These efforts are usually manifested by clumsy attempts at imitating cross-examination techniques with a series of prefatory questions aimed at striking a final smashing blow with the witness hopelessly trapped into agreement.
>
> Everyone, especially clients and non-lawyer participants, should be discouraged from turning a mediated interactive exchange of information necessary to clarify the elements of a dispute into a process aimed at winning the dispute. The objective for the opening presentation is met when the issue is delineated, not when it is decided.

As for mediators, they may ask several types of questions in the initial joint session, including inquiries to clarify a party's positions or to define and narrow down the key issues. For a long list of mediators' questions that a party should be prepared to answer during the initial joint session or private caucuses, read Appendix C, "Tough Questions: Mediator Questions Lawyers Should Anticipate," by Tom Arnold.

Truly rare—but not unheard of—is for an active mediator to ask both sides a series of pointed questions that turns the initial joint session into an extended discussion period. For a vivid real-life example, read Sidebar 8-7: "The Initial Joint Session That Swallowed a Mediation."

8.7 End the initial joint session on a productive note.

At this stage of the mediation proceeding, the negotiation phase still lies ahead. As the initial joint session concludes, and the parties are about to start private caucuses, you would like for everyone to have a good taste in their mouths. What you should do in practice depends on the specifics of the session atmosphere and feelings between the parties. But as a general rule, the more positive you can be (without looking like a dip in the face of hostility from your opponent), the better.

SIDEBAR 8-1

Do Seating Arrangements Matter?

Training for mediators often includes advice on arranging how the participants will sit during the joint sessions. One book even includes diagrams showing a variety of different options (Beer & Stief, 1997, pp.29–30).

Such considerations are relevant to a social science called proxemics, which deals with the social and communicative significance of the way people allocate space. To vastly oversimplify, sitting across the table is often associated with opposing sides. Sitting diagonally is less adversarial. Sitting on the same side is associated with allies.

For litigators, probably the most familiar seating arrangement is where the mediator sits at the head of the table and the parties face each other across it (with the lawyers usually closest to the mediator). The mediator in effect occupies the spot of a judge presiding over a hearing in chambers. As you might expect, this setup has been characterized as communicating authority on the part of the mediator (*see* Beer & Stief, 1997, p.30).

Because a side-by-side position is seen as least hostile, some mediators advocate an arrangement where the mediator sits in the middle of the long side of a table, and *both* parties (and their lawyers) sit lined up across from her along the other side (*see* Starr & Page, 2005, para. 8). This is the arrangement favored by Zena Zumeta (Ann Arbor, MI), who does some business mediation in addition to her work resolving family disputes. "My own preference for the way people are seated is that I don't like the parties glaring at each other across the table," she says. "So the tendency for me is to sit on one side and array the parties and attorneys on the other side." Sometimes opposing parties agree to sit next to each other, flanked by their lawyers.[11]

Of course, those options all presuppose a rectangular or square table. Some mediators prefer a round table, on grounds that it "fosters dialogue rather than adversity" and "promotes a sense

---

11. Zumeta made these remarks in a CLE teleconference, "The Best Impasse Breaking Technique: Preparation," sponsored by the ABA Section of Dispute Resolution (November 29, 2011).

of cooperation" (Goodman, 2004, p.42). Seating of any kind becomes more complicated where multiple parties are involved.

The mediator's preferred seating arrangement may tell you about her mediating style. For example, a mediator's choice for a round table in her conference room might imply a strongly facilitative approach, even if she has described herself as evaluative. A rare, eccentric arrangement would raise other questions.

"A lot of people put a lot of stock on who is sitting where at the table," says John DeGroote (Dallas). "I don't. It makes people uncomfortable sometimes to sit on the other party's side of the table, but those are minor issues."

The important thing to remember is that the mediator is not the boss; her choice of seating is not mandatory. You might feel a bit silly seeking an advance agreement on how the parties will sit. But if you feel uncomfortable with the arrangement, it is your prerogative to (diplomatically) object.

SIDEBAR 8-2

Why Tom Dye Asks Lots of Questions

Tom Dye (West Palm Beach, FL) views the initial joint session as a chance to do more than exchange opening presentations. A major goal is to learn as much as possible not just about the facts of his opponent's case, but also about what he calls their "emotional motivation" with regard to settlement. He does so by carefully observing the other side from the moment they enter the conference room, and by using every opportunity to ask questions.

Dye typically arrives at a mediation session well prepared to give an opening, which might include PowerPoint slides, blown-up photos and sometimes even video clips in addition to key documents. But depending on what he learns in the early part of the session, he may decide to modify—or even cancel—his presentation plan. He also uses what he learns to guide his settlement strategy.

By "emotional motivation," Dye means how strongly the other side is inclined to settle. Among other things, Dye wants to know "whether the attorney and opposing party are afraid of going to trial. If so, I will factor that into my negotiation." To learn, he tries to make use of informal chit-chat:

> I might give a little spiel: "This is not the trial, I realize that, and so we're coming in here in good faith trying to resolve the case. But I want to get some idea before we start discussing the facts of the case—because my client wants to factor it in—of the parameters of the trial and so forth, and what we can expect. I just want to see if we're on the same page, because obviously that's the cost that we're all going to have to take into account." Then I would start asking some questions. I would convey a very open and cooperative tone, but at the same time try to read their fear by my questions.

Some of those questions would be directed to the opposing attorney. For example: How long do you think the trial is going to take? How many experts do you think you're going to need? How many days will you need your expert on the stand? Dye judges the attorney not only by the competence of his answers but "by his body language and tone of voice and by his confidence as I start throwing these things out." In a world where many litigators have little (or no) trial experience, the answers can be revealing. More importantly, Dye will chat directly with the opposing client. If he senses any apprehension or reluctance about trial, he says, "I'm going to give them a more hardball opening offer."

With regard to the facts of the case, Dye wants to fill in any gaps in his knowledge before he begins his presentation. If the opposing attorney represents the plaintiff, and thus gives his presentation first, Dye is likely to follow up with informal questions. He might say something like "Okay, Joe, that was interesting, when you mentioned that. I'm not sure how you got to that. Can you explain that to me? How did you get your figure?" Or, "I had a different understanding of the facts. Where did you get that that happened on that date, and who said that?"

Through such questions, Dye believes he can potentially accomplish up to six things:

1. Obtain new factual knowledge that may affect his view of the case, or his strategy for trial if the mediation fails.
2. Learn more about his opponents' "whole approach to the case, their theory, their strategy, their witnesses." For example, he may understand for the first time why his opponents plan to call a certain witness.
3. Pick up clues about the other side's attitudes or concerns by keeping close tabs on their nonverbal behavior. "I can learn if the opposing client looks at his lawyer when I bring a point up. You know, if I see eyes askance like 'he caught us,' that's information."
4. Probe or expose weak points. If there are problems with the opposing side's account of the facts, Dye says, "I can by asking my questions show them that I know their story is full of holes."
5. Gauge whether his opponents are serious about trying to settle the case now.
6. Explore whether there are any alternative ways to "problem-solve the situation" besides payment of money.

Similarly, if Dye represents the plaintiff (and thus is expected to go first), he will put himself in a position to ask the other side some questions before he starts. He may arrange in advance for the mediator simply to say, "Tom, you have 30 minutes, and then we will give the other side 30 minutes" rather than specify that the parties will both use that time to give a presentation. Then he will start by asking the other side questions that he has formulated based on his current knowledge of the case.

For example, he might say something like: "We have expert depositions next week. But for purposes of negotiation, I need to know some of these additional things. Would you guys mind if I ask you these? Maybe you can share it with me now so that I know it's coming."

If the litigation is still in its early stages, Dye might end up spending his entire presentation period with questions and follow-ups. Otherwise, depending on the answers to Dye's questions, he may request a break to confer with his client and plan how to use the rest of his time.

He might decide to modify his planned presentation, if his view of the case has been altered. If his opponent has shown no motivation to settle and taken positions that seem very unreasonable, Dye may conclude that chances of settlement now are minuscule, increasing the probability of trial. If so, he might scuttle his PowerPoint and give a short pro forma presentation geared to reveal as little as possible about his approach to the case.

In any event, once his time is over and the other side has given a presentation, he will follow up with more questions based on his opponent's presentation.

The essence of Dye's attitude is that he wants to make the most of the initial joint session's opportunities for both information gathering and persuasion. This requires getting maximum information from his opponent before starting the persuasion phase (his presentation).

SIDEBAR 8-3

"What If I Don't Have Trial Experience?"

A reality of today's world is that many litigators practice for years without ever getting the chance to take a case to trial. Unfortunately, this is a factor that some opposing trial lawyers will consider when evaluating a dispute in the context of mediation. Even when your case is strong, its value may be discounted for settlement purposes if you lack trial experience and therefore would seem to pose less of a threat in the courtroom (*see also* Sidebar 8-2: "Why Tom Dye Asks Lots of Questions").

Unfortunately, you probably don't have the option to boost your credentials by going out and winning your first trial between now and the mediation session. But here are some things you *can* do:

1. *Prepare yourself to answer potential trial-related questions intelligently*. You don't want to look stunned at the mediation if your opponent asks something like, "By the way, if this does go to trial, how many days do you think you'll need to present your case?" If you've thought out some of the basics about a potential trial, you stand a better chance of sounding like you know what you're doing.
2. *Do a good job in your opening presentation*. Your opening represents an opportunity to demonstrate some of your abilities as a professional. Even though it differs in various respects from trial, it can bolster an impression that you could be effective in a courtroom setting.
3. *Recruit a trial figurehead*. In the event that one of your cases eventually makes it to the trial stage, you might well ask a more experienced lawyer for help. Why not advance the process? If someone with strong trial expertise agrees to join you for trial (understanding that the need is only hypothetical at present), you can talk about *that* lawyer in addition to yourself.

Of course, many other lawyers share your lack of trial background. So in some mediations, your opponent may be just as happy to avoid the topic as you are.

SIDEBAR 8-4

Conflicting Needs for Opening Presentations[12]

By Lawrence M. Watson Jr.

The presentation of the client's case in the opening phase of a mediation is a task that must meet two often-conflicting needs.

First, the client must feel his or her story has been told. Any anger, frustration, and discontent stemming from the events leading to the dispute must be relieved before focused attention

12. Excerpted from Watson, 2002, p.9.

can be given to reconciliation considerations. To one extent or another, therefore, the client must be given the chance to vent—either through counsel or directly. In all occasions, the client must feel that the merits of his or her position in the debate has been fairly presented and understood.

Secondly (and often in contradiction of satisfying the client's "venting" needs) there is a need for the opening presentations to clearly and objectively communicate the "other side of the story" to the opposition. Many clients to a dispute might be quite pleased with a lawyer that relieves built up feelings and relates their position in ominous, scolding, or even threatening terms. An overly aggressive tone or demeanor to an opening presentation in a mediation, however, can serve to turn off the opposition and the critical task of expanding their understanding of the dispute is not achieved. The better rule is to avoid hyperbole—don't give the other side any more adrenaline than they already have.

All things considered, it is probably better to shape the opening presentations in a mediation to meet the demands of the second task rather than the first. Calming the client down or providing a process to vent subliminal frustrations can be handled in other ways.[13] There is only one opportunity, however, to be in a position to bring the opposition to understand and fully appreciate all dimensions of the dispute. In instances where there are insurance representatives, claims adjusters, or other conflict management personnel involved in the decision-making for the other side, an angry or emotive presentation is a waste of time.

One acceptable method of satisfying both needs is to simply allow the client an opportunity to participate in the opening presentations to satisfy whatever venting needs exist. In that event, Counsel would prepare and execute an opening presentation geared toward communicating the reality of the dispute to the opposition in a tone and manner best suited to complete that task. The client could then add the emotive element to the presentation while satisfying his or her need to vent.

---

13. For a discussion of client "venting" in private caucuses, see Substep 9.4 and Sidebar 9-5: "The Power of Venting."

Accordingly, the best overall theme and tone of opening presentation in mediation would probably be a matter of fact description of the case to be presented at trial—firmly and unequivocally stated. It should clearly set forth the principal contentions underlying the position asserted, and the facts, principal documents, and expert opinions that support those contentions. There should be minimal argument—let the facts do the arguing.

SIDEBAR 8-5

"Should I Hold Something Back for Trial?"

"I have certainly held stuff back in mediation that I wanted to use for surprise in a trial when we got there," says Nate Cade, who does tort liability work at a law firm in Milwaukee, WI. "I didn't want to show every card I had."

Cade's comment reflects a common experience. As long as there is a possibility that a case will end up going to trial, lawyers will feel an urge to hold back information or evidence of some kind for possible use there. Mediator J. Anderson Little (Chapel Hill, NC) calls springing surprise information on opponents at trial "a pretrial fantasy of most trial lawyers" (2007, p.19).

The perceived advantage in holding something back is to have extra ammunition at trial that your opponents are not expecting, which could increase your chances for a win. The downside is that disclosing the item at mediation might potentially get your client a better settlement. And if the case settles at mediation, you will never get a chance to use the withheld information, so it won't be of any benefit to your client.

The questions are: When—if ever—is it a good idea to hold something back? If you do decide to disclose an item at mediation that you had considered holding back, when and how is it best to do so?

In John DeGroote's opinion, the general rule should be not to hold back. He says:

> There are a lot of trial lawyers that say, "I don't want to use my best evidence because I want to save it for trial." But you've got about a 3% chance of making it to trial. So I would rather monetize that good evidence in the other 97%, and hope that you are smart enough to be able to use it to your advantage anyway in the 3% likelihood event that you actually do go to trial.

"But," he adds, "that's just me."

Anderson Little's perspective as a mediator is also that holding back is generally a mistake. He observes that "what lawyers think is strategic information often turns out to be information that, if they did convey it to the other team, would help settle the case" (2007, p.21).

In some rare instances, however, even DeGroote will decide to withhold. He is most inclined to do so with material of such a nature that "by telling them now they would pooh-pooh it and come up with an excuse—where I don't think they would be able to do that on the stand." The best example that comes to DeGroote's mind is proof that the other side engaged in spoliation of evidence. "That is an area where people can think of a plausible excuse if they are given enough time."

Here is an example of where Nate Cade might hold back:

> Say we're in a personal injury lawsuit, and the plaintiff is claiming that they can't do certain things—and I have a videotape of that plaintiff, doing a sport activity or something else. Am I going to bring that up at the mediation? Probably not. Because the more time I give them to think about what I have, the more time they have to downplay it, correct it, and say "I was feeling good that day" or whatever. Playing that video as a surprise in front of a jury right then and there, that says a lot. So yeah, I would hold that back.

Tracey Salmon-Smith (New Jersey and New York) says she might withhold information "that we might be able to use on cross-examination later or something to attack our opponents' credibility. I might not share that with the mediator if I didn't have to."

For Tom Dye, the sort of evidence he might want to hold back "really depends on the case." He supplies this hypothetical:

> It may be that I find my opponents are totally missing a killer. In other words, they may be basing their case on some point while missing a document that was produced to them that totally refutes what they're saying. Apparently, they didn't read through the 5,000 pages of computer printouts my side produced in discovery to find that. I may have that document in my briefcase, but I may not pull it out at the mediation, because I want them to take that position at trial—and I'll kill them with a document that goes just the opposite. Or maybe I can get summary judgment on that down the road—I'm not going to bring it up right now. So it's really case specific.

Bear in mind that with some information, you may have the option of disclosing it in general terms rather than revealing all the specifics. That approach is favored by Steven Brom, who maintains a commercial litigation practice in Birmingham, AL. He uses an example where his opponent deposed a certain witness but "forgot to ask a certain question that turned out to be pivotal." Under those circumstances, Brom might say something like this to the mediator in a private caucus:

> I've got this information. I know that the other side has not uncovered it themselves yet. I think it's very damaging to their case, and I intend to use it fully at trial. I don't mind telling you about it—as the mediator—in full detail, because I want you to appreciate just how significant the evidence is. And I want you to be able to go into their room and to communicate to them the seriousness of the evidence. But at the same time, I don't want you to tell them exactly what it is, so that they then have a matter of months to prepare for trial with it.

Of course, there are built-in risks to telling the mediator more than you want her to tell the other side. One is that she may end up saying more—inadvertently and with the best intentions—than you meant for her to communicate.

Timing of disclosure

If you do decide to make a disclosure that favors your case, timing can be critical. As a general matter, Florida mediator Peter Grilli advises taking this step well in advance of the mediation session, so that the other side will have enough time to absorb the information and adjust expectations for the range of settlement. He says:

> If you want to impress the other side with the strength of your case, many times it's just not going to help to spring the information on them at the mediation. Even though they're supposed to have someone there with full authority to settle, very often at a corporation matters have been analyzed before the mediation in committee and so forth. And if you want the committee to weigh in on those things, you want to have that information in their hands maybe two or three weeks before the mediation, so that they have the time to think about it and react to it.
>
> It takes time to process that information. It's like the Elisabeth Kübler-Ross stages of dealing with death: The first phase is denial. So if somebody comes in with some new information that's going to turn this million-dollar case into a $5 million case, the easiest thing on the other side to do is to say, "Well, you know, we can't react to that, we just got it at the last minute. We need to check into this." So the last-minute surprising things usually don't work.

If you decide to wait until the mediation session itself to disclose confidential information that favors your position, law professor and mediator Dwight Golann (Boston) recommends that you do so no later than the initial caucuses (2009a, p.273):

> It is usually better to offer evidence as early as possible while the mediator is still focused on gathering information. . . . Evidence presented later in the process, during the bargaining phase, risks sounding like an excuse for failing to compromise. The mediator may also fail to give it full weight because he is focused on managing the bargaining.

John DeGroote agrees. He advises disclosing no later than the third "turn" (i.e., the third time the parties bat numbers back and forth in negotiations):

> The third time the mediator comes to you, this ain't about the facts of the case anymore. I kid you not—I have seen cases where fantastic evidence was saved for the sixth turn, and at that stage people just say, "Well, we are beyond that now." And you can say, "But it is a videotape!" And they'll reply, "You know, we are beyond that. We are trying to bridge the gap here." So that point will forever be lost and never be monetized.

In practice, the process of disclosure may become a kind of dance, where disclosures are made back and forth as each party gains more confidence that the other side is negotiating in good faith. This is how the process is described by Albert Watkins (St. Louis, MO):

> When you get done with the opening and go to caucus in separate conference rooms, no matter who goes first there's going to be a little bit of fear about disclosing everything. So you disclose a little bit, and you wait until they come back at you with whatever it is that they have in their bag of goodies to convince you that your case may not be worth every bit as much as you think it is.
>
> The more information you procure from opposing counsel, the higher degree of assurance you have that they're participating sincerely in the mediation process. You can tell generally by the time you've completed the first or second caucus.

Nevertheless, some information may be of such a nature that you simply do not want to reveal it unless you are relatively sure the case will settle rather than going to trial. The more probable it seems that a mediation session will result in a settlement, the more incentive there is for a lawyer to monetize such information by disclosing it. So a lawyer may decide to hold back information until reaching a point in negotiations where it seems clear that the odds of settlement are great—

then reveal it in hopes of getting a better deal (or clinching the deal).

"Towards the end of the day, if I think it can get the job done, then I might release that type of information," Tracey Salmon-Smith says. "Because you can generally get a sense of whether it's going to settle or not in midafternoon."

When you are considering the issue of whether to hold back or reveal some important point, don't forget to consult your client. As Nate Cade says, "you don't always have to hold something back. A lot of it is discussion with your client, what information do you want to reveal."

SIDEBAR 8-6

A Humanizing Video That Stunned the Defendants

David A. Hoffman (interview)

As discussed in Substep 8.4C(7), exhibits for mediation sessions can often be effective without being costly. In some cases, however, a big investment may be well worth the expense. David Hoffman (Boston) offers an extreme example.

In one case, I was serving as the mediator. The case involved a claim that a nursing home had mistreated one of the residents, and she had died as a result. The defendant was a big company. The mediation involved bringing in executives from out of town.

The first half of the mediation was a videotape prepared by plaintiff's counsel. The first part of the videotape showed advertisements for the nursing home and what a wonderful caring environment it was. Then, the remainder of the videotape showed scenes that had been secretly filmed by the family. They put a video camera in the room of their elderly relative. They had put the camera there because they thought she was being mistreated—there were bruises on her body.

It turns out those bruises were from her having fallen—which is what the nursing home said was the case—and she was not actually hit by anyone so far as people could tell after the fact. But what this camera did show is that the staff weren't feeding her properly, and she needed help. She needed assistance being fed, and the camera showed that the staff made only perfunctory efforts to actually feed her. So the fact that she withered and died was a result of a severe lack of care on the part of the staff.

The video also showed footage of her life, prior to going into a nursing home—all of the things that she had enjoyed in her life, pictures of her family. It's not entirely clear how much of this material would have been admissible if the case went to trial, although I think some of it would have been.

After half an hour of watching this videotape, you could see that the defense was stunned by what they had seen. The effect of seeing something as direct as what was shown was powerful, and it humanized the case. They weren't just talking about some person who was described on a piece of paper that the lawyers are having a debate about. There was a real talking person on that videotape. It brought this elderly, now deceased woman directly into the room.

The plaintiff's counsel obviously invested a lot of money—I would say, probably low six figures—in preparing this videotape and preparing for this mediation. They achieved a settlement that was very substantial, in part because of how powerful this material was.

SIDEBAR 8-7

The Initial Joint Session That Swallowed a Mediation

As former head of litigation worldwide for a major consulting firm, John DeGroote has been to more mediations than he can count. One might think he has seen it all. But even DeGroote was surprised by the initial joint session conducted by a nationally prominent mediator in Washington, DC, about five years ago.

This was big-ticket litigation. DeGroote's company was suing over a software deal where the amount at issue was high enough to warrant a mediator who charged about $10,000 a day—with a two-day minimum. The parties had briefed the mediator in advance, and the mediator obtained answers to some follow-up questions by e-mail.

At the mediation, DeGroote's outside lawyer was the first to launch an opening presentation, since he represented the plaintiff. He barely finished his opening line—something like "This is a case about a contract"—when the mediator interrupted.

"He said, 'Stop right there,'" DeGroote recalls. "He said, 'Isn't that really what the whole case is about?'"

From that point forward, the initial joint session was "almost like an appellate argument," says DeGroote, with the mediator focusing on the basic issue of whether a binding contract really had ever been formed. "He just fired away questions throughout. And then he looked to the other side and fired questions at them."

An hour went by, then another. Morning turned into afternoon as the initial joint session became a marathon, with the mediator leading "a carefully orchestrated give-and-take." Because the mediator knew in advance that the parties were extremely far apart on settlement numbers, he focused instead on drilling down to the fundamental issues.

"By the end of Day One," DeGroote says, "we decided that it really all came down to what one person would say in their depo." So both sides decided to postpone the second day of mediation and "negotiated a cease-fire" pending that one critical deposition.

The depo was not taken in any hurry. In fact, ultimately it was *never* taken. "Very curiously," it seemed that neither side really wanted it. "We settled without knowing what the answer was, because I think both sides were worried about how that one person was going to testify."

And that is how the initial joint session that swallowed a mediation also managed to swallow the case.

SIDEBAR 8-8

"Worry Less About the Lawyering Angle"

Charles E. Pou Jr. (interview)

Before cofounding a dispute resolution firm, Charles Pou (Washington, DC) directed the dispute resolution program at the Administrative Conference of the United States. He was one of the principal drafters of the Administrative Dispute Resolution Acts of 1990 and 1996. I asked Pou to talk about some of the mistakes that he has often seen lawyers make in mediation. Here is part of his reply.

Some lawyers tend to approach mediation much as they would a court session in litigation, as opposed to thinking that the ultimate goal here is something very different. I think some of them don't really realize what they should be trying to accomplish in a mediation—which is not to persuade me as mediator, but to persuade their opponent that they ought to take a fresh look at things and maybe be a little more forthcoming with their approach to negotiation.

It seems to me that a lot of lawyers look at mediation sessions as an opportunity to do their "lawyerly" thing and maybe impress their client. I don't know if that's prevalent, but I know it happens more than it should. Whereas frequently the smart thing to do is to let their client take a more active role, and worry less about the lawyering angle and more about the negotiating angle.

One of my concerns—and I'm sure you've heard this from others, too—is that the people who choose the mediator and run the process are the lawyers, whereas the people who have the disputes are the clients. A lot of the time, the lawyers are more focused on the legal issues, and less focused on some of the psychological, relationship, and other issues that probably had as much to do with the dispute getting out of hand as anything in the first place.

With some lawyers, the clients' interests and needs get less attention than they should, and the things that look more like what a judge would be concerned with get inordinate attention. A lot of times it is not just about the dollars and cents—it's about the relationship issues, what got them into this tangle, what would work for them psychologically or in other ways that may have very little to do with money. A lot of lawyers may have a hard time giving as much credence to these as to the kinds of things that they would focus on in court, which is usually "How much is this worth? How does this translate into a judgment of some sort?"

I've mediated a fair number of cases where—not that the money didn't matter, but the party was a lot less interested in just the size of the judgment then they were in some of the other issues that the lawyers may have not been paying as much attention to. For example, one case I mediated involved an army officer whose wife died in a government hospital due to what was pretty clearly negligence, and perhaps gross negligence, on the part of the hospital staff. This was basically a case for dollars under the Federal Tort Claims Act.

The Justice Department approached the mediation as purely a matter of "What is this case worth." But the plaintiff officer—when you actually talked to him in caucus—frankly, his wounds were a lot more emotional. His concerns were as much as anything, "Just how did this happen, and how do you keep this from happening again to somebody else down the line?" Those were concerns that the Justice Department lawyers had a hard time focusing on and dealing with and discussing in a meaningful way—even though they were really, I think, driving this lawsuit as much as anything specifically dollar related.

Ultimately, the outcome of the case was a monetary settlement. But I think the discussions that took place in the mediations let the plaintiff get some sense that maybe this lawsuit did have some positive impact on the way that these government hospitals might do business in the future—and might do some good beyond just getting him some dollars.

STEP NINE

Position Your Negotiations at the Initial Private Caucuses

The very best advocates in mediation are those that understand how to use the caucus effectively.

—John Bickerman, mediator
(Bickerman et al., 2003, p.15)

In the caucus stage of a typical mediation session, each side meets separately with the mediator, who typically shuttles back and forth until either settlement is achieved or impasse is declared. For purposes of Step Nine, we will consider your side's initial caucuses to end when your side puts its first offer or counteroffer on the table. In some mediation sessions, this might occur at the end of your side's first caucus; in others, two or more initial caucuses may take place.

After a brief overview of the stages of private caucusing at a mediation session and a preview of what to expect from a mediator in the initial caucuses, this chapter will describe eight substeps to successful completion of the initial caucus stage.

Stages of caucusing. Michael Wilk and Henry Blum (Houston) view caucuses as divided into three stages: "the opportunity to be heard," "objective skepticism," and "fight or flight" (2004, pp.18–19). In their view, a major function of the first stage is to provide a forum for the client "to freely discuss his view of the case and the impact it has had on his life." It is also a time for counsel to highlight the strength of her side's case. In addition, the mediator can "introduce the possibility of risk" to your client through questions and comments.

In the middle, "objective skepticism" caucuses, the client becomes willing (with the mediator's help) to see his lawyer turn from a "trial advocate" to a "resolution advocate" and the client goes to work toward resolution. Proposals are made and weighed. The third stage—the one that Wilk and Blum call "fight or flight"—is when the client is finally ready to make a business decision, and settlement is reached or impasse declared.

Some other mediation experts also divide caucusing into three stages, although they may be conceptualized somewhat differently. For example, in *The Mediator's Handbook* (2006), the late mediator John Cooley divided caucuses into the "problem clarification stage" (initial caucusing), the "generation and evaluation of alternatives stage," and the "selection of alternatives stage"—aka "decisional caucusing" (pp.203–304).

Mediator and law professor Dwight Golann also divides caucusing into three stages, in a somewhat different way. He classifies "the first round or two of caucusing" as the "early caucuses" (Golann, 2009a, p. 23). A distinguishing feature of the "middle caucuses," he writes, is that they "tend to mix case analysis with active bargaining and sometimes exploration of interests" (2009, p.26). In the "later" or final caucus stage, "disputants focus less on the value of their case and more on pure bargaining" (p.28).

Preview of the initial private caucus. On the topic of initial caucuses, Prof. Golann offers this preview to counsel preparing for a mediation session (2009a, p. 273):

> You can expect the following to occur in a first caucus meeting:
>
> - The mediator will focus on listening and asking questions. He will seek to gather information, both to help the parties understand their opponent's perspectives and eventually to lower their confidence about prevailing in court. Offer supportive data and supply ammunition for the mediator to use with your opponent.
> - A mediator will tend to use a principled, "let's be reasonable" bargaining style, trying to avoid tough positional tactics such as first offers intended to jolt the other side. She will expect you to show some

> cooperation and offer a concession to help the process get going. She will be looking for possible openings, or at least a private indication of flexibility. Be prepared to offer something or to explain why it is not appropriate.

Given the types of discussion and questioning that are typically involved, it is not surprising that early caucuses tend to be longer than later ones—sometimes lasting an hour or more (Golann, 2009a, p.26).

You may get some additional insight into initial caucuses by comparing Prof. Golann's preview for mediation counsel with the advice he gives mediators as to what they need to achieve in the initial caucuses (2009a, p.23):

> During the first round or two of caucusing, you will have the following goals [as mediator]:
>
> - Continue to build relationships.
> - Make the disputants feel fully heard.
> - Gather sensitive information.
> - Control negative communications.
> - Identify interests and probe for hidden obstacles.

Prof. Golann also advises the mediator to "perhaps start the bargaining process" as early as the first caucus (p.24).

Bennett Picker's description of mediator goals at this early stage includes a couple of items Prof. Golann does not mention: "The mediator will use the early phase of the initial caucus sessions to establish a rapport with the parties, to earn the trust of the parties, to *identify the negotiating styles of the attorneys* and the *identity of the real decision makers* and to *begin to shift the parties away from their initial positions*" (2009, p.33, italics added).

Mediator J. Anderson Little (Chapel Hill, NC) also discusses initial private caucuses in his book of instruction to mediators, highlighting "two important tasks" (2007, p.50). The first task he describes—echoing one of the goals listed by Golann and Picker—is "to establish rapport with the participants so that they will respond to the mediator's important and penetrating questions."

The second task of the mediator at this stage, as Little sees it, is "to frame questions that encourage the participant to think more completely about the case." He writes (p.51):

> One of the ways I have found to accomplish that difficult task is to take the material the other side has given me in either a general or private session as the basis for my inquiry. I often say things like:
>
> M: They seem to think you've got a problem linking these damages to this collision. What's your thinking on that subject?
>
> or
>
> M: The defense is telling me that you may have a problem with the fact that you asked for a second letter from Dr. Carlson. How do you evaluate that issue?

Little also notes that in his first private caucus with the plaintiff's side, he typically spends much of his time helping the plaintiff's team "get on the same page with each other about their case analysis" (p.77).

If you are outside counsel representing a company where you work with inside counsel, you may find a wide variation in the role you will be expected to play during the caucus phase. For a discussion of this, see Sidebar 9-1: "Roles of Inside Versus Outside Counsel in the Caucus Room." Your job in Step Nine—and for the remainder of the mediation session—must be adapted to fit that role. At a minimum, even where you will be following the lead of inside counsel, you may want to be prepared to offer a private word to that counsel if you feel that one of the important substeps here is being overlooked.

Your side's work in the initial caucuses involves eight substeps:[1]

1. Before the mediator joins you, discuss new observations and perspectives (as needed).
2. Confirm the ground rules on what the mediator may repeat to the other side from her private caucuses with you.

---

1. As always, these substeps are not necessarily sequential, and they will overlap to some extent.

3. Privately discuss your case with the mediator, while actively observing, listening, and probing.
4. Allow your client to vent with the mediator (as appropriate).
5. Utilize the mediator to gather and convey information.
6. Share your draft skeleton agreement with the mediator (if appropriate).
7. Take time-outs to talk privately with your client (as needed).
8. Make your first proposal for settlement.

9.1 Before the mediator joins you, discuss new observations and perspectives (as needed).

Since the mediator frequently caucuses with the plaintiff's side first, there is often downtime in the defendant's caucus room before the mediator arrives. In Sidebar 9-2 ("A Typical First Private Caucus"), litigator Michael Braun (Chicago) describes "preparing ourselves to respond to whatever the mediator comes in with" and "confirming what we think first offer will be, if we don't have a firm number in mind walking into the mediation."

This is also a good time to talk about any questions or concerns your client may have coming out of the opening joint session, including any adjustments in goals or strategy that should be considered. If you represent the plaintiff and you think developments in the opening joint session warrant some discussion alone with your client, bear in mind that you do not *have* to caucus with the mediator right away. You can always ask for a time-out first.

9.2 Confirm the ground rules on what the mediator may repeat to the other side from her private caucuses with you.

Bennett Picker recommends that in the caucus phase, you expressly confirm the mediator's pledge of confidentiality (2003, p.98). In this context, the most important element of confidentiality concerns which statements made in the privacy of your side's caucus the mediator will or will not feel free to communicate to the other side.

Susan Yates, Executive Director of the Resolution Systems Institute in Chicago, elaborates on this point. She notes that there is a wide variation as to how mediators approach the question of what they will communicate to the other side in private caucus:

> I've known some mediators who say at the very beginning of the mediation, "I'm going to assume that anything you say to me in caucus, I can say to the other party any time *unless you tell me otherwise*." In that scenario, the mediator may consider it fair game to tell your opponents things your side said in caucus about what you perceive to be your case's strengths and weaknesses or the effectiveness of your witnesses.
>
> On the other hand, you may have a mediator who says, "I'm going to check with you at the end of every single caucus and find out what it's okay to share and what isn't okay to share."

Other mediators' policies may fall somewhere in between those extremes.

Under any circumstances, Yates clarifies, "the mediator shouldn't go into the other side's caucus and say, 'Oh, you should hear—in the other room, they said "X, Y, and Z." That's not effective mediation." But mediators who do not feel bound by confidentiality on a given item could "choose to spin whatever it is that you say, however they choose."

"I think that's one of the places where a new lawyer needs to be careful, because they can find themselves saying something to the mediator that could be transferred in whatever way the mediator chooses," Yates says. "You can negotiate with the mediator about how your point of view is going to be conveyed in the other caucus room."

Confirming the ground rules on what the mediator may permissibly disclose from your caucus discussions will help prevent any misunderstandings between your side and the mediator as to what you intend to keep confidential. This will also help ensure that the ground rules have registered clearly with your client. Then, throughout the caucus phase, both you and your client will need to keep those rules in mind—and not get careless in what Yates calls the "chummy" atmosphere of the caucus room.

9.3 Privately discuss your case with the mediator, while actively observing, listening, and probing.

During discussions of the case in the initial caucuses, you can expect to see the mediator work toward the goals discussed at the beginning of this chapter, such as gathering sensitive information, trying to identify your side's underlying interests, probing for hidden obstacles to settlement, and framing questions designed to shake up your side's view of the case and facilitate shifts from your initial positions. At the same time, you will be continuing your work to position your side in the most advantageous way at the outset of the mediation session's negotiations.

Inevitably, a portion of your side's discussion with the mediator in the initial caucuses will be spillover of unfinished business from the opening joint session (assuming that one was held). "Despite the most careful preparations, what needs to be said by everyone who needs to speak doesn't always occur during the main presentations," observes mediator Lawrence Watson (Maitland, FL). "It is quite common, therefore, for the mediator initiating an early caucus to be greeted with still more positional debate" (2002, p.10).

Bennett Picker elaborates on this observation (2003, pp.32–33):

> Typically, parties will feel the need to argue the merits of their positions further at the outset of the initial caucus session. Rarely will the parties open up to a mediator quickly. Instead, they will often try to convince the mediator of the correctness of their positions in an effort to have him or her serve as an advocate in the negotiations. . . .
>
> The mediator invariably will anticipate the parties' need to reargue their positions. Given the need

> to build trust, the mediator will take time to listen to these arguments and will remind the parties that the mediator must remain impartial in order to assist the parties in resolving the dispute.

But not all discussion of the facts or issues in your dispute is just spillover—far from it. From the perspective of former in-house counsel John DeGroote (Dallas), an important function of case discussion in the initial caucus is to make sure the mediator now understands the case as thoroughly as you think she should:

> With the mediator, I think you have to highlight "our" view of the case—any twists on the facts that are not clear from the written material. You want to establish whether they read the materials or not—you've got to do that subtly—and then you add any twists on the oral presentation. And you tie together any facts that might not be particularly clear. Of course, the mediator is going to say, "Oh, I thought of that already"—but generally they haven't.

Litigator Christopher Carroll (New York and New Jersey) likes to use discussion of the case as part of what he calls "quality time" with the mediator:

> In the end, part of my job as an advocate is to try to convince the mediator to some degree of the merits of my ways and the value of our position. How I'm going to do that is by spending some quality time with him or her, answering any of their questions, certainly, and getting them comfortable. If we're going to have some form of civil diplomacy, I want to be sure the principal party to that diplomacy understands me 100%.
>
> I can establish more of a relationship with the mediator in a one-on-one session than in a joint meeting with the other side. Relationships are as critical to this process as anything else.

Here is how mediator Peter Grilli (Tampa, FL) talks about the case-discussion aspect of private caucuses:

> If somebody can persuade me of a particular strength or weakness in some aspect of the case, I think that's going to be one of the most important things. It is not all of my job; it's not even necessarily the majority of my job. But a lot of my job consists of me talking to lawyers and walking through their analysis and seeing if they have any soft spots in it. If they do, it's something their client ought to know about.
>
> I'd like to think that I've found diplomatic ways of raising those discussions. But in general, this is what I find that lawyers and sophisticated clients want me to do. They want me to look at their case and say how it looks to me, and things of that nature.

A key element of case discussion at this stage may consist of points that you did not want to discuss in your opponent's presence during the opening joint session. An example of this could be "your perspective of the personalities on the other side," as DeGroote puts it, which might relate either to negotiations or to a negative impact on your opponent's likely effectiveness at trial. In addition, this can be a time to start talking about any "Fisher and Ury interests that are beyond just the payment of money," although "you want to do that subtly, so you're not just listing them."[2]

A. Volunteering weaknesses

There is a divergence of views as to whether (or how much) you should take the initiative in bringing up any weaknesses in your side's case during your discussion with the mediator during the initial caucuses.

One view is that at that stage, your priority is to continue reassuring your client that you are a strong advocate for his position. In the opinion of Michael Wilk and Henry Blum (Houston) it is "important for your client to see that his lawyer is prepared and ready to win at the courthouse. By focusing on the strengths of your case during this first caucus, you are able to show your client that you are ready to try his case

2. For a brief discussion of interest-based negotiation theory as promulgated by Roger Fisher and William Ury in *Getting to Yes* (1981), read Substep 7.4A.

and your client is able to feel that he is bargaining from a position of strength" (2004, p.18).

By contrast, in *Mediation Advocacy* (2002) the late John Cooley advises a more evenhanded approach, including weaknesses as well as strengths(pp.142–43, italics added):

> From the beginning of the very first caucus, let the mediator know that the mediator and you are on the same team. . . . Whether representing a plaintiff or defendant, you should begin by giving an honest summary of the strong points of your case *and its weak points* together with the strong and weak points of the other side's case. If you do this, the mediator will be impressed with your preparedness and reasonableness. . . . By acknowledging your weaknesses and the other side's strengths you deprive the mediator of an opportunity to use them to adjust your first offer or demand.

Where your client is a corporation, former inside counsel Gary Poon (Washington, DC) advises that "[i]n some situations, having an open and honest discussion with the mediator about the strengths and weaknesses of your case can help you deal with any internal conflicts you may have within your organization" (2010, p.78). One or more of the corporation's executives (or inside counsel) may have strong views in favor of the strength of their case—perhaps because they played a part in the events giving rise to the dispute. Other executives may have a different view, or—for example, in the case of a higher-up in the organization who will have settlement authority at the mediation—may not previously have formed an opinion.

"When the person with settlement authority hears the strengths and weaknesses of the case [in the private caucus], particularly if he is able to gauge the mediator's reaction, there is a better chance that some of these contradictory interests could be reconciled," Poon writes (p.78).

B. Disclosing private facts that help your case

Your side may possess one or more facts or pieces of evidence that strengthen your client's position or undermine your opponent, but which you believe your opponent does not yet know. The question of whether or when you should divulge such items during mediation was discussed in Sidebar 8-5: "'Should I Hold Something Back for Trial?'" Recall Dwight Golann's and John DeGroote's advice in that sidebar that for sufficient impact on the negotiations, you should make any such disclosures in the initial caucuses if possible.

The discussion in Sidebar 8-5 concerns possible disclosures to the other side; but that is not the only option. Sometimes one side will disclose facts or evidence to the mediator with the stricture that this information not be communicated to the other side.

In Sidebar 9-3 ("The Problems With Caucusing"), mediators Gary Friedman (Mill Valley, CA) and Jack Himmelstein (New York) criticize this type of disclosure as an "opportunity for manipulation." They describe it as encouraging the mediator to "advise the other side that their case is not worth as much as they thought," without revealing why. Without passing judgment one way or another on this maneuver, the same rationale on timing may apply as to a full disclosure: It is likely to be most effective if done early, when the mediator is still gathering information and forming opinions about the case.

C. Probing by the mediator

"The parties to a dispute often intentionally distort the core issues," John Cooley wrote from his perspective as a mediator (2002, p.17). "The mediator penetrates this fog of distortion through separate caucuses in which the mediator asks direct, probing questions to draw out information that one party would not disclose in the presence of the other party."

Regardless of whether any intentional distortion is going on, the goals your mediator probably has set for herself in the initial caucuses (as noted earlier in this chapter) predictably include "gather[ing] sensitive information," "prob[ing] for hidden obstacles," and "encourag[ing] the participant to think more completely about the case."

Asking questions is the mediator's major tool for achieving these goals. "The mediator is going to be coming back to you and pushing the other side's themes on you," says John

DeGroote. "He or she is going to say things like, 'Well, didn't you agree to this contract modification?'"[3]

As counsel, you need to be ready with a response along the lines of "It's not quite that simple, Mr. Smith," DeGroote advises. "You've got to have your points at hand." For this purpose, DeGroote likes to give the mediator "a piece of paper with our primary points" that is "typed out with the point highlighted and any subpoints, in a big font."

This is similar to what mediator Larry Watson refers to as "white papers," which he highly recommends for use in caucuses. In the same vein, Watson also recommends effective use of what he calls "zingers." White papers and zingers were discussed at length earlier in this book, in Substep 6.6, Sidebar 6-7 ("Creating Positional Vulnerabilities With Zingers"), and Sidebar 6-8 ("Preparing White Papers in Advance of a Mediation Session"). Use of white papers and zingers is not confined to the initial caucuses, but they are likely to be most useful in the early caucuses, while attention is still focused on the strengths and weaknesses of each side's position in the dispute.

Whether you make use of white papers and zingers or some other method, bear in mind the request of mediator John Bickerman to give him "your best ammunition"—the best arguments he can use to shake up the other side's viewpoint—as he will use their strengths to try to shake up *your* viewpoint (*see* Sidebar 9-4: "'What I'm Looking for Is Some Good Arguments'").

By the same token, if the mediator brings up a weakness in your case to which there is no genuine counterpoint, you will enhance your credibility if you are willing to acknowledge this. "I have no problem telling a mediator, 'Look, I'm never going to pay that number,' or 'We may be wrong on this but we have to fight it,'" says inside counsel Robert Craig (Houston). "But I will also tell him if I think he's hit upon a weakness, 'You are right, that's a weakness in our case and we know that—we are working on that.'"

---

3. For an exhaustive list of questions that a mediator might ask you, see Appendix C ("Tough Questions: Mediator Questions Lawyers Should Anticipate," by Tom Arnold).

John DeGroote urges caution, however, when acknowledging a weakness that rises to the level of an admission:

> Everything you say can and will be used against you. Mediators will tell you that that's not the case, and I do not believe them. You probably think I am a cynical guy, but it's really not true—I've just been through it a lot. An admission can be used against you. So the only time you should make an admission is (a) when you don't have a choice, or (b) when it can help build your credibility, so that in areas where you don't make an admission, it looks a little bit more credible.

Especially if you represent a plaintiff, be prepared for a significant amount of probing on the topic of damages. At least, that is so if your mediator is like Anderson Little. "I like to have a significant discussion about damages in the case with the plaintiff's team before they give me a proposal," Little writes (2007, pp.51–52). "Such a discussion helps ground the plaintiff's team in the realities of their case. As a result, the plaintiff's team is more likely to formulate an opening proposal that resembles its case analysis and is less likely to make an outrageous demand that generates an equally outrageous counterproposal."

D. Direct discussion between mediator and client

In many instances, "the mediator in the caucus session will involve the party representatives by posing questions directly to them," notes Bennett Picker (2003, p.33). For example,

> [i]t is not uncommon for a mediator to direct questions to the parties such as: "How do you assess your own case?" "What are your weaknesses?" "How do you feel about this dispute?" "What do you really want?" "What do you really need?" "What do you need the most?" "What do you think the other side really wants?" These questions permit the mediator to assess the parties' real needs and open the door to possible solutions.

The obvious danger from your perspective as counsel is that the client may either "say too much—or say the wrong thing," as Michael Braun puts it in Sidebar 9-2: "A Typical First Private Caucus." Worse, there is a chance that your client will say something you did not even know about. The latter is a possibility that mediator P. Jean Baker (Washington, DC) is very much aware of:

> In the first caucus, frankly, I figure out, Did the attorney do a good job interviewing the clients? Because then basically *I* interview the client. What is it that I now can find out that your attorney doesn't know? Trust me, at some point that's going to come up.

Not surprisingly, many lawyers take the view that it is preferable for nonlawyer client representatives not to say much. "Unless I'm really comfortable with my business representative, I don't want him or her talking too much to the mediator," Michael Braun says (see Sidebar 9-2).

As pointed out in Substep 7.2E, the time to get your client on the same page with you on this topic is during your pre-session preparations. That substep also contains a discussion of what kind of oral contributions you may or may not want a client to make in caucus, including the possibility of role-playing. For best results, don't forget Dwight Golann's advice in Sidebar 7-5 ("Prepping on 'Special Aspects' of the Mediation Structure"): "[I]f you want the client to look to you, the lawyer, before answering, better have a signal system set up."

Allowing (and sometimes encouraging) a client to vent in private caucus is a function with a distinct rationale and purpose. This is addressed separately in Substep 9.4.

E. Using the mediator for a reality check

"Seasoned lawyers also use the mediator to help their client—if they need this kind of help—understand the downside risks of not settling," mediator Linda Singer (Washington, DC) points out. A common way to accomplish this is for the lawyer to "ask the mediator questions in front of their clients" that the mediator will use to point out weaknesses in the clients' case or other dangers related to going to trial.

F. Telling the mediator about your constraints on settlement

According to Singer, another characteristic of lawyers who are seasoned in mediation is that they will probably tell the mediator about any constraints on settlement at a relatively early point in the mediation session. For example, a seasoned lawyer will tell the mediator if for some reason his client could not make a settlement payment before a certain date, or if his client is concerned that settlement terms in the case at hand could have an impact on similar ongoing disputes with other plaintiffs. "It's important for the mediator not to be led on," Singer says—"to think things maybe can happen that really can't."

G. Previous history of negotiations

John DeGroote notes that the initial caucus can also be an appropriate place to bring the mediator up to speed on the previous history of negotiations between the sides. If you briefed the mediator previously on this topic as advised in Step Five, this discussion can supplement or reinforce what may have been communicated in a brief.

H. Observing, listening to, and probing the mediator

Although the mediator does not have the power to impose a settlement between the parties, she still has authority in the mediation session. A major source of this authority is that the mediator is the only person who sits in caucus with both sides—gleaning a great deal of information that she holds confidential. As a result, "she becomes the only one with the full picture" (Friedman & Himmelstein, 2008, p.174).

In a critique of the traditional caucus-based mediation procedure, Friedman and Himmelstein write, "The parties know only what goes on in the meetings in which they participate, plus whatever secondhand report the mediator is permitted and/or chooses to give of what transpired on the other side."[4]

---

4. For more on Friedman and Himmelstein's objections to the caucus procedure, see Sidebar 9-3: "The Problems With Caucusing."

(p.174) This observation underscores why you need to observe and listen to the mediator with great care in your initial caucuses and throughout your caucus-based mediation session.

Since the mediator will be the one who brings your message to the other side, you may need to ask yourself: How well is the mediator comprehending our side's arguments and point of view? How confident am I that the mediator will communicate accurately what we want her to convey? What can I do to maximize that likelihood?

Likewise, since you are dependent on the mediator for all information he or she can glean about what is going on in the other side's caucuses, obviously you will need to pay close attention to whatever the mediator says or hints in this regard. Beyond this, you may probe the mediator for anything else useful that the mediator might disclose if asked directly. In the words of Linda Singer, "the mediator may be able to share impressions that you could never get yourself."

To probe for this type of information, Singer advises, simply ask: "Ask how things have been, how did the other side react to such and such, what do you think their concerns are, what would change that, and how do you think the most effective way would be to package an offer. Mediation pros—people who use mediation a lot and use it successfully—do this quite consistently."

Dwight Golann provides another example of such probing: "If a plaintiff seems agitated in the opening session, defense counsel might later ask the mediator, 'Has Smith calmed down?' or 'If his lawyer recommends a deal, do you think he'll listen?'" (2009a, p.234). But Golann cautions that if you ask questions of this type, the mediator will probably take this as a license to answer any similar questions about *your* side if asked by your opponent.

9.4 Allow your client to vent with the mediator (as appropriate).

Your discussion of your case with the mediator, described in the previous substep, also offers a forum where you may want to allow your client to let off steam or vent. Litigator Albert

Watkins (St. Louis, MO) defines venting like this: "When I say *vent*, I'm talking about clients sharing their story in a fashion that will involve some emotion—getting that monkey off their chest."

Like many experienced mediation players, Michael Wilk and Henry Blum believe client venting serves an essential function (2004, p.18):

> Mediation does not provide the opportunity for any given side to "win." So, it is important to provide the opportunity for your client to talk about his case. He needs to know that he has been heard and understood. By creating an opening for your client to freely discuss his view of the case and the impact it has had on his life, the mediator enables your client to have his day "on the witness stand."

Substep 8.4B raised the option of actually having the client speak directly to the other side in a presentation during the opening joint session. But as noted, this could poison the atmosphere if the client becomes too aggressive or insulting as emotion builds. In the private caucus, by contrast, the client can feel the satisfaction of getting things off his chest to the mediator, without any risk of alienating the other side in the process. As mentioned previously, you may want to prearrange a signal so your client will know when you think is a good time to speak up.

For some memorable examples that illustrate venting's potential impact, see Sidebar 9-5 ("The Power of Venting") and Sidebar 2-4 ("The Power of Good Listening").

9.5 Utilize the mediator to gather and convey information.

In Substep 9.3H we explored how you can actively probe the mediator for information and observations during the course of your discussions in the private caucus. The use of the mediator in Substep 9.5 is closely related, but different. It involves engaging the mediator to go to the other side and obtain more information of various kinds, to share with you in your next private caucus with her.

For example, if the opposing side is relying heavily on a particular theory in making its case, you can request the mediator to ask your opponent to provide more facts or other data in support of that theory (Golann, 2009a, p.234). Similarly, as noted in Substep 9.8, you can ask the mediator to obtain your opponent's justification for an offer they have put on the table. At a later point, you can also ask the mediator to sound out your opponents on a settlement number or approach without attributing it to you.

9.6 Share your draft skeleton agreement with the mediator (if appropriate).

As discussed in Substep 6.7 and Step Eleven, it is very useful to prepare in advance a skeleton settlement agreement. The draft leaves blanks for terms that would need to be negotiated at the mediation session, but it includes any tailored provisions for this case that you can see in advance would be needed, such as who will give releases, confidentiality provisions, and so forth.

With regard to such draft skeleton agreements, "The worst thing that you can do is hold your proposal and then spring it on the mediator and opposing counsel just as everyone is preparing to walk away from the table," warns Jean Baker (2007b, p.6). She continues:

> Remember, effective negotiation involves reaching some degree of agreement on all the points that are essential to your client. A better approach is to provide the mediator a copy of your settlement proposal either before the process begins or during the first private caucus. This will familiarize the mediator with all the issues that must be addressed during the session, thus allowing the mediator to apportion time accordingly.

9.7 Take time-outs to talk privately with your client (as needed).

The function and importance of calling for breaks with your client are discussed in Step Ten.

9.8 Make your first proposal for settlement.

"The settlement positions of the parties before mediation should be the starting point at mediation," advises former mediator and litigator Timothy Corcoran (Tampa, FL). "Don't even think about "back striking"—offering less as your first offer at mediation than you had offered before. If that's what you're thinking, you're wasting everyone's time" (Corcoran, 2007, § 3.h.iii).

Typically, if the plaintiff has not already made a demand in a dispute—that is, named an initial number at which he is willing to settle—he will be expected to do so in the caucus phase. As a mediator, Jay Cohen describes a scene he has too often witnessed in an initial private caucus where the plaintiff's lawyer is inexperienced:

> I'm in the plaintiff's caucus room, and I say, "I don't understand. What's your demand?" And he turns around to his client and says, "Well, what do you think?" And I say, "Oh my God. This is not something that occurred to you in your planning process, guys? Mr. Lawyer? Hello?"

Cohen ranks this tentative approach among the biggest mistakes he sees rookie lawyers make in mediation. "That's a lack of preparation, lack of skills, and lack of experience," Cohen says. Such lawyers are "unsure as to what demands or offers to make, how to respond to the offers that are being made to them and try to extract the best compromise they can. They're tentative in that process." This type of mistake is not limited to plaintiff's counsel; it can just as easily be made on the defense side.

A. Discussion of possible moves with mediator

In their advice to other mediators, both Dwight Golann and Anderson Little recommend that the mediator raise the topic of negotiation tactics in the private caucus and help coach participants on effective tactics (*see* Golann, 2009a, pp.52–58; Little, 2007, pp.80–81). In the experience of mediator and law professor Wayne Brazil (San Francisco), participants frequently raise this topic themselves (2009, p.13):

> I often find that, in private caucus, parties want to identify and analyze, with me, two or more possible next steps or larger process options before they decide how to proceed. They want my input. They want to know, given what I have learned in private caucuses about the other parties and given my experience, what I think is likely to happen if they do X or if they do Y. Or, sometimes a party will tell me in advance what he or she intends to do next in the mediation, but I am very concerned that that contemplated move would inflict serious damage on the process.
>
> These occasions present ideal opportunities to engage in interactive counseling, to talk negotiation "theory" with a party (but not too abstractly). We can explore why the party thinks a move he or she is considering might be called for and how he or she thinks things will play out if that move is made. After listening, we can describe what we have seen happen in similar situations and explain why, given our experience or what we know about the other parties, following that particular course might have the same consequences in the case at bar.

In talking about advising participants on their negotiating, Peter Grilli draws a distinction between "help[ing] people decide what's the best way to *express* what they want"—which he can do as a mediator—and helping participants "*get* what they want" (which he can't):

> If somebody says, "Peter, my bottom line is going to be 250,000—how do I get there?"[5] I tell them, "Look, I can't help you get 250, nor am I allowed to help the other side hold it down to 150. But if 250 is your bottom line, I can suggest to you ways to communicate that concept to the other side without giving it away all at once." And that's part of what I consider my job to be—to just exercise *my* imagination in terms of how that information can best be communicated in a series of offers.

5. *See* Sidebar 10-8: "Should You Ever Tell the Mediator Your Bottom Line?"

In Anderson Little's case, this can mean explaining the types of "plan for movement" that we previously described in Substep 7.4B(5)(b) (*see* Little, 2007, pp.80–82).

If you have followed the advice in Steps Six and Seven of this book,[6] you have already completed a thorough economic evaluation of your case and devised a plan for movement in negotiations. Because of the discussions relating to those steps, relatively little additional advice on the topic of making an initial offer is included in this chapter.

B. Importance of an accompanying rationale

It is worth reemphasizing Prof. Charles Craver's point from Substep 7.4B(2) that you should include a rationale for whatever amount you offer. As Prof. Dwight Golann has observed, "When a money offer arrives without an explanation, the recipient must decide what it means, and disputants' tendency is to interpret ambiguous signals from an adversary in the worst light" (p.53).

John Bickerman stresses the importance of rationales in advising how to respond to a plaintiff's demand in a money dispute. If no rationale is included with the demand, ask for justification, he says: "Why is it $10 million and not $5 million? What's the reason?" Bickerman suggests enlisting the mediator to go back and get the answer from the other side before you proceed further. The other side of the coin: "If you're going to counter, have a justification too."

Like other mediation players quoted in Step Seven, Bickerman stresses the basic point that your negotiating plan needs to leave ample room for intermediate moves between your initial offer and your settlement goal. "If you have an idea where you think the settlement might be, you want to stake out a number that allows you room to get there," he says. "You don't want to go right to that number. And in subsequent iterations of the bargaining dance, you don't want to close too fast."

6. *See, e.g.*, Substeps 6.1, 7.3, 7.4B(2), and 7.4B(5).

C. Timing of first offers

Dwight Golann advises mediators that they can decide to ask for an offer either at the end of the first private caucus or during that party's second caucus (2009a, p.26). In advice to lawyers representing clients in mediation, Prof. Golann offers the following thoughts on whether to make an offer in the first caucus: "It may or may not be the best strategy. If not, don't let yourself be pushed to act prematurely. Instead of making an offer, say you would prefer to wait, for example, because you want to talk more about the issues before making decisions about bargaining" (pp.273–274).

D. Use of the mediator to convey a message with your proposal

"Typically, a mediator will ask you what he's authorized to tell the other side," says litigator John Buchanan (Washington, DC). "For example, you can tell the mediator with a kind of wink that, 'Given the proposal they just have conveyed through you, I'm afraid that this is the best we can do for now.' That conveys that you've got more movement, but that you want to communicate your client's disappointment and that the other side needs to do more."

One of John Cooley's books recommends diplomatically reminding the mediator at the end of each caucus that you want her to use your specific wording in conveying your proposal to the other side (2002, p.141). This is particularly important because otherwise, the mediator may feel entitled to modify your message on purpose if she feels it is in the best interest of negotiations (see Step Ten). If your proposal is a bit complicated, Cooley's advice is that you should actually write it down and hand it to the mediator. (Of course, you may want to get the mediator's view of how your message should be expressed, as discussed in Step Ten.)

E. Final words

Here are parting thoughts on the topic of initial offers from Timothy Corcoran (2007, § 3.h):

In making any offer, you need to do more than think what offer you want to make. You need to ask yourself what message the other side will pick up from the offer you make. Don't make that offer unless it conveys the message you want the other side to receive.

My experience teaches that the best predictor of success at mediation is each party's first move. A big, realist first move puts us immediately on the right track. A [stingy], small move is very discouraging. Victory goes to the bold. The timid, more often than not, fail.

SIDEBAR 9-1

Roles of Inside Versus Outside Counsel in the Caucus Room

If your client is a company that employs inside counsel, there is a good chance you will not be the only lawyer sitting around the table in a conference room for your side's private caucuses with the mediator. Your job in Step Seven included making sure you understood well in advance what type of role you are expected to play vis-à-vis inside counsel on behalf of this particular client in this particular mediation. Your expected role as outside counsel may vary dramatically, depending on the inside counsel's personality and practice background as well as the corporation's internal legal culture.

In some mediations, you as outside counsel may be the lead player in the initial caucus, as reflected in Sidebar 9-2: "A Typical First Private Caucus." In others, the inside counsel may take a coequal role or even restrict your role to a narrowly defined function—both in the initial caucuses and in those that follow.

For outside counsel Walter Stuart (New York), the nature of inside counsel's participation "depends on the nature of the case, and secondly, on the inside counsel's desire to get involved. Sometimes they are just burning to have a role or something to say that they feel they can really articulate better. So I'm always respectful of that." At a minimum, Stuart will review his planned initial presentation with inside counsel, along with any slides, "and really ask for active participation in that process."

Tracey Salmon-Smith (New Jersey and New York) worked for years as inside counsel for a major brokerage firm. Recalling mediations in those days, she says: "When I have outside counsel, they take the lead at the mediation in terms of doing whatever opening statements there are—but then I personally get involved in the active caucusing that goes on, because I also know the case very well. So I will be a very active participant in the individual caucuses."

That does not mean the company's outside counsel would not also be active in caucus. As an example, Salmon-Smith points to instances where the mediator may seek responses directly from a client representative or from a financial advisor directly involved in the brokerage's dispute. "We will look to outside counsel for guidance as to when to say something, because you don't want people talking out of turn," she says.

Also, Salmon-Smith sees outside counsel as instrumental in making sure the corporate representative always understands what is going on in the mediation and how developments during the course of the session may change expectations for the settlement range:

> For example, say we are having individual caucuses, and then the mediator leaves and then all of us are in the room together. It might be helpful for outside counsel to recap what happened or what the concerns were. Sometimes we as lawyers are talking over the business people's head. They are just sitting there thinking, "Okay, what's going on?" It would be helpful for outside counsel to remember that the businessperson is not a lawyer, and take the time to explain.

The view of inside counsel Hob Jordan (Lake Forest, IL) does not seem unusual: "I think it is perfectly okay for an outside lawyer to sit down and be quiet and let a party representative or let me as in-house counsel be the primary spokesman." At the extreme, your inside counsel may make it clear to you that he expects to be the dominant player. Robert Craig (Houston) is an example of this:

> My standard approach is to let my outside lawyers be the spokesmen during the joint sessions, but they should expect that *I* will be taking on the lead role in the individual sessions with the mediator. And I'm going to clearly give the impression to the mediator that I'm in charge of our team. It is my practice to really clearly get [the mediator] talking to me. He may ask the outside lawyer specific issues about the case, I'll probably let them talk about the lawsuit, our positions and so forth. But I'm usually as prepared as the outside lawyer to do that, and I do a lot of probing into whether the mediator has really inquired and pushed the other side.

(For more on probing the mediator, see Substep 9.4H and Substep 10.2.)

Likewise, John DeGroote's preference as in-house counsel is always to play the lead role after the opening joint session ends and caucuses begin. He expresses his viewpoint this way:

> I have done more mediations than most of my outside counsel. I am trained as a mediator, unlike my outside counsel. I know exactly what my client wants, unlike my outside counsel. They are the trial horses in the event the dispute cannot be resolved in mediation; I am not going to try the case. So I need to have outside counsel absolutely up to speed on the facts, to be able to give a presentation in the opening joint session that we work through together with the right tone that shows that we are prepared to proceed in the event that mediation does not succeed. Then, I need my outside counsel to serve as a member of the team and adapt to the situation in a way that they get the matter closer to resolution.

DeGroote sees outside counsel's role in caucuses as "sticking more to the facts and to the alternative to the negotiation process"—that is, going to trial if necessary. As case discussion starts taking a backseat to negotiations in the caucus phase, he says, "I expect my outside counsel's role to fade and my own role to increase throughout."

Bowen Tucker (Arlington Heights, IL) is a third example of an inside counsel who always expects to play a dominant role:

> I would tell outside counsel this very specifically—"Your role at the mediation is to tell your story about how you're going to win this case at trial and how anxious you are to try the case. My role is to be the nice guy who is there to try to get the case resolved and settled." And I don't want the outside counsel to say one word about settlement or what they think the value of the case is, other than to say they think it's a great case and he/she can't wait to try it.

SIDEBAR 9-2

A Typical First Private Caucus

Michael F. Braun (interview)

As part of his litigation practice, Michael Braun (Chicago) has participated in mediation of many securities disputes on behalf of a large brokerage firm. In this sidebar, he describes a typical first caucus at a mediation session.

If I'm representing the defendant, typically the mediator has started off with the plaintiff. We are sitting there waiting for the mediator to come in, and preparing ourselves to respond to whatever the mediator comes in with—as well as confirming what we think our first offer will be, if we don't have a firm number in mind walking into the mediation.

More often than not, we probably have a firm number in mind, unless something causes us to rethink that based on the opening statement or comments by the mediator as we go off to the private caucus.

Then, typically, you hear what the mediator has to say as to his or her visit with the other side—whatever message the mediator has been asked to convey in terms of the evaluation of the case. What the dollars are. Why the dollars are what they are. Depending on how well the mediator knows the parties involved, it may be too early in the process for the mediator to be suggesting, "This is where I think you are headed." This may still be a very initial sounding-out process.

You are obviously responding, in terms of why the facts aren't as bad as the other side makes them sound for you—why there are some key facts on your side that the other side seems to be minimizing or overlooking. And you are talking about a fairly low number in the settlement range to try to get the matter resolved. It's a feeling-out process, quite frankly, at that early stage of the mediation.

The person doing most of the talking, typically, is me as outside counsel. The inside counsel I often work with in securities cases is very effective in the mediation process and also likes to play a role. She is certainly not a potted plant in any fashion. The businesspeople I hope are sort of taking things in, but preferably not taking a real active role in pushing the mediator in terms of how they evaluate the case. Ideally, the businesspeople are letting the lawyers run with the evaluation of the case.

After that discussion with the mediator, my preference is to have the mediator step out. Then, in-house counsel and myself talk to the business representative, to answer questions that he or she may have, to get the business representative's sense as to how he or she views the information conveyed to the mediator by the other side.

Unless I'm really comfortable with my business representative, I don't want him or her talking too much to the mediator. Because I have a concern that my business representative is going to say too much—or say the wrong thing—that may result in sending the wrong message when the mediator goes back and talks to the other side.

SIDEBAR 9-3

The Problems With Caucusing

By Gary Friedman and Jack Himmelstein

As noted in Sidebar 3-4 ("A Noncaucus Model: 'Understanding-Based' Mediation"), Gary Friedman (Mill Valley, CA) and Jack Himmelstein (New York) propound a radically different model for mediation sessions, where private caucuses are never used. Their critique on caucuses is excerpted here from their influential book Challenging Conflict: Mediation Through Understanding *(2008, pp.190–192). When representing clients in a traditional caucus-style mediation, you may find it helpful to bear in mind—and try to avoid—the two potential dangers that these authors highlight.*

In the caucus style of mediation, the mediator shuttles back and forth between private meetings with each side, attempting through reason, persuasion, entreaty, or manipulation to bring the two parties together to broker a deal that will resolve their conflict. Given our goal of supporting the parties in *resolving their conflict together*, meeting separately, and very likely holding secrets, is antithetical to how we see the challenges and possibilities posed by conflict. We see two primary dangers in the caucus manner of proceeding.

Making the Mediator a Judge

The first danger is that the parties will look to the mediator as a judge, arbitrator, or informed advisor who decides on the best solution to their problem. If the mediator goes back and forth between the parties, learning more and more from each side, then only the mediator hears everything. The parties express their own views and proposals directly, and they hear the proposals and views of the other side largely secondhand, through the mediator (to the extent that the mediator transmits what has been said).

When the mediator has the fullest view, it follows that he or she is in the best position to formulate the outcome and persuade or pressure each side to accept it. All of this without necessarily having to reveal, or even being permitted to reveal, the full basis on which the chosen outcome rests. Many mediators work this way and many parties, and their counsel, naturally and readily expect them to do so.

So what's the problem? Perhaps none, if you don't believe *the parties have the primary responsibility* for resolving their conflict and you don't aspire for them *to do it together*. For many mediators, and some parties, it doesn't matter how heavy-handed the mediator is, as long as a resolution is achieved.

If the parties prefer and knowingly choose that approach, then it may make sense for them. If, on the other hand, they don't know the implications of the approach and the values behind it and if they do not know there is an alternative, which they usually do not, the matter becomes more complicated.

At a minimum, we believe that the parties should be informed of the option of staying together *and* the potential advantages of doing so. In the vast majority of mediations, however, particularly those when lawyers are present, most mediators take for granted that caucusing is the way to go and don't consider giving the parties a different opinion.

Manipulation

The second closely related danger of the caucus approach is that the parties will be manipulated, feel manipulated, or both. Manipulation occurs if the neutral takes a strong role in managing the flow of information through confidential caucuses in an effort to determine the outcome, contrary to our aim that the parties have control over the outcome. Many mediators believe that manipulating the parties to get them to reach a settlement is not only tolerable, it is their responsibility.

We would ask the parties: if you knew the mediator had such a decisive role, would you feel comfortable having the other side provide him or her with information that you are not privy to and that you may never get the chance to counter? The answer for some lawyers and parties alike might be "yes." If you were to ask those very same people if they felt similarly were the neutral to act as an arbitrator, very few would find that acceptable. Yet how different is this from a nonbinding arbitration?

At a meeting of lawyers who participate regularly in mediation, the moderator asked how many preferred to caucus rather than have the parties stay together. Most did. When asked their reasons, one statement elicited knowing smiles: "I know that I can manipulate the mediator." Often both lawyers have that same idea. The danger of manipulation is very real, either by the mediator, of the mediator, or both.

A familiar opportunity for manipulation arises in caucus when an attorney for one of the parties reveals to the mediator a trial strategy or the existence of some information or evidence that the other side is unaware of, which could increase the likelihood of a favorable outcome in court if the case ever went to trial. Such a revelation is accompanied by the admonition: "Don't tell this to the other side." Lawyers do this to show the mediator that they have a strong case. Their further intention is that the mediator will use this new knowledge without revealing the underlying information to advise the other side that their case is not worth as much as they thought.

But what is the mediator supposed to do with knowledge that must be kept confidential, particularly if that knowledge could or should influence the outcome of the case? He or she may hint to the other side or simply act as if nothing was said. More likely, the mediator will go to the other side and say something like: "I have some information that I cannot disclose to you but that convinces me your case is significantly weaker than you think. If I were you, I'd seriously reconsider their last offer." That is akin to the settlement conference model, and we believe it puts too much power and responsibility for resolving conflict in the hands of the mediator.

Working together, the parties know what the mediator knows, giving them a much greater ability to evaluate the progress of the mediation and ultimately to have much more control over the process. It also ensures that the mediator will not be delivering different messages to each side. This gives the mediator a lot less wiggle room and provides the parties and lawyers with more control and also more responsibility for finding the solution. We think this is a critical difference in our approach to mediation, because we want the parties, with their lawyers' support, to *assume responsibility* for decision making and to determine the ultimate outcome.

SIDEBAR 9-4

"What I'm Looking for Is Some Good Arguments"

John Bickerman (interview)

Unlike some mediators, John Bickerman (Washington, DC) likes to meet in person with each party ex parte in advance of a mediation session—the equivalent of a first private caucus. He makes this point here, then moves on to describe the most important thing he wants to get out of the initial private meeting.

My first caucus is before we ever get together for the mediation session. My first caucus is when I meet with the parties ex parte before we ever have the mediation date scheduled. In that meeting, what I'm looking for is for the parties to articulate their case to me. I want to know how they think they are going to prevail, what are their strengths. I am looking for them to give me some insight into the relationship with the other party, and some insights into where they recognize they have some weaknesses and some flexibility.

That's enormously helpful—but not everybody does that for me. A lot of times, the first meeting is, "We have got a great case. It's a slam dunk." That's not helpful, because if it's a real slam dunk, you wouldn't be here. Right? If it is a 90% shot in your favor, you would take your shot in court. You are here because there is some risk. So let's be serious about it, and let's figure out where your strengths and weaknesses are, and where there ought to be flexibility.

I won't characterize every mediation, but what I'm looking for is some good arguments to bring back to the other side. I'm going to play devil's advocate. I'm going to challenge and push each party on the issues, and they are going to need to respond and hopefully evaluate the things I'm saying—and maybe assess their risks differently. I need their best ammunition to go back to the other side.

So don't get upset with me. Help me understand how I can refute the best arguments the other side makes and give me some arguments to make to them. Because that's what I'm going to do. I'm the outsider, I'm neutral. So I'm just going to make the arguments, and they are going to have to defend their positions. In that way, we go back and forth.

SIDEBAR 9-5

The Power of Venting

David A. Hoffman (interview)

Many experienced mediation players stress the benefits of letting plaintiffs and defendants vent to the mediator in early private caucuses at a mediation session. The idea is that when a party vents thoughts and emotions connected with the underlying dis-

pute, the party can feel as if he or she has had a "day in court" and thus become more psychologically receptive to settlement. The story here—recounted by David Hoffman (Boston)—could not be considered typical, but it dramatically illustrates how powerful the opportunity to vent can be. (For another example, read Sidebar 2-4: "The Power of Good Listening.")

There is a case that I was involved in as a brand-new mediator, involving an elderly gentleman—a lawyer—who was being sued by a group of clients. The reason he was being sued is that he had sold stock from a foreign stock exchange to these clients, and the stock had tanked. The clients lost their investment. So did the lawyer, because the lawyer had invested in the stock also.

He was not trying to take advantage of the clients. He didn't make any money on the transaction. He didn't charge a commission. He just thought he was helping out some clients, because he had come upon what he thought was a great business opportunity. He didn't even realize that he needed to be registered with the Securities and Exchange Commission to sell stock. He was very, very sad, upset, worried about this lawsuit.

In the mediation, after some bargaining had gone back and forth, I began meeting with the parties separately. The defendant client was I would say in his seventies; the lawyer representing him looked to be maybe in his thirties.

In this private caucus session where the plaintiffs were not present, the elderly client began telling me how his wife didn't know about this lawsuit, and that they had been married for more than 40 years. And it worried him that she would find out about this; he said this would kill her to find out that he was being sued. He began talking about his alcoholism. He said that he had been an alcoholic for many, many years, and he had been sober for 30 years since then. But even today, for each of the last 30 years, the first thing he does in the morning when he gets up is, he drops to his knees and prays to God for the strength not to have a drink.

Of course, all of this had nothing whatsoever to do with the lawsuit. Nobody was accusing him of making a mistake because he had been drinking. He hadn't been drinking. He had been sober for 30 years.

While he was telling me this, his thirty-something lawyer was sitting beside him and kind of rolling his eyes and shooting me glances like, "Can you believe all these stories?" This gentleman's lawyer was barely putting up with these long, rambling digressions about his personal life.

At the end of the conversation with this elderly gentleman, where he was telling me about his alcoholism, he suddenly stood up and reached out his hand to me. So I stood up and I reached out my hand to him. We shook hands. He said, "Thank you so much. This mediation stuff is terrific. Tell the other side I'll accept their proposed settlement, and then we can settle this thing."

When he stood up, I didn't know what was happening. I thought I had blown this case. But what he needed was some acknowledgement and recognition. What he needed was somebody to hear his story—to hear how he had endured a great deal of suffering in his life, and this lawsuit was but the most recent example. He just wanted somebody to know he was a good person. I am guessing that by listening in an empathic way and being genuinely curious about him and about his life, that opened up something for him. As an impartial witness to his suffering and his difficulties, I gave him some kind of a release that enabled him to move forward in his life and resolve this case.

His lawyer perhaps could have provided that same function. It's possible that the case didn't need to go to mediation, if the lawyer might have been able to give this gentleman the opportunity to feel heard in a deep way. But maybe he really did need a mediator. Maybe part of the lawyer's job in that case—the lawyer for the defense—was to create an opportunity and to be encouraging with an opportunity for his client to be heard.

SIDEBAR 9-6

Two Kinds of Problem Cases

By C. Timothy Corcoran, III

Now a Roman Catholic priest, Timothy Corcoran previously had a long legal career as a litigator, bankruptcy judge, and mediator. Speaking on the topic of mediation at a seminar some years ago, he offered perspectives including this excerpt.

Break-out sessions often reveal two kinds of problem cases. I call them cases in which the client is following the lawyer's advice, and cases in which the client is not following the lawyer's advice. This is what I mean:

Cases in which the client is following the lawyer's advice are problems when the lawyer has created or contributed to the client's unreasonable expectations. Let's face it—the lawyer has given bad advice.

As the mediator, I can't say that. Were I to do so, I would undermine the lawyer's position and relationship with the client. So my job is to figure out how to make the lawyer look good while tearing down the expectations that the lawyer has unreasonably created. This is difficult because it pits the attorney and the mediator as rivals.

Please—don't create this kind of problem case. It is affirmatively harmful.

The second kind of problem case is the one in which the client is not following the lawyer's advice. In this case, the lawyer typically has evaluated the case well and is giving good advice. The client is just not following it.

In this case, the lawyer will seek the mediator's help in validating the lawyer's advice and persuading the client to accept it. Typically, the lawyer will directly or indirectly inform the mediator beforehand that this is the problem. By all means, share this privately with the mediator if this is your case.

The danger in this case is having the client view the mediator as the shill for the other side. But, if this is the problem you have, a strong mediator can help you get control back of the client.

SIDEBAR 9-7

One Counsel's Policy: It's Not Over Till the Mediator Says It's Over

Robert M. Craig, III (interview)

Robert Craig (Houston) managed litigation as inside counsel for a number of Fortune 500 corporations over the course of nearly 30 years. He says that early in a mediation session, his general policy was to give the mediator responsibility for deciding when or if further negotiations would no longer be fruitful. He talks more about this in this sidebar.

I usually say this in the first private caucus with the mediator. I tell my outside lawyer: "I don't care how bad it gets, how stupid the number is, how nasty things get. We are here until the mediator allows us to leave."

I have gotten mad in mediations, but I have always adhered to that rule. I will stay at a mediation until the mediator tells me that there is no longer an opportunity to settle the case, or we settle it.

I don't want my lawyers closing their books and preparing to walk out as some strategy. To the contrary, our strategy is always that we may not respond, we might increase our offer, we may do something that you don't think is very smart—but one of the things we are not going to do is walk out of the mediation.

What I do is challenge the mediator to know when it's over. We don't make that decision.

I've had lawyers who really have told me this is stupid—"We are wasting our time here"—and I said, "Probably." I have had times when they were right, and I've had times when the case broke and settled.

STEP TEN

Pursue Your Plan for Movement Through Caucus Rounds to Settlement or Impasse

It is always your next move.

— Attributed to Napoleon Hill (1883–1970)
personal-success author

Step Ten covers the sequence of caucuses that take place after an initial offer and counteroffer have been made, until the caucus phase gives way to a final joint session. For lack of a better term, we will call them the negotiating caucuses, which start from the point where each side has staked out its initial position.

These caucuses may be considered the heart of the mediation session, where settlement is ultimately achieved or blocked by impasse. They comprise the second and third stages in the various classification systems described at the beginning of Step Nine. During the course of the negotiating caucuses, the parties gradually shed their preoccupation with the merits of the case and move into a pure negotiating mode, exploring settlement possibilities and (if possible) incrementally narrowing their differences to reach an agreement that both sides can live with.

The first section of this chapter will discuss what your mediator is likely to see as her job during this sequence and the types of activities she is likely to undertake as part it. The second section will map the typical "geography" of the negotiating caucus sequence. The final section—the longest part of this chapter—will describe steps you may need to follow during the negotiating caucus phase in order to get the best outcome for your client.

A. What the mediator sees as her job during the negotiating caucuses

In written guidance for mediators, law professor and mediator Dwight Golann advises that in the early negotiating caucuses, mediators are likely to "[m]oderate the bargaining process," "[e]ncourage information exchange," "[a]sk about interests and develop options," "[r]eframe disputants' views,"[1] and "[c]hange disputants' assessments of the merits" (Golann, 2009a, pp.26–28). Boiling this down, during this stage of negotiations, your mediator is likely to focus on techniques intended to reduce each side's expectations, in order to increase the likelihood that the exchanges of offers between them will eventually be able to meet somewhere in between. To some extent, this is a continuation and amplification of techniques the mediator began to employ in the initial caucuses (*see* Step Nine).

Prof. Golann tells mediators that as the caucuses progress, among their likely activities will be to "[m]aintain momentum" (by staying in session), "[s]et up joint meetings" (i.e., among all participants or selected subgroups such as just opposing counsel or even just opposing clients), and "[o]ffer or initiate process options"—for examples, techniques such as offering a "mediator's proposal" (see Sidebar 10-2: "The 'Mediator's Proposal'") or an evaluation of one or more issues in the case (p.29). In other words, you can anticipate that your mediator will be doing everything possible to keep the negotiations from bogging down and grinding to a halt before settlement can be achieved.

You will find short description of some techniques frequently used by mediators in Sidebar 10-1: "The Mediator's Toolbox." Also read Sidebar 10-2 ("The Mediator's Proposal'"), Sidebar 10-3 ("Is Mediator Bracketing a Waste of Time?"), and Sidebar 11-3 ("Mediation and Last Offer Arbitration (MEDALOA)").

---

1. For a definition of *reframing*, see Sidebar 10-1: "The Mediator's Toolbox."

B. Geography of the negotiating caucus sequence

To be fanciful for a moment, let's think of the course of a mediation session in quest of settlement as if it comprised the geography of a quest-type computer game. If this were so, the participants would start in the Mêlée of the Merits, ballyhooing the strength of their respective cases—and their opponents' weaknesses—before beginning to negotiate in earnest. As negotiations go forward, the parties enter the world of Merits in the Mist, where facts and legal arguments fade and give way to a focus on numbers.

Moving down the path of offers and counteroffers, the parties traverse the Narrows, where numbers grow closer and closer together. At one or more spots along the way, the parties may sink into the Bog of Impasse, bringing any progress to a halt, and the mediator will try various techniques in an attempt to extricate them. Late in the afternoon (or sometimes well into the evening), participants who have made it this far may reach Crunch Time—a tipping point where they sense they are at the threshold of success or failure.

If they persevere in pressing on toward their final numbers, participants behold the Final Gap between the parties' bottom-line positions. Is a party willing to jump this gap, even though it may involve a number beyond what the party had been willing to contemplate before the session? Will both parties decide to bridge the gap and meet somewhere in the middle? Herein lies the key to whether this mediation will reach the Grail of Success.

The rest of this section will look at this mediation journey in more detail.

(1) From Mêlée of the Merits to Merits in the Mist

As noted in Step Nine, as the mediation caucuses progress, the focus shifts over time from the parties' views on the merits and value of their case to out-and-out bargaining. J. Anderson Little (Chapel Hill, NC) tracked this type of shift early in his career as a mediator. In one case where he kept track, discussion of the merits quickly faded after the second round of proposals—and rarely came up again during the subsequent 17 rounds (2007, p.27).

Steven Brom (Birmingham, AL) came to the same realization while representing clients at mediation sessions:

> Something I learned early on in my mediation experience is that at that point, your primary concern is what is the amount of money that it's going to take to get the case resolved—as opposed to who has the better argument. Clearly, you're still arguing about your positions during the mediation, but the primary concern is, "Okay, we're here. We are mediating the case, we're obviously willing to discuss settlement, and we've both got numbers in our mind as to what we're willing to do here today." What are those numbers? That's where your focus really is.

(2) The Narrows

The essence of positional bargaining, of course, is that the parties' positions come closer together as the bargaining goes forward. At the beginning, the parties' moves in some sessions may be substantial; in others, less so. But as the parties proceed, eventually the rate of narrowing is likely to slow down, with smaller increments of change.

For mediators like Anderson Little, that point calls for careful concern and analysis (2007, p.31):

> When a party makes a small move in comparison to his previous moves, is that party slowing down because he is nearing his best number, because he is reacting negatively to the other party's last move, or because he believes that the case won't settle? The mediator of civil trial court litigation spends time and effort trying to answer those questions and working with the parties to respond to and develop proposals in spite of their frustration or discouragement.

If the slowdown is merely a sign that a party's best number is near, the path may lead straight to settlement. But if there is any other cause, it is a sign that the parties are veering into territory mediators fear most: the dreaded impasse.

(3) The Bog of Impasse

Impasse may be considered the opposite of success in mediation, because by definition it occurs when the parties are unable to reach a settlement. In some cases, impasse may turn out to be inevitable because each party's sincere evaluation of its case differs so widely from the other party's that there is simply no possible way to bridge the gap completely through compromise. In other instances, however, mediations may end in impasse because of some shortcoming in the process, even though the parties might have settled if things had gone differently.

For example, one or both parties may become so frustrated or enraged by the other's bargaining positions that movement of numbers stops before the parties' best numbers are reached (*see* Little, 2007, pp.30–31, 34). Mediator and law professor Wayne Brazil (San Francisco) refers to these and other situations as "false failure" or "artificial impasse"—that is, "impasses that are premature, artificial, or unnecessary" (2009, pp.11–12). In his opening remarks at court-sponsored mediation sessions, Prof. Brazil likes to address the danger of "false failure" directly. He cautions participants about four types of mistakes that he sees as frequent sources of such failure (p.12):

> (a) "social" errors (e.g., when one person's verbal insensitivity or aggressiveness drives another person into withdrawal or rigidity);
> (b) process mistakes (e.g., when one person prematurely paints himself into a corner);
> (c) misjudging how much movement might be possible or what terms might really be accessible (e.g., as a result of excessive posturing or playing cards too close to the vest for too long); [and]
> (d) simply giving up too soon.

Those are not the *only* possible causes of false failure, of course. "In longer presentations," Prof. Brazil writes, "I identify three additional possible sources of such failures: (1) analytical error (misapprehending the applicable law or how it applies to the facts), (2) permitting competitiveness to displace judgment, and (3) ignoring or thinking too narrowly about underlying or long-range interests" (personal communication, May 29, 2012).[2]

As alluded to earlier, if impasse looms despite a mediator's best efforts in caucus, the mediator may try one or more impasse-breaking techniques in an attempt to get the parties moving again. For a quick description of some of these techniques, see some of the entries in Sidebar 10-1 ("The Mediator's Toolbox"), including those for *bracketing*, *mediator's request (for final move)*, *parallel-track negotiations*, and *range bargaining*.

(4) Crunch Time

"There usually comes a time in a mediation where I kind of have this sick feeling in my stomach—where I am at the threshold of either success or not-success," says Christopher Carroll (New York and New Jersey). "Until I get to that point, I don't think I've necessarily done my job."

This feeling alerts Carroll that the next moves will be critical to the outcome. It arises from his perception—based on signals from the other side and long experience—that his opponents have almost reached the end of the concessions they are willing to make before walking away. "It is at that time where you need to 'gut check' to make sure that you've taken every step that you need to take, you have done everything—crossed every *t* and dotted every *i*—to get to that endgame where you are right then and there."

---

2. Some potential causes of preventable impasse can take root in the mediation process long before the mediation session itself begins. One example is a party's failure to undertake a realistic evaluation of liability and damages in a case so as to arrive at a realistic goal for settlement (*see* Step Six). Another example may be a plaintiff's failure to disclose damaging facts or evidence far enough in advance for a corporate defendant to authorize a sufficient settlement number before the session (*see* Step Four).

Carroll believes that at this point it is more important than ever to make sure that your next negotiating moves will be correctly interpreted by the other side:

> You are hoping that the negotiation is going to end up where you need it to end up, and just communicating that last message in the right way—without it seeming as if you have issued an ultimatum—and letting them understand that you've done the work to get here and need them to do the work to help you. There is a lot that goes in to that last set of exchanges, because if you fail your next stage is "We're back in the soup again." That's probably where, from an experience perspective, the communication is absolutely critical, and the manner in which you're communicating is absolutely critical.

Like Carroll, Prof. Charles Craver (Washington, DC) urges the need for caution when you reach this point. For more on his views, read Sidebar 10-4: "Take Special Care in the Closing Stage of Negotiation." By this time, it is likely to be late in the day, and that in itself can sometimes lead to bad decision making. Edna Epstein (Chicago) provides an object lesson on the perils of proceeding while overtired in Sidebar 10-5: "The Fatigue Factor."

(5) The Final Gap

If the parties manage to stay on track through all this treacherous negotiation territory, their journey will finally take them to each party's internal best number or walk-away position. In order to cross that gulf, at least one party will have to go beyond the point it had privately been willing to contemplate before the mediation (i.e., the highest acceptable settlement for the defendant or the lowest acceptable settlement for the plaintiff).[3]

---

3. In those fortunate cases where the parties' internal best numbers or positions actually turn out to overlap, of course, there is no gap to be bridged in the same sense.

In Anderson Little's view as a mediator, just arriving at the point where the parties finally see each other's best number significantly increases the probability that they will manage to bridge that final gap: "In a high percentage of cases, if the real gap between the parties is known, they will find an amount of money that settles the case" (2007, p.75).

Of course, some final gaps turn out to be much too wide to be bridged at this point in the litigation (or other dispute forum). But at that point, at least it is clear that the deadlock is not the result of artificial impasse.

Can't parachute in. The route to settlement described in this section is often long, arduous, time consuming, and sometimes maddening. It is tempting to look for a shortcut or even somehow parachute in at the final stage. Sometimes "there is a sense of impatience or anxiousness to kind of 'get to it,' and some frustration that people don't settle until the end of the day," notes Prof. John Lande (Columbia, MO). But it may be basic human nature that "people are afraid of giving too much too soon," given the perceived risk that they will end up getting the worst of the bargain. As a result, Prof. Lande says, negotiators at mediation are typically not "ready to make their final concessions until it's getting closer to the end, so that they can see how much they actually have to give."

For a nutshell version of a classic, traditional bargaining session conducted through a series of private caucuses, read Sidebar 10-6: "Caucus Negotiations in 300 Words or Less." For some canny observations on the mediation process, read Sidebar 10-7: "What Maralee Eriksen Learned From Watching 40 Mediated Settlement Conferences."

C. Substeps to Step Ten

For good results at mediation, you need to formulate a negotiation plan in advance, as described in detail in Step Seven. The advice in Step Seven—including approaches to creating a plan for movement—will not be repeated in this step. Just remember: Unless you follow a plan, you will condemn yourself to negotiating reactively, which essentially puts the other side in the driver's seat.

Some of the guidance in this step will advise you on adapting your predetermined plan to new developments. You will also find a broad range of tips on how you can work the caucus rounds covered by Step Ten for best results.

Step Ten includes nine substeps:

1. Chart offers and counters in writing throughout the session.
2. Use your mediator proactively.
3. Adapt to new information about the case.
4. Examine each new move from a communications perspective.
5. Adapt to your opponent's moves in negotiation.
6. Defuse emotion in your side's decision making whenever it arises.
7. Utilize natural downtime with your client and continue calling time-outs as needed.
8. Make the most of hallway moments and breaking bread.
9. Persist until the session outcome is certain.

10.1 Chart offers and counters in writing throughout the session.

It is very important to track the series of offers and counteroffers made during negotiations at the mediation session, says Bowen Tucker (Arlington Heights, IL), a retired Associate General Counsel. By doing so, "you get an accurate sense of where these discussions are headed. By about the third exchange of offers and demands, you can pretty easily see where the other side thinks they are going. And if you aren't prepared to go there, you had better do something to change the momentum."

As a litigator in private practice, the late Andrew Berry considered charting offers to be so critical that he included the practice when asked about secrets to successful mediation (*see* Sidebar I-1: "Andrew Berry's Rules for Success in Mediation"). In Berry's view, keeping track in this way enables you to develop a clear picture of "what's negotiating to the middle, how you signal what the middle is, [and] what's a false middle." In addition to the offers themselves, Berry also advised writing down any reasons that are offered to justify the numbers.

You can be sure your mediator will be keeping track of the offers for his or her own purposes, which is another reason to record the numbers yourself. Mediator Jay Cohen (Winter Park, FL) comments as follows on his own use:

> I am always paying attention to how far apart the parties are from one another and what would happen if they split the difference right now. I'm watching that because a significant proportion of them do end up splitting the difference. The only question is, what was the difference at the time they split it?
>
> Lawyers always say at the beginning of the day, "I'm not splitting this." I tell them, "Well, I know you're not splitting it right now. You could have done that without me. The only question is, *where* are you splitting it?"
>
> Tracking of that numerical relationship between the parties is essential, because in addition to whatever you are telling a guy about how you are going to whip him down at the courthouse, he's also paying attention—if he's got any experience—to what kind of response he's getting to the give he's giving or the take he's taking. Are you giving more than he is? Are you giving less? What are you doing here? Where are we heading? That's what experienced folks pay a great deal of attention to.

Cohen adds: "The more you track your experience with those kinds of situations, numerically, the more comfortable you'll get with the decisions you'll make within that framework."

10.2 Use your mediator proactively.

Steps Eight and Nine include advice to observe your mediator closely during the opening session and initial private caucuses. Those observations will have given you at least an initial sense of how this mediator operates in practice—weaknesses as well as strengths.

"There is a big disconnect between the way people are taught to be mediators and what the legal profession really now wants in an effective mediation process," says mediator Jean Baker (Washington, DC). "You just have to accept as a reality that the mediator isn't perhaps going to understand the best way to use the process—so the advocate has to."

You are less likely to encounter this problem if the applicable mediation rules allowed you and your opponent to select the mediator (rather than have one randomly assigned—*see* Step One), and if you were able to agree on a promising candidate (*see* Step Two). If your mediator is both talented and well suited for your dispute, you will be able to put yourself in her hands with confidence.

But that does not mean you should sit back and passively depend on the mediator's skills at the expense of your own best judgment. "If the mediator is not doing his or her job effectively, an effective lawyer really should take control—should be proactive in the mediation so there is not a waste of an opportunity," says Edward Mullins (Miami). "You should not let the ineffective or even effective mediator control the situation completely and just wait and not be aggressive. You need to control the situation and control the process and try to resolve if it looks like an acceptable deal could be had."

Topics included in this substep: (1) using the mediator as a foil; (2) revealing your bottom line—or not; (3) controlling your messages to the other side; (4) getting the mediator's input; (5) receiving your opponent's message through the mediator; and (6) pressing for caucus remixing as needed.

A. Using the mediator as a foil

The primary recommendation that mediator Michael Lewis (Washington, DC) gives lawyers for using caucuses effectively is "to use the mediator as a foil" (in Bickerman et al., 2003, p.14). By this, Lewis means actively using the mediator "as someone who almost surely knows more about the other side than he or she can share with the party with whom the mediator is then working"—that is, you.

Among other specific activities, Lewis recommends using the mediator to "test ideas for settlement, test ideas for moving the dispute forward, [and] . . . help convince a recalcitrant person on the same side to move." He says:

> The ways of doing that vary. One can use questions for the mediator. What do you think, would the other side entertain this kind of a settlement? Or who on the other side of the table seems to be most willing to move and what might we do to help that person convince his or her side that we should settle this today?
>
> But the general proposition is [to] use the mediator. Use what the mediator may know but can't tell you explicitly. The mediator may know some things about the other side that he or she is not free to share with you. But at the same time, if you say to the mediator, or if you ask the mediator, well, would this work with them, if the mediator knows that it won't work, he or she is going to say, "I don't think so, based on what they've said to me thus far." Similarly, if the answer is affirmative, the mediator might say something like, "Well, now, that's a possibility; let's keep focusing on that and see if we can develop it further because then I can take it back and try it out with them."
>
> My fundamental point for advocates is to use the mediator in more ways than as simply someone to carry a message. Use the mediator's knowledge of the other side, which almost surely increases the longer the mediation lasts. The mediator will know more and more things about how the other side is viewing the world, and use that knowledge, even if the mediator can't say to you, "Well, I know exactly what or where they are on this point, and I'm happy to tell you." Because in many instances the mediator won't be free to say that. But he or she will be free to use the information that [he or] she has to move the parties closer to agreement.

Lewis's advice in this regard lines up with the shorter discussion in Substep 9.3H.

B. Revealing your bottom line—or not

Sometimes a party or her lawyer may be tempted to reveal their side's bottom line to the mediator in a private caucus. For advice on when—if ever—you should consider doing this, read Sidebar 10-8: "Should You Ever Tell the Mediator Your Bottom Line?" The ethical risks of misleading the mediator about your bottom line are discussed in Sidebar 10-9: "Ethical Risks in Misleading a Mediator."

C. Controlling your messages to the other side

You may assume that when you make a settlement proposal in private caucus, the mediator will communicate that proposal verbatim to the other side in *their* private caucus. However, this is not necessarily so. As explained by the late John Cooley in *Mediation Advocacy* (2002, pp.140–41, italics added), the mediator may choose among various "communication tactics":

> Typical communication tactics include: (1) the *conduit tactic*, in which the mediator merely reports the settlement proposals from each side to the other; (2) the *surrogate tactic*, in which the mediator additionally provides justification for the proposals; (3) the *reshaping tactic*, a more extreme tactic in which the mediator alters or embellishes the proposals with his own ideas about how the dispute may be resolved; and (4) the *clarification tactic*, in which the mediator obtains responses to specific questions or reiterates or highlights something that has already been said.

In *Mediating Legal Disputes* (2009a), Dwight Golann discusses the mediator communications tactics of rephrasing or withholding messages that a party wants to send the other side along with a settlement proposal. If a mediator deems some such comments too adversarial, she may choose to leave them out or "edit" them "into more constructive language." An example of rephrasing: "'We'll come down to fifty, but tell them if they take this thing to trial, we'll fry the defendant on the witness stand!' becomes 'They're dropping to $50,000' and 'They seem pretty confident they can make good points on cross examination of your guy'" (p.59).

Beyond these tactics, Prof. Golann raises the possibility that some mediators may even decide not to transmit an *entire offer* that they consider offensive—possibly without informing the offering party (pp.62–63).

In light of the polemical comments that some clients or even counsel may sometimes make in private caucus to accompany an offer, some judicious editing of such comments may be beneficial. However, the fundamental point here is that you must not assume the mediator will automatically convey your side's offer and accompanying explanation or other message exactly as you state it to the mediator.

If you want to control your message, you will need to take active steps to ensure that the mediator communicates that message exactly as you want. As noted in Substep 9.8D, John Cooley's *Mediation Advocacy* (2002, p.141) advises diplomatically reminding the mediator at the end of each caucus that you want her to use your specific wording in conveying your proposal to the other side—and literally writing down that wording for her if the message is complicated.

D. Getting the mediator's input

Controlling your message does not have to mean disregarding the mediator. To the contrary, you may specifically want to get your mediator's perspective on the best type of message to convey with an offer or the best wording for it, as noted in Substep 10.2A.

"Relationships, personalities, and modes of communication are as important to this process as numbers and law," observes Christopher Carroll. Your mediator may well have good insights into what message to send and how, based both on her previous mediation experience and on the relationship she has been building with your opponents in private caucus.

Naturally, the more you trust the mediator's skills, the more you are likely to seek the mediator's input. To illustrate, suppose you are about to reach your side's final number in a mediation session, with no deal on the table. Carroll mentions one mediator he knows as an example of someone with whom he can sit down and say, "It is the end for me, but I want your assistance in trying to communicate that in the most appropriate way."

E. Receiving your opponent's message through the mediator

Just as your mediator may put your message to the other side through the filter of a communications technique (*see* Substep 10.2C), the messages you receive from the other side may also be filtered. If you want to make sure you know exactly what the other side actually said, you will need to ask the mediator directly (though not confrontationally). For example, after the mediator conveys a message from the other side that accompanies its latest offer, you might say, "Thank you. Could you try to remember as best you can the exact words the other side used in saying that?"

By the same token, be aware that if the mediator was rephrasing needlessly confrontational language from your opponent, coaxing those confrontational words out of the mediator may elicit a counterproductively emotional response from your client (or even you). So there may be times when you sense it is better to let the mediator edit the message. Just be aware that such filtering may be taking place.

The communications dimension of parties' moves is further discussed in Substep 10.4.

F. Caucus remixing

In many mediations, notes John Lande,

> there is a standard pattern where there are opening statements, and then what someone called "terminal caucus"—"shuttle diplomacy" where the parties are in separate caucuses and the mediator goes back and forth, and each side doesn't communicate directly. There isn't a joint session until the end. Sometimes that works well, but part of the idea here is to be aware that there may be some situations where having one or more joint sessions may be valuable.

Caucus remixing is a technique typically used by mediators if negotiations are bogging down. This varies the typical pattern of shuttle diplomacy, where the mediator just keeps going back and forth between private caucuses for each side, and neither side ever talks to the other directly—sometimes called "terminal caucus." In caucus remixing, the mediator may try to create "a new group dynamic" by "shifting the participants into different groups" or "reconvening . . . all participants into a joint session" (Picker, 2003, p.51).

Other remixing possibilities include "speaking directly to the lawyer outside the presence of the client, suggesting a lawyer to lawyer meeting, or a principal to principal meeting" (Kennedy, 2010, p.155). Likewise, the mediator may call for a caucus in which "key decision makers meet apart," or one between experts retained by each side, or even one in which "one person meets the opposing team" (Golann, 2009a, pp.183–185).

If you diagnose terminal caucus in your own mediation, you do not have to wait and hope for the mediator to do something about it. You can actively press for some caucus remixing. Christopher Carroll describes a couple of remixing possibilities for a lawyer to suggest:

> Maybe it is just, "Hey, let me pull their counsel aside," if I see that their client is troubled or bothered or inflamed. Have a conversation that way and leave it to [the lawyer]: "You know your client. You figure out the best way to get forward movement and I'll defer to you." Or maybe it is the opposite—you've got to get the opposing lawyer out of the room. That means I have got to neutralize myself and have the clients from each side sit there and talk to each other without lawyers. I'll talk to my client about how to do it.

Thomas Dye (West Palm Beach, FL) proposes a couple of other possible variations to consider:

> Instead of separate private caucuses you could stay in the same room and make offers back and forth, and just walk out to the hall with the client when you need to talk privately. In other words, the exchange can go on between the parties. You don't have to have that mediator shuttling offers back and forth.
>
> But if the mediator does separate you out, I can still accomplish my goal. The mediator comes into my caucus room and makes whatever spiel to me and my client. After that I say, "Okay, we would like to talk." I

> ask the mediator to step out. I talk to my client. Then I tell the mediator standing out in the hall, "I will go over to the other side's conference room and deliver my response to their latest offer." So the mediator and I will walk in. And I say to the other side, "Joe, I just thought I would come over here because I wanted to explain a few things and also ask you a few questions before we respond to your offer." Then I get my questions answered. And then I watch for reaction to the other side. I get more information and then I watch them react to my offer.

Discussing remixing possibilities, Prof. Lande says, "A lot of it is just being sensitive to what's going on in the moment and what would be most productive. In some ways, this relates to the general theme of being wary about having a fixed routine and just applying the same routine to all cases."

10.3 Adapt to new information about the case.

In a court lawsuit, your degree of knowledge about the facts and evidence in the case will depend in part on how far the discovery process has advanced at the time of the mediation session. In other contexts, such as a dispute that is subject to a contractual alternative dispute resolution clause, the amount of discovery you have been able to obtain from the other side before the session is limited by the ADR procedures.

An example may be mediation as part of an ADR process in a securities dispute, such as between a broker and a customer. As Albert Watkins (St. Louis, MO) notes, "There will be an exchange of documents and information, but the problem is you can't take depositions of these witnesses. It's not like a federal court case."

If your opponent chooses to disclose more at the mediation session, the new facts or evidence will likely be negative for your side's case, since your opponent has no incentive to disclose anything that will help you. In that case, you may have to adjust your mediation plan and goals to reflect this changed dynamic. But not all new information has to be bad news. Sometimes what you learn may open the door to an unexpected interest-based settlement (in whole or part) or reveal an opportunity to "arbitrage" a deal point to your benefit.

A. Previously unknown negative information

Watkins uses a hypothetical from the securities dispute arena to illustrate how new information can change the dynamics at a mediation session:

> For example, in a variable annuity case I may say to the defendant brokerage firm: "Look—my client is 85 years old and has a heart condition, but 100% of his assets went from certificates of deposit to a variable annuity with his money tied up. This absolutely is an unsuitable investment."
>
> Opposing counsel may come back and say, "Oh, by the way, here's something that we haven't shared with you before now. Our broker was really concerned about the fact that this guy wanted to buy a variable annuity, so he brought him in for lunch and met with the branch manager. The branch manager and the broker will both testify that during lunch he made it very clear that he didn't have long to live, and he wanted the variable annuity because he wanted the death-benefit portion of the product that corresponded to that variable annuity."
>
> I turn around to my client privately and say, "I understand that in retrospect this variable annuity was an absolute raging piece of garbage. You shouldn't have purchased it. It was unsuitable. But the fact of the matter is, there are two witnesses here that say that you showed up and talked about wanting the death benefit."
>
> The client may say, "Well, yeah, I did do that. Gosh, I had forgotten about that." And of course, the dynamics of the case change.
>
> This is a bit of an exaggerated tale, but things like that do come out from time to time.

On the defense side, former inside counsel John DeGroote (Dallas) refers to such unpleasant surprises as the "CEO on spring break" phenomenon—jokingly conjuring up a scenario where embarrassing and destructive facts emerge about the behavior of the client company's chief executive. The possibility of unexpected news at a mediation session is one reason DeGroote believes it is better for a client representative to be granted a range of leeway in advance by his employer rather than being locked into an inflexible bottom line (*see* Substep 7.4B(3)).

Of course, the level of destructiveness of unexpected facts or evidence may vary greatly, depending on the particulars. Likewise, your level of ability to adapt to new adverse facts or evidence will depend both on how much they can undermine your case and on how much flexibility in settlement authority you have (or are able to obtain while the mediation is in session).

If the surprise greatly strengthens your opponent's claim for damages, or raises the total amount, such a development may result in impasse. That is the reason why a party should consider making such factual disclosures well in advance of a scheduled mediation, so that the other side has time to absorb the information and adjust settlement goals accordingly. This is especially true if the potentially surprised party is a corporation—where authorizations must often be made by committee—or if the defendant's insurance company is a major player. These points were discussed in Substeps 3.1A and 4.2D.

If the surprise disclosure is significant but not too disruptive—or if your client is an individual and insurance is not a factor—the necessary response may simply be to reset your settlement goal and modify your plan for movement accordingly.

B. Interest-based opportunities

For a discussion of interest-based negotiation and settlement, see Substep 7.4A.[4] Sometimes a new disclosure by the other side at the mediation session may actually create new

4. A good understanding of interest-based and positional ("bargaining") negotiations is essential for success at mediation. Since these topics were discussed at length in Step Seven, they are not further elaborated in this step.

opportunities for settlement. You will find a dramatic and extreme illustration of this from Thomas Dye in Sidebar 10-10: "An Example of Creative Settlement."

Although Dye's example is one of complete settlement, it more likely may become possible to use interest-based creativity for some *part* of a potential settlement where the larger part is handled by payment of money. Dwight Golann recognizes this in his article for mediators subtitled "The Special Barriers to Interest-Based Mediation, and Techniques to Overcome Them" (2011, p.26). One item of advice is that in suitable instances, mediators should "[t]reat interests as an 'add on' to money, and conduct parallel discussions":

> Plaintiffs in particular are likely to be concerned that showing a willingness to talk about creative [interest-based] options will be taken as a signal they are not serious about their money demands. Defendants are usually more open to imaginative options because they see them as a substitute for paying money. To address this concern, suggest that creative terms be considered as an addition to, rather than a substitute for, money.
>
> Propose also that monetary offers and interests be discussed in parallel, perhaps framing it this way: "We'll exchange offers, but at the same time I'd like you to think about other issues of concern. . . . I'll be asking for both offers and ideas as we go along."

Nothing prevents a party from suggesting this approach instead of the mediator. The concept of parallel negotiations is also relevant to the following section on "arbitraging" a deal point.

C. Opportunities to "arbitrage" a deal point

For purposes of this discussion, we are borrowing the concept of arbitrage from the financial markets. *Investopedia* defines *arbitrage* in part as "a trade that profits by exploiting price differences of identical or similar financial instruments, on different markets or in different forms."[5]

---

5. http://www.investopedia.com/terms/a/arbitrage.asp (accessed 11/21/11).

In the concept of settlement deals, we could consider an arbitrage situation to be one where a particular possible deal point has less value to the potential granting party (the grantor) than to the potential receiving party (the grantee). Granting such a deal point in mediation can benefit the grantor because, by doing so, the grantor will add more perceived value from the grantee's standpoint than the same point represents to the grantor.

Mediator John Bickerman points to this type of opportunity in the context of so-called win-win settlements, using the term "complementary values":

> The key element is, are there complementary values which you value higher? I mean complementary in the sense that your client is going to value something differently than the other side. As long as there is a difference in value, then there is the opportunity for trade-off.

Bickerman notes that he has seen "tons" of such trade-offs in successful negotiations he has mediated over the years.

Mediator David Hoffman provides a specific example where the difference in value of a deal point from the standpoint of each party facilitated a settlement in mediation. The dispute concerned a wrongful termination claim brought by a former airline employee who was close to retirement age, seeking a large monetary award. The plaintiff alleged age discrimination; the airline asserted that the employee's termination was simply part of a larger, legitimate workforce reduction, and had offered very little cash in settlement discussions. In private caucus, the mediator asked the plaintiff how he planned to use the money he hoped to gain from the lawsuit.

As Hoffman recounts, the plaintiff replied, "Well, at my age, I'm very close to the point where I would like to retire, and my wife and I had planned a lot of travel." So the mediator asked whether he would be willing to accept airline frequent-flier miles in place of cash. Ultimately, the plaintiff and the airline arrived at a settlement involving "a gazillion frequent-flier miles and very little cash. That worked well for the company, and it worked well for the airline employee."

What made the settlement work, of course, was that the frequent-flier miles had a substantially greater monetary value to the plaintiff—who otherwise would have had to pay full retail price for air tickets—than they did to the airline. This type of arrangement has the flavor of an interest-based settlement, and some people probably consider it to be one. But conceptually it is distinct, because it does not depend on the parties' interests related to the *underlying dispute*.[6] In Hoffman's example, the frequent-flier miles had nothing to do with the plaintiff's grievance of alleged wrongful termination. An arbitrage-based settlement could just as easily have been reached if the plaintiff had wanted to buy a used airplane, and the airline by coincidence had an old airplane it wanted to get rid of.

Construction lawyer and mediator Paul Sandars (Roseland, NJ) seems to be pointing at least in part to such arbitrage opportunities when he says there are "a lot of creative ways" to settle construction disputes:

> If you get the engineering defendants in a room, and they come up with a fix and sign off on it, and you get the contractors to agree to do it—settle the case! With some kind of mechanism to administrate the agreement, the case can settle with really no money changing hands, but with the owner getting a fix that his or her expert signs in on and agrees with the others' experts. We have done that before.

Speaking loosely, a key to the type of settlement Sandars describes is that the contractors can provide services at their wholesale cost, while the owner would have to pay a larger amount of cash at retail value from settlement funds in order to go out and buy those same services on the open market. Such arbitrage elements may also be discerned in some of the

---

6. Contrast Hoffman's story with a classic hypothetical example of an interest-based settlement, where sisters are fighting over ownership of an orange, and the resolution depends on the different plans the sisters had for using that orange (*see* Substep 7.4A(1)). The distinction applies to the real-life example in Sidebar 10-10 ("An Example of Creative Settlement"), where the resolution hinged on different uses the parties had in mind for certain intellectual property that was the basis of their dispute.

possibilities explored by Lawrence Watson in Sidebar 10-11: "Settlement Options Beyond the Money."

10.4 Examine each new move from a communications perspective.

In the context of making initial offers in Step Nine, we already discussed the usefulness of an accompanying rationale and the use of the mediator to convey a message with your proposal (*see* Substep 9.8). Beyond any accompanying verbal messages, however, the numbers themselves communicate a message. Anderson Little puts it this way (2007, p. 67):

> [N]egotiators communicate their range of settlement indirectly, through the publication of proposals. Over a series of moves, they gradually let the other side know where they can and cannot settle the case. The position of the parties and their movement from one position to another are communications about that number, range, or ballpark of settlement.

A major challenge of the negotiation phase is trying to interpret the messages of your opponent's numbers correctly, and making sure your own numbers communicate the message you intend (and are not misinterpreted by the other side).

Bowen Tucker is a retired Associate General Counsel for a large company who currently advises clients in strategic litigation management. From his experience representing his former employer in mediation, he offers the following basic example of how numbers communicate:

> In the simplest exchange, if you offer $50,000 as defendant and the other side comes back with $100,000, and you go to $60,000 and they come to $90,000, you know you're going to end up at $75,000. If you're only willing to go to around $65,000, you better start putting the brakes on at $60,500, and make it clear to the mediator you're not going to $75,000.
>
> That way, the mediator conveys an accurate report to the other side that while they may have hoped this

> was going to get resolved in the middle at $75,000, that isn't going to happen. So the plaintiff had better rethink his strategy, because it's going to be a lower number. I don't know what the number is, but it isn't going to be $75,000.
>
> That's the kind of thing that I'm saying. If you wait too long to put on the brakes you won't get a resolution, because the other side will be stunned to suddenly find out towards the end that you weren't going where they thought you were.
>
> I don't say any of this pretending the other side is dumb. I assume they should be doing their homework, just the same as I am. So it's very important not to mislead the other side that way.

John DeGroote (Dallas) agrees that an important way to convey to your opponent that you are getting near your end point is to "start slicing the ham thinner and thinner." In a mediation long ago, DeGroote once accidently miscommunicated on the plaintiff's side by taking too big a leap too late in the game:

> One of my least successful mediations was when I had gone down in a linear fashion, like 10, 8, 7, and 6½, and then the mediator said, "I have got to get you to make a big jump." So I went to 5½ off the 6½. I thought I had made what was going to be effectively my last leap—but immediately the other side put on the brakes.

In retrospect, the mistake is clear: DeGroote's opponent misinterpreted his "big jump" as a signal that he was willing to come down even further, instead of understanding that it was intended as a final (or nearly final) move.

Like Tucker and DeGroote, Anderson Little cautions that parties can sometimes inadvertently mislead each other through their sequence of offers. For more on this, see Sidebar 10-12: "How Parties Can (Mis)communicate Through Numbers."

The communications aspect of numbers is one reason why you may need to adapt your preconceived plan for movement in response to your opponent's actual moves during the session. That topic of adaptation is addressed in Substep 10.5.

10.5 Adapt to your opponent's moves in negotiation.

There is some inherent tension between two common pieces of advice about negotiating at a mediation session. One piece of advice is that you should create a plan for movement in advance of the session and follow it to avoid merely reacting to the other's side's moves.[7] This advice was explored at length in Step Seven. The other piece of advice is that you need to treat each of your opponent's moves as a form of communication—and make sure your response conveys the message that best signals to the other side where you think the negotiations should be heading (*see* Substep 10.4). By definition, this involves reacting to your opponent's moves.

In this section, we will discuss adapting your own moves in response to the other side's second number, your opponent's general negotiating approach, and highball or lowball offers.

A. Significance of the second number

"A lot of people think that the most important number in mediation is the opening number, but I was told by a very smart mediator that's really not true—the most important number is the *second* number," says John DeGroote. "Because the first number is often some fantasy B.S.—'I'll pay you $50' or 'I will take 10 million.' But if you start to bracket the settlement on the second number, you will get a much more accurate reading on where the case will resolve."

Edward Mullins agrees: "I think sometimes your second step is more important because the first step is always posturing." He gives a hypothetical example from the standpoint of both the plaintiff and defendant, where the plaintiff's first move in negotiation was a million dollars and defendant's first move in response was $100,000:

---

7. Negotiating reactively has been cited as one of the top 10 ways to doom a mediation (*see* Sidebar I-2: "How to Doom a Mediation").

> Now you're on your next move. As plaintiff, what message do I want to send to the defendant? Do I want to say, "Okay, I'm going to drop down to $900,000," to communicate that I'm really serious about settling this maybe south of $700,000? This second move tells if you are really going to settle somewhere in the middle between the million and the 100,000 from the plaintiff side.
>
> Then on the defense side, what message do you want to send with your second number? Do you want to convey to the plaintiff, "Look, I know you are going to need over $500,000, so I'm going to show you by raising my offer significantly that I am willing to go there"? Or do I want to convey, "I'm going to tell you right now, our next move is $200,000, because we are not going north of $500,000"? These are just hypothetical numbers, but that message can tell you a lot of things.

B. Opponent's general negotiating approach

By the time you and your opponent have made several moves, you will get a sense of the other side's general approach to negotiating. "It's like two boxers in a fight," Edward Mullins says. "In the first round, the bell rings, and the boxers are circling around each other, and there are a couple of jabs, kind of figuring out what kind of fighter each other is."

Switching metaphors, Mullins adds, "It's a case-by-case matter to see if the other side is just interested in horse trading or not":

> A lot of times you will get a lawyer who says, "I don't play horse-trading. This is the number I want, this is where we are at." Even so, usually the settlement is going to be different from what they've said. Some lawyers make some major moves. Other lawyers feel like they have to move in $5,000 increments.
>
> You've got to decide what kind of lawyer *you* are, and then you've got to decide what kind of lawyer the other person is. That's why they say the first moves aren't as

> important as the second and the third moves. Because then you find out what kind of lawyer they are.
>
> It can be hard to figure out. The key may not be the lawyer, it may be their client as well. A lot of times the client has been to a thousand mediations and settlements, and this is how they do it—they move in $5,000 increments. They are tough, and they don't make big moves, and they are there all night, and that's how they do it. They think that's effective for them.

Once you have figured out the other side's style, Mullins believes that to some extent "you have got to match what they are doing." For example, if your opponent's style is to make a long series of small moves, he says it is a mistake for you to make a large move. "You find yourself giving too much ground if the other side is not playing the same game."

John DeGroote expresses a similar view in discussing how best to respond to a hardball negotiator:

> There is a lesson that I have learned that nobody will ever believe until they learn it themselves. I believe that strength is best met with strength and conciliation is met with conciliation. When the other side does something in a mediation that is an effort to show their negotiation strength, your only response is to respond in kind. I virtually never respond to a hostile action with a conciliatory motion.

C. Lowball or highball offers

Mediators Herbert Stettin (Coral Gables, FL) and John Bickerman (Washington, DC) have somewhat different views on the best way to respond to an opponent's initial highball or lowball offer. As Stettin notes, a common response to a lowball offer is for the recipient to "start by a very low offer also." But he recommends an alternative:

> The smart response would be to say, "I don't think that's a realistic number." Say to them, "Make a realistic response," and tell them there won't be anything

> like that again unless they get into realistic territory. Meaning that you'll overlook what you think is simply childishness on their part one time. Or two times. But it's very difficult when you get an unrealistic opening number.

Bickerman's advice is this:

> If they stake out an extreme number, you have got to stake out an extreme number. I don't think it's enormously helpful when parties say, "Oh that's such a ridiculous number we are not going to respond." Then it puts the mediator in a position of trying to go back and tell the other side to respond, and they say, "Oh, we are not going to respond if they don't respond," and we waste a lot of time. So if it's a ridiculous extreme number, put out a ridiculous extreme number on your side to signal that you think it's a ridiculous extreme number.

If your opponent's highball or lowball offer reflects too much intransigence, it may be that neither type of response will ultimately lead to settlement. A fundamental problem is that a highball or lowball offer from the other side is likely to inflame your own client—and then either declining to respond or responding with an extreme offer of your own may only reinforce the other side's bad attitude. You and your client will have to figure out which approach is best for your situation, based on your best understanding of your opponent's psychology and the entire context of your negotiations.

Either way you go, you will need to pay very careful attention to the communications aspect. For example, if you respond with an extreme number, you may want to accompany that with a carefully crafted verbal message. If you decline to respond instead, it may make a difference exactly how you phrase that refusal.

In order to arrive at the best choice, you want a discussion with your client that is driven by clearheaded calculation rather than emotional reactivity—a specific example of the importance of defusing emotion in your side's decision making whenever it arises (*see* Substep 10.6).

(1) Adaptation without reactivity

Now that we have talked so much about adapting your plan for movement to the other side's actual moves during the session, let's circle back and remember the danger of losing sight of your own strategy and merely becoming reactive. In this context, take a look at Anderson Little's discussion in Sidebar 10-13: "Control Theory in Mediation."

10.6 Defuse emotion in your side's decision making whenever it arises.

During the mediation session, anger and related emotions may arise or continue in the negotiating caucuses, but you can make an effort to counter this both in your client and yourself. *Feeling* angry can be different from *acting* angry, which some lawyers use as a tactic. Although *reactive devaluation* (discussed in part D of this substep) is conceptually different from anger per se, it is another documented psychological phenomenon that you will want to be aware of and avoid for best results.

A. The temptation of emotion

"As the parties swap proposals, they become frustrated and angry with each other," Anderson Little observes in *Making Money Talk* (2007, p.34). "They react negatively and emotionally to proposals they don't like and, thus, formulate their responses reactively."

When Little began serving as a mediator of civil court cases many years ago, this intensity of emotion came as a real surprise to him (p.62). With experiences probably similar to those of many other mediators, he soon found that helping the parties subdue their emotions and resulting reactivity took up far more of his time as a neutral than did assisting with case analysis.

Moreover, emotional responses are not limited to clients; all too often, lawyers do the same thing. Little has made this observation (2007, p.30); so has mediator Linda Singer (Washington, DC). When asked in an interview about the most common things lawyers do in mediations that drive her crazy, Singer responded: "React like an emotional client to an offer. Say, 'It's an insult, and this case will never settle!'" Singer offers at least a partial explanation for this phenomenon: "Lawyers get enamored of their own cases. They've only been talking to people on their own side for a long period of time, so that when somebody starts disagreeing with them, they get upset."

B. Avoiding the emotion trap

How can you try to avoid the trap of emotion as a lawyer at a mediation session? The most obvious tactic is simply to remind yourself of this temptation in advance. Then try to maintain a conscious awareness of your own reactions in private caucuses when the mediator delivers an offer or message from the other side.

Similarly, you may be able to lessen your client's level of emotion in response to offers by talking about this phenomenon with her during your preparations before the session. Discuss emotional reaction as a common temptation for both clients and lawyers in mediation—even the most sophisticated. You might compare negotiations at the session to a game of chess, and point out how counterproductive it would be to react emotionally to your opponent's moves. Then, during discussion of offers in private caucuses, you can endeavor to set the tone for your side by treating negotiations as a serious game with real consequences, but one where cold logic will serve better than a hot head to advance your interests.

C. Acting angry rather than being angry

As noted in Substep 7.2E(2), some mediation players like to assign roles to members of their team, such as having the client act as the "tough guy" while counsel plays a more conciliatory part. In keeping with such roles, one participant may want to show obstreperous reactions at some points. Without addressing the effectiveness (or not) of such an approach, obviously acting angry at times is not the same thing as being angry, so the danger of its affecting analytical judgment is not similarly present.

D. Reactive devaluation

The term *reactive devaluation* "refers to the fact that the very offer of a particular proposal or concession—especially if the offer comes from an *adversary*—may diminish its apparent value or attractiveness in the eyes of the recipient" (Ross, 1995, p.28; *see also* Golann, 2009a, p.105). As psychology professor Lee Ross (Stanford, CA) explains in an influential article on the topic (1995, pp.26–42), this devaluation does not necessarily stem from emotional hostility as such. For example, a concession by an adversary may cause a party to inflate its own level of expectation as to what the party might ultimately be able to gain through continued hard-nosed bargaining (*see* p.37)—which makes the adversary's concession seem smaller in relation to the party's (new) goal.

Of course, there may be times when the nature or extent of the other side's concessions objectively indicates that your opponent is not an effective bargainer or feels more weakness than you suspected. However, knowing about reactive devaluation, you may want to be very cautious about reaching such a conclusion, because it can potentially damage the further course of negotiations.

For example, an opponent might decide to make an ample concession as a test of your side's sincerity, to see whether you will respond with a concession of your own in the same spirit. If you come back with a hardball response because reactive devaluation has raised your expectation that further toughness on your part will reap greater gains, your opponent may conclude that your side is not serious about settlement. The result of your misjudgment might be that both sides then slow the pace of concessions to a tiny trickle, ultimately leading to unnecessary impasse.

As with emotional reactivity, simply being aware of reactive devaluation as a psychological phenomenon may possibly help avoid it. At a minimum, if you believe you are starting to see such devaluation in your client as you discuss your opponent's latest offer, you have a specific label for it that may make your warning about it more convincing. Similarly, you might want to include a mention of reactive devaluation in your client prep for the session. To what extent such forewarning actually works "is an empirical question worthy of investigation" (Ross, 1995, p.40).

10.7 Utilize natural downtime with your client and continue calling time-outs as needed.

Downtime here means any type of lull or break that occurs naturally as part of the course of a mediation session. A time-out is a break that you actively decide to call for during the session. Both are important elements to use in the mediation process.

A. Using downtime

Perhaps the greatest amount of downtime during a typical mediation session occurs while one party waits for the other party to finish a private caucus with the mediator. In Jay Cohen's opinion, how a lawyer utilizes this time is one of the characteristics that separate those who are inexperienced in mediation from those who are experienced:

> An inexperienced lawyer will not use the time between when I leave the room and when I come back in exploring what their options are and planning for what they're going to do in the series of events that might occur when I come back. In other words, they need to plan for what could happen here. They know I'm coming back with a number. Okay, what are we going to do if it's *this*? What are we going to do if it's *that*? I had a law partner who used to call that "Which way is the frog going to jump?" What's their response going to be? And how far ahead are they planning?

In his years as inside counsel, John DeGroote always used caucus downtime in mediation to make sure the corporate representative understood what was going on, as well as to discuss next moves. "Every time the mediator leaves the room, you need to explain to the business client what just happened and what's going to happen next," he says (assuming that the client is not already well versed in such matters).

To illustrate, DeGroote offers a hypothetical where the mediator has just said that she does not think the plaintiff will settle unless your client pays at least $200,000, and the client tells her, "I'm not going to pay $200,000." When the mediator returns to the other side's caucus, you might tell your client something like this:

> As you know, they have demanded $400,000 and we've offered $82,000. In their next demand, they are not going to want to signal that they are willing to go under 200 grand, so they are probably going to come in at $345,000. $350,000 is too round a number, but they've got to make a real move. So they are going to come in somewhere between $320,000 and $350,000, because they are going to want to signal that they are going to hold well into the twos. We need to signal that we are not going to go too deep in the twos. So when they come in at $335,000 or $345,000, our next counter should probably be something like $98,000.

After you have been right a couple of times in predicting your opponent's next moves, your client will "trust that you know what's happening," DeGroote says. Of course, sometimes you won't get it right. In that case, you can tell your client something like, "Oh, these guys are giving me the blah-blah treatment." But the more times you prove correct, the more credibility you will build with your client.

In an article titled "Mediation: An Effective Way to Connect With Clients" (2009), mediator John Bates (San Francisco) recommends utilizing downtime with your client not only to help keep the mediation session on track but as a form of client development. He writes:

> During the mediation session, look for ways to engage your client and foster your relationship. As you know, there can be a lot of "downtime" when the mediator is meeting with the other side. Use this time productively to learn about your client's interests and things you have in common. Look for opportunities to share your own attributes and personal background. Spending time with your client, where

> you are both trapped in a conference room, is a bonding experience.
>
> Throughout the session, stay in touch with your client. Never abandon him or her, and always be aware of your client's needs and make sure they are met, whether they are process driven or personal. In essence, make sure your client is comfortable. This will foster communication, enhancing the chances for settlement, and it will strengthen your professional and personal relationship.[8]

A third way to utilize downtime with your client, where the circumstances are appropriate, is to do some additional drafting of a possible settlement agreement. In Substep 6.7 we discussed drafting at least the "bones" of a possible memorandum or understanding or settlement agreement in advance of the mediation session. Mediator Larry Mills (Seattle) suggests using downtime during the session to do further work on this (speaking in Bickerman et al. 2003, p.22):

> Some lawyers show up at mediations with laptop computers so that they can draft. And often, if you're following a caucus model of mediation, the lawyers have lots of time with their clients, and they can think about the settlement agreement and actually draft it in private caucuses; and then, when the settlement agreement is reached, then you have something to work with.

Memoranda of understanding (aka term sheets) and full-fledged settlement agreement documents are discussed in greater detail in Step Eleven.

---

8. Sometimes when your opponents want to talk among themselves without the mediator present, the mediator can also find herself with downtime. "I have had it happen a number of times when there is just nothing going on and the mediator is supposed to be sitting around, but the other side is contemplating," says Robert Craig (Houston). "I like it when the mediator comes in and sits with us and just sort of B.S.es. It doesn't always lead to a settlement, but what that tells me is the mediator feels like we are shooting straight with him, and that we are not playing games."

B. Calling time-outs

"Never hesitate to ask the mediator to take a timeout to talk to your client, if you've got something important that you want to share with your client, or you want to digest before talking publicly to the other side," advises John Bickerman (Bickerman et al., 2003, p.15). From his viewpoint as a mediator, he goes on to say (p.16, italics added):

> Your client, who may not be as experienced in mediation as you are, needs to appreciate the opportunity to speak with you privately. So if there are times when you're prepared to make a concession, or some new piece of information is shared with you, that is an appropriate time to ask the mediator to take a break. *One of the biggest mistakes I see as a mediator is [that] very important information is shared, or parties are about to make a significant move, and they don't take the time to consider how they're going to do it most effectively*. There is nothing wrong with asking the mediator to take a break, and to go figure out what you're going to do, and then do it. It will have greater force when you have the opportunity to come back into the room and make the concession in an intelligent and effective way.

From her experience as counsel, Joyce Mitchell (Silver Spring, MD) strongly agrees. She underscores and expands on Bickerman's advice (speaking in Bickerman et al., 2003, p.25):

> Stop and take many breaks. I have something that I do often. If I'm in an area where I can go outside, I will actually walk outside with my client. I not only change rooms, or go out into the hall, I ask for a break long enough to go outside. For me, this seems to give my clients an openness, an option, to think about what it is we're doing.
>
> If there have been some options that have been placed on the table that my client has been finding great difficulty with, I might take a walk with him or

> her outside, and I'll say, "Tell me what's going on. Is there something that you'd like to share with me that we haven't talked about?"
>
> That opportunity for the open space, for the change of venue, allows my client the time and the opportunity to think about what he or she has heard, and to help me make new options for him [or her] and to look at the criteria for those options. It has worked all of the time. And if you can find a space where you can just walk out under a tree on a [nice] day, it even works better.

Also on the subject of breaks, mediator Jay Cohen (Winter Park, FL) observes:

> More experienced lawyers will reach moments when they'll run me out of the room, because they don't want me to be sitting in there when they admit to their client, "Listen, you've got to consider some of these things the mediator is saying." If they want to change their client's mind, they'll let me talk to their client for a while, and then they'll want me out of the room when they tell the client they agree with me about something.

10.8 Make the most of hallway moments and breaking bread.

Before and during a mediation session, the quality of informal interaction—in the form or hallway moments and breaking bread—may sometimes be as crucial to good results as the structured elements.

A. Hallway moments

During many mediation sessions, there will be moments when counsel for opposing parties interact informally, out of their clients' earshot. Sometimes these interactions are spontaneous, such as when lawyers run into each other at the water cooler or on the way to the bathroom. Other times, a lawyer may intentionally engineer a chance to speak to his opposite number privately.

Edward Mullins calls these informal interactions "hallway moments," and he advises you to use them intelligently for purposes of furthering the goal of settlement. John DeGroote agrees, commenting that "the biggest movements in the case usually happen in the hallways."

Here is more of what Mullins has to say about hallway moments:

> You take the lawyer on the other side to the hallway and say, "Look, it's 5:00 in the afternoon. Where are we going? I'm not going to hold you on it, but where is your client really heading on this?" We have those hallway discussions as something you can kind of back off of. It's just a "you and I talking" type of thing.

Sometimes such a private moment with opposing counsel can be useful in order to get the picture when the opposing side seems to be just jumping through the hoops at a session—an all-too-familiar situation where court-sponsored mediation is required as part of the litigation process. Mullins supplies a hypothetical example:

> Sometimes you go to the caucus stage and make your first couple of moves, and it's pretty obvious that your opponents are not taking it seriously, because you've made some good safe moves and they have gone nowhere. That is a good time where you say, "I need to talk to Joe," the counsel on the other side. You know, "Just give me a second with this guy."
>
> You pull him aside and say, "My client took this mediation seriously. He flew in from out of state, and we are interested in seeing if we can resolve this thing. Tell me—what's going on [on] your side?"
>
> And usually the response [is] going to be, "I hear you. My guy is just being very aggressive today."
>
> Then you say, "Well, would it help if my guy talked to your guy? Or is it me—something I said during the session? Is he mad at me? Should my partner get involved?
>
> Sometimes it turns out, the guy says, "Look, I am not interested in settling today. You guys are being unrealistic. You are not moving up."
>
> "Okay," you say, "let's go on home, then."

That said, the utility of hallway moments "really depends on your relationship with opposing counsel," Mullins notes. "If it's become acrimonious—if you guys have fought at the deposition all the time, you can't stand each other—you've got to use the mediator" as a buffer throughout the session.

B. The value of breaking bread

By their nature, hallway moments involve some type of discussion related to the mediation. By contrast, meals with both sides present normally feature what one might call ordinary dinner-table conversation. From John Bickerman's experience, shared meals can contribute to the ultimate success of a mediation:

> Breaking bread with the other side and talking about what may appear to be trivial stuff de-demonizes the other side. When you start talking about your kids, baseball, and your kids' baseball, it makes parties realize that the other side is not the evildoer but is human as well, and has to go home and deal with the same sort of issues you do. The more commonality that exists between parties—even if it is unrelated—the more likely you'll find the barriers to settlement breaking down.

In his work as a mediator, Bickerman generally encourages shared meals during mediation sessions. "There are some cases where we are far along in active negotiations, and time is of the essence, and I am going to push through," he says. "But in cases where you are going to be out with these folks for a long time, lunch is a very important ingredient."

Hildy Bowbeer (St. Paul, MN), inside counsel at a major manufacturing firm, illustrates the value of breaking bread together with an anecdote involving breakfast rather than lunch (2011, p.183):

> In one case in which the parties held deep-seated suspicions of each other that threatened to derail any chance of a negotiated resolution, the mediator herself

hosted a breakfast where only the decision makers were present and all discussion of the case itself was forbidden. The attendees discussed their children, travels, hobbies, and favorite books, and in the course of the discussion learned of several mutual interests. The case was still enormously difficult to settle, but the temperature and blood pressure of the participants was significantly lower when the mediation began after breakfast, and each party was at least able to concede at the outset that it was not the devil in the other room.

10.9 Persist until the session outcome is certain.

Recall from the beginning of this chapter that "simply giving up too soon" is one of four errors identified by Prof. Wayne Brazil as a cause of unnecessary or artificial impasse in mediation. His observation underscores the importance of continuing to negotiate until it is clear beyond a reasonable doubt that settlement cannot be achieved at your mediation session.

When a possible impasse is looming, what is the cause? If the cause is artificial, like what Brazil calls a process error, is there any way it can be fixed at this point in the session? If so, little is lost by making the effort. In light of this, consider making it a general rule to keep persisting at a mediation until it is clear beyond a reasonable doubt that no further progress can be made.[9]

---

9. Christopher Carroll suggests one exception to the rule of persistence—calling a halt to the mediation if it starts doing more harm than good:

> Quite frankly, there are times where the mediator might not be as experienced as some. In an instance like that, if I think and feel that more damage is going be done through the mediation process, it wouldn't be a mistake in my mind to stop that process so that we could recommence a different process at some point in time. The decision involves taking the temperature of everything as you're going along, including how effective is your mediator, how receptive is the other side to the mediator.

SIDEBAR 10-1

The Mediator's Toolbox

"[Y]ou must be adequately prepared for the tools that the mediator is likely to use during the mediation," writes Southern California mediator Louise LaMothe (2010, p.68). "[I]f you are not, it shows." This sidebar lists some mediator techniques; it is not exhaustive, although it includes a number of the more common devices.

Active listening. Mediators engage in active listening not only by paying close attention to a session participant's words and nonverbal cues, but frequently by paraphrasing or summarizing a point after the participant has spoken and asking for confirmation that the mediator understood correctly.

Adjournment and rescheduling. If mediation participants reach the end of their scheduled session without also reaching settlement, one alternative to declaring failure is to try scheduling an additional session for a future day—or at least hold out the possibility that such a session may be held after some time has elapsed (Golann, 2009a, pp.191–194; Picker, 2003, p.63). Sometimes that later session may be held by telephone, with the mediator alternating between calls to each side.

Bracketing. "With bracketing, the mediator attempts to close the gap between the parties' positions, e.g. convincing one party to offer to settle for X dollars if the other moves to Y dollars" (Kennedy, 2010, p.155). For more on this technique, see Sidebar 10-3: "Is Mediator Bracketing a Waste of Time?"

Caucus remixing. *See* Substep 10.2F.

Decision tree. The use of decision trees in evaluating your party's case in advance of a mediation session was discussed in Step Six. During the mediation session itself, mediators sometimes help a party go through a decision-tree analysis to "encourage the decision-maker to consider options, anticipate the potential outcomes in the case and assign probabilities. The concept is to help the decision-maker realistically assess risk and thus move the parties toward settlement" (Kennedy, 2010, p.155). Louise LaMothe observes (2010, p.68): "Mediators like to use decision trees and similar tools because they have a tendency to pull the parties into a more realistic bargaining range."

Evaluative opinion. Offering the mediator's own evaluation of a party's case is the "mediator's ultimate weapon for influencing divergent case assessments"—powerful, but also potentially hazardous—in the words of mediators and law professors Marjorie Aaron and Dwight Golann (2009, p.145). Under the right circumstances, providing such an opinion "can cause litigants to question and reevaluate their own judgments and 'bottom lines,'" "satisfy a litigant's emotional desire for 'my day in court,'" and provide "psychological or professional cover" for litigants to move from entrenched positions (p.147). However, Profs. Aaron and Golann stress the risk that such opinions may "freeze the bargaining process because neither side wants to accept a settlement worse than the neutral's 'right number'—even when it would be wise to do so" (p.149). Also, "[e]ven solicited opinions are dangerous to the process because of the potential for perceived bias" (Picker, 2003, p.51).

"High/low." A variant of arbitration sometimes used in med-arb (*see* entry in this sidebar). In this procedure, the parties agree in advance to place an upper and lower limit on the settlement number that may be arrived at when the mediator acts as arbitrator in an impasse situation.

Last best offer. *See* the entry in this sidebar for *med-arb*.

Med-arb. If the parties are motivated to reach a settlement even if they are ultimately unable to agree on terms through mediation, they may opt for a hybrid process that includes arbitration if necessary. One example of this is mediation and last-offer arbitration (MEDALOA), also called baseball mediation or last best offer. For more on MEDALOA, see Sidebar 11-3: "Mediation and Last Offer Arbitration (MEDALOA)." Another variant is "night baseball" arbitration, where each party and the mediator all secretly come up with final numbers—then the number of the party that is *closest* to the mediator's number becomes binding (*see* Poon, 2010, p.82). *See also* the entry in this sidebar for *high/low*.

Mediator's proposal. This may refer to a formal, double-blind mediator's proposal of the type discussed in Sidebar 10-2: "The

Mediator's Proposal." The term may also simply refer to situations in a mediation session where the mediator floats a settlement idea to one or both parties to see if there is a favorable reaction (*see* Cooley, 2006, pp.286–289). In some instances, a mediator may propose a settlement approach to one party that the other party raised in private caucus—but present the proposal as if it were the mediator's idea. The late John Cooley suggested that this approach may be useful in cases where the proposal might be received badly if the other side were identified as the proponent (2006, p.286). An impasse-breaking technique.

Mediator's request (for final move). Toward the very end of negotiations, a mediator may, as an impasse-breaking technique, try to get a little bit more compromise out of a party by directly requesting one more move or concession as a favor, typically with the assurance that this will be the only such request (*see* Golann, 2009a, p.182–183). As part of this gambit, the mediator may promise to tell the other side expressly that the move was only granted as a favor to the mediator.

"One text" approach to reaching agreement. Bennett Picker writes: (2003, p.50)

> In the "one text" approach, the mediator will draft a document of potential agreement. The mediator will then pass it back and forth or circulate it among the parties. As the text circulates and the concerns of the parties surface, the mediator will revise the text to reflect the parties' concerns. Where there is some common ground and, especially in an effort to restructure a relationship, this approach may be a good tool for reaching agreement. However, this technique does not work well where the only issue is the payment of a sum of money.

Parallel-track negotiations. "This technique can be utilized where the parties disclose to the mediator that they are willing to compromise, but not prepared to declare that to their opponent. . . . It involves the parties confidentially disclosing how much they are prepared to concede if the other party makes the concession that they would expect of them" (Dunlop, 2008, para. 17). This approach can embrace a series of offers and counteroffers, each consented to confidentially (and theoretically) in private caucus with the mediator until the gap between the parties' positions has substantially closed. At that point, the mediator can obtain permission from both sides to disclose their consent and formalize those offers.

Prioritizing a party's concerns and interests. This technique is more or less self-explanatory. Through a series of questions, the mediator attempts not only to explore a party's underlying interests and concerns but to determine their relative ranking in the party's mind.

Range bargaining. "The mediator proposes that future bargaining will occur within a stated range of numbers. For example, if parties are at $80,000 and $200,000, a mediator might say, 'Can we agree that we will bargain from this point on between 120 and 150?'" (Golann, 2009b, para. 8). This is an impasse-breaking technique. *See also* the entry in this sidebar for *simultaneous steps*.

Reality testing. The reality being tested is the party's perception of his case's value or strength in comparison to what a neutral observer may conclude. In reality testing, a mediator will ask a series of questions on topics including potential factual or legal weak points, designed to challenge the party's preconceptions and encourage a more realistic view of the case.

Reframing. "Re-framing is a technique used by a mediator to re-word an unproductive statement made by one party to move the discussion in a more neutral or positive direction" (Austermiller, 2010, p.113). For example, if a plaintiff says to her opponent, "You breached our agreement," the mediator might re-frame that statement as "Money was not paid on time and [Ms. Plaintiff] believes this caused her difficulties in making her payment obligations to others" (p.114).

Rephrasing. This refers to a technique sometimes used by a mediator when conveying an offer or other communication from one private caucus to another, in which the mediator deliberately reshapes the wording to make it more palatable or for some other purpose (*see* Golann, 2009a, p.59). For more on this, see Substep 10.2C. When a mediator delivers a message to your side from your opponent, you may want to consider the possibility that some rephrasing has taken place (*see* Substep 10.2D).

Simultaneous steps. With this tactic, the mediator will ask both parties to agree to a mutual jump at the same time, with the plaintiff's demand coming down and the defendant's offer rising by an amount specified by the mediator. "If parties agree to make a large mutual jump, it can reinvigorate the bargaining process" (Golann, 2009b, para. 7). This is one of various ways to prompt linked moves by the parties, which the mediator may initiate by asking each party a "what if?" question.

SIDEBAR 10-2

The Mediator's Proposal

If your mediation session is nearing its end without a settlement in sight, the mediator may resort to a measure known as the mediator's proposal in an attempt to break the impasse. As used here, this term does *not* refer to instances where the mediator simply floats one or more settlement ideas in private caucuses to sound out the parties. Laura Kennedy (Phoenix, AZ) describes the mediator's proposal like this (2010, p.155):

> A mediator's proposal is a device that can be used (once!) at the end of the mediation if no agreement has been reached. The mediator chooses the terms of a settlement. Neither side knows whether the other side accepts or rejects unless both accept. The benefit to this approach is that no floor or ceiling is set for future negotiations. The downside is that, if the proposal is not accepted, the mediation with the particular mediator who made the proposal is likely over.

When Dwight Golann (Boston, MA) resorts to making a mediator's proposal, his practice is to tell parties that "the proposal will be based on a different kind of evaluation—my best assessment of what terms are likely to be acceptable to both parties, given the dynamics of the process—what I sometimes call the 'point of mutual pain'" (2007, p.19).

Linda Singer (Washington, DC) calls mediator's proposals "a last resort," although she uses them occasionally when necessary: "I don't want to do it very often because if you get a no, it's hard to restart the negotiations."

Louise LaMothe, a mediator based in Southern California, also uses mediator's proposals "if the parties remain far apart even after many hours of discussion" (2010, p.68). She typically gives the parties a deadline to respond of at least 24 hours—and sometimes as much as 72 hours. "I have found that the mediator's proposal is frequently successful if the parties take the time after emotions have cooled to seriously consider the risk of continuing versus the certainty of settlement at the suggested amount," she writes.

Like LaMothe, Prof. Golann has found that mediator's proposals "usually work" (2009a, p.248). But he recognizes "the effect is that the mediator rather than the parties dictates the final terms of agreement."

LaMothe share's Golann's discomfort with the device's coercive nature: "[I]t makes me squirm somewhat, since I can't escape the fact that I have picked the number rather than letting the parties get to it themselves." Moreover, "since it is a very evaluative step, if it is not successful it may reduce the mediator's utility as the parties may conclude that the mediator is no longer neutral" (p.68).

Mediator Margaret Shaw (New York) expresses a newer type of concern: As the use of mediator's proposals has become more widespread, sophisticated parties are now tempted to game the system. "If parties expect that the mediator may make such a proposal at some point, they may intentionally mislead the mediator about their true intentions in an attempt to set the range of the ultimate proposal" (2012, p.28). Under the circumstances, she urges mediators to "be thoughtful about whether, when and how they use this very powerful technique."

SIDEBAR 10-3

Is Mediator Bracketing a Waste of Time?

By Jobi Halper

Among the many techniques sometimes used by mediators to help parties arrive at a settlement is bracketing. In this excerpt from an article, mediator Jobi Halper (2011, pp.17–18) explains the technique and the reasons she believes it can be useful if not deployed too early in a mediation session.

Bracketing (sometimes referred to as double-bracketing) allows the mediator to suggest that if one party agrees to move to position X, the other party will move to position Y. Bracketing allows the mediator to narrow the gap between the parties and to skip a step in concessions trading.

For example, let's say that in negotiations, Party A's opening demand was $110,000, and Party B offered $7,000. Party A counter-demanded $100,000 and Party B responded with $10,000. Now it's Party A's turn, and she only wants to go to $97,000 because she believes Party B will only go to $12,000. The mediator proposes bracketing to Party A, recommending that she consider moving instead to $80,000 if Party B agrees to move to $26,000, narrowing the gap between the parties to $54,000. This turns the ocean between settlement numbers into a large lake.

Some attorneys argue that bracketing never works and the second party typically rejects the bracket so there is no benefit other than revealing over-flexibility from the first party. However, others say it is a valuable tool if done correctly.

Bracketing too early typically is not valuable because it doesn't make enough progress or promise any likelihood of settlement as an incentive to parties to make the hard choice to jump ahead. The above example is one such case. With bracketing, the $90,000 ocean between the second demand ($100,000) and counteroffer ($10,000) at best becomes a lake when the parties actually need a pond to feel that real settlement is likely. The expedited move and giving up too much too quickly (especially if Party B believes it has limited settlement authority) achieves no real value. Picture this scenario instead:

Party A has made the following demands during the day: \$110,000 ⇒ \$100,000 ⇒ \$90,000 ⇒ \$82,000 ⇒ \$78,000. Party B's offers were \$7,000 ⇒ \$10,000 ⇒ \$14,000 ⇒ \$19,900 ⇒ \$24,000. The natural next steps might be A\$72,000/B\$28,000. If the mediator proposes a bracket of A\$62,000/B\$38,000, the parties are now only \$24,000 apart and in a settlement zone. In essence, the parties have crossed the lake and now are in a small pond. This process helps the parties see that they can complete the settlement, without giving up their weighted positions.

Even where bracketing cannot move parties into a settlement zone, however, it can be used to help the mediator reveal whether the parties' general range of settlement tolerance is in sync. If for instance, in the first example, the mediator proposed the A\$80,000/B\$26,000 bracket and the defendant refused, saying he was only willing to go to \$15,000 in exchange for the \$80,000 concession, it tells the mediator that Party B's tolerance level for settlement is low. This allows the mediator to frame the next exchanges to explore the basis for low settlement tolerance with the defendant and begin to examine the possibility of an overly inflated value with the plaintiffs. Bracketing also can effectively allow parties to introduce or trade non-monetary concessions to test their value.

SIDEBAR 10-4

Take Special Care in the Closing Stage of Negotiation

By Charles B. Craver

Charles B. Craver is the Freda H. Alverson Professor of law at The George Washington University Law School in Washington, DC The passage here is excerpted from Legal Negotiation: Process and Techniques *(2011, pp.21–22, italics in original).*[10]

10. *Legal Negotiation* was written as an outline in a somewhat telegraphic manner, so certain words (such as the articles *an* and *the*) are naturally absent from the original. Such words have been added here, with Prof. Craver's permission.

There is a critical point near the end of a successful competitive phase of negotiation when parties begin to realize that an agreement within their respective settlement ranges is likely and they become psychologically committed to that result.

A. Parties who become *overly anxious* about achievement of accord frequently *move too quickly* toward closure.

   1. They forget the patience, carefully planned concession pattern, and thought-out tactics that got them to this beneficial position, and they try to move directly to a final agreement.

   2. Parties who make excessive and unreciprocated concessions in an effort to conclude transaction are likely to give up the gains they achieved during [the] prior competitive phase.

      65–75% of concessions are made during the last 20–30% of negotiation, although these position changes tend to be smaller than those made earlier.

B. Both parties need to *close the remaining gap together*. Alternating concessions of a reciprocal nature should be employed, to ensure that one side does not concede more than its fair share.

   1. During the Closing Stage, parties occasionally make concessions that are larger than those made just prior to entry into this stage of the process. This is not inappropriate, so long as the opponent is being equally generous *and* such reciprocal concessions do not unfairly disadvantage one side due to its previous position changes.

   2. Continue to use principled concessions and relevant negotiating techniques to keep the process moving inexorably toward a satisfactory conclusion.

C. As the parties enter the Closing Stage, each is concerned about the possibility of conceding too much. *Assist your opponent* by using *face-saving techniques* to resolve the remaining issues.

1. Use of *threats/warnings* during the Closing Stage is generally counter-productive, since threats/warnings are offensive rather than cooperative and are more likely to disrupt the process.
2. Use of the *promise technique* is particularly effective, since it permits parties to move together—*e.g.*, agreeing to "split the difference" between the positions currently on the negotiating table.

D. It is important to remember that the *Closing Stage* is a *highly competitive* part of the negotiation process.

1. If one party is more anxious to close than the other party, he/she is susceptible to larger and more numerous concessions, causing a poor result.
2. Once you recognize that your opponent has become psychologically committed to settlement, evidenced by such closing behavior as more rapid and more generous concessions, do not move too quickly.
   a. Be patient and encourage your opponent to close more of the remaining gap.
   b. Indicate that you have minimal bargaining room left, to induce your opponent to believe he/she must close most of the remaining gap.
   c. Emphasize your prior concessions in an effort to generate guilt that may induce your opponent to be more generous now.
   d. Be supportive of your opponent's position changes. Praise that party's reasonableness and indicate that an agreement is certain if he/she can provide you with the few additional items you need to satisfy your client's minimal goals.
   e. If your opponent prematurely offers to split the difference between the parties, you may offer to split the *remaining difference*, inducing your opponent to close 75 percent of the gap.

SIDEBAR 10-5

The Fatigue Factor

Edna Selan Epstein (interview)

Edna Epstein (Chicago) tells a mediation story from her years as a successful litigator that illustrates the importance of not allowing fatigue to cloud judgment. It also shows that sometimes, even competent mediators can sometimes inadvertently cause havoc.

Mediation takes time. Certainly the biggest mistake I ever made was in a very long mediation. It must have lasted well into eight, ten hours. The mediator wanted to present something to the other side that I knew was going to be a disaster, and I was just too tired to fight it, and it blew the mediation up.

The mediator—who was a good mediator—maybe was overtired herself by then. At that point, she presented what she thought was a rational outcome. It was a proposal that the mediator hoped would solve the dispute. I knew enough about the parties to know that it was going to be like waving a red flag in front of a bull. I knew it would never go, and it didn't. It may have been rational, but it was a red flag for the other side, and the other side wouldn't even talk after that. It really was just like throwing a bomb in at the last minute.

If I had it to do over again, I would have been much more insistent with the mediator that I really thought that was a bad idea and that my feeling was that it would have been waving a red flag. I don't think anybody was able at that point to think of another alternative, necessarily, because of the fatigue.

Maybe the first lesson is not to allow a mediation to go on that long, to the point that everybody becomes so tired they're not really functional any more. On the other hand, very often the very fact that you're committed to doing it on that day—and only that day—sometimes does get you to closure, whereas if you have to meet again it doesn't.

Every mediation has a rhythm of its own. It so depends on the parties, on the nature of the dispute, and how much emotion there is in the dispute. If there is a lot of emotion, you often need an awful lot of time to debride it, to defang it. If it's more of a commercial thing, it has a whole different quality. The range is enormous.

Maybe one ought to have planned ahead to have two days back to back. But in this case, if we stopped, the odds of bringing everybody back together were very small. On the other hand it, really blew up!

SIDEBAR 10-6

Caucus Negotiations in 300 Words or Less

John S. DeGroote (interview)

John DeGroote (Dallas) offers this nutshell version of a classic, traditional bargaining session conducted through a series of private caucuses. He uses a hypothetical traffic accident dispute as an example.

The mediator will go to the plaintiff's side and talk about the case, then go to the defendant and talk about the case. The mediator will listen and push back here and there, and then say to the plaintiff's side, "Okay, give me a number."

"$10,000."

Then the mediator goes to the defendant to push on them a little bit. "Give me your number."

"A thousand dollars."

The mediator goes back to the plaintiff's side and says, "They said 1,000."

"That's ludicrous! How about nine?

The mediator says, "Well, they told me that they don't think you are adequately valuing the red-light, green-light problem. And we all know that this is your third accident—it would be embarrassing to you." The mediator might also bring up the offer of a confidentiality agreement or whatever else.

The plaintiff's side says, "We have the videos. The red-light, green-light problem is gone. We are only going to eight."

The mediator will go to the defendant. This fourth caucus—which is the second time he's been with the defendant—is usually the last time anything very substantive is going to come up.

That defendant says, "That's ludicrous! The video camera was no good. We offer 2,000."

Then the mediator goes back to the plaintiff and this time says, "Well, the defendant said the video camera was no good. But we are beyond that now. Give me a real number."

"Okay, 6,000."

The defendant says, "Okay, four."

"How about five?"

"Done."

That's the classic.

SIDEBAR 10-7

What Maralee Eriksen Learned From Watching 40 Mediated Settlement Conferences

While Maralee Eriksen was clerking in Wyoming for a federal magistrate judge during the mid-1990s, she had the chance to observe at least 40 mediated settlement conferences from beginning to end. These were full-fledged mediations—ordered by the court about two months before a case was set for trial—in which a magistrate judge served as the mediator. Sitting in on the sessions, Eriksen made observations that have served her well in her subsequent legal career (currently as a partner in a Sacramento, CA law firm). Here is some of what she learned:

- ***The advantage of having everything at your fingertips.*** "The thing that stuck out the most was the attorneys who were prepared—whether it was substantiation of a damage amount, or a legal contention in the case, or an evidentiary ruling, or you name it. The attorneys who were prepared could say, 'Yes, I have authority for this position. Here is this case right here, and here is what it says.' They were prepared to give the tools that the mediator needed to kind of beat on the other side—or at least get them to come around a little bit. And it made a difference in the outcome."

- ***The classic tempo of the negotiation dance.*** "Of the mediation negotiations I observed as a law clerk, only one was what I would call a 'cut to the chase'—done in three moves, maybe, between the parties. The rest predominantly involved what I would call 'the waltz,' where it starts kind of slow, and then the pace tends to pick up a little bit and there is momentum, but there is all this back-and-forth and back-and-forth. The dynamics of the negotiations were that inevitably there was no real shortcut. It was a move here and a move there."
- ***The way a client's resolve can collapse.*** "Mediation is a long process, a grinding process, an emotionally tolling process. It was clear to me that some attorneys did not prepare their clients for that. As a result, you could tell the clients didn't quite have the resolve. There could have been more brought to the table by the other side, but their clients started to crumble. They hit their breaking point and that was it. They couldn't go on anymore. They just wanted to take whatever was on the table. So that was an interesting lesson for me: being sure to prepare clients appropriately for what would be the rigors—emotional, physical, mental—of going through a day-long mediation."
- ***The duty to respect your client's decision.*** "A really important ethical lesson was that ultimately it's the client's say whether or not to accept or reject an offer. You could just look at the body language and tell the attorney was recommending to take an offer, and the client was rejecting it. I learned that it's important to advise your client and make recommendations, but ultimately to remember that the call is up to the client."

SIDEBAR 10-8

Should You Ever Tell the Mediator Your Bottom Line?

Step Seven included a reminder from Homer LaRue (Washington, DC) that "the mediator's role is not to be the ally of the client or you"—and it certainly does *not* include "assisting the client to reach what the client wants" (*see* Substep 7.2E).[11] Each party's basic goal is to settle the case on the terms most favorable to its own side. The mediator's goal is related but different: to get the case settled on whatever terms both parties ultimately are willing to accept.

This reality may be a reason why Bennett Picker (Philadelphia) writes that "counsel and the client will be engaged in a *'negotiation' with the mediator* as well as adverse parties" during the mediation session (2003, p.81, italics added). In that context, Picker advises lawyers to plan in advance how much "voluntary candor" they will use in talking to the mediator (p.81):

> The degree of voluntary candor may depend upon a number of factors, including whether the mediator is more facilitative or evaluative; whether the communication involves legal arguments, underlying interests or settlement positions; and whether the mediation is in its early or late stages. . . . In the final analysis, this judgment call is likely to depend on the level of comfort with the mediator and be made in the fluid environment of the mediation sessions.

Whether, when, or how to reveal—or even hint at—your client's bottom line to the mediator is an issue related to your voluntary-candor decision.[12]

---

11. This plain fact is illustrated by a mediation session recounted by Dwight Golann (2009a, pp.210–212), where a plaintiff with a young lawyer ended up agreeing to settle a sexual-harassment claim for a pittance. The mediator knew from experience that similar cases might well be expected to settle for at least five times the agreed amount, but he reluctantly decided that it would be inappropriate for him to intervene.

12. A reminder: As discussed in Step Seven, some experienced mediation players advise against trying to find out your client's true bottom line in advance of the mediation session—or trusting what the client may tell you (*see* Step 7.4B(3)).

Certainly, some parties sometimes privately reveal their bottom line fairly early. In Substep 9.8A, mediator Peter Grilli (Tampa, FL) describes how a participant may ask him a question like "Peter, my bottom line is going to be 250,000—how do I get there?" In *The Corporate Counsel's Guide to Mediation* (2010), Gary Poon (Washington, DC) writes that under some circumstances, "it may even be appropriate to reveal to the mediator your organization's bottom line" in a presession confidential brief to the mediator (p.69).

In *Mediation Advocacy* (2002), however, the late John Cooley strenuously advises: "Do not disclose your bottom line to the mediator up front" (p.143). He offers several reasons for this rule. One is that knowledge of your bottom line puts too much control over your side of the negotiations into the hands of the mediator, since she knows what end point you will find acceptable. Another reason is that your assessment of an acceptable bottom line may change during the course of the mediation session, as the result of new information received from your opponent. A third reason is that the mediator may find herself in a difficult position ethically under certain circumstances, such as if your opponent asks her direct questions about your flexibility in settlement offers.

Recall the succinct advice of Hildy Bowbeer (St. Paul, MN) in Sidebar 5-7 ("Your Ex Parte Statement: Practices and Strategies"): "Just because the mediator is there to help you does not mean you want him to know how low you would be willing to go. If you do, you can virtually guarantee you will not do any better than that."

It is also worth noting that if you do privately reveal your bottom line at an early stage, the mediator may not believe you anyway. Mediator John Bickerman (Washington, DC) says, "I don't believe people will tell me what their real bottom line is—certainly not in the get-go, not at the beginning." Law professor Marjorie Aaron (Cincinnati, OH) puts the following advice in an article for mediators (Aaron, 2006, para. 29, italics added):

> *Don't* ask for anyone's bottom line, at least not until the end of a long day, and certainly not in joint session or in the first round of caucuses. *Most of the*

> *time, the parties won't tell you the truth* and, as soon as they announce their bottom—usually a fake one—they may become entrenched.

Even so, you may eventually reach a point in the mediation session when the mediator will ask for your bottom line or you may want to volunteer it. Note that Aaron's admonition to mediators about not asking for bottom lines also adds, "at least not until the end of a long day." Bickerman, who doubts what participants tell him about their bottom lines at the beginning, nevertheless raises the possibility that you may later want to disclose your bottom line under appropriate circumstances (speaking in Bickerman et al., 2003, p.21):

> In even the most complex cases that I've mediated, there comes a point in time where the parties want to get beyond the merits of the case and talk to you about what it's going to take to settle. You as an advocate for your client can play a very important role in helping the mediator close out the case. You can do this in a number of ways.
>
> First, you may want to share with the mediator what your bottom line is. And if you've been negotiating with the mediator long enough, there's a certain element of trust that goes both ways, where you'll trust that the mediator will not try to take advantage of that information, and the mediator will trust that you're telling him the truth. When that time comes, give the mediator the information, and let the mediator try to get the other side to get to a place that you can accept. So, at the end of the day, being very forthright with information about what works and what doesn't work is an essential step in closing a deal.

If and when you decide to be more frank with the mediator about your bottom line, there are still issues of how to handle that. In an article, mediator Peter Contuzzi (Northampton, MA) poses the question, "Are there mediation process techniques, to be employed at the end of a money negotiation that will otherwise conclude in a stalemate, which can allow a negotiating party to find out simply and without risk if its bottom line would be acceptable to the other side, and which also encourage candid responses?" (2001, para. 1). Contuzzi describes a couple of options, each of which has shortcomings in his view (para. 2):

> In a separate meeting, I can ask a party to disclose its bottom line to me and then ask the other party whether that number would be acceptable *if* it could be obtained. This garden variety "what if" technique offers some protection because the hypothetical language used does not constitute a formal settlement proposal. That can be a pretty thin veil, though, and some negotiators will speculate that the hypothetical number has already been approved by the other party. Alternatively, I can ask each party to tell me its bottom line and then advise them whether the numbers are the same or whether they overlap, are near each other, or are far apart.
>
> These common techniques lack sufficient incentives for candor and protections against manipulation. They may also leave unclear what will happen if an agreement is not reached. Given these risks and uncertainties, how candid can they afford to be?

As a possible improvement, Contuzzi goes on to describe what he calls a "safety deposit box" technique (para. 3–11), which is too complex for easy summary here. It starts with confidentially obtaining a bottom-line number from each party, followed by various additional steps depending upon the relationship those numbers have to each other.

Finally, let's circle back to the doubt expressed by mediators as to the reliability of the bottom lines stated by participants. That doubt gives rise to the question: If you purport to give the mediator your bottom line, do ethical rules require you to tell the truth? For more on this, read Sidebar 10-9: "Ethical Risks in Misleading a Mediator."

SIDEBAR 10-9

Ethical Risks in Misleading a Mediator

By Peter J. Klarfeld

Peter Klarfeld (Washington, DC) concentrates his law practice on franchise litigation. In this sidebar, abridged from an article (2010) in The Franchise Lawyer *(a publication of the ABA Forum on Franchising), he looks at ethical rules surrounding a lawyer's decision to mislead a mediator regarding a client's true bottom line in negotiations.*

If you tell a mediator that your client's insurance coverage or the authority granted by your client's Board of Directors puts a specific limit on the settlement your client can offer or accept, the mediator might work to bring the other side within that ballpark. But what if what you told the mediator were not true?

Toward the end of my portion of a program on mediating franchise disputes, I offered the following hypothetical on mediation ethics:

1. Your client is ordered by a court before which it is a defendant to participate in mediation, with one of the court's Magistrate Judges serving as the mediator.
2. In a pre-mediation meeting to discuss strategy, the CEO of your client tells you that (a) the limit of the company's insurance for claims of this kind is $1 million, and (b) that is the highest the company will go to settle the matter.
3. The mediation goes forward and by late afternoon, you sense that the party on the other side has come around to wanting to settle the case.
4. The mediator meets with your side separately and says that the time is right for your side to make its best offer.
5. You say to the mediator: "Look, it's been a long day, and we'd like to get this over with. The limit of the company's insurance coverage is $500,000. You can tell them we'll go $250,000 over that, for a total of $750,000. But that's it. That's as high as my client will go to settle this matter."

6. The mediator presents that offer to the other side and returns to say: "We have a deal at $750,000."
7. Should you (a) [a]lert the managing partner of your firm that you've just saved the client $250,000 and that this may be a good case for premium billing, or (b) [w]orry about what you would do if you could no longer practice law?
8. Would the answer be different if the mediator were not a judicial officer?

The basic question raised by the hypothetical is to what extent a lawyer is ethically permitted to bluff, puff or even lie in the course of a mediation. Three of the American Bar Association's Model Rules of Professional Conduct are worth considering in that regard:

Rule 4.1 of the ABA Model Rules provides:

> In the course of representing a client, a lawyer shall not knowingly:
>
> (a) make a false statement of material fact or law to a third person; or
>
> (b) fail to disclose a material fact when disclosure is necessary to avoid assisting a criminal or fraudulent act by a client, unless disclosure is prohibited by Rule 1.6.

Rule 3.3 (a) provides:

> A lawyer shall not knowingly:
>
> (1) make a false statement of fact or law to a tribunal. . . .

Rule 8.4 provides:

> It is professional misconduct for a lawyer to:
>
> (c) engage in conduct involving dishonesty, fraud, deceit or misrepresentation.

On their face, these rules appear to pose serious problems for the lawyer in the hypothetical. However, the ABA has put a gloss on their application to mediation that brings their effect more in line with common negotiating practice. In 2006, the American Bar Association Standing Committee on Ethics and Professional Responsibility issued Formal Opinion 06-439 titled "Lawyer's Obligation of Truthfulness When Representing a Client in Negotiation: Application to Caucused Mediation." The opinion's opening summary states:

> Under Model Rule 4.1, in the context of a negotiation, including a caucused mediation, a lawyer representing a client may not make a false statement of material fact to a third person. However, statements regarding a party's negotiating goals or its willingness to compromise, as well as statements that can fairly be characterized as negotiation "puffing," ordinarily are not considered "false statements of material fact" within the meaning of the Model Rules.

Thus, the opinion indicates that there are two types of statements that despite being "less than entirely forthcoming" are nonetheless allowed in the course of mediation. The first is a declaration of "a party's negotiating goals or its willingness to compromise"—for example, a statement such as: "My client will not accept less than (or pay more than) $750,000 to settle this matter." The second is a statement "that can fairly be characterized as negotiation 'puffing,'" which the opinion indicates would include exaggerating the strengths or minimizing the weaknesses of a client's position. For example, a lawyer might overstate his or her confidence that acceptable options are available if the negotiation fails, such as by stating that he or she is confident of prevailing on summary judgment despite actually believing that that prospect is remote. While the opinion does not attempt to rationalize these two exceptions (other than to say that they comport with generally accepted negotiating conventions), the characteristic they appear to share is that each posits an internal calculation, assessment or intention (upon which no adverse party should rely) rather than asserting the existence of an external "material fact."

Using these guidelines, counsel would be free in the hypothetical mediation to take the position that his or her client did not intend to settle for more (or less) than $750,000, even though the client had authorized a higher (or lower) settlement amount. However, when the lawyer adds that the client's maximum insurance coverage is $500,000, while knowing that the coverage is $1 million, it is likely that a violation of Model Rule 4.1(a) has occurred. The opinion points out that the same would be true of a lawyer's statement that the client's board of directors had authorized a settlement of no higher than $500,000 when the board had, in fact, authorized payment of a higher amount.

So much for Rule 4.1, but what about Rules 8.4 and 3.3? With respect to Rule 8.4, which does not by its terms limit its prohibition of misrepresentations to those of "material fact," the opinion concludes that, whatever its outer parameters, Rule 8.4 does not prohibit statements in mediations that are allowable under Rule 4.1.

However, Rule 3.3, which is titled "Candor Toward The Tribunal," may, in some circumstances, take away even the limited room to maneuver that Rule 4.1 affords. Like Rule 8.4, Rule 3.3 is not limited to statements of "material fact." Moreover, Formal Opinion 06-439 specifically concludes that Rule 3.3 applies in a court-sponsored mediation in which a judge acts as the mediator. In that setting, the duty of candor is elevated: counsel simply may not knowingly make a false statement of fact to a judge. Thus, if the mediator/judge asks counsel for his or her client's bottom-line settlement amount, counsel has only two ethical options under Rule 3.3: to decline to answer or to tell the truth.

In sum, the ABA Ethics Committee's opinion on the extent to which "truthfulness" is required in mediated negotiations provides some relief from the strict requirements of candor contained in the ABA's Model Rules of Professional Conduct, at least outside of a court-sponsored mediation. But two significant caveats are in order. First, the lines drawn in the opinion are far from clear, and it would serve you well to give the opinion a close reading before heading into the next mediation in which you are acting as counsel. Second, it is important to remember that the ABA Model Rules and ABA Ethics Committee opinions do not, in the end, contain the ethical standards governing your conduct. Instead, the operative ethical rules are those of the states in which you are licensed and practice and those of the courts in which you appear. While those rules may be based on the ABA Model Rules, they may differ substantially, in both their express terms and in their interpretation, from what has been promulgated by the ABA.

SIDEBAR 10-10

An Example of Creative Settlement

Thomas A. Dye (interview)

Talking to Thomas Dye (West Palm Beach, FL), it quickly becomes clear that he takes a generally hard-nosed approach to litigation. So it is doubly interesting that in the mediation context, Dye has a settlement story to tell that perfectly illustrates the win-win, interest-based approach to negotiating advocated by Roger Fisher and William Ury in Getting to Yes *(1981).*[13]

This happened in a dispute over rights to some intellectual property. There was a fight between two partners in a business, and they had split up. Then there was a fight over the intellectual property of the business. Both parties were taking hard-line positions, saying, "If you want to buy me out, I'll sell it to you for this amount. Otherwise, we're going to trial. We think we're going to win."

Both of them had proceeded on their own tracks to try to develop this intellectual property into a salable product. I didn't know what the other side wanted to use this invention for, and they didn't know what my client wanted to use it for. Neither party was disclosing what they had done in the last three years since the split, trying to translate it into a product. Neither party had allowed testimony to that fact in the depositions, on grounds that it was irrelevant.

At the mediation session, I said, "Well, this is mediation. It's confidential. Before we get into our presentations and all that, I just have a few questions. Maybe we can share a little bit of informa-

13. For more on the interest-based approach, see Substep 7.4A.

tion, because it might affect how we proceed in this whole mediation. You can be very general, very cryptic, but give me some idea of what you want to use this invention for. The reason I ask is, maybe it's different from what we want to use it for. Maybe we can agree that you can use it for that, and we can use it for what we're doing. And we can both be happy and go home."

In fact, that's what happened. They opened the door a little bit and said what they wanted to use it for, very cryptically.

I then went outside with my client and said, "What do you think about their idea, to use it for that?" My guy was the inventor. He said, "I know more about this than anyone in the world. I am the inventor of this. That will never work." I said, "Then why do you care? You're never going to use it for that. Why don't you give them the license to do that, for only that purpose? You retain all other rights, they go home, and you go home, and that's it." He said, "Yeah." And that was it.

So by asking those few questions—which never were allowed to be asked in the litigation—we realized both sides had different motivations, and we resolved the case. No money came out of anyone's pocket, except for the attorney's fees wasted in a couple of years of litigation. If this question had been answered early on, the legal-fee expenditure wouldn't have happened.

SIDEBAR 10-11

Settlement Options Beyond the Money

By Lawrence M. Watson Jr.[14]

One of the most important functions of a mediation caucus session is to brainstorm and develop settlement options. While a robust exploration of the full range of potential aspects of litigation is always important, that dialogue ultimately serves as a backdrop to consideration of options to settle the case.

14. Excerpted from an article (*see* Watson, 2002, pp.11–12).

In commercial cases, a systematic search for settlement options other than money should be conducted before the mediation commences. Consideration should be given to possible future business arrangements, i.e., an edge on the bid for the next project, special supply or delivery agreements, an exchange of products or services, joint undertakings or other "earn out" arrangements. Often simple things like business references, introductions, or joint public statements can serve as compelling elements of a settlement agreement in commercial disputes. If there is any way to convert a business dispute to a business opportunity, careful consideration should be given to that option in advance. In considering "other than money" settlement options careful thought should be given as to whether they are potentially doable—whether there are legal, contractual, political or physical barriers to including such terms in final settlement. The ultimate decision to actually include these terms in an agreement can be made later. In the advance planning stage, focus is on nothing more than feasibility. The settlement negotiations themselves should be entered with an "anything is possible" frame of mind.

In personal injury or intangible damage cases where the payment of money is the principal settlement consideration, there is still room for advance planning for caucus negotiations. In those cases, for example, defining realistic goals for the *use* of any settlement funds generated can focus the parties on aspects of settlement more solid than a simple dollar amount. What bills need to be paid? What are the exact amounts necessary to eliminate liens or third party claims on the settlement proceeds? After the bills are paid, what needs to be done with settlement money to address valid interests and concerns? What are the immediate and future family needs? Will immediate cash be needed to address those needs, or will long-term annuities work as well or better? College education, retirement security, even future family living support can often be met with structured settlements—either taken as part of the settlement (which, in some cases, can also generate income tax advantages), or purchased independently with settlement proceeds.

Even in the intangible damage cases, settlements are not always about money. Letters of apology, public announcements of exoneration, reinstatement, amending or destroying adverse personnel records, job references or opportunities, all can play a major role in making a final settlement more satisfying to the parties.

SIDEBAR 10-12

How Parties Can (Mis)communicate Through Numbers

By J. Anderson Little

As a mediator, J. Anderson Little is acutely aware that in the negotiating process, numbers aren't just numbers—they are a form of communication (see Substep 10.4). In this excerpt from his book Making Money Talk *(2007, pp.67–69), Little offers a simple hypothetical scenario in the context of an injury claim against an insured defendant, showing how poor communication through numbers can derail a mediation session.*

Consider this example:

> The plaintiff begins the negotiation at 100, having decided that 50 is probably his "homerun verdict," and sets 35 as his absolute bottom number.
>
> The defendant, having evaluated the case at 15 to 30, thinks 100 is "ridiculous" and counters at 2.
>
> The plaintiff gets angry at the defendant's "low ball" and counters at 98.

What has happened in this scenario? The plaintiff wanted at least 35. The plaintiff's lawyer's case analysis is that 50 is his best day in court. But on the theory that "you can't get it unless you ask for it," he went for a much bigger number than was justified by his own case analysis.

The defendant then hears the "message" that the ballpark of settlement is much higher than he can or will pay and reacts negatively to the plaintiff's proposal. . . . In an effort to tell the plaintiff he's "out of the ballpark" and that he needs to get into the defendant's ballpark, the defendant sends a "low-ball" proposal.

The message the plaintiff receives, however, is different from what the defendant intended. What plaintiff hears is, "We're not going to pay anywhere near what this case is worth." Based on that message, the plaintiff then reacts in frustration and thinks, "This damn insurance company is playing their silly games again and not bargaining in good faith. They don't want to settle for what this case is worth, so I'll just have to tell them to get serious." He then tells the mediator, "Tell them my next number is 98."

Many observers of this exchange will interpret the interaction of the parties in interpersonal terms—the parties are engaging in a contest of wills or egos. That may well be true, but the analysis does little to help us understand how to assist these negotiators. A more useful frame for this scenario is the language of communication. The parties have tried to convey a message and have failed to get their messages across. Instead of making moves that are consistent with their theory of the case, and thereby sending signals about where they can really settle, the parties have sent messages that will be misinterpreted.

The source of that miscommunication lies in the fact that they have formulated their counterproposals out of anger and frustration and in reaction to the other's proposal. When the parties formulated their counteroffers reactively, they failed to convey accurately the range in which they are willing to settle. In this example, the range that each side thinks will work for the other is much different than the range the other party actually has in mind. . . .

If they continue to send inaccurate messages, they will quickly quit the negotiation in the mistaken belief that there is a vast difference in their best numbers. This is a hallmark of traditional bargaining.

In our example, the parties' case analysis reveals that, if they each stretched to reach their best numbers (the plaintiff's bottom number and the defendant's top number), their real gap is only five, the difference between 35 and 30. If they had not been misled by each other's proposal, the negotiation may have played out much differently.

SIDEBAR 10-13

Control Theory in Mediation

By J. Anderson Little

In this excerpt from his book Making Money Talk *(2007, pp.92–93), mediator Anderson Little (Chapel Hill, NC) applies control theory—first promulgated by psychologist William Glasser—to explain why taking a reactive approach to your opponent's proposals in a mediation session can make it impossible to achieve your own objective.*

Control theory encourages us to focus parties on what they, as opposed to the other side, can do to make progress toward settlement. In the settlement of civil litigation, the parties have control over some things and no control over others. For instance, litigants cannot:

- control the behavior or decisions of judges.
- control the decisions of juries.
- control the movement their opponents make in negotiations.
- keep their opponents from evaluating the case differently than they do.
- keep their opponents from opening negotiations with low-ball or high-ball proposals.
- keep their opponents from moving slower than the litigants wish they would.

Litigants can control:

- their own case evaluation.
- their own negotiating ranges.
- their own movement at any point in time.
- their own stopping point at the end of their bargaining range.

One party cannot make the other do anything. Most importantly, one party cannot make the other go beyond the range he or she thinks is appropriate to settle the case.

When I first employed the insights of control theory in civil trial court mediations, I discovered an amazingly simple phenomenon: The party to a money negotiation who becomes reactive to the other's proposal has lost control. He has lost the ability to see the many options he has at his disposal to encourage the other side to make significant movement. Having lost control, he puts forth a proposal that succeeds only in driving the other side away and making it impossible to achieve his own objective, which is to settle the case.

SIDEBAR 10-14

Q&A on the Tripartite Relationship in Insurance Defense Cases

Steven M. Brom (interview)

Although Steven Brom (Birmingham, AL) has expanded his practice considerably over time, he cut his teeth on insurance defense work. A distinct feature of mediation in this context is that the insurance representative—not the insured client—has the final say on settlement. Moreover, particularly in smaller cases, the insurance rep may attend the session by phone rather than in person. In the discussion below, Brom talks about various aspects of dealing with the "triparite relationship" among lawyer, client, and insurer during a session.

Q: I'm interested in a situation where you're on the scene representing a defendant at the mediation session, but your client's insurance adjuster isn't necessarily going to be there in person. Somebody on the defense is going to have to start up with a number at some point. How do you usually work that?

A: Usually the insurer will tell me an initial number to start with, what our opening demand will be. Then I'll wait to hear the opposing party's reply. Upon receipt of the opposing party's reply, I will get back on the phone with the insurance person with settlement authority and convey to them the opposing party's reply—and then figure out where to go next. We'll discuss it at length, decide what is the best option for us in our response, and make our offer.

Q: So that is, in effect, your private conference caucus is taking place over the phone? Do you also have private caucuses just between you and the mediator in the course of that kind of mediation?

A: Yes, very frequently. Mediators are always trying to explain to the parties why their negotiating position isn't correct, and why they need to seriously consider the offer that they are receiving from the other side. So very frequently you'll have a mediator explain that the authority that you're receiving from the person with full and final settlement authority just isn't sufficient, and that you need to speak with them and explain to them whatever the strengths of the opposing party's case are. That's just the mediator's standard tool. They're going to do that in every single case.

Q: So then you get back on the phone with the adjuster and say, "This is what the mediator was telling me—what do you think?"

A: Yes, absolutely. Typically when I'm having the discussions with the adjuster, no one else is involved in the conversation. It would just be me with the adjuster.

This is how it typically happens: I'll be sitting in the room with the actual client. In cases of insurance, it's the insurance company who has got the real settlement authority, unless the client just happens to be willing to put their own money on the table—which never happens. So it's the insurance company's money you're dealing with, which makes the adjuster the person who has the full and final settlement authority.

The insured and I will be sitting in the caucus room waiting for the mediator to finish speaking with the opposing counsel. The mediator will come into our room and explain that he has just spoken with the opposing counsel at length. He has heard their position, and he has their initial offer. The mediator will convey the initial offer to us. I'll listen to it, and I'll listen to the mediator explain why he thinks that the opposing side has a valid argument. Then I'll explain to the mediator that I need to speak with my client and the adjuster alone, regardless of whether the adjuster is physically present or on the phone.

The mediator will typically leave the room, and I'll spend however long it takes speaking with my client and the adjuster to determine our reply. When that decision is made, I'll request that the mediator come back in the room, and explain to him our reply along with our best argument as to why we think it's a valid reply. Then the mediator will leave the room and go back to the opposing party's room and discuss it with them. And that process just goes back and forth like a tennis match all day long. Typically the settlements happen at the end of the day. Very rarely have I ever had them happen within the first few hours.

Q: It's an interesting type of situation where you have the client on the one hand, and on the other hand the insurance company, which in fact can make the ultimate decision about what the settlement would be. How does that dynamic work at a mediation session? Does the client typically end up expressing opinions in terms of what they think the settlement ought to be? Do they argue with you? How does that work?

A: Well, that is a very delicate subject, when you're dealing with the so-called tripartite relationship, which is the attorney, the insured, and the insurance company. As the attorney representing the insured, all of my duties are owed to the insured. So I have to do what is in the insured's best interest and not what is in the insurance company's best interest.

Sometimes the insured will want the case settled, but the insurance company doesn't want to accept whatever the plaintiff's final offer is. That creates a risk for the insurance company.

Because if the case does not settle, and it goes to trial and the insured is hit with a verdict for greater than the policy limits—when the case could have been settled at that mediation within the policy limits—now the insurance company has got a potential bad-faith action from the insured.

Sometimes you have the exact opposite happen, where the insurance company is prepared to settle, but the insured feels he didn't do anything wrong and is just furious about settling the case. He wants his day in court. There is nothing the insured can do in that situation, because the insurance policy virtually always has a clause in there that says the insurer has the authority to settle the case. The insured does not have to consent to a settlement in that situation, if the insurance company is willing to settle it. The insurance company can settle the case without the insured's permission. Frequently that upsets the insured greatly, because they feel they did not do anything wrong. They want their day in court, and they are not happy about the case being settled. Even though the settlement agreement will state that there is no admission of any wrongdoing, just the fact that their insurance company paid money to the opposing party tends to get some people very upset.

Q: Let's go back to the situation where the insurer is the one who doesn't want to settle. What do you do vis-à-vis the insured client when you've reached the end of that day and the insurance company says, "I won't settle," and the insured wants to? How do you handle that as a personal matter, you sitting there as the attorney and this person in the room with you?

A: In that situation, my responsibility is to make sure that the insurance company is fully aware that the insured wants the matter settled. At that point, it's the insurance company's issue to deal with. They are the ones making the decision as to whether or not they are going to settle it.

Q: What about the touchy-feely side of it? Picture a new insurance defense lawyer who is confronted at the end of the mediation by an unhappy insured client who is upset that the insurance company refused to settle. Have you found ways to smooth things over?

A: Well, one of the things I do is I explain to the insured what their rights are in that situation. The fact that if the insurance company turned down a settlement offer that was within the policy limits, and there is a verdict at trial that is in excess of the policy limits, then the insured has a potential cause of action for bad faith against the insurance company. Typically, that will alleviate any concerns that the insured may have.

STEP ELEVEN

Seal the Deal, Plan for Future Resolution, or Disengage at the Closing Joint Session

People, in handling affairs
Often come close to completion and fail
If they are as careful in the end as the beginning
Then they would have no failure

—Lao-tzu (6th century BC?)
philosopher and sage[1]

Regardless of how the caucus rounds ended, the parties and mediator typically meet all together for a closing joint session when the mediation ends. As mediator Gary Poon (San Diego, CA) has noted, the closing joint session "will occur in one of three circumstances: (1) the parties have reached an agreement on all issues; (2) the parties have made progress, but there are still outstanding issues to be resolved; or (3) the parties have reached an impasse, which in the judgment of the mediator seems insurmountable and further negotiations would not be productive or may even be counterproductive" (2010, p.82). The substeps for Step Eleven differ for each of those three scenarios.

11.1 Scenario #1: The parties have reached an agreement on all issues.

Obviously, the most desirable outcome for the mediation is one where you have been able to reach a complete settlement.

1. In Derek Lin (Trans.), *Tao Te Ching: Annotated & Explained*. Woodstock, VT: Skylight Paths (2006). Available online at http://taoism.net/ttc/complete.htm.

In this scenario, you will need to take care with three substeps in the closing joint session:

A. Review the final terms with the mediator and the other side.
B. Put the agreed-upon terms in writing.
C. Depart on positive terms with the other side to the extent possible.

A. Review the final terms with the mediator and the other side

"After you've got a deal, a good mediator will bring the parties together, if he's been meeting with them in caucuses separately, and will restate the deal publicly," says mediator John Bickerman (Washington, DC). "Make sure the mediator does that, so both parties hear the same words and the same information" (Bickerman et al., 2003, p.21).

Prof. Charles Craver (Washington, DC) amplifies this (2011, p.23, italics in original)

> Once a final agreement is achieved, the parties should carefully *review the final terms* agreed upon to make sure there has been a complete meeting of the minds. If any misunderstandings are found, this is the best time to resolve them since the parties are psychologically committed to a final accord. If misunderstandings are not found until later, they are likely to be more difficult to resolve.

Craver also warns about the danger of "nibbling," where your opponent suddenly demands one additional concession after you thought final agreement had been achieved (2011, p.29). He observes that a party that has become psychologically committed to an agreement "often concedes the requested item to preserve the accord."[2] If your opponent tries to take a

2. The document from which Prof. Craver's quotes were taken is in outline form, in which some small words such as *the* and *an* are often absent. They are supplied in this book with Prof. Craver's permission.

nibble, Craver advises your side not to focus on how much *you* want the agreement. Remind yourself that at this late stage, your opponent is unlikely to let the whole deal fall apart just because you decline his additional demand.

As an alternative to diplomatically declining, consider countering with an appropriate nibble of your own. "If the other party is sincere, he/she will be willing to discuss a reciprocal arrangement. If the other party is insincere, he or she is likely to demand honoring of the original terms agreed upon" (Craver 2011, p.29). Also, this tactic may discourage your opponent from trying any more nibbles.

B. Put the agreed-upon terms in writing

"[I]f I had one fundamental point that I think should be remembered it is: don't leave a mediation without a written settlement agreement," says mediator Larry Mills (Seattle; speaking in Bickerman et al., 2003, p.22). This opinion is almost universally shared among professionals in alternative dispute resolution, including Bennett Picker (Philadelphia): "If agreement is reached, the mediator should insist that the parties execute a written settlement memorandum before the mediation session concludes" (2003, p.51).

John Bickerman makes the point in even stronger language (2003, pp.25–26):

> It's malpractice, in my view, for anybody to leave a mediation session and not have a term sheet, not have a writing of what the deal looks like. It can be brief, it can be handwritten, and it's done at 11:00 o'clock at night or 1:00 in the morning sometimes. But you need something in writing that everybody initials. And the reason is, quite a few parties may have "buyer's regret," where they wake up the next morning and they regret what they did the night before. But if it's in writing, it stops them from trying to renegotiate the deal. So be sure you've got it in writing.

Bickerman's quote highlights one of the major reasons for getting something in writing at the closing session. Another reason is to help make sure the parties have remembered to cover all essential elements in their discussion of the deal. As Gary Poon puts it: "Indeed, the process of drafting the term sheet or memorandum of understanding may help the parties identify any areas of ambiguity that need further clarification" (2010, p.83). Mediator Lee Jay Berman (Los Angeles) elaborates (2006, para. 31):

> One reason to be sure to write a settlement agreement at the end of the mediation, even over the parties' predictable resistance after hours of difficult negotiation, is because the exercise of writing the agreement forces the attorneys, in particular, to focus on the details of the agreement. If a mediator has not inquired in advance about potential deal points such as confidentiality, payment terms, release language and who will be released, then this exercise can be like a ticking time bomb. Too often, deals blow up at the end where all parties think that they have reached agreement, only to find out that when they are tired and wrung out, frustrated and anxious to be done, there is a problem with a deal term.

A third rationale for getting the deal points in writing is to help ensure that the terms will be admissible for enforcement if one side tries to back out later. Lawrence Watson (Maitland, FL) points out in Sidebar 11-1 ("Preparing for Closure: The Settlement Agreement"), a signed settlement agreement is the only exception to the strict confidentiality provisions that are in place in almost every jurisdiction with statutory mediation programs.

In court-ordered mediation, a fourth reason is even more basic: Many jurisdictions' rules require something in writing signed by the parties at the end of a mediation session where settlement was reached (Watson, 2002, p.12).

However, a belief in the absolute necessity of a written agreement during the closing joint session is not universal. Among the huge number of disputes that Prof. Dwight Golann (Boston) has mediated, there have been dozens where the parties did not sign an agreement at the session—for example, where an insurance adjuster had to leave early to catch a plane and assented to final terms over the phone (Golann, 2009a, p.195). Golann believes the fear that a settlement will fall apart under those circumstances is exaggerated, because it has never happened in his experience. Even so, he acknowledges that it increases the risk of a dispute over exactly what was agreed.

(1) Term sheet or memorandum of understanding

In reducing the deal points to writing, you have two basic options: a full-fledged settlement agreement or an interim memorandum of understanding, also known as a term sheet.

"Now, the settlement agreement doesn't necessarily have to be a well-developed, full-fledged agreement," advises Larry Mills (in Bickerman et al., 2003, p.22). "It can simply be a list of business points that have been agreed upon. . . . Often it looks like a handwritten memo of settlement that the lawyers scratch out at the conclusion of a long day of mediation."

Mediator Peter Grilli calls term sheets a short form, and he uses this option often at closing sessions:

> I do a short-form settlement agreement. I try to put in the essential elements of an agreement. It's not going to have every jot and tittle, of course. For example, it's not going to name every employee, officer, director, agent, who's getting a release. But my hope is that I've made it detailed enough that it has the essential elements of the agreement so that if for some reason the paperwork doesn't go through—if people can't agree on the final paperwork—you still have an enforceable settlement agreement because you have the essential elements.

If done right, a term sheet "may be enforceable as a settlement agreement or even for entry of judgment" (Turitz, 2010, p.13). The term sheet does not require formal terminology and inclusion of every single detail (Golann 2009a, p.196). However, you will need to meet some minimum standards in order for the term sheet to be enforceable. For example, you will need to identify the conflict being resolved, identify the parties, and describe the significant terms clearly.

As with contract law in general, these requirements are typically governed by the state where the term sheet is signed. Sometimes a state may have individual quirks, such as the statutory presumption in California that a signed settlement memo is not enforceable unless it explicitly says so. *See, e.g., Fair v. Bahktiari*, 147 P.3d 653 (Cal. 2006). Gary Poon advises inside counsel to consult their outside lawyers as to whether the term sheet that is being signed for their specific mediation fits the enforceability requirements of that jurisdiction (2010,p.83).

(2) Full-fledged settlement agreement

Obviously, a full-fledged settlement agreement is exactly that: a formal agreement with every *i* dotted and all attachments (such as releases) in place, of the type one normally expects to see upon settlement of a lawsuit or similar dispute. The parties ultimately will end up with such a full-fledged settlement agreement either way; the only question is whether to try to accomplish all this at the closing joint session of the mediation or take a two-step approach—signing a term sheet at the session and following up with the full document later (*see* Picker, 2003, p.35).

(3) Pros and cons of each approach

There are differing views as to whether a lawyer representing a client in mediation should try to walk out of the session with a full-fledged settlement document. Term sheets seem to be very common, but some lawyers recommend getting the full-fledged agreement done if possible.

"I would not try to negotiate comprehensive settlement documentation at the mediation," advises former bankruptcy judge and mediator C. Timothy Corcoran (Tampa, FL). "If you do, you'll just get bogged down. That can be done later" (2007, § 3.i.x).

According to Bennett Picker, Judge Corcoran[3] has plenty of company in that opinion: "Many mediators discourage the drafting of a full and comprehensive agreement as part of the

3. A former bankruptcy judge and mediator, he has since left the law to become a Roman Catholic priest.

settlement process. Rather, where such an agreement is necessary, they will encourage the parties to draft the agreement at a later time in order to avoid the potential for a settlement to break down over the drafting" (2003, p.35). Drafting, reviewing, and executing a full-fledged settlement agreement could be a very daunting task at the end of a long day of mediation.

On the other hand, as Prof. Golann has seen, the proliferation of laptop computers has made this process much more doable than in times past (2009a, p.197):

> Lawyers sometimes bring a draft of formal settlement agreements to mediation or create them on a laptop. They can also provide drafts of supporting documents such as releases of liability. If the other side believes documents are being offered in good faith, such drafts can allow parties to leave mediation with an executed final settlement agreement.

Of course, this practice can also easily lead to dueling forms, where each party is offering its own laptop version. For lengthy formal documents, just the time required to scrutinize all the language of each party's proposed releases and so forth could make it impractical to execute a full-fledged agreement at the end of the day in mediation. Looking at a set of deal points in competing term sheets—perhaps in bullet-point format—is likely to be much less burdensome.

The complexity of the case and number of parties is likely to be a factor in the approach that parties take. "In relatively simple cases, the settlement agreement can be drafted and executed at the conclusion of the mediation," writes Gary Poon (2010, p.83). Gilda Turitz (San Francisco) adds, "In more complex matters, it is generally anticipated that counsel will prepare full settlement documentation after the mediation, including comprehensive releases" (2010, p.13).

On the other hand, inside counsel Hildy Bowbeer (St. Paul, MN) advocates getting a full-fledged agreement signed in mediation of intellectual property disputes, which presumably do not fall on the simple side of the scale (2011, p.206):

> [U]nless you entertain no hope of making a deal (in which case, why are you spending all that time and money on mediation?), you should always go to the

mediation with a draft agreement on a laptop computer, ready to be revised, finalized, and signed on the spot. It is unfortunately common for the parties to leave a mediation with a "settlement in principle" only to spend the next three months battling over the actual language of the agreement.

(4) Items to cover

For more guidance on specific matters to include in term sheets or full-fledged settlement agreements, read Sidebar 11-1 ("Preparing for Closure: The Settlement Agreement") and Sidebar 11-2 ("A Settlement Template"). Together, these two sidebars will give you a good sense of the universe to consider. For the less-inclusive term sheets, you will need to focus primarily on the deal points and other key elements that memorialize the substance of the parties' settlement.

Larry Mills advises that the term sheet should include "all the basic business points that have been agreed upon," plus a provision "for dismissals of any lawsuits that might be pending and releases, if appropriate, of all obligations, except what you've agreed upon in the settlement agreement." He also underlines the importance of including a dispute resolution clause related to issues arising from the agreement (in Bickerman et al. 2002, p.22).[4]

In addition, Dwight Golann advises you to include a schedule or set of deadlines for any future steps called for in the agreement (2009a, pp.196–97). Finally, if your jurisdiction requires it, Prof. Golann reminds you to include a statement that the parties intend the term sheet to be legally binding and admissible as evidence for purposes of enforcement. In fact, it might wise to put the same type of language in any term sheet or settlement agreement, anyway.

---

4. Mills continues: "Often, because the mediator has become very familiar with the subject matter of the mediation and the dispute, the parties will write the mediator into the settlement agreement as an arbitrator to resolve any disputes that should come up in the implementation of the settlement agreement. And most mediators are willing to serve in that role."

(5) Who does the drafting?

There are four obvious choices of drafter—the mediator, you, the other side, or some combination thereof.

(a) The mediator

In some mediation circles, it seems to be common for the mediator to draw up the term sheet. Nate Cade (Milwaukee) comments: "A good mediator will draft up a settlement then and there outlining at least the big issues, you know, that we have an agreement on." Recall also Peter Grilli's comment about short-form settlement agreements earlier in this chapter, which contemplated that he would be the one writing up the term sheet. (*See also* Golann, 2009a, pp.197–198.)

(b) You

In Substep 6.7, we recommended that you draft at least a skeleton settlement agreement in advance and bring it with you to the mediation session. "When the negotiation process concludes with a mutual accord, it is beneficial to *draft the final agreement*," writes Prof. Charles Craver (2011, pp.23–24). "While no attorney should contemplate the deletion or alteration of [a] term agreed upon or the addition of new provisions, since such behavior would be unethical and probably fraudulent, he/she should seize the chance to draft provisions that best reflect his/her understanding of the terms negotiated."

(c) The other side

For exactly the same reason, the other side may want to draft the settlement agreement. In that event, Craver urges you to take special care in review to ensure that it is accurate. Specifically: "1. Make sure the language selected reflects your understanding of the terms agreed upon. 2. Be certain that nothing has been added that was never agreed upon. 3. Make sure that nothing that was agreed upon has been omitted from the final agreement" (pp.23–24).

(d) Some combination

Drafting committees are common in complex insurance coverage dispute mediation, according to Richard Shusterman (Berwyn, PA). The various parties typically use a working document in checklist form of what everyone will agree to if a final settlement can be finalized. Then later, a drafting committee writes up a proposed final binding document.

C. Depart on positive terms with the other side to the extent possible

Relations between opposing parties can be prickly at best, and sometimes personal emotions can run high—even in business disputes between big corporations. Even so, consider trying to establish as positive a tone as feasible as the mediation session closes. Christopher Carroll (New York and New Jersey) says:

> I really feel the best walking out of the negotiation that's been successful with both sides being able to say, "You know, I don't dislike them. I respect their position. I don't necessarily agree with it, but they were fair, and they had integrity in the process and in how they dealt with us." That has value. If it doesn't really take hold in that mediation, it might take hold in the next mediation or have value in the next mediation or in another case with these very same parties.

The participants in a mediation are unlikely to end up exchanging hugs with everyone in the room—but a handshake would be nice, if possible (Golann, 2009a, pp.195–196).

A positive tone to end the mediation session may be especially important where the parties have signed a term sheet. Continuing goodwill should make it easier to complete the process of drafting and executing a full-fledged settlement agreement during the days or weeks afterward.

11.2 Scenario #2: The parties have made progress, but there are still outstanding issues to be resolved.

The first mediation where Daniel Terrell (Baton Rouge, LA) participated as a young lawyer did not end in settlement.

Even so, "there was value added," he says. "The parties narrowed the issues and understood the other side's positions more fully, allowing both sides to work more effectively after the mediation towards a resolution." The parties did in fact settle a few months later.

Where there has been some progress but not resolution at the mediation, here are some potentially useful substeps to take:

A. Agree together on what issues (if any) have been narrowed or resolved and how.
B. Diagnose current barriers to settlement and plan postsession steps to surmount them.
C. Consider leaving an offer on the table.
D. End on the most positive tone possible.

A. Agree together on what issues (if any) have been narrowed or resolved and how

In the same way that a mediator reviews with the parties the terms they have agreed to in a complete settlement, it is important to review any points that have been agreed upon or issues that have been narrowed or clarified during a session that did not settle the case. Gary Poon recommends that you and the other side together put both areas of agreement and outstanding issues in writing (2010, p.83).

B. Diagnose current barriers to settlement and plan postsession steps to surmount them

"If you fail to reach a comprehensive settlement agreement at the mediation, don't just quit," urges Timothy Corcoran (2007, § 3.j). "Agree on what you'll do next. Perhaps you need some additional discovery. [T]hen resume. Use the mediator to facilitate a discovery protocol, schedule, or case management order that will be helpful." He repeats once more for emphasis: "Don't just quit."

Peter Grilli also encourages this approach as a mediator:

> When it doesn't look like I am settling the case, I try to do something I call diagnosing the impasse. Why are we coming to impasse? Very often it's one factor, a disagreement on liability, a disagreement on damages, a disagreement on some fundamental legal issue.

> Once you've found out a disagreement on facts, once you've nailed in the reason that people are disagreeing, you can try to work on that reason. For example, you each realize that there is one very important witness and you are the one who is going to interview them and each one of you is assuming that that witness is going to go your way. So maybe you need to get that person deposed as quickly as possible and see who wins the argument on that level. There is always a lot of stuff like that you can do.

The point is restated in somewhat different terms by Larry Watson (2002, p.14):

> In the event negotiations to reach a final settlement stall, some effort should be put into attempting to determine why. What underlying issues in the dispute are blocking settlement? What are the fundamental disagreements between the parties preventing reconciliation?
>
> With help from a good mediator, it is not difficult to identify specific factual or legal disputes that have the parties locked from further movement toward an agreement. Perhaps there is a significant difference in how the parties have valued a personal injury case, how they have logically arrived at commercial damages claimed, or perhaps there is disagreement on whether an asserted legal defense will dispose of all or part of the claim. In many instances, some of these issues can be anticipated in advance of the mediation; in more instances, the fact of these differences in opinion come[s] to light during the mediation.

The potential usefulness of diagnosis and mediation follow-up led to a formal recommendation to mediators by the ABA Section of Dispute Resolution's Task Force on Improving Mediation Quality (2008b, p.6, italics in original):

> When mediations end without an agreement, mediators should consider asking the parties and lawyers if they would like the mediator to continue assisting on the case after the mediation session. If so, medi-

> ators should discuss *a plan* for further sessions or specific follow-up steps to be taken by the mediator, counsel and/or parties. These may include helping parties decide whether it would be useful to conduct additional discovery, obtain court rulings on specific issues, or use other ADR processes.[5]

Possible postsession steps worth discussing at the closing joint session include "downstream" mediation efforts—perhaps mixed with other resolution activities—and alternatives to mediation.

(1) "Downstream" mediation efforts

In the Northern District of California, ADR Local Rule 6-13 expressly requires the mediator and parties to decide together whether there should be mediation follow-up:

> At the close of the mediation session, the mediator and the parties shall jointly determine whether it would be appropriate to schedule some type of follow up. Such follow up could include, but need not be limited to, written or telephonic reports that the parties might make to one another or to the mediator, exchange of specified kinds of information, or another mediation session.

Larry Watson describes "'downstream mediation programs,' tailored to specifically deal with issues that are blocking settlement," which "can turn what appears to be an unsuccessful mediation effort into a success" (2002, p.14). The idea is to get the mediator's help to identify "specific factual or legal disputes that have the parties locked from further movement toward an agreement," then figure out how best to deal with them. "Programs, for example, might be agreed upon to: (a) conduct joint testing or investigation procedures to confirm or deny defects, (b) initiate focused discovery activities to establish disputed facts, or (c) conduct focus group or nonbinding adjudicatory hearings to get additional evaluative

5. The Task Force adds: "Alternatively, the lawyers and/or parties might appreciate just receiving a call from the mediator a week or two afterwards to inquire whether the mediator can do anything further."

input." In the same vein, Dwight Golann raises the possibility of seeking judicial resolution of one or more specific issues in a lawsuit before turning back to mediation (2009a, p.201).

Magistrate Judge Mary Pat Thynge (Wilmington, DE) often serves as a mediator in court-assisted mediation of intellectual property disputes. She provides this example of how both sides agreed to confidential third-party testing that helped lead to settlement (2011, pp.161–162):

> In a patent dispute involving a process to make microprocessors, the parties were stuck on whether the silicon disk was "dry" after the cleaning operation, a significant claim element. Neither would accept the other's analysis of the defendant's process. At the close of the first session, with my assistance, the parties agreed to an independent laboratory to perform defendant's process and negotiated the steps and parameters of that cleaning operation to be provided to the laboratory. The associated costs were equally shared. In addition, since this review was being done under the auspices of mediation, and thus confidential, and the findings would be provided only to me, the parties confirmed that the results would not be discoverable, and the laboratory personnel could not be deposed or used as experts or consultants in the case. In a later session, after the testing was completed and the findings reported, the parties left it to my discretion as the mediator whether to use that information in further negotiations. The matter settled during the second session.

Judge Thynge's example may be unusual in some ways, but it beautifully illustrates how varied the possibilities for downstream mediation can be.

(2) Alternatives to mediation

If your mediation is taking place under the umbrella of an arbitration process—for example, where an arbitration clause was built into a brokerage contract—arbitration automatically lies in your future if the mediation is unsuccessful. In other environments, such as court-ordered mediation of a lawsuit, you have the *option* to agree on binding arbitration if it seems like a preferable alternative to mediation or adjudication at this point (Golann, 2009a, p.201). Another possibility is a hybrid such as mediation and last-offer arbitration. For more on that topic, read Sidebar 11-3: "Mediation and Last Offer Arbitration (MEDALOA)."

C. Consider leaving an offer on the table

Even if the other side rejected your last offer during the negotiating session, you might consider leaving it open for some specific period of time—say a week—after your session ends (*see* Poon, 2010, p.84). This might be constructive if the parties are close enough together that you think the other side might possibly change its mind upon reflection and consultation with others.

D. End on the most positive tone possible

The potential benefit of ending on a cordial note where there has been progress but not resolution may be even greater than where settlement was reached (*see* Substep 11.1C). Any goodwill you can build up here in person may facilitate any additional steps toward achieving a settlement down the line.

11.3 Scenario #3: The parties have reached an insurmountable impasse and any further mediation efforts at this stage look counterproductive.

A closing joint session under these circumstances may tend to be hostile by nature, or at least stone cold. In the face of continuing aggression or overt hostility from your opponent, an attempt to be friendly or in any way conciliatory might be interpreted as a sign of weakness. But hard as it may be to imagine right then, the odds are still high that the dispute will still settle at some point down the line, even if it's on the courthouse steps. For that reason—and because you are a professional—try at least to preserve bare civility in your own conduct.

SIDEBAR 11-1

Preparing for Closure: The Settlement Agreement

By Lawrence M. Watson Jr.

Mediator Larry Watson (Maitland, FL) is among those who recommend a two-step approach to settlement agreements, beginning with a "bullet point" memorandum of understanding. In this excerpt from an article (2002, pp.12–14), Watson gives advice on this approach, including topics to cover.

All the preparation for the mediated negotiations will be for naught if the end result of those negotiations—the settlement agreement—is not properly documented at the conclusion of the mediation session. Virtually every jurisdiction with statutory mediation programs cloaks the process with strict confidentiality provisions. In other jurisdictions, concessions, admissions and even agreements reached during a mediation would normally be considered "settlement discussions" and thus generally held inadmissible in any subsequent evidentiary proceeding. The only exception to these confidentiality and evidential restraints is a signed settlement agreement. It is essential, therefore, that any ground gained in resolving a conflict in mediation be confirmed in writing immediately.

Tying down detailed, final settlement terms at the end of a mediation session, however, is not always possible. Available time, secretarial services, facilities and the temperament of the parties after a long, grueling negotiation session will often preclude closing a mediation session with a detailed and lengthy agreement. Confirming closure at the conclusion of the mediation therefore might best be accomplished in two steps. Begin with a short, handwritten "bullet point" agreement signed by the parties and counsel to seal the deal at the end of the session. That document can then be followed by more detailed agreement (with all required attachments) prepared by counsel at later date to finalize the agreement.

1. Sealing the Deal: Plan to Keep It Short and Simple.

As a general rule, it is by far the better practice to capture the essential terms of a mediated settlement agreement in a short "bullet point" written instrument signed by parties and counsel and exchanged at the conclusion of the mediation session. Many states with established mediation statutes and standards of performance for mediators flatly require the parties to sign off on the essential terms of the agreement before adjourning.[6] The agreements drawn at the conclusion of the mediation session need not be final in form. Mediated settlement agreements can be, and often are, prepared as handwritten instruments with the idea that "final" documents making up the more detailed terms of the settlement, i.e., release forms, stipulations of dismissal, etc., will be prepared by counsel in due course.

Clearly, there is something to be said for going immediately to the word processor and, while everyone is still assembled and the mediator on hand to resolve any disagreements along the way, preparing complete and final settlement documents at the end of the mediation session. If the circumstances of the case at hand will allow it, by all means, get it done then and there. Insisting that the parties and counsel go into a prolonged session reading and reviewing complicated fine print in a settlement document, however, can be counterproductive after a long hard negotiating session to reach the essence of a settlement.

People are usually physically tired and emotionally drained after prolonged or difficult settlement negotiations. Tempers are likely to be short. On many occasions, travel arrangements are imminent causing hurried thinking and reactions. After prolonged mediation sessions, there is a very good chance the parties simply aren't in the best frame of mind to make even minor decisions over detailed terminology and phrasing in a boilerplate settlement agreement. The entire settlement can be lost over a disproportional disagreement concerning relatively minor terms that is driven more by fatigue and anxiety than logic. The better course may be to simply capture the essence of the deal in a manner to create an enforceable agreement, and leave the peripheral details for a following session with counsel.

In a simple two party, one claim case between "ABC" and "XYZ", therefore, a bare-boned simple handwritten instrument capturing the following essential terms might be adequate:

---

6. *See* Fla. Stat. § 44.102(3); Fla. R. Civ. P. 1.730(b).

(a) The case style and number

(b) The date

(c) An introductory agreement and consideration clause, such as,

"In consideration for the mutual covenants [set] forth below, the parties agree as follows . . ."

(d) Who will pay how much to whom, and when and how it will be paid, such as,

"XYZ shall pay ABC the total sum of XXX dollars in full settlement of all claims asserted by ABC in these proceedings. Such sum shall be paid in ____ days by check payable to Trust Account of ________ Esq. to be held in escrow pending preparation, execution and delivery of all documents necessary to carry out the terms of this Agreement."

(e) Who will release who[m], and how the case is to be disposed of, such as,

"In exchange for the funds described in paragraph ___ above, ABC shall deliver to XYZ a General Release inuring to the benefit of XYZ (and its liability insurance carriers) and ABC and XYZ shall file in these proceedings a Joint Stipulation of Dismissal With Prejudice.

(f) A joint commitment to complete the settlement process by parties and counsel, such as;

"The parties hereto and counsel further agree to cooperate fully in the preparation, delivery and execution of all documents necessary to carry out the terms of this Agreement."

All this, of course, is followed by signature lines for all parties having a role in the settlement.

2. Plan to Deal With Special Documents and Provisions.

It is, of course, impossible to predict exactly where settlement discussions will end. Preparing a detailed settlement agreement in advance of the mediation session—even one that leaves blanks to fill in settlement amounts and basic terms—may not be entirely practical. There are, however, a number of supporting documents or special clauses unique to a given case that can be collected or prepared in advance and either signed or approved as to form by both parties at the conclusion of the mediation. In addition, certain collateral matters that must accompany a settlement agreement in certain cases should be considered in advance of the mediation session.

Thus, some thought should be given to the advance preparation of special settlement documents that may be necessary in a given case, such as;

(a) Limited releases, mutual releases, or indemnification agreements.

(b) Lien waivers, mortgage satisfactions, security instrument releases.

(c) Referral letters, employment confirmation statements.

(d) Structured settlement annuity contracts or performance charts.

(e) Close out warranties (construction cases), ongoing product warranties.

(f) Dispositive pleadings, stipulations of dismissal, stipulated final [judgments], etc.

In addition, preliminary thought might be given to advance preparation of any special provisions that might be appropriate to a settlement agreement in a particular case such as;

(g) Confidentiality clauses

(h) Mutual non-disparagement clauses

(i) Settlement fund escrow clauses

(j) Settlement agreement dispute resolution clauses

(k) Covenants not to compete

(l) Stipulated injunctive clauses

(m) Settlement agreement enforcement clauses

(n) Ongoing business relationship arrangements

Again, while a certain amount of preparation for closing a mediated settlement arrangement is in order, care should be taken to recognize the physical and mental limits of what the parties can accomplish at the time. All that is required is a simple, enforceable confirmation of the agreement. Discretion should be exercised in pushing the parties to[o] far with a detailed, lengthy final settlement agreement at the conclusion of the mediation session.

SIDEBAR 11-2

A Settlement Template

By P. Jean Baker

Jean Baker (Washington, DC) is a vice president with the American Arbitration Association. In this excerpt from an article (2007b, pp.6–7), she provides a template for use by attorneys representing clients in mediation and by mediators to provide guidance as the parties or attorneys draft a formal settlement agreement. Baker's 23-item list may also be useful in preparing a term sheet in advance of a formal settlement agreement.

Although there is no substitute for tailoring a settlement agreement to the particular facts and circumstances of the parties and the case, a template of frequently occurring terms and conditions is useful. The template will vary depending upon the nature of the dispute and specific requirements of the jurisdiction in which enforcement of the mediation settlement would be sought. For example, some states require that the settlement document specifically waive confidentiality for purposes of enforcement.

The following are some basic terms and conditions that you should consider including:

1. Preamble language designating all who are bound by the agreement, both signatories and non-signatories—important when a corporate party is involved.
2. Recitals that include a brief history of the parties' relationship; a brief description of the dispute; a statement that the parties are satisfied with the terms and conditions; a statement as to the impact of the settlement—for example, "settlement is in lieu of all civil claims, known or unknown, from the beginning of time to the date of the Agreement, except to the extent any continuing rights, claims or obligations are expressly reserved or acknowledged herein." If the client is electing to enter into a settlement against the advice of counsel it should be so noted here.
3. Include a statement concerning "no admission of liability or wrongdoing"—important if subsequent similar litigation is anticipated.
4. Representation of "no pending complaints, charges or claims in any court or administrative forum"—important when a party is a licensed professional.
5. Include specifics concerning any promises to transfer funds—how, when, who, where.
6. Allocation of damages for tax purposes—tort recoveries and punitive damages receive different tax treatment so proper characterization is a critical issue.
7. An indemnification and hold harmless provision for tax purposes—just in case the IRS or another taxing authority disagrees with the characterization of the damages allocation in item 6 above.
8. Specifics concerning the dismissal of all pending claims.
9. Specifics concerning the mutual release of all other types of potential claims, such as FDA, Fed-OSHA, EEOC, etc.
10. Jurisdiction specific waiver of claims language or enforcement language.

11. Power of revocation clause—mandatory if the claim involves age discrimination.
12. Factual differences clause—important if material, but unsubstantiated, representations formed the basis of the decision by the client and their attorney to accept specific settlement terms and conditions. The clause can either provide that should material facts later be found to be untrue the settlement is still enforceable except as provided in item 11 above; or the settlement shall be subject to termination, revocation or rescission by virtue of any difference in material fact discovered within a specified period of time.
13. Acknowledgement of representation of counsel or knowing waiver of representation by a party.
14. A "Successors and Assigns" clause to bind heirs, successors, assigns and personal representatives of the parties.
15. A "Warranty of Non-Assignment" clause that indemnifies and holds harmless against any unspecified claim, action, damage or liability arising from any such actual or purported transfer, including the payment of attorneys' fees and costs.
16. Agreement by the parties to execute any and all additional documents reasonably necessary to carry out the terms, conditions and obligations of the Agreement.
17. Integration and/or severability clauses.
18. Specifics concerning the limits of confidentiality. For example, the document can be disclosed to legal and financial advisors, members of a . . . party's family, said party's officers, directors, and managing agents, etc.
19. No publicity clause.
20. Enforceable arbitration clause—important if the parties want to ensure that any future disagreements concerning interpretation or enforcement will be resolved in a private forum.

21. Allocation of costs and fees associated with the mediation.

22. Representation of authority to settle—mandatory if a corporate party or public entity is involved.

23. Signature introduction and signature lines.

SIDEBAR 11-3

Mediation and Last Offer Arbitration (MEDALOA)

By Thomas O. Arnold

Thomas O. Arnold (1923–2009), who lived and practiced law and mediation in Houston, received a Lifetime Achievement Award from the American College of Civil Trial Mediators. In this excerpt from an article (2003a, pp.1, 4, endnotes omitted), he describes two forms of a mediation-arbitration hybrid, one of which is designed for mediation impasse situations.

A useful tool in the litigator's bag is the hybrid process of Mediation and Last Offer Arbitration [MEDALOA]. This little-known, little-used process, mediation followed by last offer arbitration (with or without the intermediate facilitated negotiation of the design of the arbitration) is the process of choice in many commercial cases. MEDALOA is useful to break impasse where small values are at risk, or to craft a customized arbitration procedure where issues are complex, stakes are high or the parties are far apart.

Impasse Breaking

In cases where relatively little is at risk or where the impasse has occurred in mediation with the parties not far apart by comparison with the burdens of a separate and independent arbitration, and where trust of the mediator is high, MEDALOA consists of

(i) Classic mediation, and if no settlement occurs, then

(ii) Summary arbitration, in which

- the mediator serves as arbitrator or, if the parties prefer, a new arbitrator is chosen;
- each party presents argument[s] to the arbitrator, or to a new arbitrator;
- each party prepares a written final or "last offer" and presents it to the arbitrator;
- the arbitrator picks the last offer which seems the most just and it becomes a binding arbitration award.

The outlined approach uses last offer arbitration, often before the same neutral, as a means of breaking impasse in a mediation. The summary arbitration procedure may be prescribed in the parties' original agreement, or negotiated by the parties in the course of the mediation. It is a quick, cheap, easy road to final disposition—very attractive in low value cases and in cases where the parties are already so close together that it would be a crime to lose settlement over so little a difference. . . .

The net effect of this process is that of a hi-lo arbitration, because the offers pending at the time that impasse arises in the mediation, either by the psychology of the process or by explicit agreement if the parties desire, constitute the "hi" and the "lo" of what the arbitrator will review as "last offers." This type of MEDALOA is a tool of efficient compromise, not a process by which to get the extreme result.

Path to Tailored Arbitration in Complex Cases

In cases, particularly complex cases, where much is at risk and/or the separation of the parties at impasse is great, MEDALOA comprises:

(i) Classic mediation, and if no settlement occurs, then

(ii) After the mediation, the mediator on the merits becomes a mediator/facilitator of a facilitated negotiation of the architecture of a binding arbitration process—not necessarily, but preferably, a "baseball" or "last offer" arbitration; a binding arbitration is tailored to the now well-understood dispute and circumstance in dozens of truly

> important ways; [and] binding arbitration is held before an independent arbitrator.

In complex commercial disputes, MEDALOA can be used to craft a suitable arbitration procedure bearing in mind the precise dispute of the parties—something they could not do when their contract was first drafted.

STEP TWELVE

Follow Up as Needed in the Postsession Period

I can give you a six-word formula for success:
"Think things through—then follow through."

—Attributed to Edward V. Rickenbacker (1890–1973)
World War I flying ace and business entrepreneur

Obviously, if your mediation session ended with a fully executed, full-fledged settlement agreement, you have little or no more follow-up to do. But in three possible scenarios, more work still needs to be done:

- Scenario #1: The parties signed a term sheet but still need to execute a formal settlement agreement.
- Scenario #2: The parties did not achieve settlement in mediation but agreed to take further steps.
- Scenario #3: The parties did not achieve settlement or agree to take further steps.

This short chapter will deal with each scenario in turn and end with a recommendation to record any lessons you have learned from mediating the dispute.

12.1 Scenario #1: The parties signed a term sheet but still need to execute a formal settlement agreement.

As discussed in Step Eleven, the parties often leave successful mediations with a signed term sheet memorializing the deal points instead of a full-fledged settlement-agreement document with all the bells and whistles. In this scenario, here are logical substeps to complete Step Twelve:

A. Reinforce your client's confidence in the deal.
B. Negotiate or mediate any essential terms that were overlooked or unclear in the term sheet.

C. Finish drafting and reviewing the full-fledged settlement document.
D. Execute the full-fledged settlement agreement.
E. Monitor compliance (as needed).
F. Enforce the agreement (if needed).

A. Reinforce your client's confidence in the deal

For many of us, it is human nature to second-guess ourselves on important decisions, and this is just as true of clients as of anyone else. You may want to be proactive in reinforcing your client's perception that your side made the best settlement possible under the circumstances of your case. This will head off any temptation for buyer's remorse.

A positive attitude toward the outcome of the case on the part of your client is important for at least two reasons: (1) It is better for your ongoing professional relationship with that client if the client feels good about the result. (2) More importantly, a positive attitude from your client will be helpful if any unexpected potholes emerge on the road to executing the full-fledged settlement agreement.

B. Negotiate or mediate any essential terms that were overlooked or unclear in the term sheet

"Let me share with you one of the mediator's true nightmares," says mediator John Bickerman (Washington, DC; speaking in Bickerman et al., 2003, p.23):

> [The p]arties work very hard. You get a deal. You put it in writing. Everybody signs the written term sheet. They shake hands. Everybody smiles, and they walk away. Two days later you get a call from one of the attorneys, and there's a critical piece of a term that nobody has bothered to deal with. And unless you can resolve that term, then the deal is going to go down the tubes.

Such nightmares probably are not uncommon. They can arise not only when an important deal point was inadvertently left unaddressed at the mediation session but also when the parties discover a significant ambiguity in the meaning of one of the deal points in the term sheet.

Also, some settlements—for example, for an environmental cleanup—may require one or more parties to undertake a complicated series of steps to complete. In such cases, procedural aspects related to implementing the agreement can also raise thorny issues when a term sheet is translated into a full-fledged settlement agreement (*see* Poon, 2010, p.88).

Here is Bickerman's advice for resolving such problems (2002, p.27):

> As an advocate, you need to be forthright and direct with the mediator, and you need to enlist the mediator's help in getting the other party back to the table to deal with this issue. And there's no substitute for being honest and direct and addressing the issue. And the sooner and the faster you do it, the better you will be.

Alternatively, you may be able to resolve some or all issues through direct negotiations with the other side.

In any event, as you suffer through this process, at least be assured that you are not alone. Gilda Turitz (San Francisco) remarks: "Such mediated settlements that are subject to full settlement documentation commonly drag on for weeks, or even months, as the parties argue over what they understand the term sheet to mean or try to negotiate additional terms and protections that were never discussed at mediation" (2010, p.13).

C. Finish drafting and reviewing the full-fledged settlement document

A settlement agreement is just like any other agreement in the demands it places on you to make sure it accurately and completely reflects your client's intent. For discussions of elements to consider for the written agreement, look back at Sidebar 11-1 ("Preparing for Closure: The Settlement Agreement") and Sidebar 11-2 ("A Settlement Template"). If part or all of the drafting was done by your opponent, make sure your review includes the steps described by Prof. Charles Craver in Substep 11.1B(5)(c).

D. Execute the full-fledged settlement agreement

Congratulations! You're done! Well, almost. Usually.

E. Monitor compliance (as needed)

Where a settlement is for dollars, the only compliance you will need to keep track of is making sure that the defendant cuts a check and the plaintiffs (and perhaps others) execute releases. In certain other types of settlement, such as for an environmental cleanup, postsettlement performance by one or multiple parties can be lengthy and complicated. In such instances, Gary Poon (Washington, DC) points out, it may be necessary for the disputants to agree on a monitoring entity such as a joint working group or an independent third party (2010, p.89).

F. Enforce the agreement (if needed)

"A settlement agreement is a contract and, as such, general principals of contract law govern its enforcement," notes Chalon Allen (Miami). Fortunately, the need for such enforcement seems rare. In a 2009 article on the mediation process, Allen estimates that well over several hundred thousand mediations take place each year (p.15). Using data from an article in the *Harvard Negotiation Law Review*,[1] Allen writes (pp.14–15, footnotes omitted):

> Between 1999 and 2003, there were only 1,223 court decisions in the United States dealing with issues arising out of mediation. Nearly 10 percent of these opinions were issued by state or federal courts in Florida. Of the 1,223 cases, 46 percent (or 568 cases) sought to enforce or set aside mediated settlement agreements. A review of these cases, which appears in the *Harvard Negotiation Law Review*, reveals that litigation to enforce settlement agreements negotiated during mediation focuses on typical contract issues,

1. Coben, J. & Thompson, P. (2006). Disputing irony: A systematic look at litigation about mediation. *Harvard Negotiation Law Review, 11*(43), 49.

such as lack of consideration, fraud, changed circumstances, and mistakes.

Courts enforced the mediated settlement, in whole or in part, in these cases 64 percent of the time. Courts refused to enforce the settlement agreements in 16 percent of the cases. The remaining cases either were remanded to lower courts for further consideration or were resolved on unrelated or procedural issues.

Thus, in light of the many thousands of mediations that occurred in the United States between 1999 and 2003, only a very small percentage of mediations fail to bring finality to the dispute and require further proceedings. Yet, if one party should decide to back away from an agreement reached through mediation, the parties may ultimately arbitrate or litigate the enforceability of the agreement, which will result in higher costs.

12.2 Scenario #2: The parties did not achieve settlement in mediation but agreed to take further steps.

In Substep 11.2, we discussed arrangements between the parties to take specific further steps toward reaching a resolution of the case after the mediation session. Such steps will consist of whatever the parties agreed at the session and in the period thereafter.

12.3 Scenario #3: The parties did not achieve settlement or agree to take further steps.

If the parties were not able to agree on further steps at the closing joint session, there is always still a possibility of progress toward settlement sooner or later. In this scenario, Prof. Dwight Golann (Boston) believes a good mediator should imitate the Energizer bunny and keep on going (in appropriate ways), if the parties will allow (2009a, p.201).

That also appears to be what many parties want. Prof. John Lande (Columbia, MO) was part of a the Task Force on

Improving Mediation Quality created by the ABA Section of Dispute Resolution, which conducted focus groups with experienced mediation players. "One of the things we've heard from the focus groups was that when people don't reach an agreement at the end of the mediation session, most lawyers and parties really want the mediator to check in and see if it would be helpful to continue working with the parties," he says. Such contacts may include making phone calls or sending follow-up e-mails.

In addition to focus groups, the Task Force also conducted surveys of mediation users. According to the Task Force's final report (2008a, p.17):

> Ninety-three percent (93%) of users thought that if a mediation session ends without agreement but has some potential to reach one, then the mediator should follow up with each side. Participants in our interview groups generally spoke favorably of mediation follow-up in an effort to resolve a matter that was not resolved at the mediation session, and some participants criticized mediators who did not do so. Eighty-two percent (82%) of users thought "exerting some pressure" was an important trait, very important or essential for a mediator to be effective. We also asked the question in reverse: whether it is important for a mediator to "refrain from using pressure," and we got consistent responses.

The Task Force comments, "It is a simple matter for mediators to contact users, after the final session, to ask how things are going and ask whether they may be of any further assistance" (2008a, p.18).[2]

Linda Singer (Washington, DC) is among mediators with long experience in helping to settle a case after initial mediation efforts have failed. "Lots of mediations don't settle 'the day of,'" she notes. "Unless things appear totally hopeless, a

2. In the context of construction disputes, but with broader potential application, Prof. Lande has written an article on how neutrals can help provide parties with early case-management services (2011b).

good mediator will follow up to see if there's any chance of movement." Such follow-up efforts can pay off—sometimes quite unexpectedly. Singer tells this story:

> I had a commercial case that had gone on for years, which had been up and down the Courts of Appeals—and nobody wanted to pay anybody anything to settle. We had failed to settle when we were together for mediation.
>
> Some time after the session, I had the plaintiff talk to me about how much money it had cost them to pursue the defendants who weren't going to pay them. I said, "So what were your attorneys' fees?" I found out what they were and said, "If you could recover them, would that do it?" Of course, the attorneys' fees were far less than what they'd been asking for.
>
> They said reluctantly, "Well, yeah, it would."
>
> I went to the other party and asked them, if I could get the plaintiffs to accept X—which I knew was the amount of the plaintiff's attorneys' fees—whether they would pay it. Their eyes got very big and they said yes they would. And so we got it done.

If the mediator who presided over your mediation is not persistent afterward, consider prodding her yourself. In any event, John Upchurch (Daytona Beach, FL) and colleagues at his mediation firm recommend that you should tickle your calendar to review your case for settlement purposes 45 to 60 days after an unsuccessful mediation (Upchurch, Sands, & Orfinger, 2011, p.6).

12.4 Memorialize the lessons you have learned.

Even the most experienced lawyers in mediation can learn something new from each experience. Yet such lessons and observations can easily fade from memory over time—no matter how vivid they may seem at the moment—unless you make an effort to preserve them. For advice on this, read Sidebar 12-1: "Record Lessons You've Learned in 'Mediation Notebooks.'"

SIDEBAR 12-1

Record Lessons You've Learned in "Mediation Notebooks"

By Laura H. Kennedy

Your experiences in each new mediation will bring you new understanding and insights into the process. You may think you will remember all the lessons learned, but they are all too easy to forget over time unless you write them down while they are fresh. In this sidebar, litigator Laura Kennedy (Phoenix, AZ) recommends preserving your experience in mediation notebooks (2010, p.163).

Although every mediation is different based upon the facts and circumstances of each individual case, something can be learned from every mediation process for use in the future. At the conclusion of each mediation, avoid the temptation to simply close the file. Take the time to prepare a memorandum on what transpired. Include the nature of the sessions, the offers made, and techniques used by the mediator. As you prepare and collect these memoranda, you will see patterns emerge, what works and what doesn't, and be able to generate ideas on how to approach and handle your next mediation. For the same reasons, consider building a "mediation library." Keep a notebook(s) on every case that has mediated. Include the correspondence and communications that have led up to the mediation, the exchanged and confidential briefs, the briefing book, any settlement agreement, follow-up correspondence and the memo prepared at the conclusion.[3] Your mediation notebooks will be a repeated source of valuable information.

---

3. [Note: Of course, this assumes that in a given instance, keeping certain documents does not violate an agreement among the parties regarding destruction of confidential materials.]

About the Author

Spencer Punnett is a member and former Co-Chair of the ABA Section of Litigation's Book Publishing Board, and a past Editor-in-Chief of *Litigation News*. He is a former shareholder in the Trial Department of Carlton Fields, P.A., an AmLaw 200 law firm with six offices throughout Florida, as well as offices in Atlanta and New York. His law degree is from Northwestern University School of Law, where he served as an editor of the Law Review and was awarded the school's Lowden-Wigmore Prize for Legal Scholarship. Before law school, he worked as a journalist.

Note on Interview Quotes and Legal Citations

Anyone who has read deposition transcripts knows that when people speak extemporaneously, their ideas generally flow much differently than the strict linear form associated with writing. Among other things, speakers tend to start and stop, interject a remark off topic, repeat themselves or loop back to expand on something they said previously, revise their words as they go along, or lose track of minor grammatical rules. To make oral quotes from interview participants more suitable for the page, I edited them freely by (for example) moving words or sentences around and deleting extraneous words and sentences, and adding words [in brackets like this] for clarity.[1] However, I did not add words *except* in brackets.

After making edits, I sent the quotes back to each interview participant for review and approval.[2] In addition, participants were free to make any edits or additions they thought appropriate. This was in keeping with my goal as author, which is to present the participants' views and recommendations clearly and accurately—not to freeze their words at some moment of the past. As part of this process, participants could choose to ratify any words I had added in brackets; if they did, I removed the brackets. Some participants allowed their quotes to remain in a conversational style, even if the final product might not have been fully grammatically correct. Some others did not.

One interview participant, Andrew Berry, passed away before this manuscript was completed. In his case, I retained brackets in his quotes and sent the materials to his former law partner, Eric Wiechmann, for review.

This book also contains many quotations from other published books and articles. In those quotes, I sometimes broke long paragraphs into shorter ones for readability. Other than that, the only edits not indicated by brackets were of a

---

1. I also sometimes deleted my questions in an interview when they intervened in a participant's answer. In addition, when creating sidebars with a Q&A format, I have sometimes edited my questions for clarity or flow.

2. Obviously, this was not possible for the interview participant who was no longer living when the manuscript was completed.

formatting nature, such as changing from boldface to italics or capitalizing a letter.[3]

In all instances, the views expressed represent those of the speaker and not the organization with which the speaker is or was affiliated.

Legal citations. At some points in the text I cite or quote statutes, procedural rules, or other legal authorities. I use them strictly as examples to illustrate various types of concerns or issues that can arise in mediation practice—*not* as a briefing on the applicable law or rules in any specific jurisdiction. Please do not rely on them for the latter. For any specific point of law or procedure in any jurisdiction, you will need to do the research yourself.

---

3. In sidebars described as an "abridgment," omitted material is not indicated with an ellipsis.

References (Other Than Interviews, Statutes, and Rules)

Aaron, M., & Golann, D. (2009). Merits barriers: Evaluation and decision analysis. In D. Golann, *Mediating legal disputes: Effective strategies for neutrals and advocates* (pp. 145–177). Chicago: American Bar Association (Section of Dispute Resolution).

Allen, C. (2009). The mediation process: Navigating the quagmire. *Conflict Management, 13*(3), 1, 13–15.

American Arbitration Association. (2007). *Drafting dispute resolution clauses: A practical guide* (as amended Sept 1, 2007). New York, NY: American Arbitration Association. Retrieved from http://www.adr.org

Arnold, T. (2003a). MEDALOA: The dispute resolution process of choice. *Conflict Management, 6*(3), 1, 4–8.

Arnold, T. (2003b). Tough questions: Mediator questions lawyers should anticipate. *Conflict Management, 6*(4), 1, 6–9.

Austermiller, S. (2010). *Alternative dispute resolution: Cambodia*. Washington, DC: American Bar Association (Rule of Law Initiative). Retrieved from http://www.americanbar.org

Baker, P. J. (2007a). Avoiding impasse during mediation. *Commercial & Business Litigation, 8*(2), 4–6.

Baker, P. J. (2007b). Drafting a mediation settlement agreement that avoids future litigation. *Conflict Management, 11*(3), 5–7.

Baker, P. J. (2011). Selecting the right mediator. *Alternative Dispute Resolution, 15*(2), 23–27.

Barr, E. (2012). Compassion in action. In E. Galton & L. Love (Eds.), *Stories mediators tell* (pp. 171–179). Chicago, IL: American Bar Association (Section of Dispute Resolution).

Bates, J., Jr. (2009). Mediation: An effective way to connect with clients. *The Brief, 36*(3), 62–64.

Beer, J., & Stief, E. (1997). *The mediator's handbook* (3rd ed.). Gabriola Island, BC, Canada: New Society Publishers.

Berman, L. (2004, January 20). Sincere opening statements bring best mediation results. *Daily Journal.* Retrieved as "The advocate's opening" from http://www.mediationtools.com

Berman, L. (2006, February 17). Impasse is a fallacy. *Daily Journal.* Retrieved from http://www.mediationtools.com

Bickerman, J. (2007). We have met the enemy and . . . he may be us. *Dispute Resolution Magazine, 13*(1), 2.

Bickerman, J., Bulmash, L., Butler, R., Cooley, J., Cutler, P., Fox, L., . . . Singer, L. (2003). *Effective advocacy in mediation* [transcript of an audio CLE panel presentation]. Chicago, IL: American Bar Association (Section of Dispute Resolution and ABA Center for Continuing Legal Education).

Bickerman Dispute Resolution, PLLC. (n.d.). *Mediation agreement* [form]. Obtained from Bickerman Dispute Resolution, PLLC.

Bowbeer, H. (2011). Preparing to successfully mediate an intellectual property dispute: A guide for counsel and clients. In H. Samaras (Ed.), *ADR advocacy, strategies, and practice for intellectual property cases* (pp. 165–207). Chicago, IL: American Bar Association (Section of Intellectual Property Law).

Bowling, D., & Hoffman, D. (2000). Bringing peace into the room: The personal qualities of the mediator and their impact on the mediation. *Negotiation Journal, 16* (1), 5–28.[1]

Brazil, W. (2009). Thoughts about impasse for mediators in court programs. *Dispute Resolution Magazine, 15*(2), 11–15, 28–29.

Calihan, R., Dent, R., & Victor, M. (2004, October). *The role of risk analysis in dispute and litigation management.* Distributed at ABA 27th Annual Forum on Franchising, Vancouver, BC, Canada. Retrieved from http://www.litigationrisk.com

1. This article was later expanded into a book with the same title.

Callahan, R. (2010). What to do when insolvency becomes an issue in mediation. *Conflict Management, 14*(2), 1, 9–12.

Contuzzi, P. (2000). Should parties tell mediators their bottom line? *Dispute Resolution Magazine* 6(3), 30–32.

Cooley, J. (2002). *Mediation advocacy* (2nd ed.). Notre Dame, IN: National Institute for Trial Advocacy.

Cooley, J. (2006). *The mediator's handbook* (2nd ed.). Notre Dame, IN: National Institute for Trial Advocacy.

Corcoran, C. T., III. (2007). *Maximizing your client's advantage: Practical tips for representing your client successfully in mediation.* Talking points for Tampa Bay Bankruptcy Bar Seminar presentation (unpublished).

Court-referred mediation survey: U.S. District Court of the Eastern District of Missouri (n.d.). Retrieved from http://www.moed.uscourts.gov

Craver, C. (2011, March). *Legal negotiation: Process and techniques.* Distributed at the Midwinter Meeting 2011 of the ABA Section of Litigation's Employment Rights & Responsibilities Committee, San Juan, Puerto Rico. Retrieved from http://www.americanbar.org

District Court, Northern District of CA (2011, rev. July). *Dispute resolution procedures in the Northern District of California.* San Francisco, CA: ADR Unit—U.S. District Court.

Dunlop, N. (2011). Getting past the impasse. *NZLawyer Magazine*[2] 158, 24–25. Retrieved from http://www.nigeldunlop.co.nz

Dye, T. (2010, February). *Winning the settlement: Keys to negotiation strategy.* Presented at ABA Section of Litigation Corporate Counsel CLE Seminar, Rancho Mirage, CA. Retrieved from http://www.americanbar.org

Fincher, R. (2010). Mediating disputes of the highly paid executive. *Conflict Management, 14*(2), 4–7.

2. Published in Auckland, New Zealand.

Fisher, R., & Ury, W. (1981). *Getting to yes: Negotiating agreement without giving in*. Boston, MA: Houghton Mifflin Company.[3]

Florida Mediation Ethics Advisory Committee. (2008). Opinion 2008-006. Retrieved from http://www.flcourts.org

Friedman, G., & Himmelstein, J. (2008). *Challenging conflict: Mediation through understanding*. Chicago, IL: American Bar Association (Section of Dispute Resolution).

Galton, E., & Love, L. (Eds.). (2012). *Stories mediators tell*. Chicago, IL: American Bar Association (Section of Dispute Resolution).

Gary, R. (2004). Mediation as a tool for settling mass tort class actions. *Conflict Management, 5*(2), 1, 3–6.

Golann, D. (2007). The changing role of evaluation in commercial ADR. *Dispute Resolution Magazine, 14*(1), 16–19, 36.

Golann, D. (2009a). *Mediating legal disputes: Effective strategies for neutrals and advocates*. Chicago, IL: American Bar Association (Section of Dispute Resolution).

Golann, D. (2009b). Dealing with impasse in commercial mediation. *GPSolo Magazine*, 26(6) [page numbers not available]. Retrieved from http://www.americanbar.org

Golann, D. (2011). Beyond brainstorming: The special barriers to interest-based mediation, and techniques to overcome them. *Dispute Resolution Magazine, 18*(1), 22–26.

Goldberg, S., & Sander, F. (2007, Summer). Selecting a mediator: An alternative (sometimes) to a former judge. *Litigation Journal,* 33(4): 40–44.

Goodman, A. (2004). *Basic skills for the new mediator* (2nd ed.). Rockville, MD: Solomon Publications.

3. Note: In more recent editions, Bruce M. Patton has also been credited as one of the authors.

Grappo, D. (2006). Questions litigators ask about mediation. In T. Carbonneau et al. (Eds.), *American Arbitration Association handbook on mediation* (pp. 185–193). New York, NY: JurisNet, LLC.

Halper, J. (2011). Ten things lawyers love/hate about mediators. *Alternative Dispute Resolution, 15*(2), 12–20.

Hoffman, D. (2012). The whistle-blower: Mediating an employment termination dispute. In E. Galton & L. Love (Eds.), *Stories mediators tell* (pp. 141–149). Chicago, IL: American Bar Association (Section of Dispute Resolution).

Holbrook, J. (2006). A unified theory of mediation using distributive, integrative and transformative negotiation principles in mediation. In T. Carbonneau et al. (Eds.), *American Arbitration Association handbook on mediation* (pp. 1–16). New York, NY: JurisNet, LLC.

JAMS. (2005). *Mediation agreement* [form]. Retrieved from http://www.jamsadr.com

Jentes, W. (2010, June). *Five key questions to answer before starting mediation*. Distributed at ABA National Institute on Mediation With the Masters: Contemporary strategies for effective advocacy in mediation, Chicago, IL.

Kennedy, L. (2010, June). *Mediation preparation*. Distributed at ABA National Institute on Mediation With the Masters: Contemporary strategies for effective advocacy in mediation, Chicago, IL.

Klarfeld, P. (2010). Ethical risks in misleading a mediator. *The Franchise Lawyer, 13*(3).

LaMothe, L. (2010, June). *Want to have more successful mediations?* Distributed at ABA National Institute on Mediation With the Masters: Contemporary strategies for effective advocacy in mediation, Chicago, IL.

Lande, J. (2011a). *Lawyering with planned early negotiation*. Chicago, IL: American Bar Association (Section of Dispute Resolution).

Lande, J. (2011b, Spring). How neutrals can provide early case management of construction disputes. *JAMS Global Construction Solutions*, 6–9. Retrieved from http://ssrn.com/abstract=1856026

Lande, J. (2012). Teaching students to negotiate like a lawyer. *Washington University Journal of Law and Policy, 39*(1), 109–144.

Lande, J., & Wohl, R. (2007). Listening to experienced users. *Dispute Resolution Magazine, 13*(3), 18–21.

Little, J. A. (2007). *Making money talk: How to mediate insured claims and other monetary disputes*. Chicago, IL: American Bar Association (Section of Dispute Resolution).

Lurie, P. (2006). Ethics and mediation: Using screening walls and advance waivers to manage conflicts of interest. In T. Carbonneau et al. (Eds.), *American Arbitration Association handbook on mediation* (pp. 255–261). New York, NY: Juris-Net, LLC.

Oberman, M. (2009, February 10). Lawyers bookshelf—*Challenging conflict: Mediation through understanding*. *New York Law Journal, 241*(27). Retrieved from http://www.mastermediation.com

O'Donnell, B. (2010). Private mediation: A checklist. *Woman Advocate, 16*(1).

Picker, B. (2003). *Mediation practice guide: A handbook for resolving business disputes* (2nd ed.). Washington, DC: American Bar Association (Section of Dispute Resolution).

Poon, G. (2010). *The corporate counsel's guide to mediation*. Chicago, IL: American Bar Association (Section of Litigation, First Chair Press).

Rosenberg, L. (2011, February). *Winning high-stakes corporate litigation*. Distributed at a CLE Meeting of the ABA Section of Litigation Corporate Counsel, Naples, FL. Retrieved from http://www.americanbar.org

Ross, L. (1995). Reactive devaluation in negotiation and conflict resolution. In K. Arrow, R. Mnookin, L. Ross, A. Tversky,

& B. Wilson (Eds.), *Barriers to conflict resolution* (pp. 26–42). New York, NY: W. W. Norton & Company.

Shaw, M. (2012). Mediator's proposals: Let me count the ways. *Dispute Resolution Magazine, 18*(2), 27–28.

Singer, L. (1990). *Settling disputes: Conflict resolution in business, families, and the legal system.* Boulder, CO: Westview Press.

Starr, A., & Page, N. (2005, March). Dealing with nonverbal cues: A key to mediator effectiveness. Retrieved from http://www.mediate.com

Task Force on Improving Mediation Quality (2008a). *Final report.* Washington, DC: American Bar Association (Section of Dispute Resolution).

Task Force on Improving Mediation Quality (2008b). *Improving civil mediation: Recommended considerations for civil mediators in private practice*. Washington, DC: American Bar Association (Section of Dispute Resolution).

Thynge, M. (2011). Mediation: One judge's perspective (or infusing sanity into intellectual property litigation). In H. Samaras (Ed.), *ADR advocacy, strategies, and practice for intellectual property cases* (pp.133–163). Chicago, IL: American Bar Association (Section of Intellectual Property Law).

Turitz, G. (2010). How in-house and outside counsel can collaborate to maximize results in mediation. *Woman Advocate, 15*(3), 1, 12–14.

Upchurch, J., Sands, K., & Orfinger, M (2011, April). *How to doom a mediation: A top ten list.* Distributed in conjunction with presentation by Alternative Dispute Resolution Committee, ABA Section of Litigation, at 2011 Section Annual Conference, Miami Beach, FL. Retrieved from http://americanbar.org

Victor, M., Glidden, C., Lea, C., & Whitworth, J. (2000). Evaluating legal risks and costs with decision tree analysis. In R. L. Haig (Ed.), *Successful partnering between inside and outside counsel* (pp. 12-1–12-21). Eagan, MN: West Group and

Association of Corporate Counsel. Chapter retrieved from http://www.litigationrisk.com

Watson, L., Jr. (2002). Effective advocacy in mediation: A planning guide to prepare for a civil trial mediation. *Conflict Management, 5*(2), 1–14.

Wilk, M., & Blum, H. (2004). Helping attorneys see beyond the case: Return to objectivity. *Conflict Management, 8*(3), 16–19.

Guide to American Bar Association periodicals

Alternative Dispute Resolution is a publication of the Committee on Alternative Dispute Resolution of the ABA Section of Litigation.

The Brief is a publication of the ABA Tort Trial and Insurance Practice Section.

Commercial & Business Litigation is a publication of the Commercial and Business Litigation Committee of the ABA Section of Litigation.

Conflict Management is the former title of a publication of the Committee on Alternative Dispute Resolution of the ABA Section of Litigation. The current title is *Alternative Dispute Resolution*.

Dispute Resolution Magazine is a publication of the ABA Section of Dispute Resolution.

The Franchise Lawyer is a publication of the ABA Forum on Franchising.

GPSolo Magazine is a publication of the ABA General Practice, Solo and Small Firm Division.

Litigation Journal is a publication of the ABA Section of Litigation.

APPENDIX A

Checklist for Pre-Mediation Conference Call[1]

By Louise A. LaMothe

Pre-mediation conferences are discussed in Step Three of this book. Louise A. LaMothe, a Southern California mediator and former Chair of the ABA Section of Litigation, developed this checklist for use at the planning conference call she typically holds in advance of a mediation session.

Conference call Date/Time: ___________

GENERAL INFORMATION

Case name

Court and case number

Counsel

Counsel on the call

BACKGROUND AND STATUS

(Please try to supply me the pleadings before the conference)

What is the case about?

What is the status?

Any previous settlement discussions?

Why are the parties interested in mediation now?

What do the parties want out of mediation?

Do they think it will require more than one session? (half day or full?)

Does the dispute encompass more than the parties to this case?

Are there issues between the parties beyond those presented in this case?

INFORMATION EXCHANGE

What is the status of discovery?

Is there unfinished document discovery?

Are there any depositions still to be taken?

Are there discovery disputes?

How will those get decided?

Can I assist in the information exchange?

What is the status of motions? Have all been filed? Trial date?

Next status conference?

Other upcoming events?

Should the parties discuss changing the pre-trial/arbitration schedule?

What steps are necessary in order to do that?

MEDIATION CONSIDERATIONS

Are there any issues as to which there is agreement?

What are the primary areas of disagreement?

What does each side feel comfortable in telling me about the client's attitude?

What are the personality issues?

What have the lawyers already discussed about the mediation process?

Should we begin in joint session?

Are there any persons who should attend? Any who should not?

Confirm that those with settlement authority will attend.

If there are corporate decision makers or others who must be consulted, confirm their availability by phone, including cell phone, during the entire session.

Does any lawyer or client participant have time constraints on the day we choose?

Should experts attend? How could their work product be used? Agree in advance.

CONFIRM SCHEDULE

Payment of full or half day deposit to confirm date—what the deposit covers—nonrefundable (see website for details).

Location, date and time to meet:

Who will bring lunch/snacks?

Any need for audio or video at the session?

Mediation briefs—exchange them and make sure the clients see them in advance of the mediation.

Give me anything confidential in a separate letter.

Date by which briefs will be exchanged:

Are there any other documents I need to see? Schedule for providing them.

FINAL PREPARATION

I will prepare the mediation confidentiality agreement and include any disclosures in it. (Agreement samples are available on my website.)

Plaintiff's/claimant's counsel—bring support for amount demanded (verdicts and settlements, e.g.).

All counsel—bring evidence, including witness statements, that might be shared as the mediation progresses.

Who will bring a laptop to the mediation with a draft agreement on it?

Either party's lawyer may get in touch with me before the mediation by phone or e-mail to Lalamothe@dispute-solutions.com to kick around ideas.

I may ask questions of the lawyers or raise issues by phone or e-mail ahead of the mediation.

The lawyers may send their briefs by e-mail, too.

Articles on my website may be of interest.

In particular, download from my website and review with your client my "Suggestions for Mediation Preparation."

APPENDIX B

Sample Agenda for Mediation Strategy and Preparation Session

Preparing with your client in advance of a mediation session is discussed in Step Seven of this book. A mediation prep agenda can help organize this preparation. Laura H. Kennedy, a Phoenix-based litigator, developed the detailed sample agenda below.

CONFIDENTIAL; ATTORNEY-CLIENT COMMUNICATION AND WORK-PRODUCT PRIVILEGED
ACME CORPORATION V. WIDGET CO.

AGENDA

MEDIATION STRATEGY AND PREPARATION SESSION

May 24, 20XX
11:30 a.m.
ABC Home City, State 01234
Client A
Client B
Attorney A
Attorney B
Attorney C
Attorney D
Paralegal A
Damages Expert A
Damages Expert B

I. MEDIATION PREPARATION AND LOGISTICS.

A. Mediation preparation essentials:
   1. Briefs:
      (a) Exchanged: To be submitted June 10, 20XX.
      (b) Confidential:
         (i) ACME brief to be submitted June 10, 20XX.

(ii) WIDGET CO.—Do not know if it will submit confidential brief.

2. Mediation briefing book in preparation.
3. Updating aspects of our case: analysis, research, damages, etc.
4. Demonstrative evidence in preparation.
5. Arrangements:
   (a) Air travel and arrival:
      (i) June 9, 20XX:
         - Attorney A, Attorney B, Paralegal A, and Damages Expert A.
      (ii) June 10, 20XX:
         - Client A, Client B, Attorney C, Attorney D, and Damages Expert B.
   (b) Accommodations:
      123 HOTEL
      1234 N. Hotel Street
      Mediation City, State 12345
      Telephone: (123) 456-7890;
      Facsimile: (123) 456-7891
   (c) Prep sessions in Mediation City:
      (i) ABC, PC:
         - June 9, 20XX—2:45 p.m.
         - June 10, 20XX—9:00 a.m.
         - June 10, 20XX—12:30 p.m.
      (ii) All-hands meeting:
         - June 10, 20XX—2:00 p.m.
   (d) Timing and dress.

B. The participants, schedule, and mediator.
   (a) Who: ACME representatives:
      (i) ACME—Client A and Client B.
      (ii) ABC, PC—Attorney A, Attorney B, Attorney C, Attorney D, and Paralegal A.
      (iii) Consultants—Damages Expert A and Damages Expert B.
   (b) Who: WIDGET CO. representatives:
      (i) WIDGET CO.—Attorney 1, Assistant General Counsel of WIDGET CO., New York (suspect).

(ii) WIDGET CO. COUNSEL—Attorney 2, Attorney 3, Attorney 4, etc., Chicago.
(c) Mediator: Joe Mediator.
(d) When: Friday, June 11, 20XX at 9:30 a.m.
(e) Where: JOE MEDIATOR & ASSOCIATES
1234 Mediation Street, Suite 1
Mediation City, State 12345
Telephone: (123) 456-7980

II. THE MEDIATION.

A. Conducted by Joe Mediator.
B. Reasonable Expectations.
  1. Mediator's chief goal: Settlement.
  2. Mediation style.
C. Mediation Format.
  1. Opening plenary session: Opening statements by each side.
  2. Possible questions.
  3. Private caucusing/shuttle diplomacy.
    (a) Lawyers only.
    (b) Principals.
  4. Divide and conquer approach.
  5. Be prepared with proof.
  6. Exaggerated expressions of ACME "weaknesses" and WIDGET CO. "strengths."
  7. Downtime—This is a *process*, a marathon, not a sprint. Be prepared for massive shifts of momentum.
  8. Often most of the action occurs in the last few hours—remain patient but vigilant.
  9. No breaks throughout the day.

III. ACME APPROACH AND STRATEGY.

A. Preparation, preparation, preparation:
  1. Mediation papers.
  2. Key documents.
  3. Demonstrative evidence.

4. Briefing book.
5. Resolve.

B. Roles of participants: ACME—ABC, PC:
   1. Plenary session—ABC.
   2. ACME role: When called upon or permitted by counsel/mediator: ACME mission, strategic vision, details of WIDGET CO.'s conduct, impact of same, WIDGET CO.'s refusal to be accountable, actual and punitive damages. Please do *not* exaggerate.
   3. Feasibility of solutions—All.
   4. Damage explanation and quantification—ABC, ACME, and damages-expert firm.
   5. Legal challenges/opportunities/realities—ABC.
   6. Settlement scenarios—All.

C. Attitudes of participants:
   1. Steeled resolve for fairness—retrospective and prospective damages.
   2. *Complete* emotional and intellectual sobriety while in session (cell phones and BlackBerries off).

D. Ready Access to ACME/ABC resources.

E. Creativity in solutions is critical, but *raise the level*!
   1. Monetary component:
      (a) Amount.
      (b) Timing.
      (c) Characterization.
   2. Viable additions/alternatives to money?

IV. ANTICIPATED CHALLENGES: WIDGET CO.'S PRIMARY DEFENSES.

A. WIDGET CO. did not make false representations.

B. ACME did not rely upon WIDGET CO.'s representations, and they were not the proximate cause of ACME's alleged damages.

C. ACME waived its claims.

D. ACME did not conduct any due diligence as respects the representations.

E. ACME would have purchased the product even if it had the information it claims it should have had.

F. Third-party witnesses are not credible, as they have received a financial benefit in exchange for favorable testimony.
G. ACME's damages are not reasonable, for X, Y, and Z reasons.
H. ACME is not entitled to punitive damages.
I. ACME's claims are barred by the statute of limitations.

V. PERORATION.

A. Highs and lows of mediation.
B. Closing thoughts, issues, and assignments.

APPENDIX C

Tough Questions: Mediator Questions Lawyers Should Anticipate

By Tom Arnold

Thomas O. Arnold (1923–2009), who lived and practiced law and mediation in Houston, received a Lifetime Achievement Award from the American College of Civil Trial Mediators. This appendix originally appeared as an article (2003b) in Conflict Management, *a publication of the ABA Section of Litigation's Alternative Dispute Resolution Committee. Don't overlook the item of advice that ends Arnold's article: "[D]espite the importance of candor, it is sometimes best to elect not to answer each and every question a mediator may pose."*

Experienced mediators frequently use a series of open-ended questions in an effort to obtain a resolution of the parties' conflict. These questions are most typically posed after the parties have ventilated their respective positions before one another, although there is no hard and fast rule. Some will be asked in joint session; others, particularly those which are likely to elicit concessions or admissions of weakness, will be posed in caucus. Through questioning, a mediator seeks a number of goals:

- to foster a relationship of trust between the party and the mediator;
- to reveal interests and desired or acceptable outcomes, as distinguished from stated positions and claims of right;
- to explore the possibility of business alternatives to the dispute;
- to bring the party and counsel to some degree of reality;

- to prompt the party to come up with a responsible offer that can be presented to the other party; and
- to help the mediator obtain information for advocacy with the other party.

The most common mediator question areas include the following:

1. Free Form Solicitations.

(a) How do you *feel* about this problem/dispute?
(b) "Is there anything more?"—e.g., anything not stated by your counsel in his opening statement, at caucus commencement, or not stated in the joint session?

2. How to Conduct the Negotiation.

(a) How do you want to conduct this negotiation?
(b) If you were the mediator, how would you set out to forge a settlement?
(c) What else do I (the mediator) need to know to do my job right?
(d) What are your best ideas as to how to keep it going [when impasse is threatened]?
(e) What's wrong with the process so far?

3. Particularization of Issues.

(a) What are the issues presented in this dispute?
(b) What claims have been/will be plead/not plead?
(c) What are the elements of these claims?
(d) What defenses have been/will be raised?
(e) What elements of proof does the law require for that claim/defense?

4. Wants, Needs, and Greeds.

(a) What interests of yours are at stake and how would you prioritize these?
(b) What future *needs* do you have? The other party? Prioritize them.

(c) What do you *want* as a result of this process? Prioritize them.
(d) What are your motivations or greeds? Prioritize them.
(e) What are your biases in looking at this? Why does the other party see it differently?
(f) What are your plans for the future?
(g) What is the importance to you of timely resolution of this dispute?
(h) "What if?" In eliciting information regarding wants, needs, and greeds, the use of a hypothetical a series of "what if" questions may prove very effective.
  (1) For example, if you feel that the plaintiff, though asking for $400,000, will settle for $200,000, you, as mediator, should commence a series of questions such as:
    "What if the plaintiff offered to accept $300,000?"
    "What if the plaintiff offered to accept $250,000?"
    "What if the plaintiff offered to accept $200,000?"
  By using such a pattern of "what if," you draw the party out without revealing a position of the other party.
(i) Hidden Agenda.
  (1) What hidden agenda, motivation, or interest do you have that is not apparent from the present status of discussion?
  (2) What is bugging you?
  (3) Who in your organization wants vindication or victory more than a reasonable business settlement? Anybody?
  (4) Repeat these questions as to the perceptions of the other party's perceived interests, what's bugging him, and who wants a combat win.

5. Inhibiting Commitments.

Has party or counsel made some commitment that has the potential to interfere with the resolution process? For example, has counsel or party negotiator told the Union Membership that they would resign prior to giving in on a certain point?

6. What are the strengths of your case?

(a) What evidence do you have in support of each required element of the claim?
(b) Is the evidence you have admissible?

7. What are the weaknesses in your case?

(a) What are you most afraid of?
(b) What fact would you like to change?
(c) What fact do you wish was not there?
(d) What additional facts would you like to exist?
(e) What law would you like to change?
(f) What are the rocks the parties will turn over in the course of this case and what is the additional information or embarrassments that may come to light?
(g) If lawyer says "None," no weaknesses, the mediator may ask the lawyer if (s)he is guaranteeing the result in this case? Will the lawyer agree to pay 90% of the damages? 65%?
(h) What other evidence do you need?
  (1) Is there anything about the other party's operations, costs, activities, profits, that might influence your attitude to be more favorable to it?
  (2) What would you want to know in order to arrive at a responsible compromise proposal and support it with good reasons?

8. Wants, Needs, Greeds, and Attitudes of the Adversary.

(a) What *wants* do they have? Prioritize these.
(b) What *needs* do they have? Prioritize them.
(c) What *greeds* do they have? Prioritize them.
(d) Have they any other *interests*? Prioritize them.
(e) What are their motivations? Prioritize them.
(f) What are their biases in looking at this?
(g) What are their plans for the future?

(h) What is the importance to them of the timely resolution of this dispute?
(i) Can we concede their true needs as some price? Their greeds?
  (1) These tend to be big trading chips.
  (2) What among their wants/needs/greeds can you provide at high value to them but low cost to you?
(j) What do they see as their best and least favorable options?
(k) How do they evaluate the case? What are their perceived odds of result X?
(l) What is the range they see for a jury award?
(m) What do you think they will settle for?

9. Empathy.

(a) How do they feel?
(b) Is that legitimate, given what he knows?
(c) How would you feel if you had to walk in their shoes?
(d) What made them feel the way they do? There must be a reason.
(e) Ask each party to tell in words what the other party said in opening statements.
  (1) Then ask the party how they, believing that story, might feel.
  (2) What would you ask for, or do, if you were in their shoes?

10. Risk Aversion Analysis.

(a) How much will you pay happily to be rid of the ancillary burdens of litigation: additional costs, risk of loss, workload burdens, discovery, turmoil, appeal, time 'till trial, time in trial, time to pay or collect judgment, and related money discounts?
(b) Even if you win, what is the likelihood of collection—judgment proof?
(c) Are you willing to accept the always uncertain decision of a jury?

(d) Are you willing to accept that, despite all honesty on your part, the decision will likely turn upon the credibility of the various witnesses as viewed by the jury after a cross-examination?

11. Probability of success and recovery.

(a) For example, when there are few elements in a claim, a party may be asked to come up with a percent chance of winning or losing on each element that (they necessarily must win in court to achieve the desired verdict). Multiply the individual percentages on each element together to reveal the likelihood of success or failure on the overall claim. 70% on element one times 80% on element two times 90% on element three times 100% on element four equals only a 50% chance of winning liability as a "risk factor." Multiply each party's risk factor for a claim times each of three likely recovery/liability sums for that claim, big, middle, and low liability sums.
(b) Do you realize that the odds of winning big are much smaller than the odds of just barely winning? A 50% chance of winning $400,000 at trial is today worth $400,000 divided by two, then less litigation burdens and time discounts.

12. Court-Trial Realism Testing.

(a) What is the range of recovery you think is responsible to estimate for this case in court?
(b) How confident are you of that? 30%, 50%, 95%, 100%?
(c) What is the probability of a good verdict on liability?
(d) What is your fondest hope as to damages number?
(e) What is your realistic expectation as to damages number?
(f) What is your best option? The likelihood of getting it from the court?
(g) What is your least favorable alternative if mediation fails? The likelihood of getting it from the court?

(h) What trial result are you most scared of? How likely is it? How costly?
(i) What other hurdles will you have to get over in court (e.g., summary judgment motions, motions in limine, attorney-client privilege issues)?
(j) How much will it cost to try and appeal the case? In money? In turmoil?
(k) How long will it take for trial and appeal? How much do you discount money received/paid then rather than now?
(l) Where will you go from here if no settlement is obtained?

13. Settlement Structure.

What are the likely settlement . . .

(a) Terms?
(b) Dollars?
(c) Services?
(d) Performance?
(e) Product?
(f) Rescission?
(g) Apology?
(h) Injunction?

14. Maintenance of Relations.

(a) What is the nature of the relationship between you and the other party, and what needs are satisfied by the relationship?
  (1) What would be ideal, as to a future relationship?
  (2) What would be your hopes for a future relationship?
  (3) What are your needs for the continued existence of a relationship?
  (4) Who would be hurt most if the relationship ceased to exist?
(b) If the controversy involves domestic relations or neighborhood controversy . . . .

(1) How was the relationship before the controversy arose?
(2) Did the parties belong to the same organizations (e.g., church)?
(3) Did your children/do your children play together?
(4) Did your children/do your children go to the same school?
(5) What are the likely consequences to you if the relationship ceases to exist?
(6) What are the likely consequences to the other party if the relationship ceases to exist?

15. The Offer.

(a) What do you want to offer?
(b) How or why did you arrive at the offer you are proposing?
(c) Given the nature of the "dance" of offers and counters, what signals does this offer or the recent pattern of offers send to the other party?
(d) What signals do you want to send with this offer?
(e) How does the offer influence your credibility, the adversary's expectations, or the likelihood of a counter offer?
(f) If you were the other party, how would you react to the offer?

Any questions which solicit a denigration of a party's case usually should be reserved for private caucus, lest the asking of those questions make the mediator both appear and be non-neutral. Indeed, those reality testing questions are an important reason for frequent use of the caucus model of mediation. Used in private, they get the party/counsel to persuade themselves of an objective, no-stars-in-their-eyes view of their case.

Before embarking upon a mediation, parties and counsel should familiarize themselves with the foregoing questions and prepare answers which meet the client's needs. This will have the added effect of forcing the client to evaluate the dispute in a structured, logical way. Additionally, the lawyer may elect to develop instructions to be used to tell the client not to answer certain questions, because in mediation, despite the importance of candor, it is sometimes best to elect not to answer each and every question a mediator may pose.

Expanded Table of Contents

For Summary Table of Contents, see page v.

STEP ONE
Check Out the Governing Rules and Plan Accordingly 19

STEP TWO Agree on a Mediator (If You Have a Choice) 47

STEP FOUR

Exchange Information With Your Opponent, Including an Exchanged Memo for the Mediator (As Warranted) 127

STEP FIVE
Confidentially Brief the Mediator (As Allowed or Required) 149

STEP SIX

Bios of Interview Participants

P. JEAN BAKER (Washington, DC) is a vice president with the American Arbitration Association in their Washington, DC, office. She oversees the association's Commercial Division activities in New Jersey, Pennsylvania, Delaware, Maryland, Virginia, and Washington, DC. Ms. Baker assists businesses with the design and implementation of commercial ADR programs and serves as a mediator for the American Arbitration Association on special projects. Ms. Baker is Co-Chair Emeritus of the ABA Section of Litigation's ADR Committee. She has served as an adjunct professor at Georgetown University Law Center and Catholic University Columbus School of Law. She has been included since 1996 as an ADR professional in *Who's Who in American Law*. Ms. Baker earned her JD degree from California Western School of Law, an MBA from Northeastern University, and her BS (summa cum laude) from Wright State University. See http://abaiplspring.org/coursematerials2011/speaker-bio.html#2 for more.

ANDREW T. BERRY was a partner in the Newark, New Jersey, office of McCarter & English, LLP, where he chaired the firm's Executive Committee. His experience with litigation and alternative dispute resolution included mass torts, securities, and insurance coverage disputes. Mr. Berry held a BA cum laude from Princeton University (1962) and an LLB from Harvard Law School (1965). He was a Fellow of the American College of Trial Lawyers, the American Academy of Appellate Lawyers, and the American Bar Foundation. He passed away in July of 2009. In an obituary (July 26, 2009), the Newark *Star-Ledger* quoted this praise from one of Mr. Berry's former partners: "Drew exhibited all of the attributes people think lawyers should have. He thought you should be honest and up-front dealing with people and that one of the most important things about a lawyer and a firm is its reputation, and doing the best work and having the highest ethics."

JOHN BICKERMAN is an internationally recognized arbitrator and mediator, specializing in complex, multiparty, high-value, commercial, insurance coverage, environmental, and public policy disputes. In the last 20 years, he has logged over 20,000 hours and has resolved more than $3 billion in claims in more than 35 states. More than two dozen *Fortune* 100 companies and one dozen states have retained him to arbitrate or mediate their disputes. Mr. Bickerman is a former Chair of the ABA Section of Dispute Resolution, has taught at Cornell University, and is a former Adjunct Professor of Dispute Resolution at Georgetown University Law Center. He received his law degree from Georgetown University Law Center, magna cum laude, and undergraduate and graduate degrees from Cornell University. See http://www.bickerman.com for more.

JOHNATHAN C. BOLTON (Honolulu, HI) is Counsel at Goodsill Anderson Quinn & Stifel, focusing on U.S. and international bankruptcy and insolvency matters. He is licensed to practice law in Hawaii, New York, and Texas and is admitted as a solicitor in the United Kingdom. He is Board Certified in Business Bankruptcy Law by the American Board of Certification and the Texas Board of Legal Specialization. Previously, he was a senior associate in the Houston office of Fulbright & Jaworski. He holds a JD from Baylor Law School (2000), where he was Assistant Managing Editor of the Law Review, and earned a BA cum laude from the State University of New York at Stony Brook (1997). See http://www.goodsill.com for more information.

MICHAEL F. BRAUN (Chicago, IL) is a shareholder in the law firm of Schuyler, Roche & Crisham, PC. His practice includes litigation and counseling in the areas of employment and benefits, business and commerce, securities, commodities, and intellectual property. While litigation and preparation for trial still constitute a substantial portion of his practice, counseling clients about avoiding or resolving litigation has become an increasingly important aspect of his representation. Earlier in his career, he helped establish an appellate advocacy course at Northern Illinois University College of Law. Mr. Braun holds a JD (1981), magna cum laude, and a BS in Political Science and Economics (1978) from the University of Illinois (Champaign-Urbana). See http://SRCattorneys.com for more.

STEVEN M. BROM (Birmingham, AL) is the managing member of the Brom Law Firm, LLC, where he practices primarily in the areas of business and commercial litigation, alternative dispute resolution, and appeals. He received his JD from the University of Colorado (2001) and his BA from the University of Georgia (1998). Mr. Brom was selected as a member of the 2010 Alabama State Bar Leadership Forum, 2011 Leadership Vestavia Hills, and Birmingham Inns of Court. He has served on a number of committees for the Alabama State Bar and Birmingham Bar Association, including the Board of Editors for the *Alabama Lawyer*. See http://www.bromlawfirm.com for more.

JOHN G. BUCHANAN III (Washington, DC) is a partner at Covington & Burling LLP, where he has engaged in insurance coverage advocacy, dispute resolution, and counseling since the early 1980s. He earned an AB, magna cum laude, from Princeton University (1972), a BA with First Class Honors from Oxford University (1974), and a JD from Harvard University (1978). He teaches a graduate-level insurance litigation course at the Insurance Law Center of the University of Connecticut Law School; serves as an Adviser to the American Law Institute's Principles of the Law of Liability Insurance Project; and is Website Coeditor-in-Chief for the ABA Section of Litigation's Complex Insurance Coverage Litigation Committee. Previously, he was a member of the ABA Dispute Resolution Section's Task Force on Improving Mediation Quality. See http://www.cov.com for more.

NATHANIEL (NATE) CADE JR. (Milwaukee, WI) is a partner and general counsel at Gonzalez Saggio & Harlan LLP. He handles products and professional liability cases, as well as complex commercial litigation, construction law, and other matters. He has first-chaired more than a dozen bench and jury trials. He holds a BA from the University of Pennsylvania (1993) and a JD from the University of Michigan School of Law (1996), where he served as Associate Editor of the

Journal of International Law. Mr. Cade is a Co-Chair of the Products Liability Committee of the ABA Section of Litigation. He currently sits on the ABA's Standing Committee on Ethics and Professional Responsibility and serves in the House of Delegates. See http://www.gshllp.com for more.

CHRISTOPHER R. CARROLL (New York and New Jersey) is a founding member of Carroll, McNulty and Kull LLC. His practice focuses on resolution of insurance coverage disputes (including environmental, toxic tort, and asbestos issues) through litigation or alternative dispute resolution. He has represented clients in insurance coverage disputes in all 50 states, Puerto Rico, and Europe. He also provides counsel to corporate clients on general business matters, contract negotiation, environmental litigation and compliance, and all types of commercial disputes. Mr. Carroll holds a BA from St. Josephs College (1988) and a JD from St. Johns University School of Law (1991). Among other activities, he has served on the Advisory Board of *Insurance Law & Litigation Week*. See http://www.cmk.com for more.

JAY M. COHEN (Winter Park, FL) is a mediator who has conducted more than 4,000 mediations since 1990. He has also taught courses in negotiation at the Roy E. Crummer Graduate School of Business at Rollins College. Mr. Cohen holds a BA from Temple University and a JD from George Washington University. After graduation, he was a trial lawyer for 23 years. He is a founding member of the American College of Civil Trial Mediators. Mr. Cohen is a member of the Florida Bar Association Grievance Mediation panel and was selected by the Judicial Relations Committee of the Orange County Bar Association to deal with disputes between the judiciary and the trial bar. See http://www.jmcohenpa.com for more.

ROBERT M. CRAIG III (Houston, TX) managed litigation over decades for a number of *Fortune* 500 corporations. He has participated in many dozens of mediations in venues throughout the United States. Mr. Craig is currently available as a mediator and arbitration panelist in his role as a Vice President at Charles River Associates, a global consulting firm that offers economic, financial, and business management expertise to major law firms, corporations, accounting firms, and governments around the world. He holds a JD from the University of Virginia School of Law (1973) and a BA in journalism from Texas Christian University (1970). Mr. Craig is a former Co-Chair of the Committee on Corporate Counsel of the ABA Section of Litigation, and a former Co-Director for the Division on Substantive Areas of Litigation. See http://www.crai.com for more.

JOHN DeGROOTE (Dallas, TX) served at the global technology consulting firm BearingPoint, Inc., and its predecessor, KPMG Consulting, LLC, from 2000 through 2009, first as Chief Litigation Counsel, then Chief Legal Officer, and ultimately as President. He now serves as settlement counsel to select clients and as the court-appointed trustee or receiver to significant corporate and probate estates, including the BearingPoint, Inc. Liquidating Trust and other interests, through John DeGroote Services, LLC. Mr. DeGroote received a JD from the Duke University School of Law (1990), a BA from Mississippi State University (1986), and mediation training from Pepperdine University's Straus Institute for Dispute Resolution (2005). He has represented clients in hundreds of mediations across 20 states. He is also a cofounder of the online decision tree tool Resolution Tree (http://www.resolutiontree.com) and comments on litigation management, settlement techniques, and negotiation strategies at http://www.settlementperspectives.com.

THOMAS A. DYE (West Palm Beach, FL) is a shareholder at Carlton Fields, PA. He is a trial lawyer handling commercial, intellectual property, product liability, tax, environmental/real estate, telecommunications, and consumer class action cases. He also has extensive insurance litigation experience, including insurance coverage and bad faith, property insurance, product liability, mass torts, and other business torts. Mr. Dye holds a JD, cum laude, from the Miami School of Law (1981) and a BA in Economics from the College of William and Mary (1976). He is a Co-Chair of the Property Insurance

Subcommittee of the Business Torts Committee of the ABA Section of Litigation, and former Editor of the *Business Torts Journal*. See http://www.carltonfields.com for more.

EDNA SELAN EPSTEIN (Chicago, IL) has practiced in her own law firm since 1989. She has handled a wide variety of litigated matters, including employment discrimination, pension fraud class actions, medical and legal malpractice, and business torts, generally on the plaintiff's side. Previously, she was a partner at Sidley & Austin. Ms. Epstein received her law degree, cum laude, from the University of Chicago (1973), where she served on the Law Review and was elected to the Order of the Coif. Before law school, she earned a PhD in Romance Languages and Literatures from Harvard University and taught as an assistant professor. She is on the Book Publishing Board of the ABA Section of Litigation and is the author of *The Attorney-Client Privilege and the Work-Product Doctrine*.

MARALEE ERIKSEN (Sacramento, CA) is a principal in the litigation group of Boutin Jones Inc., where she devotes much of her practice to intellectual property, officer and director liability, probate and trust, and corporate disputes. She also has substantial experience in cases involving software and technology, trade secret misappropriation, shareholder disputes, antitrust and unfair competition claims, and commercial contracts. Ms. Eriksen holds both a BA (1993) in Russian and a JD (1996) from the University of Wyoming, where she served as an editor of the *Land and Water Law Review*. She is a member of both Phi Beta Kappa and the Order of the Coif. See http://www.boutinjones.com for more.

WILLIAM T. GARCIA is Principal and Chief Legal Officer at Eagle Key Consulting LLC, which provides consulting and coaching to law firms, law departments, and professional services firms in areas including inside-outside counsel management, value-based engagements, and client service program development. In March 2011, he was appointed by the partnership dissolution committee of Howrey LLP, and subsequently by the Bankruptcy Trustee, to serve as part of the wind-down team for that firm. He previously served as inside counsel at Gannett and later as Vice President of Compliance Oversight at MCI. Mr. Garcia holds a JD from the University of Chicago Law School and an AB from Harvard University. He also has held several leadership posts at the ABA Section of Litigation, including Co-Chair of the Committee on Corporate Counsel. See http://www.linkedin.com/in/billgarciadc for more.

PETER J. GRILLI (Tampa, FL) has mediated more than 4,000 cases since opening his mediation practice in 1993, including the then-largest employment class action ever certified and a public school system desegregation case. Before becoming a mediator, he litigated in private practice and served as a law clerk for the Hon. Ben Krentzman (U.S. District Court, Middle District of Florida). Mr. Grilli earned his law degree from Georgetown University (1977), where he served on the Executive Board of *Law and Policy in International Business*, after receiving his BA, cum laude, from Yale University (1973). He is a Fellow of the American College of Civil Trial Mediators. See http://www.grillimediation.com for more.

HOWARD A. HERMAN (San Francisco, CA) is Director of the ADR Program for the U.S. District Court, Northern District of California. He is a 1983 graduate of the University of California Hastings College of the Law (where he now teaches ADR-related courses), and a 1979 graduate, with high honors, of the University of California at Berkeley. A mediator, mediation trainer, and early neutral evaluator, Mr. Herman previously served as Director of ADR Programs for the Contra Costa County Superior Court. He also spent four years as a settlement conference attorney for the United States Court of Appeals for the Ninth Circuit, ultimately serving as a codirector of that court's settlement conference program. He is a member of the Executive Committee of the ABA's Section of Dispute Resolution. See http://www.uchastings.edu/faculty-administration/faculty/adjuncts/herman.html for more.

DAVID A. HOFFMAN (Boston, MA) is the founding member of the Boston Law Collaborative, LLC, and teaches the Mediation course at Harvard Law School, where he is the John H. Watson, Jr. Lecturer on Law. He has published two books on the subject of dispute resolution: *Massachusetts Alternative Dispute Resolution* (with Prof. David Matz; 2d ed. 1996) and *Bringing Peace Into the Room: How the Personal Qualities of the Mediator Impact the Process of Conflict Resolution* (with Daniel Bowling; 2003). He earned his JD, magna cum laude, from Harvard Law School (1984), where he served as an editor of the Law Review. He also holds an MA from Cornell University (1974), as well as a BA, summa cum laude, from Princeton University (1970). He is a former Chair of the ABA's Section of Dispute Resolution. See http://bostonlaw collaborative.com for more.

HORACE (HOB) W. JORDAN JR. (Lake Forest, IL) is a founder, Executive Vice President, General Counsel, and Secretary of Kingsbridge Holdings, LLC—a privately held company that provides financing to customers regarding equipment acquisitions. He is responsible for the legal and administrative operations of the company. Since going in-house, he has served as corporate counsel in dozens of mediation proceedings. Mr. Jordan is a former Co-Chair of the Committee on Corporate Counsel of the ABA's Section of Litigation and a former partner at Jenner and Block. He received his law degree, cum laude, from Northwestern University and his undergraduate degree, magna cum laude, from Tufts University. See http://www.kingsbridgeholdings.com for more.

JOHN LANDE (Columbia, MO) is the Isidor Loeb Professor and former director of the LLM Program in Dispute Resolution at the University of Missouri School of Law (Columbia, MO). He holds an AB in Psychology from the University of Michigan (1974), a JD from Hastings College of Law at the University of California (1980), and an MS (1991) and PhD (1995) in Sociology from the University of Wisconsin. In 1994–1995, he was a Fellow in the Program on Negotiation at Harvard Law School. Prof. Lande has served on the Council of the ABA Section of Dispute Resolution, as well as on its Task Force on Improving Mediation Quality. He is the author of *Lawyering With Planned Early Negotiation*. See http://law .missouri.edu/lande for more.

EDWARD M. MULLINS (Miami, FL) is a founding shareholder of Astigarraga Davis (Miami), handling international commercial litigation and arbitration, as well as defamation and privacy, communications and media, class actions, and intellectual property disputes. He is also an arbitrator and mediator. Mr. Mullins holds a JD (1990) and BA (1986) from the University of Florida. In law school, he served as Editor-in-Chief of the Law Review and was elected to the Order of the Coif. In the ABA Section of Litigation, he has served (among other posts) as Co-Chair of the ADR Committee, as Co-Chair of the International Litigation Committee, and Co-Editor of the *International Litigation Quarterly*. For the Florida Bar, he is a former Chair of the International Law Section and the Florida Appellate Courts Rules Committee, and a former Co-Editor of the *International Law Quarterly*. See http://www.astidavis.com for more.

CHARLES E. POU JR. (Washington, DC) has served as a mediator of public policy and other government and private disputes and has assisted many agencies in establishing ADR programs. For more than 10 years, Pou directed the dispute resolution program at the Administrative Conference of the United States, where he was a principal drafter of the Administrative Dispute Resolution Acts of 1990 and 1996 and headed a team carrying out the conference's lead responsibility within the federal government for ensuring agencies' implementation of consensus-based decision-making methods. A cum laude graduate of Rice University and Harvard Law School, Mr. Pou is a former Co-Chair of the Dispute Resolution Committee of the ABA Section of Administrative Law and Regulatory Practice.

SHARON B. PRESS (St. Paul, MN) is an Associate Professor at Hamline University School of Law and Director of the school's Dispute Resolution Institute. Until 2009, she was Director of the Florida Dispute Resolution Center, based in Tallahassee, Florida, which is a joint program of the Florida Supreme Court and Florida State University College of Law. In that role, she provided technical assistance to local courts who wished to establish court mediation programs, and worked with Florida Supreme Court Committees to develop policies, procedures, court rules, and legislation for implementation of court-connected ADR programs for the state court system. Ms. Press received her BA and JD degrees from The George Washington University. She has received awards including the Mary Parker Follett Award for Excellence and Innovation in Dispute Resolution. See http://law.hamline.edu/disputeresolution for more.

TRACEY SALMON-SMITH (Florham Park, NJ) is Counsel with the Commercial Litigation, Labor and Employment Law, and Securities Law groups of Bressler, Amery & Ross. Previously, she was a Director and Associate General Counsel for UBS Financial Services Inc., where she defended the firm and its brokers in Sales Practice arbitration matters before FINRA. She was also an Assistant U.S. Attorney in the EDNY. Ms. Salmon-Smith holds a JD from Villanova University School of Law and an AB from Dartmouth College. She serves as Co-Director of Division VI of the ABA Section of Litigation and has previously held posts including Co-Chair of the Committee on Corporate Counsel and Cochair (Retention) of the Membership Committee. See http://www.bressler.com for more.

PAUL ALAIN SANDARS III (Roseland, NJ) is a member of the law firm of Lum, Drasco & Positan, LLC. He concentrates his practice in construction and complex commercial litigation, alternative dispute resolution, construction law, taxation, and zoning matters. He holds an LLM in Taxation from New York University (1987), a JD from Boston University, and a BS, cum laude, in economics from the Wharton School at the University of Pennsylvania (1978). Mr. Sandars has served on the Council of the ABA Section of Litigation, as Co-Director of Division I (Administration), Co-Chair of the Alternative Dispute Resolution Committee, and Co-Chair of the Construction Litigation Committee. He is also a former Council member and Long Range Planning Officer of the ABA Dispute Resolution Section. See http://www.lumlaw.com for more.

RICHARD M. SHUSTERMAN (Berwyn, PA) is the founder of Shusterman Arbitration & Mediation Services (shustermanr @verizon.net). He is a former partner of a large Philadelphia law firm, where he chaired its Commercial Litigation Department and its ADR, Insurance Coverage, and Reinsurance Practice Groups and served on the firm's Executive and Compensation Committees. Mr. Shusterman earned his law degree, cum laude, from the University of Pennsylvania (1964) and a BA, magna cum laude, in History from Lafayette College (1961). He also serves as a member of the panel of Distinguished Neutrals of the CPR International Institute for Conflict Prevention & Resolution, is a certified ARIAS US mediator and arbitrator, and is a certified ReMedi mediator.

LINDA R. SINGER (Washington, DC) is a mediator, arbitrator, lawyer, teacher, and author and has been president of the Center for Dispute Settlement since 1971. She also is a principal in JAMS. In 2012, Ms. Singer received the D'Alemberte-Raven Award from the ABA Section of Dispute Resolution, in recognition of her contributions to the field. Ms. Singer holds a BA, magna cum laude, from Harvard University (1963) and a JD with highest honors from George Washington University Law School (1968). She has taught as an adjunct professor at Georgetown, American, George Washington, and Harvard law schools. She has also been a visiting lecturer at the University of New Mexico, Stanford, and UCLA. She is also the author of *Settling Disputes: Conflict Resolution in Business, Families, and the Legal System*. See http://www.cdsusa.org for more.

SARA SOTO (Miami, FL) is a Member at the law firm of Bressler, Amery & Ross, PC, where her practice encompasses a broad range of business litigation and arbitration matters. She has represented brokerage firms, banks, corporations, and individuals in arbitration and litigation involving customers, employees, other institutions, and other individuals. Her experience includes more than 25 years representing broker dealers in arbitrations brought by customers involving a variety of financial products. Ms. Soto holds a BA, magna cum laude, (1975) and a JD (1978), cum laude, from the University of

Miami. In law school, she was a Harvey T. Reid Scholar and served on *Lawyer of the Americas* (now the *Inter-American Law Review*). See http://www.bressler.com for more.

RICHARD C. SPENCER is a sole practitioner in Los Angeles whose practice includes mediation and arbitration services. As a mediator, in addition to private mediation, he serves on panels of mediators for the Superior Court, the State Appellate Court, and the local bar association's Attorney-Client Fee Dispute Service. His current law practice comprises primarily litigation and transactional work in business, corporate, and real estate matters. In the past, Mr. Spencer has also had a substantial plaintiff's personal injury litigation practice.

HERBERT M. STETTIN (Coral Gables, FL) is a retired Miami-Dade Circuit Judge who has also served extensively as a certified mediator and an arbitrator. In 2009, he was appointed as Chapter Eleven Trustee to recover assets of Rothstein Rosenfeldt Adler, PA, in connection with an alleged Ponzi scheme by that law firm's former chairman. Judge Stettin holds a BA from Queens College, an MA from Harvard University, and an LLB from the University of Miami School of Law, where he served as editor of the *University of Miami Law Review* (1961–1962).

WALTER B. STUART (New York, NY) is a partner at Freshfields Bruckhaus Deringer, in the litigation practice group. Previously, he was Managing Partner in the New York office of Vinson & Elkins, where he cochaired the firm's Securities Litigation and Enforcement Practice Group. Mr. Stuart received his law degree with honors from Tulane Law School, served as Editor-in-Chief of the Law Review, and was elected to membership in the Order of the Coif. A coauthor of *Lender Liability: Theory and Practice*, Mr. Stuart has also written numerous articles for legal publications and has been listed in *Best Lawyers in America* for business litigation, corporate law, and banking law. See http://www.freshfields.com for more.

DANIEL S. TERRELL (Baton Rouge, LA) is Vice President and General Counsel for the Fabrication & Manufacturing

Group of The Shaw Group Inc. (NYSE: SHAW), a *Fortune* 500 company. In that role, he serves as principal legal advisor for the largest U.S. specialty contractor of fabricated piping systems to power, refinery, petrochemical, and industrial markets. Formerly, Mr. Terrell practiced law in the New Orleans office (Northshore location) of Baker Donelson Bearman Caldwell & Berkowitz, PC, where he assisted clients in resolving commercial disputes relating to construction projects. He received his JD and BCL from Louisiana State University. He is a former chair of the Dispute Resolution Committee of the ABA Young Lawyers Division and a former YLD Liaison to the ABA Forum on the Construction Industry. See http://www.shawgrp.com for more.

BOWEN H. TUCKER (Arlington Heights, IL) is a retired Associate General Counsel for FMC Corporation, where he was responsible for the direction of all litigation. He both developed and managed FMC's Litigation Department within the Law Department. He has also served in leadership positions including Chairman of the Lawyer's Council of the Construction Industry Manufacturers Association and Chairman of the Product Liability Advisory Council. After graduating from Brown University and the University of Michigan Law School, Mr. Tucker spent several years as a trial lawyer with the Hinckley, Allen law firm in Providence, Rhode Island, and later joined the Law Department of Caterpillar, Inc. (Peoria, IL). He is a member of the American Law Institute and serves as an Arbitrator for the Cook County (IL) Mandatory Arbitration Program. See http://bowentucker.com for more.

ALBERT S. WATKINS (St. Louis, MO) is a managing member of Kodner Watkins & Kloecker, LC, whose practice includes representing claimants in securities disputes, as well as banking and general civil litigation. He earned his BA (1982) and JD (1985) from St. Louis University. Mr. Watkins was a founding member of the Board of Directors of the U.S. Chamber Institute for Legal Reform. He has been appointed to the Board of Arbitration of the New York Stock Exchange, Arbitration for the Financial Industry Regulatory Authority (FINRA), the National Association of Securities Dealers, the

American Arbitration Association, and the Chicago Board of Trade. He is a Senior Counsel at both the American College of Barristers and The College of Master Advocates & Barristers. See http://kwklaw.net for more.

LAWRENCE M. WATSON JR. (Maitland, FL) is a principal at the mediation firm of Upchurch, Watson, White & Max. Throughout his legal career, he has practiced exclusively in litigation and alternative dispute resolution, with an emphasis on complex multiparty commercial problems and construction claims. In 1988, while serving as Senior Litigation Counsel for the Carlton Fields law firm, Mr. Watson became one of the first civil trial mediators certified by the Florida Supreme Court. He is a past President, Founder, and Fellow of the American College of Civil Trial Mediators, from which he received a Lifetime Achievement Award. At the ABA Section of Litigation, he has served in posts including Division Director and Chair of the ADR Committee. See http://www.uww-adr.com for more.

DANIEL M. WEITZ is the Deputy Director, Division of Professional and Court Services and Coordinator, Office of ADR and Court Improvement Programs for the New York State Unified Court System. As Coordinator of ADR/CIP, he oversees a statewide program of court-annexed ADR initiatives involving mediation, arbitration, neutral evaluation, and summary jury trials as well as the Community Dispute Resolution Centers Program. He has served as mediator in a wide range of matters, including general civil, family, employment, and human-rights cases. Mr. Weitz is also an Adjunct Clinical Professor at the Benjamin N. Cardozo School of Law. He holds a JD from Cardozo (1996) and a BA from New York University (1991).

The views expressed by Mr. Weitz for this book are his alone and do not reflect those of the New York State Unified Court System.

RACHEL WOHL (Annapolis, MD) is the founding Executive Director of the Maryland Judiciary's Mediation and Conflict Resolution Office. She is a mediator, facilitator, and attorney, and has helped design, strengthen, and expand a variety of conflict resolution programs. Ms. Wohl served as Co-Chair of the ABA Dispute Resolution Section's Task Force on Improving Mediation Quality. She is a recipient of ACR's Mary Parker Follett Award for Innovation in the Field of Conflict Resolution. Before becoming a lawyer, she earned a master's degree as a filmmaker and worked in film production. She was a civil litigator for many years, focusing on the rights of children, domestic violence survivors, and the disadvantaged. See http://www.courts.state.md.us/macro for more.

SUSAN M. YATES is executive director of Resolution Systems Institute (RSI) in Chicago. In this role, she is responsible for implementing the organizational mission of strengthening justice by enhancing court ADR through technical assistance to courts that are establishing or improving their ADR programs; monitoring and evaluating court ADR programs; and maintaining the Court ADR Resource Center (http://www.courtADR.org), a national online resource center. Ms. Yates holds a BS in Industrial and Labor Relations from Cornell University. She has been a mediator since 1983, currently focusing on employment discrimination and foreclosure disputes. She coedited the *ADR Handbook for Judges* (2004) and served as a member of the ABA Dispute Resolution Section's Task Force on Improving Mediation Quality. See http://www.aboutrsi.org for more.

Bios of Authors and CLE Panelists Quoted

Although it is unusual for a book to provide biographical information about authors quoted in the text, it seems appropriate here. Since these authors' views and suggestions appear alongside those of interview participants as part of the "conversation" about mediation practice, you may be interested to know about their backgrounds.[1] *The same logic applies to CLE panelists quoted.*

MARJORIE CORMAN AARON (Cincinnati, OH) is Professor of Practice and Director of the Center for Practice at the University of Cincinnati College of Law. A mediator of legal disputes for more than twenty years, she is the former Executive Director of the Program on Negotiation at Harvard Law School and former Vice President and Senior Mediator at Endispute, Inc. (now JAMS).

CHALON T. ALLEN (Miami, FL) is an attorney with Broad and Cassel. Her practice is focused on various complex litigation matters, including general commercial litigation. See http://www.broadandcassel.com for more.

THOMAS O. ARNOLD (1923–2009) was an intellectual property lawyer, mediator, arbitrator, and special master. He served as a past Chair of the ABA Section of Intellectual Property Law. In 1998, he received a Lifetime Achievement Award from the American College of Civil Trial Mediators.

P. JEAN BAKER—*see Bios of Interview Participants.*

ELEANOR BARR (Los Angeles, CA) has mediated disputes for more than 13 years in the areas of employment, real estate, environmental, business, insurance coverage, and personal injury. She is a Distinguished Fellow of the International Academy of Mediators and has taught mediation as an Adjunct Professor at Pepperdine School of Law. See http://www.eleanorbarr.com for more.

1. Some authors who were quoted fleetingly are not represented in these bios.

JOHN BATES JR. is commencing his 21st year as a full-time mediator and has mediated several thousand matters across the country (including Hawaii). Previously he was a partner at Cooley, Godward in San Francisco. He is a cofounder of JAMS. He has been a member of the ABA since 1974 and can be reached at jbates@jamsadr.com or 415-774-2614.

LEE JAY BERMAN (Los Angeles, CA) has been a commercial mediator since 1994. He is a former Director of Pepperdine Law School's Mediating the Litigated Case program. See http://www.leejayberman.com for more.

JOHN BICKERMAN—*see Bios of Interview Participants.*

HENRY J. BLUM (Houston, TX) has practiced law since 1988 and mediated full-time since 2000. He is a past Chair of the Houston Bar Association ADR Section. See http://www.blum-mediations.com for more.

HILDY BOWBEER is Assistant Chief Intellectual Property Counsel at 3M Innovative Properties Company, where she manages 3M's intellectual-property litigation. Previously, she managed product liability and mass tort litigation with 3M's Office of General Counsel. Before joining 3M, Ms. Bowbeer was a founding partner of Bowman and Brooke, where she had a national trial and appellate practice in the defense of products liability litigation.

WAYNE BRAZIL (Berkeley, CA) is a Professor from Practice at the University of California Berkeley School of Law, a former magistrate judge, and a mediator, arbitrator, and special master with JAMS. In 2009, he received the ABA Section of Dispute Resolution's D'Alemberte-Raven Award, recognizing leaders who have contributed significantly to the field of alternative dispute resolution by developing new or innovative programs. See http://www.jamsadr.com/brazil for more.

PETER CONTUZZI is an attorney-mediator based in Massachusetts. His practice since 1984 has been concentrated in the mediation of civil cases characterized by high stakes, complex issues, or multiple parties. See http://www.contuzzi.com for more.

JOHN W. COOLEY (1943–2009) was a federal magistrate judge, mediator, arbitrator, and adjunct professor at Northwestern University School of Law. He authored half a dozen books, including *The Mediator's Handbook* and *Mediation Advocacy* (both for the National Institute for Trial Advocacy).

C. TIMOTHY CORCORAN III (Tampa, FL), a Roman Catholic priest ordained in 2012, is a former federal bankruptcy judge, mediator, and litigator. He was previously active in leadership of the ABA Section of Litigation.

CHARLES B. CRAVER (Washington, DC) is Freda H. Alverson Professor of Law at The George Washington University. He is a member of the American Law Institute and formerly served as secretary to the ABA Section of Labor and Employment Law. He has authored many books, including *Alternative Dispute Resolution: The Advocate's Perspective*. See http://www.law.gwu.edu/Faculty for more.

NIGEL DUNLOP (Auckland, New Zealand), a private mediator, has been a barrister since 1996 and prior to that was a solicitor for 18 years. He is a past President of the Canterbury District Law Society and Council member of the New Zealand Law Society. See http://www.nigeldunlop.co.nz for more.

THOMAS A. DYE—*see Bios of Interview Participants.*

RICHARD D. FINCHER (Phoenix, AZ) is the managing partner of Workplace Resolutions LLC. Before establishing his practice as a neutral, he served as a senior executive in law and human resources with three *Fortune* 500 corporations. See http://workplaceresolutions.com for more.

GARY FRIEDMAN (Mill Valley, CA) is a cofounder and codirector of The Center for Understanding in Conflict. Before starting to practice and teach conflict resolution, he was a trial lawyer in Bridgeport, Connecticut. He is a coauthor (with Jack Himmelstein) of *Challenging Conflict: Mediation Through Understanding*. See http://www.understandinginconflict.org for more.

ERIC GALTON (Austin, TX) of the Lakeside Mediation Center has mediated cases since 1989. Previously, he was a litigator in areas including personal injury, commercial, and consumer law. He is a former Chair of the ABA Section of Dispute Resolution. See http://www.lakesidemediation.com for more.

ROBERT GARY (Lorain, OH) is a member of Gary, Naegele & Theado. His experience includes more than 35 years of litigating class actions. He has participated in the mediation of numerous class actions. See http://www.gntlaw.com for more.

DWIGHT GOLANN (Boston, MA) is Professor of Law at Suffolk University, where he teaches mediation and negotiation. He is a recipient of the ABA Legal Educators Award and formerly served as Chair of ADR programs for the ABA's Sections of Litigation and Business Law. He is the author of *Mediating Legal Disputes: Effective Strategies for Neutrals and Advocates*. See http://www.golann.com for more.

JOBI HALPER (San Diego, CA) has offered arbitration and mediation services on a full-time basis since 2008. Previously, she was a litigator whose practice included class actions and commercial disputes. See http://www.adrservices.org/neutrals/jobi-halper.php for more.

JACK HIMMELSTEIN (New York, NY) is a cofounder and codirector of The Center for Understanding in Conflict. He previously taught at Columbia Law School and was also a founder of the City University of New York School of Law. He is a coauthor (with Gary Friedman) of *Challenging Conflict: Mediation Through Understanding*. See http://www.understandinginconflict.org for more.

DAVID A. HOFFMAN—*see Bios of Interview Participants.*

WILLIAM R. JENTES (Chicago, IL) is an arbitrator and mediator. His ADR work has been spread across the United States and internationally, with the parties coming from 17 countries. Previously, he was a principal litigating partner at Kirkland & Ellis, LLP, for almost 40 years. See http://www.williamrjentes.com for more.

LAURA H. KENNEDY (Phoenix, AZ) is a member of Cohen Kennedy Dowd & Quigley, where her law practice is concentrated in commercial litigation. She has been active in leadership of the ABA Section of Litigation, where she has cochaired a number of committees and task forces. See http://www.ckdqlaw.com for more.

PETER J. KLARFELD (Washington, DC) is a principal in the Franchise & Distribution Practice Group of Gray Plant Mooty, where he concentrates his practice on franchise litigation. He is a former member of the Governing Committee of the ABA Forum on Franchising. See http://www.gpmlaw.com for more.

LOUISE A. LaMOTHE, based in Southern California, devotes her practice exclusively to providing professional services as an arbitrator and mediator. She is a past Chair of the ABA Section of Litigation and previously practiced as a business litigator. See http://www.dispute-solutions.com for more.

JOHN LANDE—*see Bios of Interview Participants.*

HOMER C. LaRUE (Washington, DC) is a professor at Howard University School of Law, where he teaches courses including Alternative Dispute Resolution. He has also served as an arbitrator and mediator for more than 20 years, and is a former Chair of the ABA Section of Dispute Resolution. See http://www.law.howard.edu for more.

MICHAEL K. LEWIS (Washington, DC) is a mediator with JAMS. In 2001, he received an award in recognition of Outstanding Achievement for ADR Education/Training from the American College of Civil Trial Mediators, and in 2012 he shared the Section on Dispute Resolution's D'Alemberte-Raven Award with Linda Singer. See http://www.jamsadr.com/lewis for more.

J. ANDERSON LITTLE (Chapel Hill, NC) is a mediator and mediation trainer in North Carolina. He chaired the North Carolina Dispute Resolution Committee and also chaired legislative and rule-drafting projects for mediation programs in state trial and family courts. He is the author of *Making*

Money Talk: How to Mediate Insured Claims and Other Monetary Disputes. See http://www.ncmediators.org/anderson-little for more.

LAWRENCE MILLS (Seattle, WA) of Mills Meyers Swartling is a mediator and arbitrator whose law practice emphasizes business law and commercial transactions. See http://www.millsadr.com for more.

JOYCE MITCHELL (Silver Spring, MD) is a business and employment lawyer and alternative dispute resolution professional, mediating and arbitrating complex employment and securities cases nationwide. She also teaches as an adjunct professor at the University of Maryland Francis King Carey School of Law. See http://www.law.umaryland.edu/faculty for more.

BRUCE E. MEYERSON (Phoenix, AZ) regularly serves as a mediator in virtually all aspects of commercial, employment, construction, real estate, and business litigation, in cases ranging in value up to $1.5 billion. He is a former appellate judge and former Chair of the ABA Section of Dispute Resolution. See http://www.brucemeyerson.com for more.

MICHAEL S. OBERMAN (New York, NY) is a partner at Kramer Levin Naftalis & Frankel and head of its Alternative Dispute Resolution Practice Group. He has litigated a wide variety of complex civil cases at the trial and appellate levels and in arbitration. See http://www.kramerlevin.com for more.

BEATRICE O'DONNELL (Philadelphia, PA) is a partner at Duane Morris, LLP, where she maintains an active practice in areas including mass tort, products liability, and commercial litigation. She is a Co-Chair of the Mass Torts Committee of the ABA Section of Litigation. See http://www.duanemorris.com/http://www.duanemorris.com for more.

MICHAEL S. ORFINGER (Daytona Beach, FL) is a shareholder in the ADR firm of Upchurch, Watson, White & Max. Previously, he was a litigator and appellate practitioner. See http://www.uww-adr.com for more.

JOHN R. PHILLIPS (Kansas City, MO) is a partner at Husch Blackwell, where he counsels boards of directors and others on employment matters and traditional labor relations. He also serves as a mediator and arbitrator in complex cases. See http://www.huschblackwell.com for more.

BENNETT G. PICKER (Philadelphia, PA) is Senior Counsel at Stradley Ronon, where he maintains an active ADR practice as a mediator and arbitrator of business disputes. In 2010, he received the American Bar Association's Lawyer as Problem Solver Award. He is the author of *Mediation Practice Guide: A Handbook for Resolving Business Disputes*. See http://www.stradley.com for more.

GARY P. POON is a Washington, DC, lawyer, business advisor, and mediator now residing in San Diego, California. In addition to offering outside "general counsel" services to corporations, nonprofit organizations, private clients, and other entities, he is a mediator and a partner in Global InterMediation PLLC, an international mediation service. He is the author of *The Corporate Counsel's Guide to Mediation* (also translated into Russian). See http://www.poonlaw.com for more.

LAWRENCE D. ROSENBERG (Washington, DC) is a partner at Jones Day, where he has tried cases and argued appeals in cases throughout the country. He is a former Co-Chair of both the Trial Practice and Appellate Practice Committees of the ABA Section of Litigation. See http://www.jonesday.com/ for more.

KIMBERLY SANDS (Daytona Beach, FL) is a shareholder in the ADR firm of Upchurch, Watson, White & Max. Previously, she was a civil trial attorney and is currently a Florida Supreme Court Certified Circuit Trial Mediator. See http://www.uww-adr.com for more.

MARGARET L. SHAW has maintained an active mediation practice for more than 30 years. She was also for more than 25 years an adjunct professor of law at NYU Law School, where she taught ADR and negotiation. See http://www.jamsadr.com for more.

LINDA R. SINGER—*see Bios of Interview Participants.*

V. HEATHER SIBBISON (Washington, DC) is a partner at SNR Denton and a member of the firm's Public Policy and Regulation practice. Her practice focuses on Indian law and tribal representation. See http://www.snrdenton.com for more.

MARY PAT THYNGE (Wilmington, DE) is a Magistrate Judge of the U.S. District Court for the District of Delaware. She initially developed and has managed the ADR program of that court, while also serving as a mediator.

GILDA R. TURITZ (San Francisco, CA) concentrates her practice on business litigation in federal and state courts and arbitration tribunals. In addition to representing clients as an advocate, she is an arbitrator, mediator, and early neutral evaluator. See http://www.sideman.com for more information.

JOHN J. UPCHURCH (Daytona Beach, FL) is a principal at the ADR firm of Upchurch, Watson, White & Max. Previously he was Chief Judge of the 7th Judicial Circuit of Florida and managing partner of Cobb Cole & Bell. See http://www.uww-adr.com for more.

LAWRENCE M. WATSON JR.—*see Bios of Interview Participants.*

MICHAEL S. WILK (Houston, TX) has practiced law since 1966 and has been an active mediator since 1990. He has served as Chairman of the State Bar of Texas ADR Section and National President of the Association of Attorney-Mediators and is a member of the International Academy of Mediators and a credentialed distinguished mediator with the Texas Mediator Credentialing Association. See http://www.hirschwest.com for more.

RACHEL WOHL—*see Bios of Interview Participants.*

ZENA ZUMETA (Ann Arbor, MI) is a mediator and national mediation trainer with one of the longest-standing mediation practices in Michigan. She is president of the Mediation Training and Consultation Institute and of The Collaborative Workplace. See http://zenazumetamediation.com for more.

Index

Note: page numbers followed by *n* indicate material found in footnotes.

M

S

INVITATION TO READERS

Would you like to share a memorable, instructive personal experience on the topic of representing clients in mediation? Do you have any thoughts or comments for improvement of this book? You might be able to join the voices of other mediation advocates and mediators in an expanded second edition. Contact the author at spencerpunnett@earthlink.net.